BLITZKRIEG

OSPREY
PUBLISHING

EDITED BY DR STEPHEN HART AND DR RUSSELL HART

BLITZKRIEG

THE INVASION OF POLAND TO THE FALL OF FRANCE

OSPREY PUBLISHING
Bloomsbury Publishing Plc
Kemp House, Chawley Park, Cumnor Hill, Oxford OX2 9PH, UK
29 Earlsfort Terrace, Dublin 2, Ireland
1385 Broadway, 5th Floor, New York, NY 10018, USA
E-mail: info@ospreypublishing.com
www.ospreypublishing.com

OSPREY is a trademark of Osprey Publishing Ltd

First published in Great Britain in 2021

In the compilation of this volume we relied on the following previously published Osprey titles: CAM 3: *France 1940* by Alan Shepperd, CAM 107: *Poland 1939* by Steven J. Zaloga, CAM 183: *Denmark and Norway 1940* by Douglas C. Dildy, CAM 218: *Maginot Line 1940* by M. Romanych and M. Rupp, CAM 219: *Dunkirk 1940* by Douglas C. Dildy, CAM 264: *Fall Gelb 1940 (1)* by Douglas C. Dildy, and CAM 265: *Fall Gelb 1940 (2)* by Douglas C. Dildy.

BEV artworks by The Black Spot, previously published in CAM 107: *Poland 1939* (pp. 46–47, 52–53 and 70–71), CAM 183: *Denmark and Norway 1940* (pp. 112–113, 128–129 and 140–141), CAM 219: *Dunkirk 1940* (p. 246–247), CAM 264: *Fall Gelb 1940 (1)* (pp. 198–199 and 204–205) and CAM 265: *Fall Gelb 1940 (2)* (pp. 182–183 and 190–191).

Battlescene artworks previously published in CAM 107: Poland 1939 (pp. 38, 50 and 65), CAM 183: *Denmark and Norway 1940* (pp. 120, 130 and 142), CAM 218: *Maginot Line 1940* (pp. 262 and 277), CAM 219: *Dunkirk 1940* (pp. 234, 242 and 248), CAM 264: *Fall Gelb 1940 (1)* (pp. 206, 218 and 222) and CAM 265: *Fall Gelb 1940 (2)* (pp. 180, 214 and 234).

Maps by www.bounford.com, previously published in *Atlas of the Blitzkrieg*.

A catalogue record for this book is available from the British Library.

ISBN: HB 978 1 4728 4787 4; eBook 978 1 4728 4789 8; ePDF 978 1 4728 4788 1;
XML 978 1 4728 4790 4

21 22 23 24 25   10 9 8 7 6 5 4 3 2 1

Index by Zoe Ross
Printed and bound in India by Replika Press Private Ltd.

Imperial War Museums Collections
Many of the photos in this book come from the huge collections of IWM (Imperial War Museums) which cover all aspects of conflict involving Britain and the Commonwealth since the start of the twentieth century. These rich resources are available online to search, browse and buy at www.iwm.org.uk/collections. Imperial War Museums www.iwm.org.uk

Osprey Publishing supports the Woodland Trust, the UK's leading woodland conservation charity.

To find out more about our authors and books visit **www.ospreypublishing.com**. Here you will find extracts, author interviews, details of forthcoming events and the option to sign up for our newsletter.

CONTENTS

INTRODUCTION

During the first ten months of World War II in Europe – from September 1939 through to June 1940 – the *Wehrmacht* (German Armed Forces) stunned the watching wider world with the astonishingly fast and decisive military successes that they achieved. These awesome combat triumphs completely transformed the balance of power within the continent of Europe. First, in a mere 36 days (some 860 hours) during September and October 1939, the Wehrmacht invaded Poland and, with the assistance of a subsequent Soviet invasion from the East, quickly conquered the entire country. Then, in April 1940, German forces invaded and overran the small neighbouring country of Denmark in a mere matter of hours. In addition, over the course of 60 days of combat from April to June 1940, German expeditionary forces mounted successful amphibious assaults on the Norwegian coast and subsequently overran that country; in the process they also forced the withdrawal of the Anglo-French intervention forces that had landed to prevent the Wehrmacht occupying the whole of Norway.

Thirdly and finally, on 10 May 1940 the Wehrmacht took on by far the biggest martial challenge it had yet faced. German forces invaded the Netherlands, Belgium, Luxembourg and France, as well as engaging the British Expeditionary Force (BEF) that had deployed to northern France. During the Great War of 1914–18 German Imperial forces had failed to overwhelm the Allied military defence of Belgian and French soil along the trench-systems of the Western Front, despite four years of intense combat amid a wider context of increasingly total war mobilisation. Astonishingly, in the space of just ten short days, 10–20 May 1940, the German Armed Forces' *Fall Gelb* (Case Yellow) invasion conquered all of the Netherlands and most of Belgium, as well as driving a powerful *Panzer* (armoured) wedge through the difficult forested hilly terrain of the Ardennes in the weakly defended Allied centre.

On 20 May 1940 the headlong westward charge of these massed German Panzer and mobile infantry divisions reached the Channel coast near Abbeville.

Here a detachment of German cavalry parades through conquered Paris near the Arc du Triumph in mid-June 1940. The elite armoured and motorised infantry divisions were each equipped with several thousand armoured vehicles, including tanks, half-track infantry carriers, lorries and tracked engineering vehicles. However, the rest of the German Army – its regular infantry divisions – still employed hundreds of thousands of horses as their main mobility assets. (Photo by Heinrich Hoffmann/Timepix/The LIFE Picture Collection via Getty Images)

This successful penetration of the Allied centre cut off in a pocket the significant Allied forces – French, British and Belgian – deployed in the northern flank of the theatre. Most of these forces capitulated, although significant elements managed to escape via the maritime evacuation operations carried out around the town of Dunkirk between 27 May and 4 June 1940. This was a staggering military success that dwarfed the triumphs achieved by the Imperial German forces' execution of the Schlieffen Plan invasion of France and Belgium back in the summer of 1914. Finally, over the course of the ensuing 20 days of the German *Fall Rot* invasion of the rest of France (5–25 June 1940) the country was brought to strategic defeat and humiliating capitulation. Indeed, in just 47 days – a mere 1,120 hours – the Wehrmacht had strategically defeated the most potent military power in Europe.

In trying to comprehend the causes of all three of these staggering German early-war martial successes, the Allies focussed heavily on trying to understand German strategy, operational methods and tactics. The Allies became fixated with the so-called German military doctrine popularly, though misleadingly, named *Blitzkrieg* ('Lightning War'). This radical new operational method envisaged the utilisation en masse of strategically concentrated, rapidly moving, all-arms armoured forces. The German operational method initially envisaged quickly breaking through the initial enemy defences (the tactical zone of prepared defence, typically located along the national border) through exploiting surprise and shock action, with these actions being backed by extensive aerial strikes.

Once the German Panzer divisions had got beyond the tactical zone of defence, they would conduct audacious, risk-embracing, rapidly executed strategic deep penetration. These bold armoured advances deep into enemy territory, carried out with scant regard to their exposed flanks, would overrun enemy rear-area headquarters, depots, transportation nodes, and reserve forces' assembly areas, increasingly inflicting dislocation, paralysis and shock action on the enemy at the tactical and operational levels. The tempo and momentum that the German Panzer divisions developed were significantly greater than that developed by the enemies that these formations engaged. The rapid execution of German operations enabled their forces to get well inside their enemies' decision-making cycles (Observe-Orientate-Decide-Act, or OODA loops). This helped paralyse their enemies' reactions; by the time some Allied tactical response had been crafted, the German advances in the intervening period of time had so changed the tactical (and sometimes operational) situation, that the planned Allied response had become an irrelevance before it had even been initiated.

In fact, the Germans had no such explicit doctrine as Blitzkrieg. The principal German capstone doctrinal work remained the 1936 version of *Truppenführung* (The Command of Troops). Rather Blitzkrieg was an operational method that was developed, and fervently believed in, by a small number of forward-looking German commanders – officers such as Heinz Guderian, Erwin Rommel and Ferdinand Schaal. In these campaigns – but particularly during the 1940 Western campaign – these far-sighted apostles of fast-paced mobile operations proved through success in battle the validity of their vision. This was often in the face of the qualms experienced by the more conservative higher German commanders at army and army group level. These officers – like Rundstedt and Kleist – were deeply worried about the vulnerable flanks created by these rapid Panzer advances.

From 1935 to 1940 many of Germany's older, conservatively minded, senior commanders – like GenObst Fedor von Bock and GenObst Gerd von Rundstedt – remained sceptical about the vision of fast-paced, risk-embracing, mechanised warfare put forward by more junior commanders like Heinz Guderian and Erwin Rommel. Gen d.Inf Johannes Blaskowitz, an army commander in the 1939 Polish campaign, shared these doubts. He is seen here (right) being taken into Canadian Army custody in Apeldoorn, the Netherlands, on 14 June 1945. (Photo courtesy of Libraries and Archives Canada, PA-138038)

Seen here on 1 November 1918 is a German A7V tank, captured by the French, on display in the Place de la Concorde, Paris. Unlike Britain and France, Germany had only extremely limited experience with tanks in the Great War, with just 22 examples of the unwieldy A7V tank design being built. But it was upon these slender foundations that the Germans built Blitzkrieg during the interwar years. (Photo courtesy of Libraries and Archives Canada, R11203-388-9-E)

Indeed, Guderian only managed to be allowed to continue his charge west to the Channel coast by resigning in the midst of battle and by insubordinately using whatever tactical ruse he could find to avoid his superior's orders to halt. His superiors wished to stop the Panzers temporarily, so as to allow the more slowly moving follow-up infantry divisions to catch up and establish defences along these vulnerable flanks. But such conservative risk-aversion violated the fundamental principles upon which Blitzkrieg was based. It was only by continuing to advance as quickly as possible deep into the enemy rear that the Panzer spearheads could keep generating tactical surprise, momentum, tempo and shock action, and thus keep within the enemy's decision-making cycle. The exposed flanks of the armoured wedges were not a threat if the enemy was too overwhelmed with the unfolding offensive to do anything about counter-attacking these exposed flanks.

Yet the German journey to implementing Blitzkrieg during 1939–41 was an evolutionary one that looks more linear with hindsight than it did at the time. It did not necessarily unfold naturally during the interwar period. During the 1939 Polish campaign, for example, fast-paced mobile operations by Panzer, light-mechanised and motor-infantry formations played a key part in the German success. That said, in this campaign the Germans did not employ the massed strategic concentration of armour as seen during the 1940 Western campaign in the form of Panzer Group Kleist's eight mobile divisions. Equally, given the expeditionary nature of the spring 1940 German campaign in Norway, and the largely mountainous terrain, these operations did not feature armoured fighting vehicles on any significant scale. Instead, the Germans exploited the Blitzkrieg principles of surprise, speed, shock, mobility, and rapid decision-making cycle – but without the employment of all-arms tank-centered mobile formations.

Indeed, it was only during the 1940 German invasion of the West that the execution of the so-called Blitzkrieg approach neared its apogee. The eventual Wehrmacht plan exploited the German understanding of Allied strategic intentions and the latter's consequent ensuing maldeployment. Into the weak Allied centre, the Germans infiltrated Panzer Group Kleist's concentrated armoured wedge; further north the rapid advance of other Panzer formations was critical to fixing the best Allied forces in a bitter contact battle raging in central Belgium. The Germans had no clear plan beyond the establishment of a bridgehead across the Meuse, from which they could subsequently launch threatening offensives to the north, west, south and southeast. Yet the Panzer commanders – men like Guderian, Hoth, Rommel and Stever – were determined to seize this opportunity with daring, risk-embracing, high-tempo armoured thrusts that eventually reached the Channel coast. Even without an official Blitzkrieg doctrine during the 1940 campaign, this crop of audacious Panzer commanders nevertheless realised in action their forward-looking dream of the so-called Blitzkrieg-style of fast-paced, strategic-level, all-arms mechanised warfare facilitated by dedicated aerial support.

The indirect doctrinal and tactical roots of this new German style of strategic mechanised warfare can be traced back to all the belligerents' experiences of the 1914–18 Great War. Ideas about the future possibilities of mobile warfare first arose out of the bitter impasse of trench stalemate on the Western Front – an utterly unexpected and truly painful tactical reality that led over the course of four years of bitter combat to the slaughter of hundreds of thousands of young European soldiers.

One particular antecedent of Blitzkrieg was the German development and employment of *Stoßtrupp* ('Storm Troop') tactics during the final period of the Great War in 1917–18. The elite Storm Troop units, powerfully reinforced with organic firepower, used infiltration tactics to enter enemy trenches by surprise and overcome the defenders. The German Storm Troops relied upon speed and flexibility when on the offensive, to generate confusion and paralysis within the enemy while simultaneously outmanoeuvring them. The Panzer division – a well-balanced all-arms formation built around a mass of tanks – was in many ways the late 1930s doctrinal descendent of German Storm Troop tactics.

During most of the interwar period Britain, France, the US and the Soviet Union initially led the way in developing mechanised warfare capabilities. A small number of far-sighted tacticians within these armies believed that the tank – which uniquely combined the elements of lethal firepower, potent protection and high mobility – could take the Storm Troopers' approach to a geographically larger and faster scale. While Germany lagged behind the other nations in this area, such ideas about the future employment of mechanised formations fell on fertile ground. This was because these ideas dovetailed nicely with the traditional elements of Prussian, and later, German military strategy. This strategic approach emphasised the importance of deep penetration operations, envelopment and encirclement movements, and *Vernichtungsschlacht* (the decisive battle of annihilation). These basic principles formed the bedrock of the Schlieffen Plan invasion of Belgium and France. These interwar notions on future mechanised warfare capability, therefore, connected neatly with both pre-existing Prussian/German strategic principles and with Storm Troop tactics.

The conditions that pertained for the interwar military of the new German Weimar republic, however, were far from conducive for the audacious development of a costly and unproven revolutionary new form of mechanised warfare. The 1919 Treaty of Versailles that ended the Great War's Western Front campaign had reduced Germany to a 100,000-man army, curtailed offensive weapons development, and completely prohibited tank development and procurement. Yet ironically the severe limitations imposed on the interwar German military by the Versailles settlement compelled the *Reichswehr* (the German Army) to embrace innovation. The emasculated German Armed Forces could not effectively defend the Weimar Republic against powerful hostile neighbours. The hand-picked brains of the numerically tiny German Army grasped at developing any advantage their forces could gain through tactical innovation.

During 1920–26 the Commander-in-Chief of the German Army, *GenObst* (Colonel-General) Hans von Seeckt, set the foundation for the future development of Blitzkrieg methods. Seeckt transformed the seemingly obsolescent post-war German cavalry into a semi-motorised strategic reserve and directed his forces' focus on the use of speed and mobility to offset the Reichswehr's numerical and material inferiority. He emphasised the employment of coordination between combat arms, which provided a key backdrop to the effective combat power that the future well-balanced all-arms German Panzer divisions would develop in the first, tumultuous year of World War II. Under Seeckt's tenure, the first covert German tank research occurred both in Sweden and, perhaps surprisingly, in the Communist Soviet Union – the fellow pariah state of the League of Nations' new world order.

Perhaps the key event in this haphazard, meandering, gradual German journey toward the development of Blitzkrieg operational approaches was the coming to power of Hitler's Nazi Party in 1933. The violently nationalistic, militaristic, racist,

GenObst Hans von Seeckt was the German Army Commander-in-Chief from 1920 to 1926. His innovations helped set the doctrinal foundations that enabled the German Blitzkrieg approach to be realised during the 1930s. After a career in German politics in the years 1930–32, he became military advisor to Chiang Kai-Shek during the Chinese Nationalist Army's internal war against the Chinese Communist guerrillas before his death in 1936. (Photo by Imagno/Getty Images)

ABOVE The support Luftwaffe aircraft provided to the rampaging Panzer divisions on the ground proved crucial to deliver the success of Blitzkrieg. Here a squadron of Junkers Ju 87 Stuka dive-bombers from *Stukageschwader* 2 fly in formation over France in a close air support mission on 30 May 1940. Luftwaffe aircraft also performed vital counter-air, interdiction, reconnaissance, airborne-landing/ air assault and transportation missions. (Photo by Hulton Archive/Stringer/ Getty Images)

LEFT During 1937–38 the German Condor Legion fought alongside Franco's Nationalist forces in the Spanish Civil War. This all-arms and combined air-and-ground force deployed 180 light Pzkpfw I and II tanks and several air squadrons. The Germans garnered valuable tactical lessons from the Legion's combat experiences in Spain. (Photo by Heinrich Hoffmann/ullstein bild Dtl. via Getty Images)

anti-Semitic Nazi movement, headed by the utterly expedient and politically-astute demagogic Adolf Hitler, the German *Führer* (leader), had very different foreign policy objectives to those of the Weimar Republic. Adolf Hitler saw the use of war as the first, preferred, instrument of the Nazi state in its quest of territorial expansion. The Nazi regime wished to regain the 'German' lands lost in the Treaty of Versailles, as well as to secure the subjugation of eastern Europe to provide *Lebensraum* (living space) for the economically self-sufficient (autarchic) German nation of the future. Hitler wanted a military capability to take the offensive, to meet his aggressive foreign policy objectives. The development of German mechanised formations from 1935 fitted very well with the Nazi *Weltanschauung* (world-view) that naked raw military power could be used forcibly to reshape the political face of Europe.

Within the German Panzer divisions, most of the supporting artillery pieces and field guns (that is indirect and direct fire support assets) were towed by fully-tracked or half-tracked prime movers. Here a German Sdkfz 7 medium half-track tows a howitzer past Cleopatra's Needle in Paris, on 23 June 1940. (Bettmann / Getty Images)

Propelled forward by Hitler's fervent approval and a massive rearmament programme, during 1935 the Reichswehr formed, within its recently-created Mobile Troops Command, its first three Panzer divisions. These were well-balanced formations, built around a brigade of tanks, together with motorised infantry, semi-motorised artillery and anti-tank guns, as well as other mobile supporting arms, such as engineers, recce forces and a dedicated motorised *Luftwaffe* (German Air Force) air-support liaison detachment.

It was now possible for Germany to create this Panzer force structure because in 1934, Hitler – completely ignoring the restrictions of the Treaty of Versailles – ordered German factories to commence production of two interim light training tanks, the PzKpfw I and II. Meanwhile, German manufacturers were also designing the heavier PzKpfw III and IV combat tanks. Next, the German Army grouped these three Panzer divisions under the command of the XVI Corps (Motorised). In so doing, the Germans created the first ever mechanised corps that was intended for employment on strategic operations.

Subsequently, the German Army created the 4th and 5th Panzer Divisions during 1938 and in November appointed *Obst* (Colonel) Guderian as Chief of the newly-formed Mobile Troops Command. During 1937–38, moreover, the Germans had dispatched 180 PzKpfw I light tanks to support General Franco's Nationalist forces during the Spanish Civil War. In this conflict the Germans gained useful combat experiences that highlighted the limitations of this light tank's design, and which established the first basic tactical arrangements for air-ground co-operation.

The bloodless March 1938 German *Anschluss* (annexation) of Austria, the October 1938 occupation of the Sudetenland, and the March 1939 conquest of the rump Czech state revealed the many organisational and tactical deficiencies of the new German mobile force. In the meantime, the larger and more effective PzKpfw III and IV were entering German service in small numbers, as did the former inventory of the Czech Army, redesignated as the PzKpfw 35(t) and 38(t) tanks.

By the summer of 1939, moreover, the German Army's *Panzerwaffe* (armoured branch) had – in the space of just six years – developed into a reasonably effective combat force. With the spring 1939 raising of the 10th Panzer Division, the German Mobile Force fielded on the eve of World War II some six armoured divisions, four light (mechanised) divisions, one cavalry division and four motorised infantry divisions; two infantry-support tank brigades also existed. By summer 1939 the German Army fielded a total of 3,197 tanks, of which 1,946 served within its six Panzer divisions. However, serious deficiencies remained. Germany's Panzer formations could only field small numbers of half-tracked armoured personnel carriers, and thus had to rely instead on lorries for infantry transport. Equally, these divisions had insufficient numbers of the heavier and PzKpfw III and IV combat tanks.

That said, by late August 1939 the German Army had developed a more effective fast-paced strategic mobile warfare capability than any of her European opponents; the militaries of all Germany's potential enemies also suffered from significant doctrinal, structural, organisational and tactical deficiencies that the German forces would go on to ably exploit. The raw power of German offensive operations was clearly demonstrated from 1 September 1939 when the Wehrmacht invaded Poland. The stunning German successes in the 1939 Polish campaign introduced to the watching world the devastating combat power unleashed by the German strategic and operational approach the world came to describe as Blitzkrieg. In ten short months Hitler's use of Germany's superior military power – executed in the manner of Blitzkrieg – would utterly transform the face of Europe. Regrettably, these stunning Nazi martial triumphs would plunge many tens of millions of Europeans into the heinous deprivations of brutal and rapacious Nazi occupation. The when, what, how and why of these three German Blitzkrieg wars fought during 1939–40 – the autumn 1939 Polish, the spring 1940 Danish and Norwegian, and the May–June 1940 Western campaigns – are examined in detail in the pages that follow.

The German Blitzkrieg swiftly overran the Netherlands, Belgium, Luxembourg and France during May–June 1940. Here in mid-May 1940, the crew of a Panzer tank stop to chat to some fellow German infanteers near a windmill in newly occupied Dutch territory, while a young local boy looks on with mixed feelings of curiosity, awe and fear. (Photo by Hugo Jaeger/Timepix/The LIFE Picture Collection via Getty Images)

1

THE AUTUMN 1939 POLISH CAMPAIGN

INTRODUCTION

The German invasion of Poland on 1 September 1939 signalled the commencement of World War II in Europe. The outcome was a foregone conclusion since the invasion pitted Europe's best military and greatest industrial power against an impoverished eastern neighbour. To seal defeat, Germany had secretly agreed that the Soviet Union would invade Poland two weeks after the German attack. Polish strategy hinged on Anglo-French entry into the war, diverting German forces to the Western Front; but this strategy collapsed when France remained overwhelmingly on the defensive, well protected behind the fortifications of the Maginot line.

The German campaign's nature was not similarly defensive. Even if the outcome of the 1939 Polish campaign was predictable, the nature of the fighting was not. The 1939 campaign represented the first demonstration of the Blitzkrieg style of warfare. The German assault was spearheaded by Panzer divisions whose firepower and shock action were further amplified by the use of Junkers Ju 87 Stuka dive-bombers to provide close air support (that is, aerial fire support to the contact battle). The Polish army of 1939 was not as backward as is often portrayed, and its stubborn defence gave the Germans the occasional surprise, for example during the Bzura counter-offensive. The German military's novel tactics were certainly imperfect, and casualties were therefore relatively heavy for such a short campaign. The Polish campaign proved to be a crucial learning experience for the Wehrmacht. It uncovered the shortcomings in German training and doctrine.

The German forces vigorously addressed these weaknesses over the winter of 1939–40, during an intensive period of tactical self-reflection and adaptation. These tactical and organisational improvements made possible the stunning decisive victory the Wehrmacht achieved in the 1940 Western campaign.

If a single image dominates the popular perception of the Polish campaign of autumn 1939, it is the imagined scene of Polish cavalrymen bravely charging the advancing German Panzers with their lances. Like many other details of the campaign, it is a myth that was created by German wartime propaganda and perpetuated by sloppy scholarship. Yet such myths have also been embraced by the Poles themselves as symbols of their wartime gallantry, achieving a cultural resonance in spite of their variance with the historical record. Given the many advantages the Germans had at the start of the campaign, which were augmented when the Soviets invaded Poland from the east, it is surprising that on a good number of occasions the defending Polish forces fought with great determination and effectiveness.

THE ORIGINS OF THE CAMPAIGN

A platoon of Polish cavalry troops exercises adjacent to East Prussia, prior to September 1939. (Bettman / Getty Images)

If Hitler's rise to power in the early 1930s was nourished by Germany's humiliating defeat in the Great War, the perceived harsh settlement terms imposed by the Allies in the Treaty of Versailles and the loss of former German territory in the east

to Czechoslovakia and Poland were bitterly resented by the German population. The Nazis ruthlessly exploited this popular resentment in their rise to power. Tensions were further amplified by the fetid stew of Nazi racial ideology that linked the resurgence of the German nation with the violent seizure of *Lebensraum* (living space) from the allegedly subhuman Slavs on Germany's eastern frontier.

Having rejected the demilitarisation of the German Armed Forces soon after taking power, by the late 1930s Hitler was increasingly using Germany's growing military might to further his political ambitions. In September 1938, he pressured France and Britain to accept his seizure of the Sudetenland (the border areas of Czechoslovakia with the most ethnic Germans within it). The appeasement of Germany by Britain, France, and Italy, represented respectively by Neville Chamberlain, Édouard Daladier, and Benito Mussolini at the 1938 Munich conference (Czechoslovakia and the Soviet Union, also interested parties, did not attend), served as a catalyst for the ensuing war. It convinced Hitler that Anglo-French leaders were timid men who could be bluffed, bullied and coerced into making further territorial concessions to Hitler's expansionist foreign policy objectives. It similarly convinced Josef Stalin, the leader of the Soviet Union, that France and Britain would not honour their commitments to east-central European states, so Stalin reached his own accord with Germany. The Bolshevik Soviet Union had also lost territory after the Great War and shared a desire to overthrow the existing territorial boundaries. While the ideological beliefs of the two nations – Marxism and Nazism – were diametrically opposed, their national state interests temporarily converged in an expedient fashion during 1939.

GenObst Wilhelm List (1880–1971), who commanded the German Fourteenth Army during the 1939 Polish campaign, is photographed here on 5 April 1939. (Photo by Keystone/Stringer/Getty Images)

The Munich concessions were famously hailed by then British Prime Minister Neville Chamberlain as offering 'peace in our time'; but by spring 1939 the leaders of both Britain and France began to recognise that Hitler's territorial demands were insatiable. The situation further deteriorated after 15 March 1939 when German troops seized the remainder of Czechoslovakia and formed an Axis puppet Slovak state.

In late March 1939, Hitler informed the senior leaders of the Wehrmacht that the 'Polish question' would have to be solved by military means. Hitler used lingering resentment over German territorial losses to Poland during 1918–22 as the pretext for war. The most significant irritant for Germans was the separation of East Prussia from the rest of the *Reich* (Empire) by the former German territory now known as the Pomeranian Corridor. In addition, the major German Baltic port of Danzig had been converted to a 'free city', and Germans also chafed over Polish control of eastern Pomerania and Silesia, ceded to Poland in the early 1920s, all of which contained substantial German minorities. From October 1938 onwards Hitler pressured Poland for an extra-territorial road through the Corridor to East Prussia. He also demanded the return of Danzig to Germany.

German Foreign Minister Joachim von Ribbentrop (right) being congratulated by Hitler in the Reich Chancellery, after his return from Moscow with the Molotov–Ribbentrop Pact, signed 29 August 1939. (Photo by Heinrich Hoffmann/ullstein bild via Getty Images)

Poland's strategic plans hinged on its alliance with France. Paris had attempted to create a strategic grouping of Allied states in east-central Europe as a bulwark against German or Soviet expansion. By the 1930s, however, the 'Little Entente' was falling apart. Poland and Czechoslovakia, embroiled in petty bilateral territorial disputes, could not form a military alliance against their threatening German neighbour.

Warsaw rejected the German diplomatic moves of 1938–39, correctly reading them as pretexts for territorial aggrandisement. After the cessation of the Sudetenland, Warsaw was concerned that Germany would similarly attempt to annex the Pomeranian Corridor, Danzig, and Silesia. On 31 March 1939, the British government announced its guarantee of Polish security, including the maintenance of the status quo of the city of Danzig. The Soviet Union was excluded from these discussions, largely due to Polish fear that Soviet military intervention was tantamount to eventual occupation.

Although both Britain and France were interested in involving Moscow in an anti-German coalition, they could not overcome Warsaw's deep suspicions about long-term Soviet aims. A combination of German diplomatic success and Anglo-French vacillation led Stalin eventually to a treaty with Germany. Stalin had his own territorial ambitions in the region, and desired to cash in on any future German territorial seizure. Much of eastern Poland had been Russian until 1918, and the large numbers of Byelorussians and Ukrainians in eastern Poland provided the nationalist pretext for Soviet territorial absorption. In addition, Stalin sought to regain strategically important former Russian territory, including the Baltic states, Moldova, and parts of Finland. During summer 1939, the Germans and Soviets hashed out a treaty. The 25 August 1939 announcement of the Molotov–Ribbentrop Pact, between these two arch ideological enemies, stunned the world. But for both Adolf Hitler and Josef Stalin, the Molotov–Ribbentrop Pact was nothing more than a cynical temporary expedient marriage of convenience that would last but two short years. It did nothing to change the prospect of a future titanic military struggle between the two countries.

The Molotov–Ribbentrop Pact effectively gave Hitler the green light to invade Poland. He was convinced that weak Anglo-French leaders would avoid war, and that even if they did declare war, their response would be indecisive. On 23 August 1939, Hitler set the invasion date for the 26th, but hesitated when Britain pledged military support to Poland. Last-minute diplomatic efforts sought to discredit the Polish government internationally. A border violation was fabricated to provide an excuse for invasion. While these diplomatic shenanigans unfolded, on 31 August 1939, Hitler ordered the invasion for the following day.

CHRONOLOGY: POLISH CAMPAIGN

1938

29 September	At the Munich conference Britain and France agree to the German demands that Czechoslovakia cede the ethnically German Sudetenland region to Germany.
1–7 October	German troops occupy the Sudetenland region.
23 October	Hitler demands an extra-territorial road connection through the Pomeranian Corridor from Germany's eastern borders to East Prussia. The Polish government rejects the demand.

1939

15 March	The German Army invades the remainder of Czechoslovakia, occupies Bohemia–Moravia and eventually allows Slovakia to form an Axis puppet state.
22 March	The German Armed Forces seize the Baltic port of Memel from Lithuania.
25 March	Hitler orders OKW and OKH to start preparations for an invasion of Poland.
28 March	The Polish Army begins partial mobilisation in response to German diplomatic pressure to cede Pomeranian Corridor and allow return of the Free City of Danzig to Germany.
31 March	The British government announces its guarantee of Polish security, including maintaining the status quo of the city of Danzig.
May	The Polish and French General Staffs hold meetings in France, during which France pledges to launch a major offensive against Germany two weeks after a German invasion of Poland.
23 August	Hitler sets the date for the invasion of Poland as being on 26 August.
24 August	Britain gives written assurances of assistance to Poland in the event of war with Germany.
25 August	The German foreign minister Ribbentrop and Soviet foreign minister Molotov announce the German–Soviet Non-aggression Pact (the Molotov–Ribbentrop Pact). This treaty includes secret clauses in which the two parties agreed that they would cooperate in a two-front invasion of Poland that will lead to that country's dismemberment.
26 August	Hitler planned to start the Polish campaign on this day, but postpones the attack in wake of the British security announcement of the 24th.

The old German battleship *Schleswig-Holstein* bombards the Polish defences at Westerplatte, 1 September 1939. (Photo by Hulton Archive/ Stringer/ Getty Images)

31 August	Hitler irrevocably commits to launching the invasion of Poland on the following day, 1 September. As a consequence, German border provocations escalate.
1 September	The Polish campaign begins at 0400hrs with the old German battleship *Schleswig-Holstein* firing on the Polish garrison on Westerplatte near Danzig. German forces cross Poland's borders. Polish cavalry units counter-attack astride the River Brda. The German Third Army advance from East Prussia initially stalls. Army Group South advances toward Katowice. Large Luftwaffe air strike on Warsaw is ineffectual.
2 September	German forces advancing out of East Prussia force the Polish Army Modlin to withdraw to the River Vistula line.
3 September	France and Britain declare war on Germany. The last two remaining major Polish warships are sunk in an air attack. The Army Pomorze begins its withdrawal behind the River Vistula. Army Group North forces the Pomeranian Corridor.
4 September	Polish forces retreat from the town of Mława.
5 September	The Polish town of Piotrków falls, and the gateway to Warsaw is opened to the German Panzers. In the evening, the Armies Łódź, Kraków, and Poznań are ordered to begin the retreat behind the River Vistula. Army Group North forces the River Narew. The Army Modlin is encircled. The Polish strategic reserve, Army Prusy, is committed astride Piotrków.
6 September	Polish fighters abandon the air defence of Warsaw, leaving it protected only by anti-aircraft guns. The Polish Army Prusy withdraws behind the River Vistula.

7 September   German armoured formations reach outskirts of Warsaw but are thrown back in intense street fighting. *Marszałek* (Marshal) Rydz-Śmigły decides to shift the Polish High Command headquarters from Warsaw to Brześć nad Bugiem (Brest-Litovsk). Westerplatte surrenders. Poles constitute a new strategic reserve, Army Lublin. Tarnów falls. French launch half-hearted offensive into the Saar.

9 September   The Army Poznań launches counter-attack along the River Bzura, catching the German Eighth Army off-guard. The Germans are driven back in disorder.

10 September   Full-scale Polish strategic withdrawal behind the River Vistula ordered. New Northern and Southern operational fronts formed.

11 September   Germans fully occupy Upper Silesia. Bzura counter-offensive stalls. Polish strategic withdrawal in south into Romanian bridgehead ordered.

12 September   A Polish counter-attack recaptures Łowicz. France halts its Saar offensive after gaining minimal territory.

13 September   The Army Kraków faces the predicament of encirclement.

14 September   Germans clear and fully occupy Danzig. The Polish Northern Front is routed.

German frontier guards on duty at Danzig on the last day of peace patrol on a road near Zoppot barricaded with anti-tank entanglements. (Photo by Keystone/Stringer/Getty Images)

A German self-propelled light anti-aircraft gun guards against an attack by Polish aeroplanes on 25 September 1939, possibly around Warsaw. (Bettman / Getty images)

| 15 September | Units from the German Army Group North reach the northern outskirts of Warsaw. The siege of the capital resumes. Soviets sign armistice with Japan. |
| 16 September | Polish forces along the River Bzura subjected to massive German artillery and air attack. Polish retreat to Warsaw ordered that evening. The Luftwaffe sinks last remaining Polish warships. |

17 September	The Soviet Red Army begins to invade Poland from the east. Initial Polish resistance is minimal. This second surprise attack seals Poland's fate.
18 September	Polish intelligence officers escape to France with copy of Enigma decoding machine. The bulk of the Armies Lublin, Pomorze and Poznań surrender in the Bzura Pocket. Polish resistance against the Soviet advance increases.
19 September	The Army Kraków attempts to break out towards Romania through the area around Tomaszów Lubelski.
20 September	Most forward German units begin withdrawal to agreed Soviet-German demarcation line. The largest armoured clash of the campaign occurs astride Tomaszów Lubelski as Poles drive toward the Romanian bridgehead. The Army Kraków capitulates.
21 September	The last units from the Polish Bzura counter-offensive finally surrender.
22 September	Encircled by German and Soviet troops, the city of Lwów finally surrenders to the Soviets.
23 September	Massive German assault on Warsaw stalls in the face of determined resistance.
25 September	'Black Monday', a massive Luftwaffe attack on Warsaw causes heavy civilian casualties; Germans renew all-out assault.
26 September	German assaults capture the southern Warsaw forts, rendering the continued defence of the capital strategically untenable.
27 September	The Warsaw garrison surrenders; some 140,000 Polish troops are captured.
29 September	The fortified Modlin garrison surrenders.
1 October	The Polish garrison on the Hel Peninsula surrenders.
2 October	The remnants of the Polish Northern Front capitulates at Nisko.
5 October	The Germans hold a victory parade in Warsaw.
6 October	A Polish battle group under *Generał Brygady* (Brig) Franciszek Kleeberg surrenders after a four-day battle around Kock. This is the last major Polish unit in the field to capitulate, thus ending the conflict.

THE OPPOSING COMMANDERS

The German Commanders

The choice to go to war was clearly made by the leader of the Nazi German Third Reich, the Führer **Adolf Hitler**. The Führer usurped the control of grand strategy from the *Oberkommando des Heeres*, OKH (German Army High Command) even before the war began. He forced the resignation of the Chief of the General Staff, Ludwig Beck, in August 1938, when his lack of confidence in Adolf Hitler's belligerent schemes became apparent. The senior Wehrmacht leadership was unenthusiastic for the campaign, fearing that it would precipitate a general European war. Most German military leaders at the time thought that the Wehrmacht was not yet ready for war with the Western powers. In the 1939 Polish campaign Hitler played the traditional role of supreme political leader but left operational planning to the officer corps.

The senior German generals remained ambivalent towards Hitler. They rejoiced at his avid support of the military, his rejection of the restrictions of Versailles, and his rejuvenation of German national pride. Yet, as traditional, conservative, authoritarian aristocrats, they disdained the Nazis as upstarts and

Hitler visits German ground forces at the site of an overrun Polish gun battery. To the left of Hitler is Gauleiter Albert Forster, and on the right is GenObst Keitel, September 1939. (Photo by Heinrich Hoffmann/ullstein bild via Getty Images)

many questioned the virulence of Nazi ideology. They resented the former corporal Hitler's attempts to usurp their domination of professional war planning. A few such senior officers dallied with half-hearted schemes for an army coup but younger officers were more supportive of Hitler's Nazi ideology and goals. Hitler was a highly able politician, and skilfully manipulated the senior army leadership by installing pliable officers in senior positions.

Before the war Hitler had abolished the old War Ministry and assumed the position of Commander-in-Chief, overseeing the Oberkommando der Wehrmacht, OKW (Armed Forces High Command). **GenObst Wilhelm Bodewin Keitel** headed the OKW. Like so many other senior German staff officers in World War II, Keitel had been an artillery officer in World War I at a time when artillery was the dominant branch of service. After being wounded in 1914, his abilities brought him to the attention of the general staff, on which he served for the remainder of the war. Keitel replaced the former war minister, Werner von Blomberg, in 1938 following a personal scandal that led to his downfall. Keitel's new position was largely administrative and his quest for unified control of the armed forces never materialised, as control of the Luftwaffe remained in the hands of one of Hitler's cronies, *Reichsmarschall* (Marshall of the Reich) Hermann Göring.

Keitel was ably served by **Alfred Jodl**, Chief of the Operations Office. Jodl, was a former Great War artillery officer, and his evident abilities led to his appointment to the clandestine general staff after the war's end in 1918. He rose quickly in the interwar army and joined the OKW in 1938. In August 1939 Keitel elevated him to be his operations chief. Nevertheless, the key planning for the Polish operation fell to the army, not to the OKW.

The German Army's Commander-in-Chief (namely, the head of the OKH) was **GenObst Walther Heinrich Alfred Hermann von Brauchitsch**. He was a Silesian aristocrat and former Great War staff officer; during this war he received the coveted Iron Cross. He was deeply indebted to the Nazi party financially and for keeping secret sordid aspects of his messy divorce and remarriage. Suitably compromised, he offered no resistance to Hitler's offensive plans even if he had personal doubts about their wisdom.

The Chief of the German General Staff was **GenObst Franz Halder**, who had replaced Beck in the midst of the Czech crisis in 1938. Under Hitler, the general staff no longer had the influence it had during the days of Moltke and Schlieffen in Germany's two previous wars – the Franco-Prussian War of 1870–71 and World War I. Halder, who was a monarchist and a practising Christian, was another Prussian general with little personal enthusiasm for the Nazis. He was regarded by other German generals as a competent if mediocre commander. Once at his post, Halder took up his assignment with enthusiasm and brought together a superb team under GenObst von Rundstedt to plan the Polish operation.

Field command in the autumn 1939 Polish campaign was split between the German Army Groups North and South. **GenObst Karl Rudolf Gerd von Rundstedt** commanded the larger force, Army Group South. Rundstedt, a Prussian aristocratic officer, had had a distinguished Great War career. While apolitical, Rundstedt's expertise catapulted him into senior command.

Army Group North was commanded by **GenObst Moritz Albrecht Franz Friedrich Fedor von Bock**, whose career had parallels to Rundstedt's. He had enjoyed a brilliant interwar career. Both these commanders, buoyed by their successful operations during the autumn 1939 Polish campaign, would each go on to lead one of the three army group commands deployed for the spring 1940 Western campaign, of which we will hear much more later.

The Polish Commanders

The greatest influence on Polish commanders was **Józef Piłsudski**, the Polish leader until his death in 1935. Piłsudski, a socialist, attempted during the Great War to entice the Austro-Hungarians to form Polish military units to fight the Russians. Fearing separatist nationalism, the Austrians imprisoned Piłsudski. But Józef Piłsudski's Legion attracted many young fervent Polish nationalists, many of whom later become key military leaders.

The collapse of empires in 1918 permitted the recreation of an independent Polish state in 1919. Yet Poland's independence had to be secured by force of arms. A war immediately broke out between Poland and Bolshevik Russia (1919–20). Piłsudski's inspired wartime leadership led most Poles to regard him as a national saviour. Piłsudski initially withdrew from public life after the war, but then in 1926 overthrew Poland's fractious democracy in a bloodless seizure of power. Piłsudski became the power behind the throne, remaining politically influential. His death in 1935 left the country adrift, as his successor, Generał (General) Edward Rydz-Śmigły, could not fill the shoes of so talented a political leader.

The 1920s Polish army was created from scratch. Experienced officers came from Germany, Austro-Hungary, and Tsarist Russia. Piłsudski was generally successful in moulding together a cohesive officer corps. The Polish experience of war in the years 1918–22, however, was quite different from the Great War static trench fighting, principally experienced on the Western Front. Thus, Polish military doctrine stressed improvisation and manoeuvre.

Marszałek Edward Rydz-Śmigły headed the General Inspectorate of the Polish Armed Forces (GISZ), which had been created by Piłsudski in the late 1920s to control the armed forces instead of the general staff. Rydz-Śmigły had headed the Legion after Piłsudski was imprisoned. He was one of Piłsudski's most talented and trusted field commanders, leading the Polish units that seized Wilno (summer 1919), Dunaberg (in Latvia, during late 1919) and Kiev (in the Ukraine,

A bomber wing of Junker Ju 87 (Stuka) dive-bombers on a mission against Polish ground targets sometime in September 1939. (Photo by ullstein bild/ullstein bild via Getty Images)

in 1920). During the defence of Poland against the Bolsheviks in 1920, Edward Rydz-Śmigły defended Warsaw and campaigned in Galicia.

Piłsudski selected him as his successor because the latter was apolitical. Unfortunately, during the 1930s Rydz-Śmigły increasingly floundered in both the political and military realms. Poland had several capable generals in 1939, but Rydz-Śmigły's army politicisation and the cult of amateurism and improvisation led to poor command and control. All nine field army commanders reported directly to Rydz-Śmigły. Given the relatively poor communication links between Warsaw and the field armies, this fatally delayed decision-making, enabling the Germans to get inside the Poles' OODA loop.

The Soviet Red Army Commanders

The Soviet Red Army was still crippled by the consequences of Stalin's 1930s purges when it entered Poland in September 1939. Since Stalin had liquidated much of the senior army leadership, he struggled to fill key positions with competent officers. Several survivors, including **Georgi Zhukov**, were in the Far East at the time, fighting the Japanese at Khalkin Gol. Thus, one of the last survivors from Stalin's Civil War military circle, **Semyon Timoshenko**, commanded the main strike force, the Ukrainian Front. The Byelorussian Front was led by an inexperienced and lacklustre corps commander, **M. P. Kovalev**. The same situation was repeated through the lower levels of the force. The 1939 Polish campaign did offer the Soviet Red Army some opportunity to identify talented young commanders who had precipitously risen through the ranks due to the purges, for example, Vasily Chuikov, later a hero of the bitter 1942–43 battle of Stalingrad.

THE OPPOSING GERMAN AND POLISH STRATEGIC PLANS

Fall Weiss (Case White) envisioned a double envelopment to annihilate the Polish military west of the River Vistula and fatally disrupt Polish mobilisation. The Third Army attacking from East Prussia and the Eighth Army in lower Silesia would conduct the inner pincer. For the outer pincer, Fourth Army would force the Polish Corridor, traverse East Prussia, and attack east of Warsaw. The Tenth Army led the main southern effort, aiming for Warsaw. Polish plans predicted German strategy.

Their Plan Z correctly identified the main southern effort, but the Poles had to forward deploy both to prevent German land-grabbing and to shield mobilisation in the west. Forces would then fight a delaying defence back to the Vistula waiting for the promised major French offensive, which never materialised. The Molotov-Ribbentrop Pact complicated Polish planning and Soviet intervention destroyed any prospects of protracted Polish resistance.

THE OPPOSING PLANS

The German Plans

World reaction to the annexation of Czechoslovakia in March 1939 and the ensuing partial Polish mobilisation rendered initial German plans for a surprise seizure of Danzig and the Pomeranian Corridor unlikely. As a result, Hitler ordered the OKH to plan a full-scale invasion, codenamed *Fall Weiss* (Case White). Poland's geography simplified planning. With Slovakia a German pro-Axis puppet state, German armed forces could attack Poland from three sides. Furthermore, Poland had few natural defences: most of western Poland was flat farmland. The only natural obstruction was the Carpathian mountain chain between Poland and Slovakia.

Because of the fear of Anglo-French intervention, the Germans planned a rapid destruction of the Polish Army so that forces could be quickly shifted westward to defend the Reich. The objective became the envelopment and destruction of the Polish Army west of the Vistula and Narew rivers. A German double envelopment launched from Prussia and Silesia would envelope the Polish forces in western Poland. The heaviest concentration of forces was with Rundstedt's Army Group South. The main southern blow would be struck from Silesia towards the north-east, aimed at Warsaw. A secondary southern blow would be directed out of the former Czech territories and the Slovak puppet state to neutralise the Polish forces deployed in Galicia.

Geography made the German Army Group North's task more challenging. Its mission was to force the Pomeranian Corridor and link up with East Prussia. Then Bock's Army Group North would push southward towards Warsaw. Bock's task was complicated by the wooded, riverine Prussian frontier. The initial planning aimed at a direct assault on the Polish capital, Warsaw, from the north, along the western bank of the River Vistula.

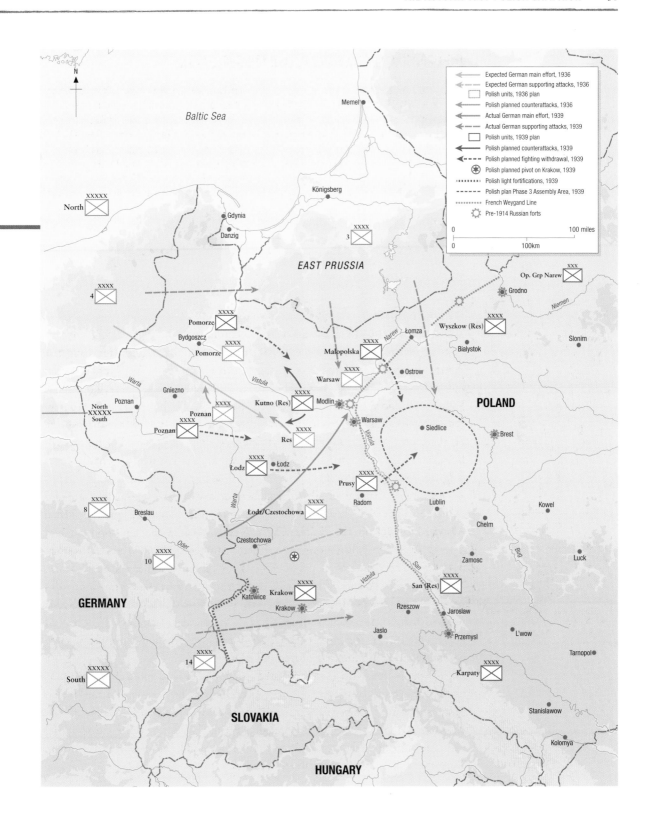

Baltic Sea

Memel

Königsberg

Gdynia

Danzig

North

EAST PRUSSIA

3

Expected German main effort, 1936
Expected German supporting attacks, 1936
Polish units, 1936 plan
Polish planned counterattacks, 1936
Actual German main effort, 1939
Actual German supporting attacks, 1939
Polish units, 1939 plan
Polish planned counterattacks, 1939
Polish planned fighting withdrawal, 1939
Polish planned pivot on Krakow, 1939
Polish light fortifications, 1939
Polish plan Phase 3 Assembly Area, 1939
French Weygand Line
Pre-1914 Russian forts

0   100 miles
0   100km

4

Op. Grp Narew

Grodno

Niemen

Slonim

Pomorze

Bydgoszcz

Pomorze

Malopolska

Narew   Łomza

Wyszkow (Res)

Bialystok

Warta

Warsaw

Vistula

Ostrow

POLAND

Gniezno

Poznan

North
XXXXX
South

Poznan

Kutno (Res)

Modlin

Warsaw

Siedlice

Brest

Poznan

Res

Łodz

Łodz

Vistula

Prusy

Lublin

Kowel

8

Breslau

Łodz/Czestochowa

Radom

Chelm

Luck

Czestochowa

Oder

Warta

Zamosc

10

San

Krakow

Krakow

Katowice

San (Res)

Jaroslaw

Rzeszow

L'wow

GERMANY

Vistula

Jaslo

Przemysl

Tarnopol

14

South

Karpaty

Stanislawow

SLOVAKIA

Kolomya

HUNGARY

The Polish Plans

The Polish High Command had a good appreciation of German dispositions and a clear understanding of the likely German plan. A new Polish war plan, codenamed Plan Z, was formalised in early March 1939 but was quickly reformulated after the German seizure of the rump Czechoslovakian state on 15 March. The revised plan correctly identified the main effort as coming from Silesia, striking to the north-east.

In May 1939, discussions with the French left Polish leaders convinced that the French Army would launch a major attack against Germany within two weeks of an attack on Poland. Unfortunately, the French had no detailed plan for such an operation. Instead, unknown to the Poles, on 31 May 1939, the French reduced the scale of the planned offensive to the combat power of merely a probe. The French expected that the Poles could hold out for four months, more than enough time to prepare and launch a major operation against Germany's western border. The illusory Polish belief in an immediate French attack in the west dominated Polish strategic planning in 1939.

The Poles examined two broad strategic options. The first was to rely on the old Russian fortification line along the Narew, Vistula, and San river lines. This line fitted Polish operational doctrine, since such a defensive grouping would not overextend the limited Polish forces. Its main problem was political. For such a plan to succeed, the Polish Army would have to be fully mobilised and deployed,

Non-operational Polish bombers, Okezie airfield near Warsaw, during the German invasion of Poland. (Photo by Hugo Jaeger/Timepix/The LIFE Picture Collection via Getty Images)

since most Polish troops had to be called up from the more populous provinces west of this line. Plan Z presumed that Germany would strike before mobilisation could be fully implemented; thereby, much of the Polish Army's manpower would be lost before it could reach the eastern mobilisation areas. Moreover, there was considerable concern that if Poland's defences were situated far to the east, the Germans would simply seize the Pomeranian Corridor as well as the western provinces of Pomerania and Silesia unopposed, just as they had taken the Sudetenland. The Polish government was therefore unequivocally opposed to any plan that could lead to a repeat of Czechoslovakia's uncontested demise.

Polish TKS tankettes lined up before going into action, somewhere in south-eastern Poland, 22 September 1939. (Bettman / Getty Images)

The second, alternate, plan was to position Polish troops well forward near the western frontier. It was presumed that it would take 15 days to fully mobilise the army, so defending the western borders would shield the mobilisation of forces in the most populous sections of western Poland. This was especially critical as Poland was an ethnically diverse country and only 60 per cent Polish: most Poles lived in western Poland. In addition, a strong defence of western Poland would oblige Britain and France to honour their commitments to declare war on Germany. The Polish planners had no illusions about their chances of victory. Their only hope was to prolong the defence long enough for France and Britain to mobilise and strike Germany in the west.

While the resulting plan placed most Polish forces in western Poland, the objective was to shield western Poland long enough to enable general mobilisation, and to permit a gradual withdrawal of forces eastward to prolong the war by avoiding decisive battle. Polish defensive concepts were based largely on the experience of the 1920 manoeuvre war with Russia. Marszałek Rydz-Śmigły's intention was gradually to withdraw the army eastward and to avoid decisive battle west of the River Vistula.

This plan had several major flaws. It stretched deployed Polish forces so thinly that forward divisions were unable to slow the German advance effectively without becoming deeply engaged and destroyed. In addition, the plan seriously underestimated the pace of fighting. Although the Poles planned a war of manoeuvre, they failed to appreciate the mechanisation of their opponent. Concentrated, fully mobilised German formations rapidly penetrated the low-density, understrength Polish divisions and the Wehrmacht could more rapidly exploit a breakthrough than the Poles could react. The German tempo of operations was greater than that the Polish forces could obtain.

The Poles were not alone in underestimating the potential of the new style of mechanised warfare (the Germans did too). Like most other European armies, they had been misled by the lessons of the Spanish Civil War. The Polish predicament was that the river defence option, while militarily superior, failed to address Poland's political and strategic dilemmas. The forward defence plan, while addressing Poland's political and strategic concerns, was militarily unsound. Poland was thus caught in a hopeless situation. The situation became dire in late August with the announcement of the Molotov–Ribbentrop agreement. The Polish government was unaware of the secret invasion protocols to the non-aggression pact, and so it was unclear whether the Soviet Union would intervene in a war between Poland and Germany. Given the paucity of forces available to the Polish Army, the eastern borders remained thinly guarded by token border forces.

THE OPPOSING FORCES

The German and Polish Forces Compared

The Wehrmacht enjoyed numerous advantages over the Polish military in both quality and quantity. German superiority was in no small measure due to the enormous economic disparity between the two countries. Between the years 1935 and 1939, Germany had defence budgets totalling about £5.52 billion; 30 times greater than Poland's expenditure of £175 million during the same period. In terms of peacetime strength, the German Army was more than three times the size of the Polish; about 600,000 men compared to about 210,000. The sheer mobilisation potential of Germany was also considerably greater, with an active force of 51 divisions and a wartime force of 102 divisions. Poland was able to muster only 30 divisions, though theoretically another 15 reserve divisions could eventually be deployed in a protracted conflict, if defeat had been successfully staved off.

The Wehrmacht also committed its best divisions to the autumn 1939 Polish campaign and left units with less training and equipment facing the French on the Western Front. The two German army groups between them deployed a total of 37 infantry, one mountain, four motorised infantry, four light (mechanised), and six Panzer (armoured) divisions, as well as a solitary cavalry brigade. Bock's German Army Group North fielded some 630,000 personnel while Rundstedt's German Army Group South deployed around 886,000 troops.

The Polish Army deployed 23 infantry and three reserve infantry divisions, as well as eight cavalry, one motorised, and three mountain brigades. Along the major avenues of attack, the Wehrmacht enjoyed a 2.3:1 force advantage. In field artillery, the Wehrmacht had a force advantage of 2.8:1 overall and 4.4:1 along the main avenues of attack. The force disparities were greatest in armoured

vehicles with the Wehrmacht deploying 2,511 tanks to Poland's 615, for an advantage of 4.1:1 overall and 8.2:1 along the main avenues of attack.

These numerical comparisons underestimate the German strength advantages, since many Polish formations were only partially mobilised while German units were on war footing at the very outset of the campaign. The most obvious qualitative disparity between the two forces was in the greater mechanisation of the German forces. The German Army had formed six Panzer and four light (mechanised) divisions, while Poland fielded a single mechanised brigade. When German remilitarisation began in 1933 under Hitler, the groundwork had already been established for further mechanisation.

In contrast to many other armies, the Wehrmacht committed none of its total tank strength to separate battalions for close infantry support. Instead, the available German tanks were entirely concentrated into well-balanced all-arms Panzer divisions designed to overcome enemy defences by shock and firepower. Once the enemy's main line of resistance had been penetrated, their mobility would allow them to rapidly exploit the penetration by either enveloping the enemy from the rear in a pincer movement or racing deep into enemy territory to attack key command and supply nodes. The views of the armoured warfare theorists were criticised by some older, more conservative, German generals but won Hitler's approval.

The Panzer divisions mixed tanks, motorised infantry, motorised artillery, and mobile engineer and recce elements. Their combat power came from their ability to exploit the virtues of multiple branches of service combined. In addition, one

German tanks and motorcycle-mounted troops drive into Poland on 1 September 1939. (Photo by Pictorial Parade/Getty Images)

The Polish Mechanised Brigade undergoes inspection near Warsaw, 15 April 1939. (Photo by Popperfoto via Getty Images/ Getty Images)

of the Panzer division's least appreciated advantages was its extensive deployment of radios. Guderian was a signals officer and realised the need for radios to coordinate fast-moving mobile formations. Unlike Allied vehicles, nearly all German tanks had radio receivers. In addition, unit leaders utilised *Befehlspanzer*, a command tank variant that sported a powerful transmitting radio. Most of the 215 Befehlspanzer in service in 1939 were a turretless type based on the PzKpfw I chassis, but 38 were the more capable PzBefWg III on the medium-tank chassis. The widespread use of radio in German tanks allowed for enhanced communication and thus better execution of synchronised tactical actions.

The light divisions were an attempt to mechanise the German cavalry and were intended to conduct the traditional cavalry role of strategic reconnaissance and flank security. German tanks in 1939 were not particularly impressive in terms of either firepower or armour. The majority were light tanks including 1,223 of the machine-gun armed PzKpfw I and 1,445 of the 20mm gun armed PzKpfw II that could penetrate the armour of all Polish tanks. Some 98 PzKpfw III medium tanks armed with a 37mm gun existed, a dozen in each Panzer division. Moreover, 211 of the larger PzKpfw IV, possessing a short-barrelled 75mm gun were in service, normally six per regiment. Germany also benefitted from absorbing the Czech tank force. A total of 196 PzKpfw 35(t) and 78 PzKpfw 38(t) were in service in 1939. Of the 3,466 tanks available on 1 September, 2,626 were committed to the 1939 Polish campaign.

Poland's armoured force was weak compared to Germany's. The Poles had become enamoured by the tankette and built their armoured force around 450 small, machine-gun-armed TK and TKS tankettes. Neither vehicle had anti-armour capability and their speed and mobility were poor. Poland had purchased 38 British Vickers 6-ton tanks and license-produced an improved model, the 7TP light tank. The final 95 of these carried a Bofors 37mm gun superior to most German tanks in 1939 but there were too few to make much difference. The Poles equipped two battalions – with a third forming – as independent units. Poland also acquired a battalion of French Renault R-35 infantry tanks but too late to make an impact.

In contrast to Germany, in 1939 Poland still maintained large cavalry formations, most notably its eight cavalry brigades that were viewed as the army's elite forces. Horse cavalry was essential in the marshy eastern borderlands, where Polish defensive actions might be needed to thwart any future Soviet invasion from the east. As the German threat from the west grew, the Polish Army debated mechanising the cavalry. But the puny Polish defence budget limited this. Two cavalry brigades were mechanised, though only one was actually operational on 1 September. This command was *Pułkownik* (Colonel) Maczek's 10th Mechanised Brigade. In fact, most of the Polish cavalry troops generally fought as dismounted infantry in this campaign.

The German and Polish infantry divisions were better matched in organisation and equipment. Both formations averaged some 16,500 personnel organised into three infantry regiments. Both sides employed the Mauser 98k as their principal rifle. The German squads were beginning to receive the *Machinenpistole* (MP) 38 submachine gun in small numbers, while the Poles had a handful of the new Mors submachine gun as well. The German Army was deploying the *Machinengewehr* (MG) 34 light machine gun in significant numbers, while the Polish Army employed a licenced copy of the American Browning Automatic Rifle (BAR) as its principal squad automatic weapon. The German divisions had more firepower at most organisational levels, however.

Anti-tank defence was a similar situation. The German Army used the 37mm PaK 36 anti-tank gun, while Polish infantry used the licence-manufactured Swedish Bofors 37mm anti-tank gun. They had similar performance and could penetrate any tank of the period. The Poles deployed theirs in platoons at battalion level for a total of 27 per division. The Germans deployed theirs in regimental companies of 12 guns and added a divisional anti-tank battalion, typically of three companies.

The firepower disparity between the German and Polish forces was greatest in artillery. While German divisions averaged 68 guns versus the Polish 48, the German salvo power was about double that of the Poles. The Wehrmacht relied on the 105mm leFH 18 as its principal field gun, which was more powerful than the Polish 75mm field gun. In addition, German infantry divisions had some 20 75mm and 150mm infantry guns for direct support, whereas the Poles had none. Superior ammunition supply and fire control procedures accentuated German firepower advantages. Greater use of radios ensured far superior German artillery fire control. In addition, greater motorisation meant that German divisions carried more ammunition and could replenish more rapidly.

Although both sides relied on horses as their principal method of transportation, German infantry divisions were more motorised. In terms of command and

Stuka Attack, September 1939

The Junkers Ju 87B Stuka dive-bomber has remained the icon of Blitzkrieg warfare. The demoralizing howl of the Stuka in its bombing dive terrified soldiers and civilians alike. Here we see an attack by a pair of Junkers Ju 87B Stukas of Stukagruppe 1 **(1)**, which operated out of Elbing in East Prussia. Air attack introduced a third dimension to the modern battlefield, enabling powerful attacks deep behind enemy lines. Cooperation between the Wehrmacht and Luftwaffe was still in its infancy during the 1939 Polish campaign. Contrary to the popular image of Stukas as a form of close air support, there was a lack of adequate radios and appropriate doctrine for such tactics. Instead, Stukas were used mainly to carry out preplanned air attacks against selected targets, with the targets generally selected by the Luftwaffe staff, not the Wehrmacht. During the first days of the campaign, their primary mission was to destroy the small Polish air force, a task made very difficult by the dispersion of Polish aircraft to concealed bases prior to the outbreak of the war. As a result, there were numerous encounters between Polish fighters like the PZL P.11c seen here **(2)**, and the attacking Luftwaffe squadrons. The P.11c had been a formidable fighter when it first entered service in the early 1930s. Its monoplane gull-wing design was advanced for its day when many other air forces, including both Britain

and Germany, were still relying on biplane fighters. Unfortunately, the Polish budget did not match its defence needs. Polish plans to introduce a modern fighter with an enclosed cockpit and retractable landing gear, the PZL P.50 *Jastrząb*, failed to materialise in time due to a lack of funds. A single prototype was completed and flew in 1939, but the fighter force depended entirely on aircraft that were a generation behind Germany's. Indeed, the Stuka was as fast as a P.11c and unless careful, Polish fighters could fall victim to a skilled Stuka pilot. In fact, one of the first air-to-air battles of the war saw a Stuka shooting down a P.11c in the Kraków area. Heavy combat attrition of the Polish fighter force in the first few days of the campaign gave the Luftwaffe mastery of the air and Stukas were later able to bomb their targets with impunity. They were especially effective in attacking columns of troops and equipment moving to the front, and they helped to disrupt and paralyse Polish reinforcement of their battered defences. By the later stage of the campaign, the Wehrmacht and Luftwaffe began to cooperate in planning Stuka missions, laying the groundwork for the development of true close air support tactics. The Stukas were used with considerable success in the counter-attacks against the Polish Bzura river counter-offensive. (Artwork by Howard Gerrard, © Osprey Publishing)

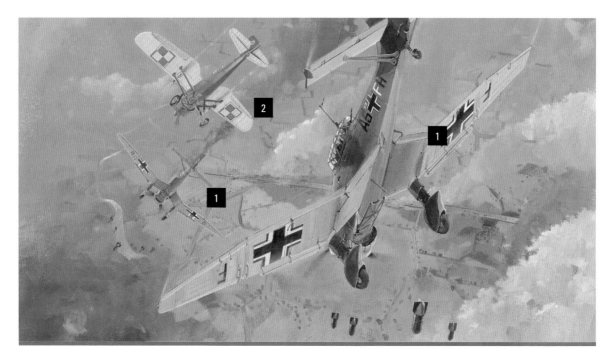

control, German divisions utilised both radios and field telephones, whereas the Poles relied mainly on field telephones. In a war of rapid manoeuvre, radios were a vital ingredient in German victory acting as a repeated force multiplier and allowing synchronised exploitation faster than the Poles could react.

The Germans also enjoyed substantial advantage in air power. German air strength on 1 September was 3,368 combat aircraft, 64 per cent of which was committed to the east. The main striking force comprised the *Luftflotte* 1 (First Air Fleet), which supported Army Group North, and the Luftflotte 4 (Fourth Air Fleet), which provided dedicated support to the German Army Group South. These two commands included 800 medium bombers, 340 Junkers Ju 87 Stuka dive-bombers, 520 fighters and 250 transport aircraft. In addition, 262 spotting and liaison planes directly supported the two army groups. Total front-line German aviation strength was 2,152 aircraft. The German bomber force was made up primarily of the Heinkel He 111 and Dornier Do 17, with a handful of Junkers Ju 88s. The fighter force comprised 440 single-engine Messerschmitt Bf 109s and 80 twin-engine Bf 110 aircraft. During the 1939 Polish campaign, the German Air Force committed its entire Junkers Ju 87 Stuka dive-bomber force, 70 per cent of its bombers and half its fighters to the onslaught in the skies above Poland.

Although the Polish air force had a nominal strength of 1,900 aircraft, 650 were trainers and another 700 were obsolete and often non-operational. The real strength was 392 front-line aircraft including 158 fighters, 114 scout bombers and 36 medium bombers. The Polish fighter force comprised 128 PZL P.11 and

Squadron of German Ju 87 dive-bombers on a mission against enemy positions in Poland, *c.* 2 September 1939. (Photo by ullstein bild/ullstein bild via Getty Images)

Light German naval vessels docked in the recently captured harbour of Gdynia, Poland, late September 1939. (Photo by Mondadori Portfolio via Getty Images)

30 PZL P.7 fighters. The PZL P.23 *Karaś* ('Crow') was an army cooperation scout bomber. The best Polish plane was the PZL P.37 *Łoś* ('Elk') medium bomber, but it was only just entering service. The air force was divided into two main components – Strategic Aviation and Army Aviation. The Strategic Aviation force comprised the Bomber Brigade (36 P.37 *Łoś* and 50 P.23 *Karaś*) and the Pursuit Brigade (43 P.11 and ten P.7 fighters). The Army Aviation typically deployed with each army one scout squadron, at least one fighter, and an observation squadron. In total, the strategic aviation units contained 206 aircraft, while army aviation possessed 288 aircraft.

The navies on both sides played a minor role in the conflict. The Polish navy was configured primarily for operations against possible Soviet operations in the Baltic. Its main ports were so near Germany that in the event of war, they could be quickly smothered from the air. The main element was the destroyer flotilla, comprising four destroyers. The submarine flotilla included three minelaying and two ocean-going submarines. The only other major vessel was a minelayer. The German *Kriegsmarine* (war navy), aware of the Polish minelaying capability and submarine force, limited its operations in the Baltic, and left the Luftwaffe to neutralise the threat. Meanwhile, the Polish destroyer flotilla departed for Britain on 31 August. The German Naval Group East deployed four older warships including the cadet-training battleship *Schleswig-Holstein*, 14 submarines, nine destroyers, 34 torpedo and patrol boats, and 26 minesweepers.

THE ORDERS OF BATTLE: THE GROUND FORCES

THE POLISH ARMY ORDER OF BATTLE (1 SEPTEMBER 1939)

THE ARMY POMORZE – Generał Broni (Lt Gen) W. Bortnowski

Directly Subordinated:

9th Infantry Division – *Pułkownik* (Col) J. Werobej

15th Infantry Division – *Generał Brygady* (Brig) Z. Przyjałkowski

27th Infantry Division – Generał Brygady J. Drapella

Group Wschód – Generał Brygady M. Bołtuć

4th Infantry Division – Pułkownik T. Lubicz-Niezabitowski

16th Infantry Division – Pułkownik S. Świtalski

Group Czersk – Generał Brygady Grzmot-Skotnicki

Pomorska Cavalry Brigade – Pułkownik A. Zakrzewski

THE ARMY MODLIN – *Generał Dywizji* (Maj Gen) E. Krukowicz-Przedrzymirski

Directly Subordinated:

8th Infantry Division – Pułkownik T. Furgalski

20th Infantry Division – Pułkownik W. Lawicz-Liszka

Nowogródzka Cavalry Brigade – Generał Brygady W. Anders

Mazowiecka Cavalry Brigade – Pułkownik Jan Karcz

Operational Group Wyszków – Generał Brygady W. Kowalski

1st Legion Infantry Division – Generał Brygady W. Kowalski

41st Reserve Infantry Division – Generał Brygady W. Piekarski

Special Operational Group Narew – Generał Brygady C. Młot-Fijałkowski

18th Infantry Division – Pułkownik S. Kossecki

33rd Reserve Infantry Division – Pułkownik T. Kalina-Zieleniewski

Podlaska Cavalry Brigade – Generał Brygady L. Kmicic-Skrzyński

Suwalska Cavalry Brigade – Generał Brygady Z. Podhorski

THE ARMY POZNAŃ – Generał Dywizji T. Kutrzeba

Directly Subordinated:

14th Infantry Division – Generał Brygady F. Wlad

17th *Wielkopolska* Infantry Division – Pułkownik M. Mozdyniewicz

25th Infantry Division – Generał Brygady F. Alter

26th Infantry Division – Pułkownik A. Brzechwa-Ajdukiewicz

Wielkopolska Cavalry Brigade – Generał Brygady R. Abraham

Podolska Cavalry Brigade – Pułkownik L. Strzelecki

THE ARMY ŁÓDŹ – Generał Dywizji Juliusz K. Rómmel

Directly Subordinated:

2nd Legion Infantry Division – Pułkownik E. Dojan-Surówka

10th Infantry Division – Generał Brygady F. Dindorf-Ankowicz

28th Infantry Division – Generał Brygady Boncza-Uzdowski

Kresowa Cavalry Brigade – Pułkownik S. Kulesza

Group Piotrków – Generał Brygady W. Thommée

30th Infantry Division – Generał Brygady L. Cehak

Wołyńska Cavalry Brigade – Pułkownik J. Filipowicz

THE ARMY PRUSY – Generał Dywizji S. D b-Biernacki

Directly Subordinated:

13th Infantry Division – Pułkownik W. Zubosz-Kaliński

29th Infantry Division – Pułkownik I. Ozierewicz

Cavalry Operational Group – Generał Brygady R. Dreszer

19th Infantry Division – Generał Brygady K. Kwaciszewski

Wileńska Cavalry Brigade – Pułkownik K. Drucki-Lubecki

***Skwarczyński* Operational Group – Generał Brygady Skwarczyński**

3rd Legion Infantry Division – Pułkownik M. Turkowski

12th Infantry Division – Generał Brygady G. Paszkiewicz

36th Reserve Infantry Division – Pułkownik B. Ostrowski

THE ARMY KRAKÓW – Generał Brygady A. Szylling

Directly Subordinated:

6th Infantry Division – Generał Brygady B. Mond

7th Infantry Division – Generał Brygady I. Gąsiorowski

10th Mechanised Brigade – Pułkownik Stanisław Maczek

Krakowska Cavalry Brigade – Generał Brygady Z. Piasecki

Group Slask – Generał Brygady J. Jagmin-Sadowski

23rd *Gornoslaska* Infantry Division – Pułkownik W. Powierza

55th Reserve Infantry Division – Pułkownik S. Kolabinski

Group Bielsko – Generał Brygady M. Boruta-Spiechowicz

1st Mountain Infantry Brigade – Pułkownik E. Zondolowicz

21st Mountain Infantry Division – Generał Brygady J. Kustroń

THE ARMY KARPATY – Generał Dywizji K. Fabrycy

Directly Subordinated:

2nd Mountain Infantry Brigade – Pułkownik A. Stawarz

3rd Mountain Infantry Brigade – Pułkownik J. Kotowicz

***KORPUS OCHRONY POGRANICZA* (The Border Defence Corps) – Generał Brygady W. Orlik-Rückemann**

THE GERMAN ARMY ORDER OF BATTLE (1 SEPTEMBER 1939)

THE ARMY GROUP NORTH –*GenObst* (Colonel-General) Fedor von Bock

THE FOURTH ARMY –*Gen d.Art* (General of Artillery) Günther von Kluge

XIX Corps (Motorised) – *Gen d.Pztr* (General of Armoured Troups) Heinz Guderian

2nd Motorised Infantry Division – *GenLt* (Lt Gen) P. Bader

3rd Panzer (Armoured) Division – GenLt Geyr von Schweppenburg

20th Motorised Infantry Division – GenLt M. von Wiktorin

Infantry Regiment 'Großdeutschland' – *ObstLt* (Lt Col) Schwerin

II Corps – *Gen d.Inf* (General of Infantry) Erich Straube

32nd Infantry Division – GenLt F. Boehme

3rd Infantry Division – *GenMaj* (Maj Gen) W. Lichel

III Corps – Gen d.Art Curt Haase

Netze Division – GenMaj Freiherr von Gablenz

50th Infantry Division – GenLt K. Sorsche

Army Reserve:

218th Infantry Division – GenMaj W. Freiherr Grote

Frontier Guard Command – *Gen d.Flg* (General of Aviation) Leonhard Kaupisch

207th Infantry Division – GenMaj K. von Tiedemann

THE THIRD ARMY – Gen d.Art Georg von Küchler

XXI Corps – GenLt Nikolaus von Falkenhorst

228th Infantry Division – GenMaj H. Suttner

21st Infantry Division – GenLt K. H. von Both

I Corps – GenLt Walter Petzel

1st Infantry Division – GenLt Joachim von Kortzfleisch

12th Infantry Division – GenLt L. von der Leyen

Corps *Brand* – GenLt Fritz Brand

Lötzen Brigade – GenMaj Offenbacher

Goldap Brigade – *Obst* (Col) Notle

The Army Reserve:

10th Panzer (Armoured) Division – GenMaj Ferdinand Schaal

217th Infantry Division – GenMaj R. Baltzer

Eberhard Brigade – GenMaj Eberhard

Army Group Reserves:

73rd Infantry Division – GenMaj F. von Rabenau

206th Infantry Division – GenLt H. Hoefl

208th Infantry Division – GenLt M. Andreas

THE ARMY GROUP SOUTH – GenObst Gerd von Rundstedt

THE EIGHTH ARMY – Gen d.Inf Johannes Blaskowitz

X Corps – Gen d.Art Wilhelm Ulex

24th Infantry Division – GenLt F. Olbricht

30th Infantry Division – GenMaj K. von Briesen

XIII Corps – *Gen d.Kav* (General of Cavalry) Maximilian Freiherr von Weichs

10th Infantry Division – GenLt C. von Cochenhausen

17th Infantry Division – GenMaj H. Loch

THE TENTH ARMY – Gen d.Art Walter von Reichenau

The Army Reserve:

3rd Light (Mechanised) Division – GenMaj A. Kuntzen

1st Light (Mechanised) Division – GenMaj F. von Loeper

XI Corps – Gen d.Art Emil Leeb

18th Infantry Division – GenMaj F. Cranz

19th Infantry Division – GenLt G. Schwantes

XVI Corps (Motorised) – Gen d.Kav Erich Hoepner

4th Panzer (Armoured) Division – GenLt Hans-Georg Reinhardt

1st Panzer (Armoured) Division – GenLt R. Schmidt

14th Infantry Division – GenLt P. Weyer

31st Infantry Division – GenLt R. Kaempfe

IV Corps – Gen d.Inf Viktor von Schwedler

46th Infantry Division – GenMaj P. von Hase

4th Infantry Division – GenMaj E. Hansen

XV Corps – Gen d.Inf Hermann Hoth

2nd Light (Mechanised) Division – GenLt G. Stumme

XIV Corps (Motorised) – Gen d.Inf Gustav von Wietersheim

13th Motorised Infantry Division – GenLt M. von Faber du Faur

29th Motorised Infantry Division – GenLt J. Lemelsen

THE FOURTEENTH ARMY – GenObst Wilhelm List

XXII Corps – Gen d.Kav Ewald von Kleist

1st *Gebirgsjäger* (Mountain Infantry) Division – GenMaj L. Kubler

2nd Gebirgsjäger Division – GenLt V. Fuerstein

VIII Corps – Gen d.Inf Ernst Busch

8th Infantry Division – GenLt R. Koch-Erpach

28th Infantry Division – GenLt H. von Obstfelder

5th Panzer (Armoured) Division – GenLt Heinrich von Vietinghoff gennant Scheel

XVII Corps – Gen d.Inf Werner Kienitz

44th Infantry Division – GenLt A. Schubert

45th Infantry Division – GenLt F. Materna

7th Infantry Division – GenMaj E. Ott

XVIII Corps – Gen d.Inf Eugen Beyer

2nd Panzer (Armoured) Division – GenLt Rudolf Veiel

4th Light (Mechanised) Division – GenMaj Dr Alfred Ritter von Hubicki

3rd Gebirgsjäger Division – GenLt E. Eduard Dietl

The Army Group Reserve:

239th Infantry Division – GenMaj F. Neuling

221st Infantry Division – GenLt J. Pflugbeil

213th Infantry Division – GenMaj R. de L'Homme de Courbiere

62nd Infantry Division – GenMaj W. Keiner

68th Infantry Division – Obst G. Braun

27th Infantry Division – GenLt F. Bergmann

THE (SLOVAK) ARMY GROUP BERNOLÁK

1st *Janošík* Division – *Plukovník* (Colonel) A. Pulanich

2nd *Škultéty* Division – *Generál* (General) A. Čunderlík

3rd *Rázus* Division – *Podplukovník* (Lieutenant Colonel) A. Malár

Mobile Group *Kalinciak* – Podplukovník J. Imro

THE CAMPAIGN

The Opening Moves: Mobilisation and Provocations (26 August–1 September 1939)

Adolf Hitler had first planned to invade Poland on 26 August 1939 and German forces began to move to their start lines the afternoon before. The announcement of the Anglo-Polish security pact on the afternoon of 25 August 1939 left Hitler considerably shaken, however, and he ordered the army to postpone the attack while further diplomatic ventures with Italy were pursued. Not all units received the message and there were a number of small border incidents. One of these included an attempt by a German *Brandenburger* special forces commando unit to seize a rail junction and tunnel in the key Jablonka pass leading through the southern Carpathian mountains. In the ensuing days the German guerrilla units in western Poland stepped up their sabotage activity, and the Luftwaffe continued their high-altitude reconnaissance flights over Polish territory. Although the Poles spotted the aircraft, there was little they could do as their obsolete fighters could not reach the

high altitudes of the specialised German reconnaissance aircraft.

Meanwhile, the Poles had mobilised some 700,000 troops by late August 1939, but Anglo-French pressure constrained full-scale mobilisation. Dark memories of how the 1914 mobilisations had triggered the Great War haunted the senior British and French military commanders. German activity across the frontier, however, made it clear to the Poles that their neighbours planned war and Rydz-Śmigły ordered full mobilisation on 30 August. In spite of the ominous situation on the frontier, the French embassy nevertheless pressured Rydz-Śmigły to rescind the call-up. The Polish government realised that British and French military support was their only hope of resisting German attack, and reluctantly agreed again. Poland's small fleet of ships was dispersed from its ports. On 30 August, Operation *Pekin* was put into motion and the Polish destroyer flotilla left for Britain and cleared the Danish straits before war broke out.

On 31 August, the situation along the borders became so grave that Rydz-Śmigły again ordered full Polish mobilisation. However, the delayed and confused mobilisation served only to make Poland's precarious situation worse. While the Wehrmacht was able to attack in a fully mobilised condition, the Polish Army had been able to mobilise only about 65 per cent of its strength before the war broke out, with many of the reservists in transit when Germany struck.

Hitler continued to hope that the Western powers would refrain from militarily aiding the Poles, and so concocted a pretext to try to shift the blame on to the Polish forces. Under Operation *Himmler*, SS troops dressed in Polish uniforms staged a phoney attack on the German border radio station at Gleiwitz and broadcast inflammatory messages to the Polish minority in eastern Germany to take up arms against Hitler. The bodies of German concentration camp victims dressed in Polish uniforms were left behind as evidence of this naked Polish aggression for the foreign journalists the Germans had brought to the scene. The amateurish charade fooled nobody and Europe grimly braced itself for the horrors of a new general war.

The Initial German Attacks (1–3 September)

The war was scheduled to start at 0445hrs on 1 September 1939, but in fact it began earlier, around 0400hrs, when the old Kriegsmarine cadet-training battleship *Schleswig-Holstein* slipped its moorings in Danzig harbour and began a bombardment of the neighbouring Polish base on Westerplatte. Owing to treaty restrictions, the Poles were forbidden from fortifying the peninsula, but in fact had reinforced the walls of many buildings. As a result, the small garrison held out for a week despite intense bombardment and repeated assaults.

The Polish fleet was smothered by German air attack. The submarine flotilla dispersed into the Baltic to lay mines and hunt for coastal transports, while the only remaining major Polish surface combatants – the destroyer *Wicher* and the minelayer *Gryf* – began minelaying operations off the coast. The small Polish naval air detachment was wiped out in German air raids during the first few days of fighting. On 3 September, the Kriegsmarine sent two destroyers towards the Polish naval bases, but they were repulsed by the coastal guns located at Hel, on the Hel peninsula, and by gunfire from the *Wicher* and the *Gryf*. The Luftwaffe responded with a highly effective air raid, which sank Poland's two remaining operational major warships. The smaller Polish coastal minelayers escaped repeated air attacks until 16 September, when German aerial strikes finally sunk them.

Fighting in the League of Nations' Free City of Danzig was conducted by paramilitaries on both sides and was especially savage. Polish postal workers barricaded themselves in their office but were eventually overwhelmed by a motley amalgam of German forces: the SS *Heimwehr Danzig* militia, German naval assault troops and other paramilitaries. Many of the Polish workers were summarily executed after surrendering.

THE DEFENCE OF WESTERPLATTE

1–7 September 1939, viewed from the south-east, showing the initial bombardment by the German battleship *Schleswig-Holstein* and the Polish garrison's week-long resistance under intense artillery and air attack and repeated infantry assaults.

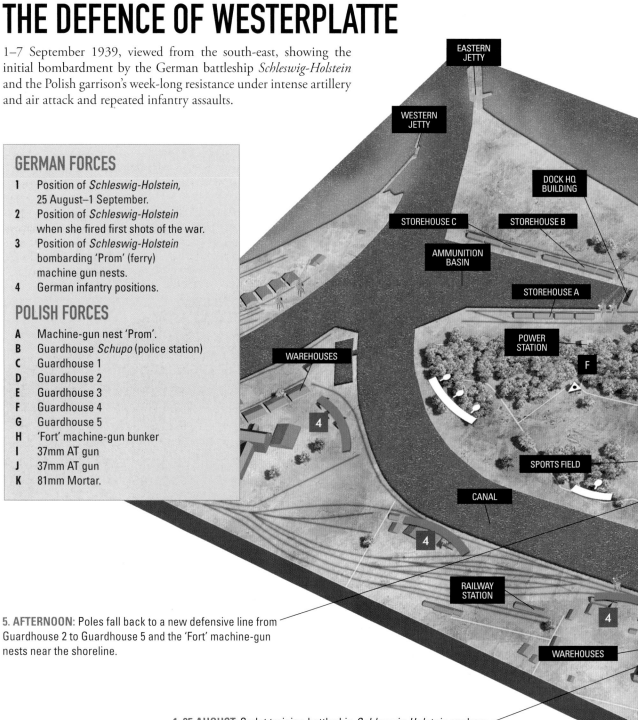

GERMAN FORCES

1 Position of *Schleswig-Holstein*, 25 August–1 September.
2 Position of *Schleswig-Holstein* when she fired first shots of the war.
3 Position of *Schleswig-Holstein* bombarding 'Prom' (ferry) machine gun nests.
4 German infantry positions.

POLISH FORCES

A Machine-gun nest 'Prom'.
B Guardhouse *Schupo* (police station)
C Guardhouse 1
D Guardhouse 2
E Guardhouse 3
F Guardhouse 4
G Guardhouse 5
H 'Fort' machine-gun bunker
I 37mm AT gun
J 37mm AT gun
K 81mm Mortar.

EASTERN JETTY

WESTERN JETTY

DOCK HQ BUILDING

STOREHOUSE C

STOREHOUSE B

AMMUNITION BASIN

STOREHOUSE A

POWER STATION

F

WAREHOUSES

4

SPORTS FIELD

CANAL

4

RAILWAY STATION

4

WAREHOUSES

5. AFTERNOON: Poles fall back to a new defensive line from Guardhouse 2 to Guardhouse 5 and the 'Fort' machine-gun nests near the shoreline.

1. 25 AUGUST: Cadet training battleship *Schleswig-Holstein* anchors opposite the Polish Westerplatte transit port in the port canal, which connects Danzig to the Baltic sea.

2. 1 SEPTEMBER: Before dawn *Schleswig-Holstein* moves down canal to better firing position. 0448hrs. War begins with a salvo from *Schleswig-Holstein* against *Schupo* guardhouse.

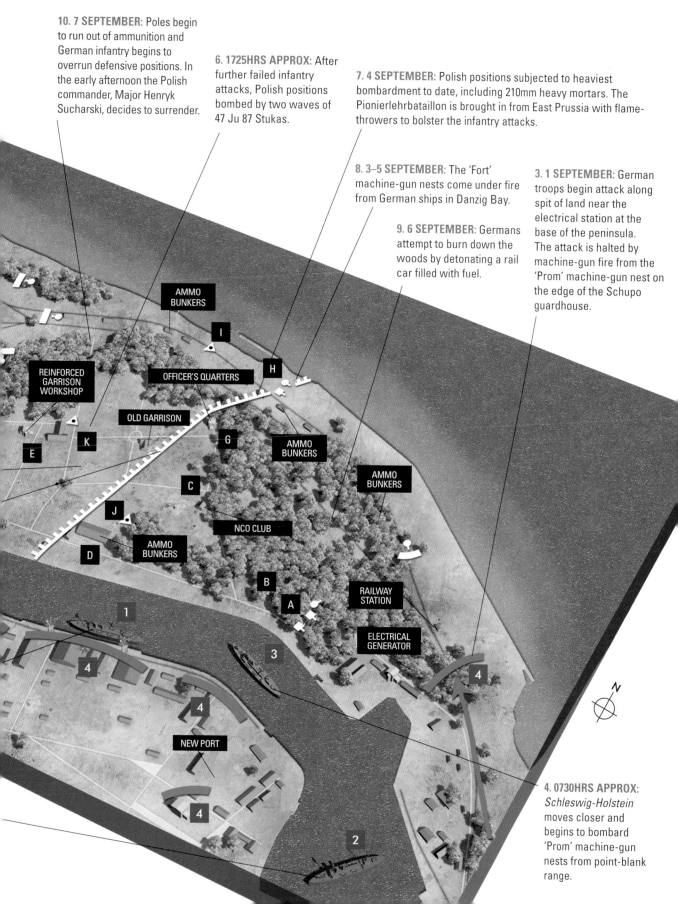

10. 7 SEPTEMBER: Poles begin to run out of ammunition and German infantry begins to overrun defensive positions. In the early afternoon the Polish commander, Major Henryk Sucharski, decides to surrender.

6. 1725HRS APPROX: After further failed infantry attacks, Polish positions bombed by two waves of 47 Ju 87 Stukas.

7. 4 SEPTEMBER: Polish positions subjected to heaviest bombardment to date, including 210mm heavy mortars. The Pionierlehrbataillon is brought in from East Prussia with flame-throwers to bolster the infantry attacks.

8. 3–5 SEPTEMBER: The 'Fort' machine-gun nests come under fire from German ships in Danzig Bay.

3. 1 SEPTEMBER: German troops begin attack along spit of land near the electrical station at the base of the peninsula. The attack is halted by machine-gun fire from the 'Prom' machine-gun nest on the edge of the Schupo guardhouse.

9. 6 SEPTEMBER: Germans attempt to burn down the woods by detonating a rail car filled with fuel.

AMMO BUNKERS

I

H

REINFORCED GARRISON WORKSHOP

OFFICER'S QUARTERS

OLD GARRISON

K

E

G

AMMO BUNKERS

C

AMMO BUNKERS

J

NCO CLUB

D

AMMO BUNKERS

B

A

RAILWAY STATION

ELECTRICAL GENERATOR

1

4

3

4

4

NEW PORT

4

2

4. 0730HRS APPROX: *Schleswig-Holstein* moves closer and begins to bombard 'Prom' machine-gun nests from point-blank range.

N

Commanded by Generał Broni Bortnowski, the weak Polish
Army Pomorze, which was deployed in the Pomeranian
Corridor, comprised two infantry divisions and a cavalry
brigade. Their deployment was more political than tactical, since
Warsaw feared that the Germans might attempt to seize the
Corridor in surprise actions that fell short of a full-scale war, as
they had done previously in the Sudetenland. The Polish units
were positioned to resist such German action. Once full-scale
war broke out, their political mission became moot, and they
effected a fighting withdrawal southward to more defensible
positions. In the rearguard, Pułkownik Zakrzewski's *Pomorska*
Cavalry Brigade fought GenLt von Wiktorin's German 20th
Motorised Infantry Division along the River Brda.

In the late afternoon, the commander of the Polish 18th Lancer Regiment,
Pułkownik Mastelarz, led two understrength squadrons in a raid behind the lines.
Galloping out of the forest, they caught a German infantry battalion in the open
and mounted a successful sabre charge that decimated the startled German
formation. Towards the end of the skirmish, several German armoured cars
arrived and began firing at the mounted troops. About 20 Polish troopers were
killed, including the commander, before the cavalry could withdraw to safety. The
following day, Italian war correspondents were brought to the scene by the
Germans and were told that the Polish cavalry troopers had been killed while
fearlessly charging the German tanks. This much embellished story became the
most enduring myth of the 1939 Polish campaign. Despite the Polish cavalry's
defensive actions, GenLt von Schweppenburg's 3rd Panzer (Armoured) Division
was nevertheless able to force a crossing of the Brda.

While the Fourth Army was fighting its way across the Pomeranian Corridor, Gen d.Art von Küchler's German Third Army, deployed in East Prussia, attacked south towards the Polish capital, Warsaw. Two German corps that between them deployed two infantry divisions and the ad hoc Panzer Division Kempf began the assault, which soon became entangled in the Mława fortification line. Mława was one of the few locations with any significant modern fortifications, as it was the obvious approach route to Warsaw from the north. Manned by the Polish 20th Infantry Division, the fortifications held out against repeated enemy assaults. In the meantime, the German *Wodrig* Corps attempted to outflank the town of Mława to the east. Simultaneously, the German 1st Cavalry Brigade attacked Pułkownik Karcz's *Mazowiecka* Cavalry Brigade along the River Ulatkowka, in one of the very few genuine cavalry-versus-cavalry battles of the campaign. By the end of the first day of fighting, however, the German Third Army was stalled.

The driving force in the Wehrmacht's assault on Poland, however, was GenObst von Rundstedt's more powerful Army Group South. The point of main effort for Army Group South's operations fell upon its two northern flank formations, the German Eight and Tenth Armies in Silesia. These formations intended to smash through the opposing Armies Łódź and Kraków, cross the River Warta, envelope the Polish forces along the western frontier and drive on Warsaw. As a result, these two armies had a disproportionate share of the Panzer and light (mechanised) divisions that the Wehrmacht possessed.

German 37mm anti-tank gun opening fire in a camouflaged emplacement in woodland, Poland, September 1939. (Photo by Mondadori Portfolio via Getty Images)

Cavalry Defence at Mokra

Although the myth of Polish cavalry charging German Panzers has dominated the popular image of the 1939 campaign, the actual combat record was considerably different. The most dramatic encounter between cavalry and Panzers took place on the first day of the campaign when the *Wołyńska* Cavalry Brigade confronted the 4th Panzer Division near the small village of Mokra. The resulting battle was a reminder of the high morale and excellent training of the Polish cavalry, but also of their limitations in contemporary combat. Polish defences at Mokra hinged on the two principal types of anti-tank weapons: anti-tank rifles and the Bofors 37mm anti-tank gun. The scene here shows one of the Bofors 37mm anti-tank guns in action (**1**). This small weapon was license-produced in Poland, and was capable of knocking out any contemporary German tank. Defending the Bofors from German infantry is a squad automatic weapons gunner to the right (**2**). The standard Polish squad automatic weapon in the campaign was a license copy of the Browning Automatic Rifle, familiar to US infantry as the BAR. During the afternoon fighting around Mokra, the German Panzer companies managed to break through the forward Polish defences, and a few infiltrated as far as the railway line running behind the village. The *Wołyńska* Cavalry Brigade was supported by Armoured Train 53 *Śmiały* (**3**), and the Panzers were taken under fire at close range, with several

Panzers being knocked out (**4**). These trains had two artillery cars (**5**), each armed with two turreted guns and several machine guns. They also had an assault company of infantry in a special armoured car, and a few tankettes on special flat-cars that could disembark for scouting or attack. Armoured trains had played a prominent role in the fighting on the eastern front in World War I, and were especially important in the Russian Civil War and the related conflicts such as the 1920 Russo-Polish War. They provided a unique blend of mobility, protection, and firepower compared to the road-bound armoured cars of the day. They were used by both the German and Polish forces in 1939, though their day had passed. Although effective in some battles such as Mokra, they were extremely vulnerable to air attack, as shown when *Śmiały* was damaged on 1 September. In 1939, Blitzkrieg was still in its infancy, and the German attack at Mokra demonstrated the need for further refinement of Panzer division tactics. The early Panzer divisions lacked the infantry necessary to overcome a determined, prepared defence like the Polish defence at Mokra. In the future, the Wehrmacht would rely on their infantry divisions to effect the breakthrough, then use the superior mobility of the Panzer divisions to exploit the breakthrough – as the 4th Panzer Division would demonstrate a few days later in the race for Warsaw. (Artwork by Howard Gerrard, © Osprey Publishing)

The most intense battle in this sector occurred around the village of Mokra, held by Pułkownik Filipowicz's *Wołyńska* Cavalry Brigade. Repeatedly attacked by GenLt Stever's 4th Panzer Division, the cavalry held it off and inflicted significant losses. At least one of the German attacks was repulsed with the assistance of the armoured train *Śmiały* in one of several encounters between Panzers and armoured trains during the campaign. Eventually, however, *Wołyńska* Cavalry Brigade's losses became so severe that it was forced to withdraw that evening.

The Germans achieved more extensive tactical success against the Army Kraków, commanded by Generał Brygady Szylling, further to the south. The Army Kraków had one of the most difficult tasks of all the Polish higher formation commands, since it faced the heaviest German force concentration: no fewer than four Panzer divisions and four light (mechanised) divisions. In addition, its wide sector spanned the frontier from the gritty and sooty towns of the Upper Silesian industrial region right through to the Carpathian foothills in the south.

In the initial German assault, GenLt Schmidt's 1st Panzer Division drove a wedge between the *Wołyńska* Brigade and the Polish 7th Infantry Division to its south. The latter division was attacked frontally by the German 46th Infantry Division, and its southern flank was threatened when GenLt Stumme's 2nd Light (Mechanised) Division pushed in the defences of the *Krakowska* Cavalry Brigade. Next, two more German infantry divisions attacked the hapless Polish 7th Infantry Division. Less progress was enjoyed to the south when the German

A German Messerschmitt Bf 110 fighter in flight over Poland, September 1939. (Photo by PhotoQuest/ Getty Images)

CAVALRY V. ARMOUR AT MOKRA

1 September 1939, viewed from the south-east, showing the repeated attacks by the 4th Panzer Division around the village of Mokra on the *Wołyńska* Cavalry Brigade, which determinedly holds its ground, inflicting significant losses on the poorly coordinated tank and infantry attacks.

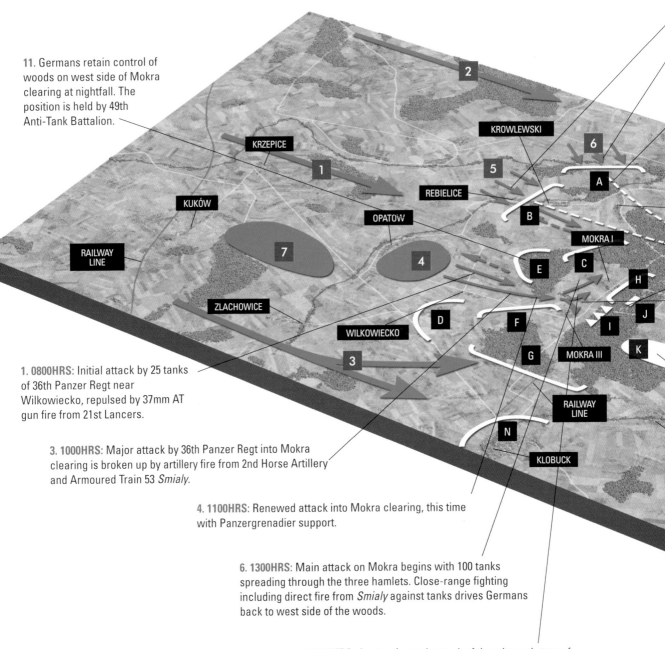

11. Germans retain control of woods on west side of Mokra clearing at nightfall. The position is held by 49th Anti-Tank Battalion.

KRZEPICE

KROWLEWSKI

1

5

6

A

REBIELICE

B

KUKÓW

OPATOW

MOKRA I

RAILWAY LINE

7

4

E

C

H

ZLACHOWICE

D

J

I

WILKOWIECKO

F

G

MOKRA III

K

3

RAILWAY LINE

N

KLOBUCK

1. 0800HRS: Initial attack by 25 tanks of 36th Panzer Regt near Wilkowiecko, repulsed by 37mm AT gun fire from 21st Lancers.

3. 1000HRS: Major attack by 36th Panzer Regt into Mokra clearing is broken up by artillery fire from 2nd Horse Artillery and Armoured Train 53 *Smialy*.

4. 1100HRS: Renewed attack into Mokra clearing, this time with Panzergrenadier support.

6. 1300HRS: Main attack on Mokra begins with 100 tanks spreading through the three hamlets. Close-range fighting including direct fire from *Smialy* against tanks drives Germans back to west side of the woods.

9. 1600HRS: Last major tank attack of day pits tankettes of 21st Armored Troop against Panzers. The German attack is broken up by artillery and anti-tank rifle fire.

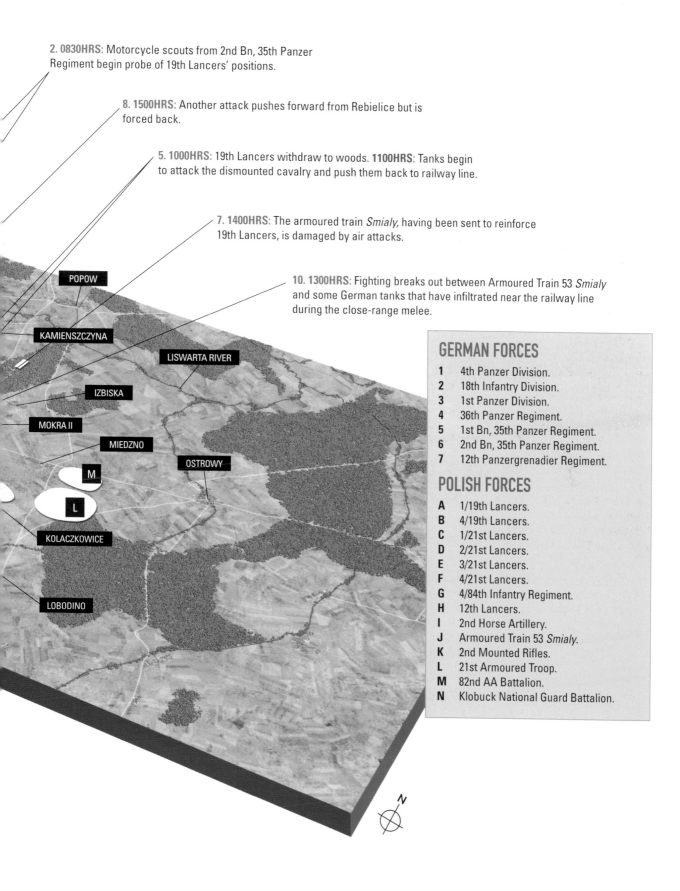

2. 0830HRS: Motorcycle scouts from 2nd Bn, 35th Panzer Regiment begin probe of 19th Lancers' positions.

8. 1500HRS: Another attack pushes forward from Rebielice but is forced back.

5. 1000HRS: 19th Lancers withdraw to woods. **1100HRS:** Tanks begin to attack the dismounted cavalry and push them back to railway line.

7. 1400HRS: The armoured train *Smialy,* having been sent to reinforce 19th Lancers, is damaged by air attacks.

10. 1300HRS: Fighting breaks out between Armoured Train 53 *Smialy* and some German tanks that have infiltrated near the railway line during the close-range melee.

POPOW

KAMIENSZCZYNA

LISWARTA RIVER

IZBISKA

MOKRA II

MIEDZNO

OSTROWY

M

L

KOLACZKOWICE

LOBODINO

GERMAN FORCES

1 4th Panzer Division.
2 18th Infantry Division.
3 1st Panzer Division.
4 36th Panzer Regiment.
5 1st Bn, 35th Panzer Regiment.
6 2nd Bn, 35th Panzer Regiment.
7 12th Panzergrenadier Regiment.

POLISH FORCES

A 1/19th Lancers.
B 4/19th Lancers.
C 1/21st Lancers.
D 2/21st Lancers.
E 3/21st Lancers.
F 4/21st Lancers.
G 4/84th Infantry Regiment.
H 12th Lancers.
I 2nd Horse Artillery.
J Armoured Train 53 *Smialy*.
K 2nd Mounted Rifles.
L 21st Armoured Troop.
M 82nd AA Battalion.
N Klobuck National Guard Battalion.

N

Polish bomber, Okezie military airport near Warsaw, early September 1939. (Photo by Hugo Jaeger/Timepix/The LIFE Picture Collection via Getty Images)

8th and 239th Infantry Divisions assaulted the fortified zone around the gritty industrial city of Katowice. Meanwhile, the neighbouring German 28th Infantry Division and GenLt von Vietinghoff gennant Scheel's 5th Panzer (Armoured) Division struck the defensive positions manned by the Polish 55th and 6th Infantry Divisions.

Aside from these large-scale regular conventional military operations, there was also considerable turmoil erupting in the Polish rear areas. This chaos was primarily due to the operations of German guerrilla units that had been formed prior to the war by the *Abwehr* (Military Intelligence). The province of Silesia, which had been German territory before 1919, also still had a sizeable pro-Nazi German ethnic minority. Consequently, numerous small-scale skirmishes occurred as regular Polish Army and police units faced attacks from German guerrilla and paramilitary militia groups.

The German XXII Corps, operating out of Axis-puppet Slovakian territory, began a determined attack on Polish mountain defences along the Dunajec river. GenLt Veiel's 2nd Panzer Division manoeuvred past Dunajec, obliging Generał Szylling's Army Kraków to commit the Polish Army's only mobile force, the 10th Mechanised Brigade. The German advance was finally stopped later in the day when Generał Brygady Mond's Polish 6th Infantry Division arrived. Meanwhile, the German 1st and 2nd Gebirgsjäger Divisions, supported by Slovak units, tried to force the Carpathian Mountains in the sector controlled by Generał Dywizji Fabrycy's Army Karpaty. But these attacks made no serious territorial gains thanks to the highly challenging terrain, which favoured the defending side.

The Initial Air Operations (1–8 September)

The doctrine of the Luftwaffe focused on initially gaining air superiority. Consequently, most missions flown on the first day attacked Polish airfields. One of the myths of the campaign was that the Polish Air Force was destroyed on its fields on 1 September. In fact, the air force dispersed to improvised air strips on 31 August. The only airfield attacked in strength, Rakowice, lost 28 unserviceable aircraft that could not be flown out. While the dispersion saved Polish aircraft from the initial German attack, it also made operations more difficult since the units were operating from grass strips with limited technical support. The Luftwaffe had considerable trouble locating the dispersed Polish bases, and only about 24 Polish combat aircraft were destroyed on the ground during the campaign. Other Luftwaffe missions targeted a wide variety of pre-identified objectives, including key road and rail targets. In September 1939, the German Air Force was not yet prepared to carry out close air support missions on demand from the army.

Polish bomber crews, after briefing for an upcoming mission, travel in the back of a van to their planes. (Photo by Keystone Features/Stringer/Getty Images)

A two-turreted armoured truck knocked out in Fortress Modlin in late September 1939. (Photo by Hugo Jaeger/Timepix/The LIFE Picture Collection via Getty Images)

After the first few days, the Luftwaffe shifted to support the ground forces. Once again, these were not close air support missions, but rather targets previously selected. The Luftwaffe was highly effective in interdicting Polish troop movements along road and rail lines. Attempts to use the Luftwaffe in direct close support of ground operations did take place later in the campaign, notably the attacks against the Bzura counter-offensive in the second week of the war and the attacks on Warsaw in late September.

The Luftwaffe met serious resistance over the capital city, Warsaw. Reichsmarschall Hermann Göring planned a major first day air attack on Warsaw, codenamed Operation *Wasserkante* (Water's Edge). However, the attack was ineffectual due to low clouds and the Polish Pursuit Brigade's fighters shot down 16 German aircraft at a cost of ten fighters lost. The Pursuit Brigade, moreover, proved the most effective Polish aviation unit with 42 credited kills in the first six days of the war. However, these modest losses failed to stop the repeated German attacks. By 6 September 1939, the Pursuit Brigade had lost 38 fighters, and had transferred to airbases located east of Lublin. After this, the defence of the capital fell to the numerous Polish anti-aircraft guns located there. The Polish Army fighter squadrons were involved in numerous air battles with German combat aircraft. Indeed, Polish fighter aircraft shot down no fewer than 126 of the 285 German aircraft shot down during the campaign.

The Polish Bomber Brigade proved less successful in these initial operations. Its best asset, the new *Łoś* bomber squadrons, were still working up. The first major bombing mission was conducted by 24 P.23 *Karaś* light bombers on 2 September 1939. The Polish pilots pressed their attacks with considerable courage, but their losses were high. The *Łoś* medium bombers were first committed on 3 September, but ten were lost to flak on 4 September alone. On 7 September, the Bomber Brigade was shifted to the northern front to attack Army Group North's armour. By this stage, the deteriorating fuel and maintenance situation severely reduced its capabilities. The brigade was reinforced with local army *Karaś,* but these aircraft were in poor shape after a week of operating from rough grass strips. The army *Karaś* units conducted numerous bombing raids but by 6 September 1939 had already lost half their aircraft. During the campaign, about 260 Polish aircraft were lost to enemy action including 70 lost in air-to-air combat.

Continuing Combat in the East Prussian Theatre (2–5 September)

During 2 September GenObst von Bock's Army Group North continued its attempts to break eastward across the Pomeranian Corridor so as to link up with the German forces deployed in East Prussia. As planned, the northernmost Polish forces had withdrawn southward, leaving the Seacoast Defence Forces, including the Westerplatte garrison, completely isolated along the Baltic coastline. The heaviest fighting in the Corridor centred around the Tuchola Forest, with Schweppenburg's 3rd Panzer Division forcing the main Brda river. From East Prussia, two German infantry divisions penetrated the eastern side of the Pomeranian Corridor. By the end of the day, two Polish divisions were nearly trapped. On 3 September, the German 27th Infantry Division fought its way southward to Bydgoszcz, but the other formation was encircled and suffered heavy casualties. That day Army Pomorze also began withdrawing behind the River Vistula, because of the collapse of the Mława defences to the east. In total the Poles lost about 10,000 troops in the Pomeranian fighting. With the Polish defences evaporating, Bock's Army Group North transferred forces into East Prussia for the main assault against Warsaw.

Unable to penetrate the fortified positions of the Polish 20th Infantry Division near Mława, the ad hoc Panzer Division Kempf instead penetrated the badly over-extended Polish *Mazowiecka* Cavalry Brigade. Even the commitment of the Polish 8th Infantry Division could not restrain the German advance. By evening, the Polish defensive line had ruptured and Generał Dywizji Krukowicz-Przedrzymirski's Army Modlin headquarters ordered a withdrawal southward to the main Vistula line. Yet on the evening of 2–3 September the *Podlaska* Cavalry Brigade raided a quiet sector of the East Prussian front, the only Polish operation on German soil of the war. The Polish 20th Infantry continued to hold out in Mława, slowing the German advance.

The Polish forces withdrew towards fortified Modlin. The Panzer Division Kempf managed to cross the Narew river near Różan on 5 September despite the opposition of the 41st Infantry Division. The breach of the defences was widened the next day with another river crossing at Pułtusk. Rydz-Śmigły ordered Krukowicz-Przedrzymirski's Army Modlin to retreat once again behind the San river. The Modlin garrison continued to hold out even though surrounded.

A German motorcycle detachment launches a surprise attack somewhere in Poland during September 1939. (Photo by ullstein bild/ullstein bild via Getty Images)

The German Breakthrough in Silesia (1–7 September)

Since the German plan called for an encirclement of the Polish forces in western Poland, Army Groups North and South were separated from one another by Pomerania. Generał Dywizji Kutrzeba's Army Poznań defended this region; its original political mission had been to prevent an uncontested German seizure of this disputed territory. Kutrzeba, who had been heavily involved in prewar planning, was well aware that the Germans were making their main thrusts around his formation. Communications with Warsaw were finally restored on 3 September. Kutrzeba vehemently argued that his forces should begin operations against the northern flank of Rundstedt's command, namely against Gen d.Inf Blaskowitz's Eighth Army. Rydz-Śmigły refused, since he wanted to avoid a decisive battle west of the River Vistula that would lead to the premature destruction of Kutrzeba's forces.

Indeed, Rundstedt feared the very attack that Kutrzeba had proposed to Rydz-Śmigły. His concerns centered on his vulnerable flank, which was merely defended by GenMaj von Briesen's over-extended 30th Infantry Division. Nonetheless, Rundstedt pressed his main assault to the north-east through Silesia. The *Wołyńska* Cavalry Brigade held up the 4th Panzer Division on 2 September 1939, but the Polish 7th Infantry Division to the south was in a dire predicament, pitted against GenLt Kirchner's 1st Panzer Division as well as against two infantry divisions. Its withdrawal towards Częstochowa allowed the 1st Panzer Division to force the Warta river. The German Tenth Army next committed GenMaj Kuntzen's 3rd Light (Mechanised) Division. As a result, Generał Brygady Piasecki's *Krakowska* Cavalry Brigade had one of its regiments overwhelmed, and by 4 September, the Polish 7th Infantry Division had been shattered. The 2–4 September battles along the boundary between Armies Łódź and Kraków proved critical as they opened the gateway to Warsaw. Since the German Tenth Army contained most of the German mechanised force, the advances in this sector held the greatest potential for deep exploitation toward Warsaw amid the mostly flat farmland. In these actions, GenMaj von Richthofen's *Fliegerführer zbV* (Special Purpose Air Command) provided Tenth Army's units with some rudimentary and limited amounts of aerial support.

The battlefield situation along Army Kraków's southern flank was brighter, owing to the Polish 10th Mechanised Brigade's skilful defence against GenLt Veiel's 2nd Panzer (Armoured) Division. Nevertheless, the steady German advances obliged Generał Brygady Szylling's Army Kraków to withdraw towards Kraków. The mountainous terrain aided in the defence, and an orderly withdrawal prevented the Germans from penetrating the gap between Szylling's Army Kraków and Generał Dywizji Fabrycy's Army Karpaty.

The Polish High Command was deeply shocked by the sheer pace of the unrelenting German advance. Correctly anticipating that the main German thrust would emanate out of Silesia towards Warsaw, Generał Dywizji Dąb-Biernacki's Army Prusy was deployed as the main strategic reserve here. It comprised three infantry divisions and a cavalry brigade. The main threat was the rapid advance of the 4th and 1st Panzer Divisions towards Piotrków. Here, one of the few tank-on-tank engagements of the campaign occurred when the Polish 2nd Tank Battalion's 7TP tanks knocked out 33 AFVs for a loss of only two tanks. But the Polish armour was not concentrated and thus its effects were inconsequential.

By the evening of 5 September, the boundary between Generał Dywizji Rómmel's Army Łódź and Szylling's Army Kraków had fully ruptured, and Dąb-Biernacki's Army Prusy was unable to staunch the flow. Two Panzer divisions punched through to Piotrków, and the German Tenth Army pushed back the Army Kraków's northern flank, opening the way to Kielce. The Polish defence of the approaches to Warsaw was on the verge of collapse. On 5 September 1939, Rydz-Śmigły ordered the Armies Łódź, Kraków and Prusy to withdraw behind the Vistula. In addition, Kutrzeba's Army Poznań was also ordered eastward to the River Vistula.

The situation in the south had become equally bleak for the Poles. The Germans had finally broken out of the mountains and were pressing towards Kraków. The only effective Polish mobile formation, Pułkownik Maczek's 10th Mechanised Brigade, was eventually overwhelmed by the attacks mounted by

German troops observe, while in the far distance a Polish village burns. (Bettman / Getty Images)

GenLt Veiel's 2nd Panzer Division, as well as by those of GenLt Dietl's 3rd Gebirgsjäger Division. On 5 September, the Polish units were ordered to fall back behind the Dunajec river to protect the southern approaches to the city of Kraków.

During 5 September both sides felt compelled to reassess their plans. The OKH had been hesitant to commit divisions eastward for fear that they would have to be turned around to respond to a French attack. With no evidence of any French attack developing, this fear waned. German commanders recognised that the Poles were attempting to avoid a decisive battle west of the Vistula and urged that they should push further east to envelop and destroy individual chunks of the Polish Army. The German Army's Commander-in-Chief, GenObst von Brauchitsch, changed his position on 9 September, when it was blatantly evident that the Poles were conducting a strategic withdrawal and that French activity was limited to merely a token offensive.

The Polish strategic situation was now extremely grim. The Germans were advancing faster than the Poles could retreat. Rydz-Śmigły's main objective remained avoiding decisive battle west of the Vistula to keep the army in the field until the anticipated French counter-offensive. The collapse of Dąb-Biernacki's Army Prusy led Rydz-Śmigły to form a new strategic reserve, designated the Army Lublin. By 7 September, Rydz-Śmigły was convinced that the Germans would surround Warsaw within a week. He therefore decided to move the Polish High Command eastward to the city of Brześć nad Bugiem (Brest-Litovsk).

This move was a serious mistake, as Brześć was unprepared to handle the communications to the field armies. At the most critical time, coordination from the High Command was disrupted. Units received contradictory orders from Warsaw and Brześć, and some armies were essentially cut off from the high command. The position of Szylling's Army Kraków was the most perilous. Late on 7 September, the German 5th Panzer Division forced the Holy Cross mountains and began to move behind the main Polish defensive lines from the north-west. On the other flank, GenMaj Ritter von Hubicki's German 4th Light (Mechanised) Division and GenLt Materna's 45th Infantry Division between them seized the key town of Tarnów on 7 September 1939. This success occurred after the forces of the Army Małopolska withdrew from the Nida river line against orders from above. A day-long battle ensued as Szylling's Army Kraków tried to fight its way out of the noose being quickly tightened around it.

The four other central Polish armies continued to retreat towards the Vistula, but the rapidly advancing German mechanised units outpaced them. The most serious situation existed in the ruptured boundary between the Armies Łódź and Prusy, with both Kirchner's 1st Panzer and GenLt Reinhardt's 4th Panzer Divisions racing through the gap towards the Polish capital, Warsaw. Desperate counter-attacks mounted by units of Krukowicz-Przedrzymirski's Army Modlin were unsuccessful. As the OKH's opinion shifted, Bock was finally permitted to thrust down the eastern bank of the River Vistula, to threaten the rear areas of the Polish defences established along the river line.

Germans tanks cross a river deeper into Polish territory during 6 September 1939. (AFP via Getty Images)

Inaction in the West (3–12 September)

On 3 September 1939, France and Britain had both declared war on Germany. The Polish leaders in Warsaw rejoiced: salvation was anticipated. Unfortunately, French mobilisation was slow, and no detailed staff plans existed for a major offensive against Germany. Despite the promise of offensive support made to the Poles by *Général d'Armée* Maurice Gamelin, the French Chief of the General Staff, French strategic planning remained defensive: the army intended to shield itself behind the Maginot line to thwart a major German incursion into France. The French believed that they could defeat the Germans using a defensive strategy, since they were convinced that the Great War had taught that defence was the stronger method of war. Gamelin was in no rush since he expected that the Poles would hold out for months. The French, like the Poles, badly underestimated the pace of the new style of warfare.

In fact, Gamelin's May 1939 assurance to the Poles was insincere. The problem was not capability but will. Confined within the straitjacket of France's defensive strategy, in early September, Gamelin vetoed a hastily planned offensive. The general staff had prepared plans for an offensive into the Saar in 1938 during the Czech crisis. The plan was dusted off in a half-hearted attempt to honour France's commitments to Poland. Nine divisions crossed into Germany along a 25km (16 mile) front on 7 September, took minimal casualties, advanced 8km (five miles) to the Siegfried line and stopped. Disturbed by the grim news from Poland, Gamelin halted the Saar offensive on 12 September 1939. Britain's actions were no bolder. The BEF would not begin to arrive in France for months. British military action was limited to a campaign of leaflet raids on Germany, derided as 'confetti warfare'. Hitler had hoped that Britain and France would abandon Poland altogether. Their extremely timid response nevertheless still left the Poles to their fate.

THE POLISH BZURA COUNTER-ATTACK – THE FINAL STAGE, 14–18 SEPT

The Germans overreacted to the Bzura counter-offensive by diverting much of Rundstedt's Army Group South, plus elements of Army Group North. On 13 September, Rundstedt committed the Eighth and Tenth Armies to the Bzura River area. The Eighth Army counter-attacked from the west and south, while Tenth Army attacked westward from in front of Warsaw. Finally, a corps of Army Group North pursued from the northwest. The German counter-offensive, initiated on 14 September, compelled Kutrzeba to retreat due east. By the 16th, the Germans had so constricted the defenders' perimeter that Kutrzeba ordered his forces to break out eastwards through the Kampinos Forest. Elements of four formations fought their way out into Warsaw. Organised resistance collapsed on the 18th though mopping up continued through the 21st, with over 120,000 POWs taken. Kutrzeba avoided capture. The Polish Bzura counter-attack succeeded beyond the wildest Polish dreams of diverting German forces from Warsaw and brought the destruction of the counter-attacking forces. The German overreaction to the offensive did buy appreciable time for the Poles to organise a protracted defence of Warsaw.

Polish cavalry moving up to engage the German invaders, 18 September 1939. (Bettman / Getty images)

The Polish Bzura Counter-offensive (9–21 September)

With catastrophe looming, Rydz-Śmigły finally allowed Kutrzeba's Army Poznań to counter-attack the exposed flank of Blaskowitz's German Eighth Army to relieve pressure on Army Łódź and permit a more orderly withdrawal to Warsaw and the Vistula. Rundstedt continued to warn Blaskowitz about the threat. In the counter-attack along the Bzura river the Poles for once enjoyed modest numerical superiority: three infantry divisions – the 14th, 17th and 25th – supported by the *Podolska* and *Wielkopolska* Cavalry Brigades. The counter-offensive started on 9 September and after heavy fighting the Polish forces seized Piątek. Indeed, by the next day, 10 September, both GenLt Olbricht's 24th and Briesen's 30th Infantry Divisions were in full retreat. By then the surprise Polish riposte had taken 1,500 prisoners of war from these two German formations, which were subordinated to Gen d.Art Ulex's X Corps.

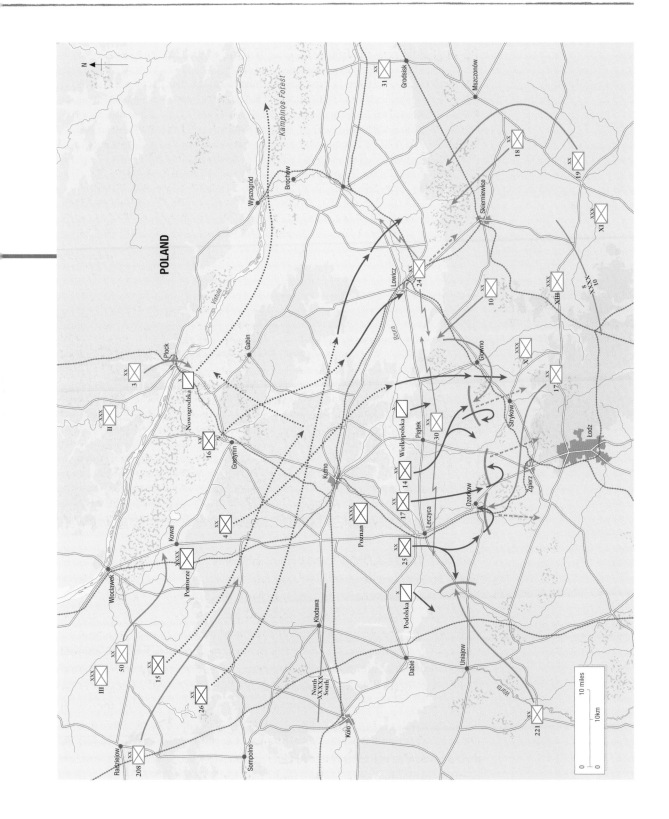

N

POLAND

Kampinos Forest

Vistula

Bzura

Warta

Grodsisk
Mszczonów
Skierniewice
Brochów
Wyszogród
Łowicz
Płock
Nowogrodzka
Gabin
Gostynin
Kutno
Głowno
Stryków
Łódź
Zgierz
Wielkopolska
Piątek
Leczyca
Ozorków
Kowal
Włocławek
Pomorze
Poznań
Kłodawa
Dabie
Podolska
Uniejów
Radziejów
Sompolino
Koło

North
XXXX
South

10 miles
10km

31
18
19
XI
XXXX
8
IX
24
10
X
17
30
14
17
25
4
16
3
II
50
15
26
208
221

German infantry tightening their encirclement of Warsaw, 15 September 1939. (Photo by ullstein bild/ullstein bild via Getty Images)

The German reaction was swift and forceful. Rundstedt ordered the encirclement and destruction of the Polish concentration. The 1st and 4th Panzer Divisions, on the outskirts of Warsaw, turned westward and blocked any attempts by Kutrzeba's Army Poznań to slip into the capital. Within two days, the Polish attacks had bogged down, and the Germans restored numerical superiority. The Polish High Command ordered Kutrzeba to attack towards Radom aiming to break through and withdraw southward towards Romania.

The Polish plan was sheer fantasy. By this time, the Polish forces, which numbered nine infantry divisions and two cavalry brigades, faced 19 German divisions. Kutrzeba instead tried breaking out eastward towards Warsaw via Sochaczew in concert with elements of the Army Pomorze. Wehrmacht commanders demanded more air support. The Luftwaffe responded with a massive air attack on 16 September: 820 aircraft dropped a total of 328,000kg (723,000lb) of bombs on the Polish ground units.

On the ground, Gen d.Kav Hoepner's German XVI Corps (Motorised) attacked that day with considerable fury and Kutrzeba was compelled to order his units to break out through a gap north of Sochaczew. Taking advantage of their mobility, the troopers of both Generał Brygady Abraham's *Podolska* Cavalry Brigade and Pułkownik Strzelecki's *Wielkopolska* Cavalry Brigade managed to break through into the Kampinos Forest on the northern edge of Warsaw. Behind them elements of the Polish 15th and 25th Infantry Divisions also successfully managed to reach the suburbs of Warsaw. The remaining Polish forces held out

Street Fighting in Warsaw, 7 September 1939

Having suffered a bloody nose at Mokra, the 4th Panzer Division crunched through the battered Polish lines during the following two days. With the brittle Polish defences cracked wide open, the 4th Panzer Division was able to take advantage of its mobility to carry out one of the most successful Panzer missions of the campaign, exploiting its breakthrough and racing to Warsaw. Reaching the outskirts of Warsaw a week after the start of the campaign, the 4th Panzer Division pushed into the Ochota suburbs in the south-western approaches to the city. The ensuing battle highlighted the problems with operating mechanised forces in urban areas. By the time the 4th Panzer Division reached Ochota, the Poles had managed to scrape up a number of units to defend the capital. Lacking dedicated anti-tank weapons the Poles deployed 75mm field guns to cover key street intersections. The German Panzers of 1939 were not the impregnable steel fortresses of later years, and were vulnerable to nearly any weapon heavier than a light machine gun. They could be blown open by a 75mm field gun, and a confrontation between a Panzer blindly stumbling through unfamiliar streets and a well-placed field gun behind a barricade had predictable results. Many Panzers were lost. The solution was to use infantry to locate and eliminate the field guns. But the early Panzer divisions had too few

infantry for such a mission, especially when faced with Polish infantry blockaded in houses and behind barricades. Furthermore, the 4th Panzer Division had advanced so quickly that German infantry divisions were days behind. Here, a PzKpfw II light tank **(1)** cautiously advances with Panzergrenadiers **(2)** in support. Tank–infantry cooperation in urban environments was extremely difficult as the infantry had no way to communicate with the tanks, lacking a radio link except at battalion level. The experiences of tank use in Warsaw would convince German Panzer commanders that urban battles were better left to the infantry, a lesson that still resonates with contemporary armour officers. The attack of the 4th Panzer Division petered out after a couple of days of hard fighting, due to events occurring further west. While the 4th Panzer Division had been racing to Warsaw, Generał Kutrzeba's Army Poznań had launched a surprise counter-attack on German infantry divisions moving on Warsaw. The ensuing battle along the Bzura River temporarily halted the attacks on Warsaw and they did not resume until later in the month after the Polish forces were surrounded and crushed. (Artwork by Howard Gerrard, © Osprey Publishing)

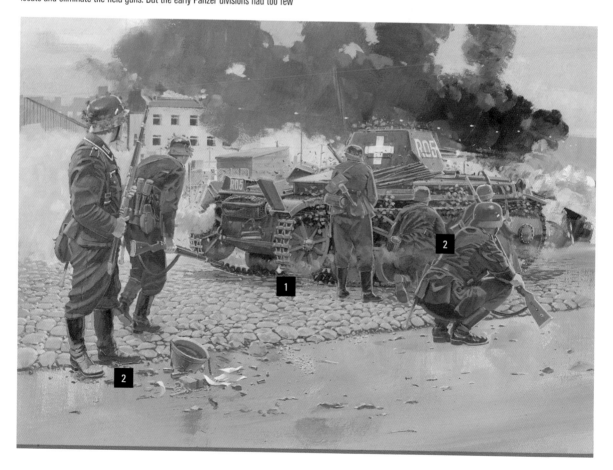

THE BATTLE FOR WARSAW, 5–27 SEPT 1939

The 4th Panzer Division entered southwestern Warsaw on 8 September but was bloodily repulsed. Thereafter, the Poles launched their Bzura counter-attack, which diverted substantial German forces. The remnants of Armies Łódź and Modlin retired into Warsaw, joined by the survivors of the Bzura debacle. The Germans launched probing attacks from 15 September. The Third Army attacked first in the east, against the Praga suburb and in the north as the Germans invested Warsaw with Eighth Army's

13 divisions. On 20 September, massive air and artillery attacks heralded the final assault. The Germans stepped up attacks on the 23rd and on 'Black Monday', the 25th, they reached unprecedented ferocity. The same day, the major defensive forts fell, and on 27 September Generał Dywizji Juliusz Rómmel surrendered with 140,000 soldiers. Nearly 10,000 civilians had perished, and half of the city's buildings were damaged

for two more days. Organised defence collapsed on 18 September, though it took three more days for the Germans to mop up the last resistance. Some 120,000 Polish troops were captured and the Armies Pomorze and Poznań were wiped out. The Bzura counter-offensive, however, provided several short-term benefits for the Polish Army. It bought the Armies Warsaw and Lublin time to prepare the defence of the capital, and temporarily derailed the main German thrust towards Warsaw by about a week.

The Siege of Warsaw (7–29 September)

The rupture achieved between Rómmel's Army Łódź and Dąb-Biernacki's Army Prusy enabled the 1st and 4th Panzer Divisions to race to the outskirts of Warsaw on 7 September. At that moment the Polish plans for Warsaw were in flux. The city was gripped by panic when the Polish High Command transferred to Brześć and many believed the rumours that its entire male population was to form up east of the capital. This last order was countermanded by the Warsaw Defence Command of Generał Walerian Czuma and the city's mayor, Stefan Starzyński. The mayor urged Warsaw residents to help erect defences on the outskirts of the city. Warsaw was acting as a magnet for retreating and partially mobilised Polish units, and Polish commanders in the city decided on mounting as prolonged a defence as was possible.

German tanks from GenLt Reinhardt's 4th Panzer Division first probed the Ochota suburbs on 8 September but encountered accurate point-blank Polish artillery fire. The German tanks were not adequately supported by infantry and took heavy losses from anti-tank and field guns positioned at street intersections. The fighting petered out on 9 September when Reinhardt's 4th Panzer Division was recalled westward to help thwart the Polish Bzura river counter-offensive.

When the attack on Warsaw resumed on 15 September it came from the north, from the German Army Group North since Army Group South was preoccupied with the Bzura fighting. Army Group North's spearhead consisted of

N

Kawęczyn

61

XXX I

Wawer

XX 11

21

Praga

III 26/6

III 8

Goclaw

21

I 136

Czerniakowski

XX 46

Czerniakowski

217

III 80/20

III 79/20

XX 20

II XIx

III 78/20

Vistula

II 21/8

IV

Dabrowski

Sluzew

XX 3

Warsaw

II 41/29

Mokotow

XX 10

Citadel

IV 30/10

III 60/25

III 61/45

III 60/25

II 144/44 Res

II 40/5

XXX XIII

XX 18

II 41 Res

Wola

III 40/5

Ochota

Rakow

Powazki III 114

Kolo

Bem

Szczesliwicki

XXX XI

Wawrzyszew

II 26/5

III

V 360

Wolsk

Okecie

XX 31

XX 24

I 360

XX 19

Groty

Odolany

XX 4

1 mile

1km

0   0

the units of Küchler's German Third Army. The German mid-September change in plans allowed Bock to deploy his forces on both sides of the River Vistula, so Küchler's German Third Army sensibly attacked down both banks of the river. The Germans were not able to encircle the city of Warsaw until the Bzura fighting subsided, and so the second wave of fighting focused on the northern suburbs.

By 20 September 1939, the last battered remnants of Kutrzeba's Army Poznań had managed to struggle back into Warsaw, mainly through the Kampinos Forest north of the city. With the fighting on the Bzura largely over by 21 September, the Wehrmacht gradually encircled the city with 13 divisions, about a third of their entire forces in Poland. Rundstedt's Army Group South again closed off the southern and western edges of the city. For the final assault, 1,000 German artillery pieces were brought up. The first major attempt occurred on 23 September, but it made few gains as the Poles were by then well prepared.

The next attack, on 25 September, was preceded by an enormous artillery and air bombardment, which went down in city legend as 'Black Monday'. Some 1,200 aircraft participated, even including Ju 52 transports employed expediently in the improvised bomber role. Though the air attacks were not immediately decisive, the following day German infantry finally overwhelmed the three old Tsarist fortresses (the Forts Mokotów, Dąbrowski and Czerniaków) located to the south of the city. Hitler gave instructions to his commanders to forbid civilians to

TOP In the battle of Warsaw during late September 1939, German troops demarcate their control with swastikas to orientate Luftwaffe planes and minimise the risk of friendly fire accidents. (Photo by ullstein bild/ ullstein bild via Getty Images)

ABOVE German tank burned out during the street fighting in the Polish capital, Warsaw. (Photo by Hugo Jaeger/Timepix/The LIFE Picture Collection via Getty Images)

leave the city, presuming that the overwhelming need for food and water for the populace would eventually force the city's defenders to capitulate. The stratagem worked. On 27 September, the new commander of Army Warsaw, Generał Dywizji Rómmel, capitulated and some 140,000 Polish troops surrendered. The siege had been enormously costly with over 40,000 civilians killed, and half the city's buildings destroyed or damaged. The nearby Modlin garrison held out until 29 September when Generał Brygady Thommée surrendered the remaining 24,000 Polish troops.

Further Major Polish Setbacks (10–16 September)

Although the Polish High Command had hoped to defend on the eastern bank of the Vistula, their plans collapsed. In the north, Krukowicz-Przedrzymirski's Army Modlin and Generał Brygady Młot-Fijałkowski's Special Operational Group Narew had been thwarted by the assault out of East Prussia that forced the Vistula. Likewise, in the south, German forces had advanced over the Vistula in several places during the second week of the fighting.

Rydz-Śmigły attempted to improve the confused situation by creating two new operational commands on 10 September, the Northern and Southern Fronts. His plan took account of the geography of the area, as it was bisected by the Pripyat marshes at its centre. The Northern Front, placed under the command of Dąb-Biernacki, was unable to create a coherent defence. Its main assignment was to prevent the German forces from penetrating southward towards Brześć by holding a series of east-west river lines. But Bock had committed Guderian's

Hitler, Heinrich Himmler (left), head of the SS, and Hans Frank (right), Governor General of Poland, observe German troops in Poland sometime during September 1939. (Photo by Ann Ronan Pictures/Print Collector/Getty Images)

THE BATTLE FOR WARSAW

8–26 September 1939, viewed from the south-west, showing the initial attacks on the city's southern suburbs by 4th Panzer Division, the retreat of the remnants of Army Poznań into the city, and the subsequent German siege and assault.

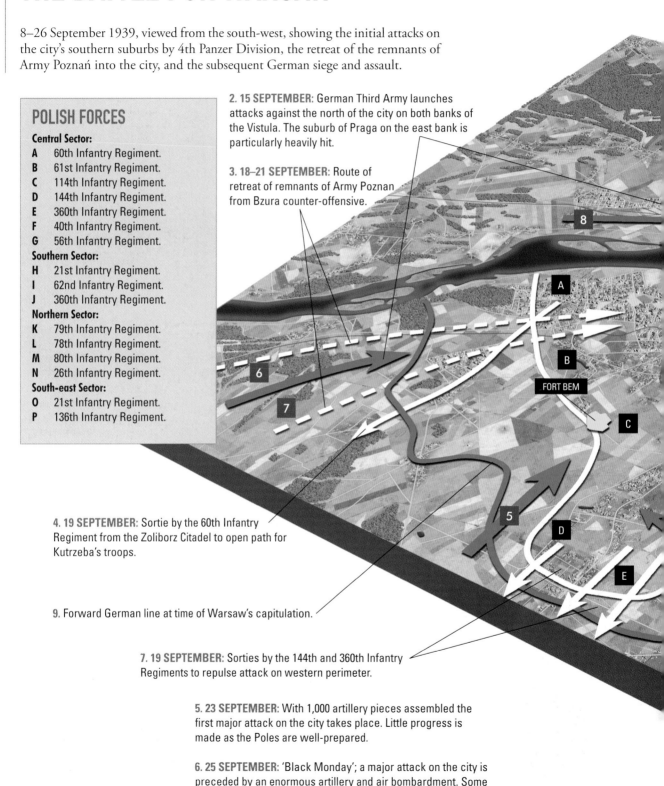

POLISH FORCES

Central Sector:
A   60th Infantry Regiment.
B   61st Infantry Regiment.
C   114th Infantry Regiment.
D   144th Infantry Regiment.
E   360th Infantry Regiment.
F   40th Infantry Regiment.
G   56th Infantry Regiment.

Southern Sector:
H   21st Infantry Regiment.
I   62nd Infantry Regiment.
J   360th Infantry Regiment.

Northern Sector:
K   79th Infantry Regiment.
L   78th Infantry Regiment.
M   80th Infantry Regiment.
N   26th Infantry Regiment.

South-east Sector:
O   21st Infantry Regiment.
P   136th Infantry Regiment.

2. 15 SEPTEMBER: German Third Army launches attacks against the north of the city on both banks of the Vistula. The suburb of Praga on the east bank is particularly heavily hit.

3. 18–21 SEPTEMBER: Route of retreat of remnants of Army Poznan from Bzura counter-offensive.

FORT BEM

4. 19 SEPTEMBER: Sortie by the 60th Infantry Regiment from the Zoliborz Citadel to open path for Kutrzeba's troops.

9. Forward German line at time of Warsaw's capitulation.

7. 19 SEPTEMBER: Sorties by the 144th and 360th Infantry Regiments to repulse attack on western perimeter.

5. 23 SEPTEMBER: With 1,000 artillery pieces assembled the first major attack on the city takes place. Little progress is made as the Poles are well-prepared.

6. 25 SEPTEMBER: 'Black Monday'; a major attack on the city is preceded by an enormous artillery and air bombardment. Some 1,200 aircraft take part in the attacks.

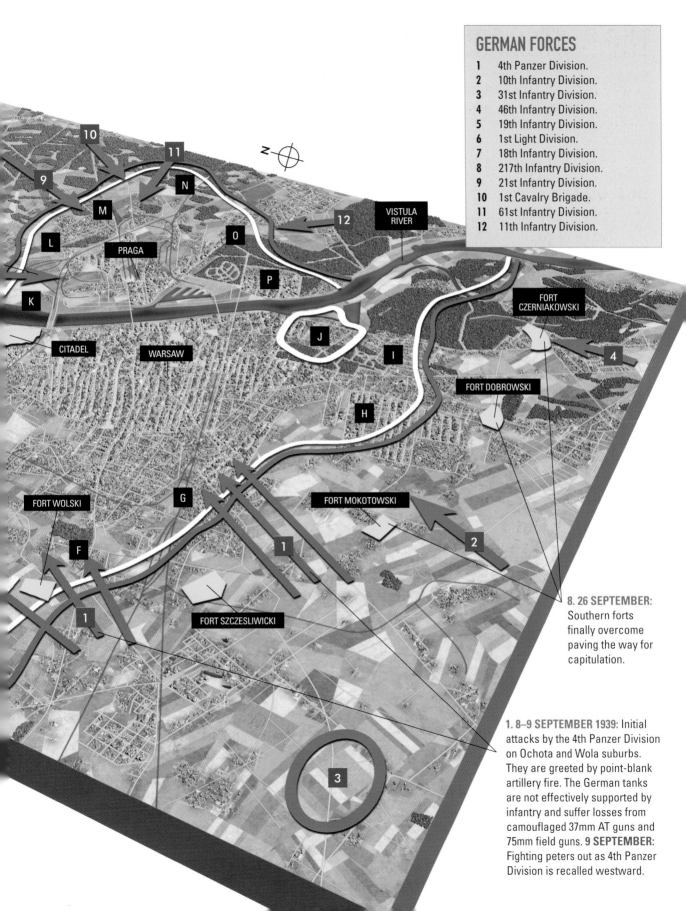

GERMAN FORCES

1. 4th Panzer Division.
2. 10th Infantry Division.
3. 31st Infantry Division.
4. 46th Infantry Division.
5. 19th Infantry Division.
6. 1st Light Division.
7. 18th Infantry Division.
8. 217th Infantry Division.
9. 21st Infantry Division.
10. 1st Cavalry Brigade.
11. 61st Infantry Division.
12. 11th Infantry Division.

VISTULA RIVER

FORT CZERNIAKOWSKI

FORT DOBROWSKI

PRAGA

CITADEL

WARSAW

FORT MOKOTOWSKI

FORT WOLSKI

FORT SZCZESLIWICKI

8. 26 SEPTEMBER: Southern forts finally overcome paving the way for capitulation.

1. 8–9 SEPTEMBER 1939: Initial attacks by the 4th Panzer Division on Ochota and Wola suburbs. They are greeted by point-blank artillery fire. The German tanks are not effectively supported by infantry and suffer losses from camouflaged 37mm AT guns and 75mm field guns. **9 SEPTEMBER:** Fighting peters out as 4th Panzer Division is recalled westward.

XIX Corps (Motorised) on 9 September. Its spearhead, GenMaj Schaal's 10th Panzer Division, soon plunged south towards the Bug river and the Polish High Command at Brześć. The Polish Northern Front found that some of its units were fighting their way through German units that had already moved south of them. By the end of 10 September, the German 10th Panzer Division was south of the Biebrza river and had completely pinned-down Generał Brygady Podhorski's *Suwalska* Cavalry Brigade. Poland's defence in the north-east was on the verge of immediate collapse.

The imminent disintegration of the Polish Northern Front prompted Rydz-Śmigły to order the withdrawal of Polish forces to the so-called Romanian bridgehead on 11 September. His intention was to preserve surviving Polish forces in south-east Poland until the start of the anticipated French offensive six days hence. The desperate order was entirely unrealistic. The forces west of the River Vistula were either occupied in a life-and-death struggle along the Bzura river, or in the process of retreating to the Vistula. Furthermore, the Southern Front was not as secure as Rydz-Śmigły might have hoped. For GenMaj Kubler's German 1st Gebirgsjäger Division had managed to fight its way through the Carpathian Mountains. On 12 September Kubler's advancing troops had reached and secured the regional capital of Lwów. Even more ominously, the Soviet Union had announced a general military mobilisation on 11 September.

By 14 September, the Polish Northern Front had been completely routed. Młot-Fijałkowski's Special Operational Group Narew had disintegrated. The remnants of Krukowicz-Przedrzymirski's Army Modlin east of the Vistula succeeded in withdrawing, but had suffered heavy losses. With German spearheads closing in on Brześć, Rydz-Śmigły and the Polish High Command began withdrawing to the town of Kołomyja in the Romanian bridgehead. By this stage, national coordination of the Polish defence effort had collapsed because of insurmountable communication problems. The continuation of Polish resistance now fell to the initiative and determination of local commanders in the face of overwhelming odds.

The situation on the Polish Southern Front also had continued to deteriorate. The front commander, Generał Broni Sosnkowski, attempted to withdraw both the Army Kraków and the Army Małopolska east to Lwów. He was stymied, however, when the rapidly advancing German 2nd Panzer and 4th Light (Mechanised) Divisions drove a wedge between them. Veiel's 2nd Panzer Division advanced so fast and so deep behind the Polish forces that it encircled the Army Kraków. On 14 September, Army Lublin, renamed as the Central Front, began arriving from the north to reinforce the Army Kraków. By this stage, the army was fighting a desperate battle with German forces that were closing in on three sides and which had already managed to isolate the Polish 21st Mountain Infantry Division.

The Soviet Invasion from the East (17 September–6 October)

On 17 September 1939, the Polish ambassador in Moscow was informed that the Soviet Red Army was intervening in eastern Poland, allegedly to protect its fraternal Byelorussian and Ukrainian populations from German occupation. The Polish high command, which had expected the start of the French offensive that day, suddenly faced an unexpected new calamity. The Soviet invasion from the east destroyed any hopes for a prolonged defence of Poland.

The Soviet operations in eastern Poland had been anticipated in the secret protocols of the Molotov–Ribbentrop Pact. Stalin's delay in attacking Poland was in part due to uncertainty over the reaction of the Western Allies, the unexpectedly rapid pace of the German advance, the distraction of military operations in the Far East and the time needed to mobilise the Soviet Red Army. Besides the dramatic events in Poland, Stalin was preoccupied with the undeclared war between the Soviet Union and Japan, which culminated in the decisive Soviet victory at Khalkin Gol in September 1939. An armistice was signed with Japan on 15 September, and with German formations already operating east of the proposed Soviet–German demarcation line, Soviet leader Josef Stalin was forced to act sooner than he had planned.

The decapitation of the Soviet officer corps by Stalin's purges hindered the Red Army's execution of the operation. The Soviet Red Army estimated it needed several weeks to mobilise. The German advance had proceeded much more quickly than the Soviets had anticipated, forcing a hasty commitment of the ill-prepared Red Army to secure the spoils of the treaty agreement. The Red Army was organised into two fronts and deployed 25 rifle and 16 cavalry divisions plus 12 tank brigades with a total strength of 466,516 troops. Its tank forces sent into Poland exceeded the German and Polish

German and Soviet military units linked up at Brest-Litovsk. A Soviet political commissar and German officers discuss the impending capitulation of the city, *c.* 21 September 1939. (Photo by ullstein bild/ullstein bild via Getty Images)

THE SOVIET INVASION OF EASTERN POLAND, 17–29 SEPT 1939

In the Molotov–Ribbentrop Pact's secret protocols the Soviet Union and Germany carved up Poland between them. On 17 September, Soviet forces invaded eastern Poland. The Belorussian Front's three armies and one cavalry-mechanised group fielded 16 divisions, while the Ukrainian Front's three armies and one cavalry-mechanised group deployed 21 divisions. They were opposed by less than 11,000 Polish frontier guards and remnants of frontline formations. Red Army forces advanced across the entire 1,290km (800 mile) Polish–Soviet border with minimal resistance from the confused Poles at up to 97km (60 miles) a day in the initial stages. Yet major command and control and maintenance challenges hamstrung the Soviet advances and about 100,000 Poles escaped. On the 22nd, the Germans withdrew fully to the demarcation line. A week later, the two countries formalised the Bug and San Rivers as their new mutual border.

inventories combined, amounting to 3,739 tanks. The Red Air Force was also committed in strength, totalling about 2,000 combat aircraft. Fighters made up 60 per cent of the attacking force, along with medium bombers accounting for another 30 per cent.

Polish defences had been stripped bare in the east. Normally Generał Brygady Orlik-Rückemann's *Korpus Ochrony Pogranicza* (The Border Defence Corps, or KOP for short) guarded the frontier with a strength of some 12,000 troops. These forces were essentially light infantry. Furthermore, many of the KOP's border units had been ordered westward as desperately-needed reinforcements to help stem the eastward German onslaught. As a result, only a token border force remained stationed on the Polish-Soviet border. The resulting force ratio was ludicrously one-sided, with roughly one Polish battalion battling an enemy force the size of an entire Soviet corps command.

That said, Soviet Red Army mobilisation was chaotic at best. Due to the upcoming harvest, it was difficult to fill out the units with war-mobilisation civilian trucks. Consequently, Soviet formations were seldom at half vehicle strength. Soviet formations were often deployed haphazardly, loosely configured as regional groups. As a result of their belated and haphazard mobilisation and the almost non-existent opposition they faced, the Soviet Red Army relied on mechanised groups created around cavalry divisions reinforced by tank brigades to sweep rapidly into Poland.

There was considerable confusion on the Polish side when news of the Soviet invasion first filtered through. At first there was some hope that the Soviets might be intervening to aid Poland, a delusion that was quickly exposed. Nevertheless, the Polish High Command on 17–18 September ordered the KOP not to engage Soviet forces except in self-defence or if the Soviets interfered with their movement to the Romanian bridgehead. However, the order was not widely received. Instead Orlik-Rückemann, on his own initiative, ordered his troops to fight. Skirmishes between the KOP and Soviet Red Army units took place all along the frontier,

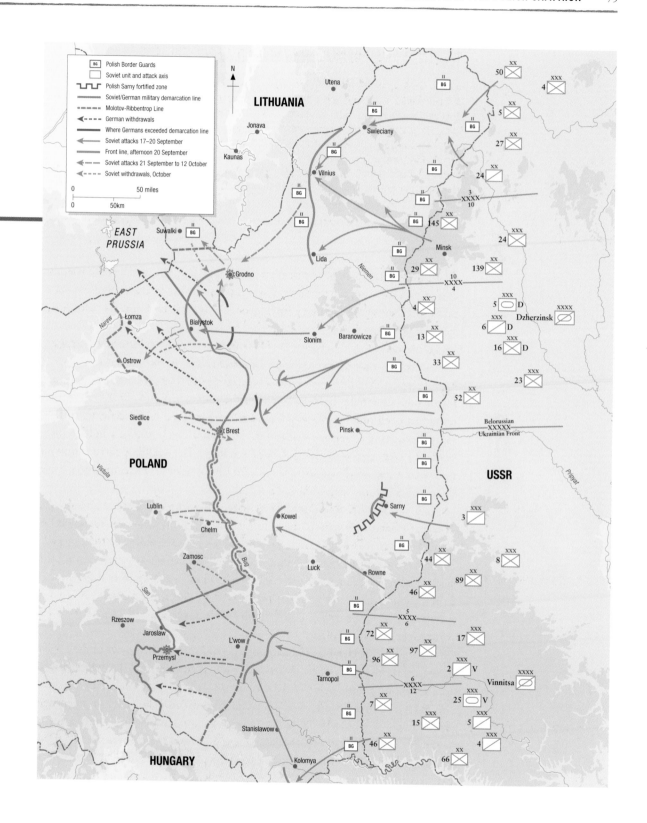

Polish Border Guards

Soviet unit and attack axis

Polish Sarny fortified zone

Soviet/German military demarcation line

Molotov-Ribbentrop Line

German withdrawals

Where Germans exceeded demarcation line

Soviet attacks 17–20 September

Front line, afternoon 20 September

Soviet attacks 21 September to 12 October

Soviet withdrawals, October

N

0   50 miles

0   50km

LITHUANIA

Utena

Jonava

Kaunas

Swieciany

Vilnius

Lida

EAST PRUSSIA

Suwalki

Grodno

Narew

Łomza

Bialystok

Ostrow

Slonim

Baranowicze

Niemen

Minsk

Dzherzinsk

POLAND

Siedlice

Brest

Pinsk

Belorussian Ukrainian Front

USSR

Vistula

Lublin

Chelm

Kowel

Sarny

Bug

Luck

Rowne

Dnieper

Rzeszow

Zamosc

L'wow

Jaroslaw

San

Przemysl

Tarnopol

Vinnitsa

Stanislawow

HUNGARY

Kolomya

50   XX
4   XXX
5
27   XX
24   XX
3   XXXX   10
145   XX
24   XXX
29   XX   10   XXXX   4   139   XX
4   XX   5   XXX   D
6   XXX   D
13   XX   16   XXX   D
33   XX   23   XXX
52
3   XXX
44   XX   8   XXX
89   XX
46   XX
5   XXXX   6
72   XX   17   XXX
96   XX   97   XX
2   XXX   V
6   XXXX   12   Vinnitsa
7   XX   25   XXX   V
15   XX   5   XXX
46   XX   4   XXX
66   XX

especially near the towns of Wilno (Vilnius) and Grodno. The heaviest fighting occurred in the region of Galicia in south-eastern Poland, where retreating regular Polish Army units had gravitated.

The region of Galicia was also the only real area of significant and sustained aerial combat. This occurred mostly on the first day of the Soviet invasion, as the surviving Polish air force units had been ordered to escape into Romania. On 17 September 1939, Polish fighters downed three Soviet aircraft but the following day the Polish Pursuit Brigade evacuated to Romania with its last 43 aircraft. Several Soviet aircraft were lost in subsequent fighting, mostly to ground fire.

The Germans had not been forewarned about the date of the Soviet invasion and were caught unprepared. Some German forces had already advanced beyond the boundaries set by the Molotov–Ribbentrop Pact, especially Guderian's XIX Corps (Motorised). On 17 September, the OKW demarcated the furthest points east units could advance. On each succeeding day, the OKW issued new boundary lines, gradually pulling back, and minimizing encounters with the Soviet Red Army. On 20 September, Adolf Hitler explicitly ordered units to stop any combat operations east of the boundary line. All German troops were to withdraw to the definitive line laid down in the Molotov–Ribbentrop Pact by 21 September. On 22 September, a ceremony was held in Brześć and the Germans formally handed over the fortress to the Soviet forces. Despite the extensive precautions taken there still were some unintended clashes with the Soviet Red Army, especially around the city of Lwów.

Soviet intervention led Rydz-Śmigły, now recognising that his forces could not prevent the country from being overrun, in desperation to order all Polish units to retreat southwards into Romania. The aim was to preserve the Polish military for later reconstitution in France to continue the struggle against the Germans. However, Soviet intervention was to make the retention of a Romanian bridgehead impossible, thereby greatly reducing the number of Polish troops able to escape.

The Army Kraków's recently formed Warsaw Mechanised Brigade spearheaded its attempted breakout through the German lines near Tomaszów Lubelski on 18 September. The attack was partially successful in penetrating the lines of Hubicki's 4th Light (Mechanised) Division. However, Veiel's 2nd Panzer Division counter-attacked and prevented a breakout. The attacks were repeated on 20 September precipitating the largest tank-versus-tank engagements of the campaign. The failure of these attacks compelled Szylling's Army Kraków to surrender on 20 September.

The continuing defence of the city of Lwów by the Poles presented one of the more ticklish diplomatic situations as there were German forces on the city's western side and Soviet units on its eastern side. The Polish commander, Generał Brygady Władysław Langner, surrendered on terms to the Soviet Red Army on 22 September. Ostensibly, the capitulated officers were permitted to find their way south to Romania but in fact the NKVD rounded up the officers before massacring them at Katyn the following year in one of the more infamous atrocities of the war.

The last units of the shattered Polish Northern Front were halted by the Wehrmacht. Eventually, the last operational force still extant, about 2,000 troops under the command of Pułkownik Zieleniewski surrendered near Nisko on 2 October. The KOP border units and other scattered forces in the north could not reach the Romanian frontier so Generał Brygady Kleeberg drove 16,000 troops toward Warsaw, not knowing that Warsaw had already fallen. After a four-day battle around Kock, Kleeberg finally surrendered on 6 October 1939. With the defeat of Kock's forces, the Polish campaign finally came to an end. Despite the puny size of Polish forces deployed in the eastern border areas, the Soviet Red Army still lost 996 soldiers killed and 2,383 wounded in the fighting. Tank casualties amounted to 42 combat losses and a further 429 mechanical breakdowns and other non-combat losses.

The Soviet invasion shortened the 1939 Polish campaign by several weeks. The immediate tactical consequence for the Polish Army was to prevent troops retreating eastward from reaching Romania. The Soviet Red Army had captured 99,149 Polish troops by 2 October 1939. Later records state that they eventually captured 452,536 Polish troops, but this number included many non-military personnel arbitrarily rounded up to 'de-Polonise' the region. Subsequently, the Soviets, in 1940 in the Katyn fortress, murdered most of the Polish officers – some 8,000 persons – who had been captured in the 1939 invasion of Poland. In addition, the Soviets deported tens of thousands of Polish armed forces personnel, to the Gulags of Siberia, along with many tens of thousands of Polish government officials, civic leaders, teachers, intelligentsia, and clergy.

The German leader Hitler viewing the victory parade in Warsaw, 5 October 1939. (Photo by Hugo Jaeger/Timepix/ The LIFE Picture Collection via Getty Images)

THE AFTERMATH

Polish casualties in the 1939 campaign amounted to 66,300 dead, 133,700 wounded, and around 687,000 prisoners. German casualties were 16,000 killed and 32,000 wounded. A total of 674 German tanks were knocked out, of which 217 were total write-offs. For the German Army, the Polish campaign was a vital learning experience that prepared it for the Western campaign. It tested German men and machines. The new tactics, training and technology were proven. The fighting highlighted the skills of the better commanders and troops while also providing many German divisions with their first combat experience. It was especially valuable in validating the Panzer divisions and the revolutionary potential of combined arms warfare. Some French and British observers dismissed the outcome of the campaign as the result of poor Polish performance, thereby underestimating the importance of the new tactics. The Germans were not so dismissive of Polish performance in 1939. More perceptive British observers dubbed the new combined arms tactics as 'Blitzkrieg', a word that entered the military vocabulary a few months later following the stunning defeat of France.

While German Army performance in Poland had been good, the campaign revealed numerous shortcomings that the Germans vigorously addressed. The light divisions had proven a failure and were upgraded to Panzer divisions for the French campaign. Many aspects of combined arms operations needed improvement. The Panzer divisions were tank heavy and infantry light. Tank and infantry co-operation had proven poor. The Luftwaffe had played an important role in the campaign, gaining air superiority, and conducting interdiction missions, but greater air-ground coordination was required.

The Soviet Red Army, concentrating on its victory over Japan at Khalkin Gol in the same period, learned some lessons from the Polish experience but ignored most others. The level of training of all ranks was poor, with weaknesses in the senior officer ranks. GenObst Halder concluded that it would take them a decade to return to the level of competence of the early 1930s prior to the purges. Almost 15 per cent of the Soviet Red Army's tank force was lost during two weeks of operations against a token opponent. For the German commanders, the 1939 Polish campaign suggested that the Soviet Red Army was a mere paper tiger, emboldening Hitler's long-term ideological aggression against the Soviet Union.

View of a targeted Polish city from the cockpit of a German He 111 medium bomber, September 1939. (Photo by Galerie Bilderwelt/Getty Images)

A total of some 100,000 Polish troops escaped into Romania, Hungary, and the Baltic republics. Of these, around 35,000 made their way to France where they served in four infantry divisions and a mechanised brigade during the 1940 campaign. At the core was the remnants of Pułkownik Maczek's 10th Mechanised Brigade, which had performed so well in 1939. Maczek later commanded the mechanised brigade in France in 1940 and, thereafter he organised the 1st Polish Armoured Division in Britain, which fought under his command in 1944–45. The II Polish Corps was created in the

Mediterranean from Polish survivors of the Soviet POW camps, released by Stalin after 1942. These units won fame for their capture of Monte Cassino in Italy in 1944.

If the 1939 Polish campaign had revealed the technical excellence of the Wehrmacht, it also began to reveal its dark side. The scale and brutality of German reprisals in Poland in 1939 were unusually savage. The worst atrocities were committed by German paramilitary formations and the SS units. Indeed, the heinous actions of the SS led some morally minded and highly courageous Wehrmacht commanders such as Gen d.Inf Blaskowitz to complain directly to Adolf Hitler; his reward for this moral rectitude was never to be promoted throughout the remaining five of years of war. These atrocities were only hints of far worse to come, as warfare in eastern Europe would degenerate into appalling savagery later.

For Poland, World War II was an unredeemed tragedy. One in six Poles died under brutal Nazi and Soviet occupation. Europe's most thriving Jewish community was annihilated, and the names of the German death camps in Poland – Auschwitz, Belzec and Treblinka – have become synonyms for genocide. The Allied victory in 1945 brought little solace, as Poland was then subjected to nearly 50 years of communist rule. The consequences of the 1939 Polish campaign were felt for decades afterwards. Despite being nominally allied to Poland after the German invasion of 1941, Stalin insisted that the Soviet Union be allowed to keep the half of Poland it seized in 1939. In compensation, Poland was allotted territory in eastern Germany. Instead of gaining *Lebensraum* in the east, Germany contracted: East Prussia disappeared and the German populations in the east were forcibly displaced. In swallowing western Ukraine, the Soviet Union contributed to its own demise in the guise of Ukrainian nationalism, which was one of the many catalysts for the dissolution of the Soviet Union.

THE BATTLEFIELD TODAY

Today, an interested person's attempt to retrace the events of the September 1939 campaign in Poland is highly complicated, thanks to the complex interplay of the impacts of geography, history and politics. Poland's borders shifted dramatically during World War II. The eastern half of the old Polish republic was taken over by the Soviet Union in 1939 and it remained in Soviet hands until the collapse of the Soviet Union in 1991. Now, these territories are part of the newly independent countries of Belarus, Ukraine and Lithuania. Since Poland and the Soviet Union were nominally allies from 1941 to 1945, Stalin suggested that Poland be compensated for the loss of its territory with German territory. As a result, Poland shifted westward, with Berlin now nearer the Polish border. East Prussia no longer exists, having been absorbed by Poland except for the area around the city of Königsberg (which is now the Russian city of Kaliningrad). As a result, even the

Pro-German victory parade in Danzig after the city's 'liberation', early September 1939. The banner reads, 'Danzig greets its Führer!' (Photo by Keystone-France/Gamma-Keystone via Getty Images)

most basic facts, such as the establishment of the location of the former borders of 1939 Poland, are difficult to achieve without a really good map of the period.

An individual's attempts at retracing the sites of the battles waged during autumn 1939 is further hindered by later history and politics. Poland was a battleground on several later occasions during World War II, and so the 1939 campaign competes with other commemorations. Poland's former eastern provinces were the site of the opening phase of Operation *Barbarossa* in June 1941. In 1944 the Red Army swept through eastern Poland in the wake of Operation *Bagration*, ending up along the eastern banks of the Vistula. Warsaw was the most severely damaged of Poland's cities. The Jewish quarter of the capital was razed in the wake of the Warsaw ghetto uprising of April 1943, while the rest of the city was systematically destroyed by German engineer troops as a reprisal against the city-wide Warsaw Uprising of August 1944. When the Red Army marched into the city in January 1945, there was nothing but ruins. As a result, Warsaw has been rebuilt from scratch since the war, and its Old City is a reconstruction.

The old royal capital of Kraków miraculously escaped extensive war damage, but it did not figure prominently in the 1939 fighting. Danzig, now Gdansk, was also severely damaged during the 1945 fighting. It still retains the flavour of a German Baltic port. The communist government, which took power in Poland after the war, favoured the commemoration of battles by the Polish People's Army (LWP), which fought alongside the Red Army from 1944 to 1945. The prewar Polish army was regarded, at least by the government, as the tool of the old bourgeois regime. In this climate battlefields like Studzianki, site of the 1944 Vistula crossing, were amply preserved, while other battlefields from 1939 were either ignored or received minimal attention.

There were some notable exceptions to this post-war attitude of disinterest and neglect. Perhaps the most notable was the preservation of the base of the Westerplatte garrison. In spite of the tendentious attitude of the government, the Poles' fascination with their military history meant that the memories could not be totally ignored. Other monuments were created as a result of local initiatives. The post-1945 Polish army did not share the politicians' viewpoint and sponsored many studies of the 1939 campaign.

The collapse of communism in Poland in the 1980s has had the paradoxical effect of giving the Poles the opportunity to freely study their past history and to freely ignore it. The political and economic turmoil of the 1990s has prevented any extensive government expenditure on historical preservation, though there have been many local initiatives. At the national level, the *Muzeum Wojska Polskiego* (Museum of the Polish Army) in Warsaw now has a more comprehensive exhibit on the 1939 campaign than was possible during the communist period.

Unfortunately, after the devastation of German and Soviet occupation and a half-century of neglect, the artefacts of war are few. The museum has no example of a Polish armoured vehicle from the war, while combat aircraft are limited to a single P.11 fighter preserved in Kraków. There are larger collections of small arms and some artillery. The German Army captured large quantities of Polish equipment after 1939, so Polish equipment has shown up in a surprisingly wide variety of locations. A partial TKS tankette was recovered in Sweden, having been used by German units in neighbouring Finland during the war. The Yugoslav Army museum in Belgrade had an ex-German TK tankette on display for many years, though its status at the moment is not clear, given the recent conflicts in the Balkans. A C2P artillery tractor turned up on the Franco-Spanish border and was preserved in a private collection in Belgium.

Some Polish aircraft from the 1939 period that were exported shortly prior to the war are today in foreign collections. Polish small arms are widely found in international military museums. For example, the United States' Army's Ordnance Museum at Aberdeen Proving Ground has two examples of the 46mm infantry mortar, the 7.92mm anti-tank rifle and other rifles and pistols that were captured by the United States Army from the Wehrmacht in 1944–45. The Soviet Union also captured a considerable amount of Polish equipment in 1939 but little of it has been preserved. The sole surviving Polish 7TP tank was scrapped. The Russian central armour museum at Kubinka outside Moscow, however, still has a Polish TKS tankette. This museum also has on display a Renault R-35 tank, which is probably the example the Red Army captured from the Polish 21st Tank Battalion in autumn 1939. No Polish aircraft from the 1939 campaign are known to survive in former Soviet collections.

Due to the de-Nazification of Germany after the war and widespread anti-war sentiment, there has been little government effort in Germany to preserve artefacts from the war except for documents and photographs. There are few surviving German items that can be directly linked to the 1939 campaign. It is possible that some preserved armoured vehicles took part in the 1939 Polish campaign, such as the PzKpfw 35(t) preserved at the Ordnance Museum at Aberdeen Proving Grounds in the United States. However, few early German armoured vehicles have survived the war, and the same is the case for 1939-period aircraft.

Concrete bunkers tend to survive longer than other military artefacts and this has been the case with the 1939 campaign. A significant number of 1939-era defensive works are still intact, though access is hampered in some cases due to their location on military bases or private land. There are a number of bunkers still intact around Mława. The fortified garrison of Modlin can also be visited. A number of the forts around Warsaw have survived, and the Polish Army museum is converting one of them into an armoured vehicle museum. Some effort is needed to find fortifications, not only due to their dispersion in the countryside but also because of the steady accretion of foreign fortifications in Poland over the centuries, which often makes the exercise quite confusing.

The German Army, it should be remembered, built a number of bunker complexes in Poland after 1939 that might be easily confused with the earlier bunkers constructed by the Polish armed forces. There are even a few Soviet bunkers from the Stalin defence line that were built in 1940–41 near the town of Przemyśl. Fortunately, there has been a resurgence in interest in military architecture in Poland in the past decade, which has resulted in many fine books and journals such as the magazine *Forteca*. These publications are an excellent aid in tracking down specific examples of fortifications.

Much of the documentation on the 1939 campaign has been lost over the years owing to the destruction of the Polish military archives by the Germans during the 1939–44 occupation and the destruction of much of the German military archives during the later years of the war. Still, much has been preserved and can be found in major military archives such as Freiburg in Germany and Rembertów in Poland. There are also some significant archives outside Germany and Poland. Many of the Polish soldiers who escaped in 1939 made their way to Britain where they were re-formed into new units that fought alongside the Allies for the remainder of the war. Their records are preserved at the Sikorski Institute near Hyde Park in London, which also has a collection of uniforms from the 1939 period. Other Polish archives were formed abroad, such as the Piłsudski Institute in New York, which has also preserved prewar and wartime records.

The 1939 Polish campaign has been the subject of a number of documentaries and films. One of the first was the German propaganda film *Kampfgeschwader Lützow* (Bomber Wing Lützow), a pseudo-documentary on the war that includes staged footage of a Polish cavalry charge against tanks. This film occasionally reappears in television documentaries as authentic footage. For political reasons, Polish films about the 1939 campaign were not favoured during the communist years, though there were some important exceptions. Poland's premier film director, Andrzej Wajda, grew up in a cavalry garrison in eastern Poland before the war. His 1959 film *Lotna*, about a cursed horse and the fate of its doomed cavalry troop in 1939, was an epitaph to prewar Poland. Its surrealistic imagery of a cavalry charge against tanks helped enshrine this myth in Polish national legend, becoming a symbol of the undoubtedly brave but doomed military struggle waged across Polish soil during autumn 1939.

Wrecked Polish military planes seen at Kraków airfield, September 1939. (Photo by ullstein bild/ullstein bild via Getty Images)

2

THE SPRING 1940 CAMPAIGNS IN DENMARK AND NORWAY

THE ORIGINS OF THE CAMPAIGN

The rapid German conquest of Poland during the autumn of 1939 did not bring lasting peace to the continent of Europe. Indeed, the German military onslaught against Poland subsequently proved to be but the first taste of the awesome power of the operational method the world retrospectively labelled 'Blitzkrieg'. Just six months later, the German Armed Forces swiftly conquered Denmark and Norway. The subjugation of these Scandinavian countries was not originally part of Adolf Hitler's designs for the conquest and domination of Europe. However, the Kriegsmarine – still smarting from the professional ignomy of being bottled up at Kiel and Wilhelmshaven during most of World War I – pressed for an operation to secure Norwegian ports soon after the Polish campaign had ended; the seizure of Narvik and Trondheim was particularly desired. *Großadmiral* (Grand Admiral) Erich Raeder ordered the Naval War Staff to study it and discussed it with Hitler on 10 October 1939. He argued that securing the Norwegian ports, especially Trondheim and Narvik, would broaden the navy's operational basis against the Royal Navy. Hitler, who understood these ports' strategic significance from the point of view of the Kriegsmarine, was strongly attracted by the idea.

Vidkun Quisling, former Norwegian Foreign Minister (1931–33), further encouraged the proposal. He and his Norwegian *Nasjonal Samling* (National Union) Fascist party were half-heartedly planning a *coup d'état* and requested German occupation to guard against British interference. When Quisling visited Berlin on 11 December, however, Raeder disliked both Quisling's idea and his lack of

The Tribal-class British destroyer HMS *Cossack* figured prominently in the Norwegian campaign. It rescued British prisoners from the German auxiliary *Altmark* in Norwegian territorial waters. Two months later *Cossack* was badly damaged in the Second Battle of Narvik. (Photo by Haynes Archive/ Popperfoto via Getty Images/ Getty Images)

indigenous support. However, Quisling mentioned that the Norwegian government had decided not to resist Allied landings. Dutifully, Raeder discussed Quisling's revelation with Adolf Hitler, who found British occupation of Norwegian ports unacceptable. Three days later, Hitler ordered studies to begin on how to seize Norway: he feared possible Allied intervention because of their support for Finland in the Winter War against the USSR (30 November 1939–12 March 1940). To aid Finland, an Allied expeditionary force would have to occupy Narvik in northern Norway and secure the railway running through Sweden to Finland. This would also prevent Swedish iron ore shipments reaching Narvik.

The possibility of unilateral Allied action was sharply focused in mid-February 1940 when HMS *Cossack* audaciously boarded the German auxiliary vessel *Altmark* in the Jøssingfjord, and freed 299 British merchant seamen captured by the pocket battleship *Graf Spee*. This demonstrated to Hitler that Norway could not defend its neutrality. From Raeder's point of view, if Britain could seal off the North Sea from Scapa Flow to Stavanger, it would create an unbreakable blockade. He also feared interdiction of Swedish iron ore sailing out of Narvik all the year round, shipments essential to the Nazi war machine. German ore ships steamed down the Norwegian coast, predominantly inside Norwegian waters immune from British interception. If the Allies occupied Narvik, the ore shipments would be halted, denuding the German war economy of indispensable raw materials: this dearth could fundamentally undermine the German war economy.

Therefore, on 27 January 1940, Hitler ordered a new study under the cover name 'Unternehmen *Weserübung*' (Operation *River Weser Exercise*). A month later he insisted that it must occur before the invasion of the West. Once the decision was made to take Norway, Denmark fell into the invasion plan too because of the need to secure staging airfields in northern Jutland. The Luftwaffe also favoured occupying Denmark to extend their air-defence belt further north since RAF bombers outflanked the air-warning network, threatening the key naval ports of

Hamburg and Kiel. Thus, all three German armed services desired the occupation of both Norway and Denmark.

CHRONOLOGY: DANISH AND NORWEGIAN CAMPAIGNS

1939

1 September	Germany invades Poland, beginning World War II.
3 September	Britain and France declare war on Germany.
Early October	Großadmiral Raeder orders the Naval War Staff to study capturing important Norwegian ports.
10 October	Raeder suggests to Hitler the desirability of securing Trondheim and Narvik as bases for the Kriegsmarine surface fleet as well as for her U-boat submarines.
30 November	The Soviet Union attacks Finland, starting the Winter War. The Allies begin making plans to aid Finland, through Norway and Sweden if need be.
11 December	The leader of the Norwegian Fascist movement, Vidkun Quisling, meets with Raeder requesting German forces to support his proposed *coup d'état* to prevent British interference – he fails to enlist German support but motivates Hitler to consider action.
14 December	Hitler orders a study undertaken to seize Norway in order to pre-empt an Allied intervention.

1940

27 January	Hitler orders the original staff study for occupying Norway be developed into an operational plan, codenamed 'Unternehmen *Weserübung*' (Operation *River Weser Exercise*).
16 February	The British destroyer HMS *Cossack* attacks the German navy auxiliary *Altmark* in the Jøssingfjord, freeing 299 British seamen and violating Norwegian neutrality. This convinces Hitler that Norwegian neutrality might easily be exploited by the Allies.
19 February	Hitler orders the detailed planning for *Weserübung* to proceed with the assignment of units from all three German military services.
21 February	General von Falkenhorst presents concept of operations plan for *Weserübung* to Hitler, who approves the plan.
1 March	Germans constitute the XXI Group to oversee development of the operational plan and to lead the execution of *Weserübung*.

3 March	First meeting of the German service chiefs to be informed of and review the plan for Operation *Weserübung*. Hitler decides *Weserübung* will precede *Fall Gelb* (the planned Case Yellow invasion of the West).
12 March	Finland accepts Soviet terms, this ends the Winter War.
21 March	In France, the failure to support the Finns causes the government of Édouard Daladier to fall; he is replaced as Prime Minister by Paul Reynaud.
28 March	Paul Reynaud attends his first Allied Supreme War Council and supports Winston Churchill's proposal to mine the Norwegian Leads to disrupt German iron ore traffic from Narvik, a contingency plan subsequently designated Operation *Wilfred*.
2 April	Hitler meets with his senior operational commanders and reviews plans and preparations – the next day he gives the go-ahead order for the invasions of Denmark and Norway.
Early April	Allies develop contingency plan R4 to occupy the major Norwegian ports of Narvik, Stavanger, Bergen, and Trondheim to pre-empt a German attempt to occupy Norway.
6-8 April	The German battle squadron and other warships depart their ports, beginning *Weserübung*.
7 April	British Home Fleet sets sail from Scapa Flow and 2nd Cruiser Squadron departs from Rosyth.

The British Army contingent destined for operations in Norway was composed primarily of battalions of Territorial Army reservists who had been gathered into independent brigades. Here the reservist soldiers wait on the quayside to board their troopship bound for Norway.
(© IWM, N 3)

The German Fliegerkorps X included one wing of long-range Ju 87R Stuka dive-bombers. The pinpoint accuracy of dive-bombing proved especially effective against Allied warships and transports penned in the narrow fjords along Norway's coastline.
(© IWM, HU 2924)

8 April	British destroyers sow mines in Norwegian territorial waters; Royal Navy destroyer HMS *Glowworm* is sunk by the German heavy cruiser *Admiral Hipper*. The German transport *Rio de Janeiro* is sunk by Polish submarine *Orzel* in the Skagerrak. Luftwaffe bombs Scapa Flow, but British Home Fleet had already put to sea.
9 April	German naval units, infantry divisions, and German Air Force squadrons begin the invasion of Denmark and Norway. Danish and Norwegian forces partially mobilise. Falster bridge, Vordingborn Fort, and Vaeloese airfield all seized. Copenhagen is seized by coup de main. The Royal Life Guards resolutely defend the Amalienborg Palace. King Christian X orders Danish forces to capitulate that morning. The Norwegian capital Oslo and the ports of Kristiansand, Stavanger, Bergen, Trondheim and Narvik are occupied. HMS *Renown* ineffectually engages the *Scharnhorst* and *Gneisenau*. *Fliegerkorps* (Air Corps) X sinks the British destroyer *Gurkha*.
10 April	The First Battle of Narvik: 2nd British Destroyer Flotilla (five destroyers) sinks two German destroyers and six merchantmen for the loss of two ships. Also, Fleet Air Arm air attack at Bergen sinks the light cruiser *Königsberg*. HM Submarine *Truant* sinks light cruiser *Karlsruhe*. HM Submarine *Spearfish* cripples heavy cruiser *Lützow*.
11 April	The Royal Navy launches its first ever, albeit abortive, carrier-based air attack on German destroyers in Trondheimfjord. Germans commence two-pronged ground advance from Oslo toward Trondheim. *Oberst* (Col) Otto Ruge is promoted major general and assumes command of the Norwegian Army.

13 April	The Second Battle of Narvik: The battleship HMS *Warspite* and nine destroyers eliminate the remaining eight German destroyers deployed at Narvik while the Fleet Air Arm sinks German U-boat *U-64* anchored in the Herjangsfjord near Bjerkvik.
14 April	The Norwegian 1st Infantry Division withdraws into Sweden and is interned. The British 24th (Guards) Brigade begins landing at Harstad. The British 146th Brigade is diverted to Namsos in order to retake Trondheim. A German paratrooper company is overrun and captured at Gudbrandsdalen.
15 April	The Norwegian 3rd Infantry Division surrenders to Germans in southern Norway.
16 April	The British 146th Brigade begins landing at Namsos and moves towards Trondheim. It becomes the core of Mauriceforce.
17 April	The cruiser HMS *Suffolk* and four destroyers ineffectually bombard Sola airfield. Luftwaffe counter-strike cripples *Suffolk*.
18 April	The British 148th Brigade begins landing at Åndalsnes and moves to Lillehammer. It forms the foundation of Sickleforce.
19 April	Germans capture Hamar and Elverum. French 5e Demi-Brigade *Chasseurs Alpins* disembark at Namsos.
21–23 April	Sickleforce conducts a delaying defence of the Gudbrandsdalen valley.
22 April	The Battle of Lillehammer – the first meeting in World War II of German and British troops in combat. Mauriceforce abandons its attempt to recapture Trondheim.
23–24 April	The Battle of Vist – the British 146th Brigade is driven back to Namsos.
23 April	The British 15th Brigade arrives at Åndalsnes. RAF No. 263 Squadron arrives at Lake Lesjaskog the following day. It is wiped out in two days. Norwegian 2nd Infantry Division renews its advance toward Narvik; it retakes and then loses, Gratangsbotn.
24 April	HMS *Warspite*, three Royal Navy cruisers and a destroyer bombard Narvik.
24–25 April	The Battle of Kvam, German advance delayed but not stopped.

A precursor to the June 1944 D-Day landings: British landing craft conduct the Allies' first amphibious assault of World War II, landing French legionnaires to retake Bjerkvik from the Germans during 12–13 May 1940. (© IWM, HU 93723)

28 April	The French 27e Demi-Brigade Chasseurs Alpins arrives in the Narvik area and moves to engage the German 139th *Gebirgsjäger* (Mountain Infantry) Regiment. British War Cabinet orders the evacuation of all British expeditionary forces from Norway.
30 April	The Norwegian 4th Infantry Division surrenders, ending the fighting in southern Norway. Luftwaffe sinks British AA cruiser HMS *Bittern*.
2 May	The evacuation of the British Sickleforce intervention command from Åndalsnes is complete.
3 May	The evacuation of the Anglo-French intervention group Mauriceforce from Namsos is complete; the Norwegian 2nd and 5th Infantry Divisions surrender to Germans, ending the fighting in central Norway. The Luftwaffe sinks the French destroyer *Bison* and HMS *Afridi* during the evacuation.
4 May	French mountain troops attack the Labergdal Pass.
6 May	French troops arrive in the Narvik area.
9 May	The Polish 1st Carpathian *Podhale* (Highland) Brigade arrives in the Narvik area.
10 May	The *Fall Gelb* German invasion of the Netherlands, Belgium, Luxembourg and northern France begins.
11–31 May	The British 24th Brigade is transferred to Bodø and withdrawn.
12–13 May	Allied attack seizes north bank of the Ofotfjord.
13 May	The Battle of Sedan, France – Guderian's armoured divisions breaks through French defences. Near Narvik French units engage the German 139th Gebirgsjäger

	Regiment. Maj Gen Auchinleck arrives to replace Maj Gen Mackesy.
14 May	German Navy proposes to sortie capital ships to attack British shipping off Harstad in a mission designated Operation *Juno*. Hitler approves and sets a 4 June launch date.
15 May	British troopship *Chrobry* sunk. The heavy cruiser HMS *Effingham* grounds and is abandoned.
20 May	In France, the German Panzer spearheads reach the Channel coast near Abbeville, thus cutting off the Allied forces located to the north.
21 May	A re-equipped RAF 263 Squadron returns and is based at Bardufoss. It is reinforced by No 46 Squadron equipped with Hurricanes.
25 May	British tanker *Oil Pioneer* sunk.
26 May	Operation *Dynamo* – the evacuation of the BEF from France – begins. The Royal Navy anti-aircraft cruiser HMS *Curlew* is sunk at Skanland. British liner *Orama* is sunk.
27 May	Final Allied assault on Narvik commences.
28 May	French and Norwegian forces retake Narvik.
4 June	Evacuation of Allied forces from Narvik begins; German battle squadron returns to the campaign, steaming unobserved into the Norwegian Sea in Operation *Juno*.

Adm Raeder was willing to risk his two most powerful warships, the battle-cruisers *Gneisenau* and *Scharnhorst,* in the campaign. Here, led by the tanker *Dithmarschen*, the *Gneisenau* and *Scharnhorst* depart Germany, bound for operations in the Norwegian Sea during Operation *Juno*. (© IWM, HU 2224)

5 June	The German *Fall Rot* campaign – the final conquest of the remainder of France – begins.
7 June	The evacuation of Rupertforce from Narvik complete.
8 June	The Norwegian 6th Infantry Division surrenders to Germans near Narvik. The aircraft carrier HMS *Glorious* sunk during Operation *Juno*, as are its escorting destroyers HMS *Ardent* and HMS *Acasta*.
13 June	Royal Navy launches abortive carrier strike from HMS *Ark Royal* on German battle-cruisers *Scharnhorst* and *Gneisenau* in Trondheimfjord.

THE OPPOSING PLANS

The German Plan

On 1 March 1940 Adolf Hitler established the operational planning staff, XXI Group, which developed the plan. In final form, it called for 'daring actions and surprise execution' of simultaneously trans-shipped three divisions, landing at five seaports – Oslo, Kristiansand, Bergen, Trondheim and Narvik – while two other divisions occupied Denmark. The greatest threat was from British naval and air striking forces, especially at Narvik and Trondheim. Covering the assault groups were the battle-cruisers *Gneisenau* and *Scharnhorst* and a screen of 28 U-boat submarines.

Oslo was to be taken by a combined airborne attack on Fornebu airfield and seaborne assault. The German Air Force would provide defensive air cover, anti-shipping attacks and air support for the ground forces. With airbases secure, the Luftwaffe would mount an air bridge to resupply the advancing ground forces. Fighters would arrive in Norway to establish local air superiority and dive-bombers would follow to drive off the British fleet. Denmark would be overrun in a simultaneous ground assault across Jutland, an airborne assault to secure the critical Ålborg airfields, as well as a seaborne attack to seize Copenhagen harbour.

The complex German plan required close coordination and precise timing to secure the initial objectives. It was also intricately interdependent, requiring that each service accomplish its objective in a timely manner or risk the failure of the whole enterprise.

The Allied Plans

The Danes realised that, because of their vulnerable frontier and meagre means, defence against a determined German invasion was impossible and instead relied on the German–Danish Non-Aggression Treaty of May 1939 that confirmed the existing friendly relations that were based on being neighbours. Thus, the Danish government took extraordinary steps to prevent provoking the Germans.

The Norwegians spurned Nazi overtures to sign a similar treaty and the military planned to repulse either German or Soviet attacks. But, since these antagonists would have to force their way through Denmark and Sweden, respectively, Norway anticipated having time to mobilise. Since the Royal Navy 'ruled the waves' the high seas were not considered a viable German avenue of approach. This assumption ensured that defences were strongest in the south – to meet a crossing of the Skagerrak and Kattegat – with only vital points being defended along the long coastline.

The Allied plan to counter a German invasion began as a proposal to save the Finns from defeat. However, the Finns surrendered before the Allies could implement it. At the Allied Supreme War Council (28 March 1940), the new French Prime Minister Paul Reynaud endorsed Winston Churchill's proposal to mine the Norwegian Leads and disrupt the German iron ore shipments from Narvik. Operation *Wilfred* thus came into being.

An anticipated consequence of this neutrality-violating operation was that the Germans might invade Norway to secure the ore supply route. For this contingency Plan R.4 was devised, which allotted an infantry brigade to occupy Narvik, and battalions to hold Stavanger, Bergen, and Trondheim. Plan R.4 assumed

The Allied Narvik operation was 'my pet project' said First Lord of the Admiralty Winston Churchill. Here Churchill meets with RAF officers at their headquarters in France during the period of the Norwegian campaign. (© IWM, C 368)

Anglo-French troops would arrive ahead of the enemy. These forces were to hold the ports against German amphibious assaults while the Norwegian Army defended in the south. Plan R.4 was naïve, inadequate, and amateur in comparison to Operation *Weserübung*. It was also reactive, forfeiting the initiative to the enemy, and its resources were pitifully inadequate. Moreover, the absence of any planned air cover for *Wilfred* condemned it to failure.

THE OPPOSING COMMANDERS

The German Commanders

The German officers chosen for Operation *Weserübung* were well matched in training, background, and experience for the daunting task ahead. Gen d.Inf von Falkenhorst was in overall command. He had served in 1918 as an operations officer in the Baltic and Finland where he worked with the navy. He commanded XXI Corps in Poland, defeating the Pomorze Army on the lower Vistula. He presented on 21 February 1940 a concept of operations that Hitler liked, leading the Führer to entrust Operation *Weserübung* to him.

The Norwegian king, Håkon VII, and Crown Prince Olaf during the Norwegian campaign. Without King Håkon's resolute determination to fight the Nazi invaders, this campaign, and all the lessons it taught the Allies, would have never occurred. (© IWM, HU 55637)

GenLt Kaupisch and his XXXI Corps staff was selected to command the forces conquering Denmark. He was an experienced artillery officer, World War I veteran, and twice retired general. In August 1939, he was recalled and drove across the Danzig Corridor.

GenLt Dietl commanded the Gebirgsjäger headed for Narvik. A tough Bavarian mountaineer, he rose rapidly after participating in the infamous Munich Beer Hall Putsch. Dietl commanded the 99th Alpine Regiment in the Anschluss of Austria and the 1939 conquest of Poland. He was then given command of the German 3rd Gebirgsjäger Division and put in charge of the Narvik mission.

VAdm **(Vice Admiral) Günther Lütjens** led the naval forces assigned and personally commanded the battle-cruiser squadron. He had previously commanded the Kriegsmarine's torpedo boats and served as Destroyer Leader in the 1939 Polish campaign before becoming Commander-in-Chief Reconnaissance Forces in spring 1940. He led the largest deployment of German warships since 1918.

GenLt Hans Ferdinand Geisler's Fliegerkorps X provided the air support. As a former naval officer who, in 1939, became responsible for anti-shipping operations, Geisler was a good choice for commanding air forces supporting maritime operations.

The Norwegians had seven small but capable destroyers, as seen here on manoeuvres, circa spring 1940. This photo, published by the Norwegian Information Service to demonstrate the strength of their navy, was sent to British media on the very morning that the Germans invaded the country. (© IWM, HU 91801)

The Neutrals

The Danish king, Christian X, was the Commander-in-Chief of the Danish armed forces. Commanding the army was General Wilhelm Prior and the navy chief was Viceadmiral H. Rechnitzer. Norway's King Håkon VII commanded the Norwegian armed forces. *Generalmajor* (Maj Gen) Kristian Låke, old and conservative, led the Norwegian Army. An able administrator, he was unsuited to wartime command, and King Håkon VII quickly replaced him with the dynamic, industrious Oberst Otto Ruge, the Inspector General of Infantry. Admiral Henry Diesen commanded the numerically small Norwegian Navy.

The Allies

Admiral William Boyle, the 12th Earl of Cork and Orrery, a dynamic and dedicated naval officer, led the British expeditionary force to Norway. In April 1940 Churchill recalled the retired Admiral of the Fleet to service and ordered him to turn the enemy out of Narvik. As Flag Officer Narvik, Boyle had overall responsibility for the Allied operation. His ground forces commander was Maj Gen Mackesy, commander of the 49th (West Riding) Division. Mackesy had distinguished himself in Southern Russia (1919–20) and in Palestine. He was armed with amplifying orders from Gen Sir Edmund Ironside, the Chief of the Imperial General Staff. These instructed him to establish a firm base first from which to advance upon Narvik. Mackesy thus insisted on a deliberate, incremental advance on the port-city. Boyle, on the other hand, favoured an immediate storming of Narvik. Ostensibly in charge of the entire operation, Boyle's authority ended where Mackesy's began. Consequently, Boyle petitioned London to replace Mackesy with Maj Gen Auchinleck, who had distinguished himself during the Great War and between the wars, having led two successful campaigns on India's north-west frontier. Promoted major-general, he took command of the British IV Corps. He was then reassigned to the Narvik campaign in early May, but arrived too late to impact the campaign in any significant fashion.

Instead, tactical ground authority eventually passed to the French commander *Général de Brigade* (Brig) Béthouart. A St Cyr military academy graduate, dynamic and determined, he was promoted brigadier on 15 April and given command of the 1ère *Division Légère de Chasseurs*, formed specifically for the spring 1940 Norwegian campaign. Béthouart proved to be the ablest Allied commander involved in the 1940 Norwegian campaign.

THE OPPOSING FORCES

The German Forces

The German Army's Forces

The total ground forces initially assigned to Falkenhorst's German XXI Corps were one mountain formation, seven infantry divisions, a paratrooper battalion, and a handful of old training tanks plus three experimental German NbFz B heavy tanks. For the subjugation of Denmark, GenLt Kaupisch's German XXXI Corps comprised three main formations. These were GenMaj Wittke's 170th Infantry Division, Obst Günther Angern's 11th Motorised Rifle Brigade, and GenMaj Röttig's 198th Infantry Division. In addition, these formations were supported by three German motorised machine-gun battalions and two light tank companies.

For the more challenging expeditionary invasion of Norway, Falkenhorst had been allocated some six divisions, excluding reserves. In the first wave were two German infantry divisions. GenMaj Tittel's 69th Infantry Division was to land at Bergen, while simultaneously GenMaj Engelbrecht's 163rd Infantry Division was to disembark at Oslo. In addition, Dietl's 3rd Gebirgsjäger Division was bound for Narvik and Trondheim. The second wave consisted of three German infantry divisions to reinforce the ground advance northwards from Oslo.

The German advance into the interior would initially be supported by one light tank company and later by a platoon of experimental prewar heavy tanks; Norway did not offer much suitable terrain over which armour could manoeuvre. The German campaign would thus reflect the broad Blitzkrieg-inspired principles of surprise, speed of action, high momentum, shock action, audacity and envelopment – just without any tanks being involved in most actions. From Dietl's division, the 139th Regiment was to secure Narvik while the 138th Regiment was to be landed at Trondheim.

The Kriegsmarine Forces

The scale of Operation *Weserübung* required essentially the employment of the entire Kriegsmarine. The most powerful element was the battle-cruiser squadron, which deployed the *Gneisenau* and *Scharnhorst*. Supplementing these was the pocket battleship (armoured ship or heavy cruiser) *Lützow*, and the modern heavy cruisers *Admiral Hipper* and *Blücher*. Additionally, the Kriegsmarine deployed four light cruisers: the *Emden, Karlsruhe, Königsberg*, and *Köln*. Additionally, all 20 operational destroyers in German service were allocated to

The German VAdm Günther Lütjens proved a most formidable adversary in the Norwegian campaign, leading the German capital ships committed to the battle. But in May 1941 he was killed when the much-feared German battleship *Bismarck* was sunk by massed Allied naval forces. (Photo by Keystone/Stringer/Hulton Archive/Getty Images)

the invasion. The Germans also impressed numerous merchant ships, tankers, and cargo vessels into the naval armada, to transport the thousands of troop reinforcements needed for the invasion. All these vessels were escorted by a myriad collection of small German combat vessels, ranging from torpedo boats, minesweepers, minehunters, patrol boats and U-boat submarines.

The Luftwaffe

The German Fliegerkorps X, the Luftwaffe's specialised anti-shipping command, provided the air component for Operation *Weserübung*. It consisted of two wings each with three groups of Heinkel He 111 bombers and a third of Junkers Ju 88s, plus *Kampfgruppe* (Bomber Group) 100, equipped with the experimental X-Gerät radio-guided bombing system. These were highly experienced anti-shipping units. Two groups of Messerschmitt Bf 110C twin-engine fighters reinforced them for long-range escort, along with one group of Messerschmitt Bf 109E single-engine fighters to defend captured airfields, and one group of Junkers Ju 87 Stuka dive-bombers. In total, the command fielded 527 combat aircraft, including 317 bombers.

Additionally, Geisler's Fliegerkorps X was required to conduct the first German airborne assaults of the war, and then establish an extensive aerial bridge across the waters to Norway. For the first mission, three groups from the 1st Special Operational Battle Wing were assigned to drop paratroopers and air-land follow-up infantry. For the second, six transport groups flew the Junkers Ju 52/3m tri-motor transport and a seventh fielded four-engine transport aircraft. An eighth transport floatplane group was used for water reinforcement landings. The 40 transport squadrons totalled 533 aircraft. One battalion of experienced paratroopers was supplied from the German 7th Fallschirmjäger Division.

Danish Armed Forces

The Danish Army had just two divisions – one deployed across Jutland and the other one across Zealand. Between them, these two formations fielded seven infantry regiments, two cavalry, the Royal Life Guards and three field artillery regiments. However, the divisions were actually small administrative staffs that trained 6,600 conscripts annually, rather than being fighting headquarters. The Danish Army Aviation Troops comprised two fighter squadrons equipped with Gloster Gauntlet biplanes and new Fokker D.XXI monoplanes, and two more with Fokker C.V scout biplanes. All four squadrons were entirely based at Værløse near Copenhagen. The Danish Navy was likewise based at Copenhagen harbour and had 1,500 personnel working some 58, mostly old, naval vessels. The best warships were two old coastal defence ships and the most modern were three torpedo boats and four submarines. The Danish Naval Flying Service composed two squadron-sized air flotillas, one of ancient Heinkel HE 8 floatplanes based at Copenhagen and a fighter unit with elderly Hawker Nimrod Mk II biplanes stationed at Avnø.

Norwegian Armed Forces

Norway was a sparsely populated country with few resources and no real martial tradition. Consequently, the nation adopted a territorial army concept, utilizing trained reservists to fill its ranks. The country was divided into six military districts, headquartered at Halden, Oslo, Kristiansand, Bergen, Trondheim and Harstad. Each region reorganised to field a division upon general mobilisation. Norwegian infantry divisions comprised two or three infantry regiments and either an artillery regiment or a mountain artillery battalion. They possessed no armour or anti-tank weapons since the rugged terrain precluded the execution of mechanised operations. Horse-mounted cavalry regiments or bicycle/ski scout companies conducted reconnaissance duties.

The Norwegian Army Air Service provided army cooperation using obsolete Fokker C.V biplanes, organised into three reconnaissance flights. Additionally, a fighter flight with nine Gloster Gladiator biplanes based at Fornebu defended the capital and a light bomber flight with twin-engine Caproni Ca.310 and Fokker C.V-E light bombers was deployed at Sola airbase near Stavanger.

The Norwegian Navy was a small coast defence force. The strongest ships were two ancient monitors, the *Norge* and *Eidsvold*. These were deployed to Narvik at the

Supplementing the British forces deployed to Norway were six French battalions of Chasseurs Alpins. These mountain troops were the best trained and most effective of the Allied units in the fight against the German Gebirgsjäger around Narvik. (Photo by Keystone-France\Gamma-Rapho via Getty Images)

first sign of invasion. The navy's seven small destroyers were scattered between Oslo and Narvik, supported by 17 torpedo boats, nine coastal submarines, eight minesweepers, ten minelayers, nine patrol boats, and 49 patrol vessels. The Norwegian Naval Air Service had three squadrons based at Horton, Bergen and Tromsø. These were equipped primarily with Høver M.F.11 reconnaissance biplanes and new German-supplied Heinkel He 115A twin engine torpedo-bombers.

Allied Expeditionary Forces

By the time Plan R.4 was approved, the BEF – which fielded Britain's most combat-effective formations – had already deployed to northern France. What remained behind in the United Kingdom were four combat brigades, including the 24th (Guards) Brigade from Mackesy's 49th Division, which were earmarked for operations in Norway. These brigades comprised three infantry battalions, an anti-tank company, and a support company. However, only a single artillery battery supported the brigades.

The French Chasseurs Alpins were best prepared to face the German Gebirgsjäger in northern Norway and were the only troops trained and equipped for mountain/winter warfare. Six Chasseurs Alpins battalions were organised into two *demi-brigades* of the 1ère Division Légère de Chasseurs Alpins. The 13e Demi-Brigade of the *Légion Étrangère* (the French Foreign Legion (two battalions)), reinforced the alpine troops along with a tank company. Also sent was the Polish army-in-exile's 1st Carpathian *Podhale* Brigade. Commanded by Général Brygady Bohusz-Szyszko, the *Podhale* Brigade fielded two demi-brigades, each of which deployed two mountain infantry battalions.

The Royal Navy

The Royal Navy's Home Fleet was at this time the most powerful armada afloat. On the eve of the campaign, it boasted three battleships, two battle-cruisers, one aircraft carrier, 13 cruisers, 17 destroyers and 20 submarines. The battle-line comprised the three battleships HMS *Rodney*, *Valiant* and *Warspite* and the two battle-cruisers HMS *Renown* and HMS *Repulse*. The submarine service commander, Vice Admiral Horton, anticipated the German invasion, and pre-positioned 12 submarines off the Norwegian coast. Convinced that Operation *Wilfred* would precipitate a German invasion, he dispatched another six submarines on 7 April 1940 to interdict the German assault forces crossing by sea. The Home Fleet's greatest deficiency was limited air cover. The aircraft carrier HMS *Furious* was undergoing a refit and HMS *Ark Royal* was in the Mediterranean.

The RAF

The RAF was poorly positioned for the spring 1940 Norwegian campaign. Its Bomber and Fighter Commands naturally concentrated in south-east England, close to the continent and Germany. Coastal Command was spread thinly, mostly facing the Western Approaches from south-west England to search for German U-boat submarines. The remainder of its forces was based in Scotland, but few could reach Norway even from there. Its 18th Group was responsible for maritime reconnaissance and convoy protection in the North Sea. But only its No 204 Seaplane Squadron, based at Sullom Voe in the Shetland Islands, was fully operational, equipped with the Short Sunderland four-engine flying boat. The group was supported by three squadrons of Lockheed Hudsons, a makeshift maritime patrol bomber.

Eventually, two fighter squadrons were committed to provide cover for Allied ground forces in Norway. First was the new RAF No 263 Squadron equipped with Gloster Gladiator biplanes. Reinforcing later was the No 46 Squadron, an experienced Hawker Hurricane unit. Against the might of the Luftwaffe, the RAF initially deployed just 36 fighters. The inability to maintain even local air superiority doomed the Allied campaign to failure.

With no suitable airfields in the area, No. 263 Squadron's Gloster Gladiators were forced to operate from the frozen surface of Lake Lesjaskog. But they were extremely vulnerable to enemy air attack and during 25–26 April all of the squadron's Gladiators were lost during relentless Luftwaffe air attacks.

THE ORDERS OF BATTLE
THE ALLIED ORDER OF BATTLE

THE NORWEGIAN FORCES

NORWEGIAN ARMY – *Generalmajor* (Maj Gen) Kristian Låke
(replaced by Oberst Otto Ruge, 11 April 1940)
1st Infantry Division – Generalmajor Carl Erichsen
2nd Infantry Division – Generalmajor Jacob Hvinden Haug
3rd Infantry Division – Generalmajor Einar Liljedahl
4th Infantry Division – Generalmajor William Steffens
5th Infantry Division – Generalmajor Jacob Laurantzon
6th Infantry Division – Generalmajor Carl Fleischer

NORWEGIAN ARMY AIR SERVICE – Oberst (Col) Gulliksen
Fighter Wing
Bomber Wing
Training Wing
Flying School

NORWEGIAN NAVY – *Kontreadmiral* (Rear Admiral) Henry
Diesen
1st Sea Defence District – Kontreadmiral J. Smith-Johannsen
Oslofjord Flotilla
Kristiansand Flotilla
2nd Sea Defence District – Kontreadmiral C. Tank-Nielsen
Bergen Flotilla
Trondheim Flotilla
3rd Sea Defence District – Kontreadmiral L. Hagerup

NORWEGIAN NAVAL AIR SERVICE
1st Squadron
2nd Squadron
3rd Squadron

ALLIED EXPEDITIONARY FORCES IN NORWAY

ALLIED GROUND FORCES
Mauriceforce – Maj Gen Adrian Carton de Wiart
British 146th (Territorial) Infantry Brigade – Brigadier
Charles Phillips

French 5e Demi-Brigade Chasseurs Alpins – Commandant
Brunelli
Sickleforce – Maj Gen Bernard Paget
British 15th Brigade – Brig Herbert Smyth
British 148th (Territorial) Infantry Brigade – Brig Harold de
Riemer Morgan
Rupertforce – Maj Gen Pierse Mackesy
British 24th (Guards) Brigade – Brig The Hon William
Fraser
French 1ère Division Légère de Chasseurs – Général
Antoine Béthouart
French 27e Demi-Brigade Chasseurs *Lieutenant-Colonel*
Valentini
French 13e Demi-Brigade de Légion Étrangère –
Lieutenant-Colonel Magrin-Verneret
Polish 1st Carpathian *Podhale* (Highland) Brigade –
Generał Brygady Zygmunt Bohusz-Szyszko
British 6th Anti-Aircraft Brigade, Royal Artillery – Brig F.
Rosseter
51st Heavy Anti-aircraft Regiment, Royal Artillery
55th Light Anti-aircraft Regiment, Royal Artillery
56th Light Anti-aircraft Regiment, Royal Artillery
82nd Heavy Anti-aircraft Regiment, Royal Artillery

ROYAL AIR FORCE – Group Captain M. Moore
No 46 Squadron
No 263 Squadron
RAF Bomber Command:
2nd Group: Nos 107 and 110 Squadrons
3rd Group: Nos 9, 37, 38, 75, 99, 115 and 149 Squadrons
RAF Coastal Command:
18th Group: Nos 201, 204, 209, 220, 224, 233, 240 and 254
Squadrons
RAF Fighter Command:
Nos 29, 43, 111 and 605 Squadrons

THE ALLIED NAVAL FORCES

THE ROYAL NAVY HOME FLEET – Admiral of the Fleet Sir Charles Forbes

2nd Battle Squadron – Vice Admiral L. Holland

Battle Cruiser Squadron – V Adm William J. 'Jock' Whitworth

Aircraft Carrier Squadron – V Adm L. Wells

1st Cruiser Squadron – V Adm John Cunningham

2nd Cruiser Squadron – V Adm Sir George Edward-Collins

18th Cruiser Squadron – V Adm G. Layton

2nd Destroyer Flotilla

3rd Destroyer Flotilla

4th Destroyer Flotilla

5th Destroyer Flotilla

6th Destroyer Flotilla

8th Destroyer Flotilla

10th Destroyer Flotilla

12th Destroyer Flotilla

2nd Submarine Flotilla

6th Submarine Flotilla

REINFORCING NAVAL ASSETS

BRITISH:

Royal Navy:

Aircraft carriers HMS *Ark Royal* and HMS *Glorious*

20th Cruiser Squadron (anti-aircraft cruisers) – Rear Admiral J. Vivian

Anti-Aircraft Flotilla (anti-aircraft sloops) – Captain A. Poland

1st Destroyer Flotilla

7th Destroyer Flotilla

20th Destroyer Flotilla

Fleet Air Arm:

800 Naval Air Squadron

801 Naval Air Squadron

803 Naval Air Squadron

804 Naval Air Squadron

810 Naval Air Squadron

816 Naval Air Squadron

818 Naval Air Squadron

820 Naval Air Squadron

821 Naval Air Squadron

823 Naval Air Squadron

FRENCH: Naval Group Z – *Amiral* E. Derrien

POLISH: Three destroyers; two submarines

THE GERMAN ORDER OF BATTLE

THE GERMAN GROUND FORCES

XXI CORPS (GROUP XXI) – *Gen d.Inf* Nikolaus von Falkenhorst

Military Operations in Norway

2nd Gebirgsjäger Division – GenLt Valentin Feurstein

3rd Gebirgsjäger Division – GenLt E. Eduard Dietl

69th Infantry Division – GenMaj Hermann Tittel

163rd Infantry Division – GenMaj Erwin Engelbrecht

181st Infantry Division – GenMaj Kurt Woytasch

196th Infantry Division – GenMaj Richard Pellengahr

214th Infantry Division – GenMaj Max Horn

Panzer Abteilung zbV 40 (40th Special Purpose Tank Battalion)

Military Operations in Denmark

170th Infantry Division – GenMaj Walter Wittke

198th Infantry Division – GenMaj Otto Röttig

11th Motorised Rifle Brigade – Obst Günther Angern

KRIEGSMARINE

NAVAL GROUP COMMAND WEST – *Generaladmiral* (four-star Admiral) Alfred Saalwächter

Battleship Force – VAdm Günther Lütjens

Battlecruiser *Gneisenau* – *Kapitän zur See (KzS)* (Captain) Harald Netzbandt

Battlecruiser *Scharnhorst* – KzS Kurt-Caesar Hoffmann

FIRST NAVAL GROUP – *Kdr* (Commodore) Friedrich Bonte (Narvik)

First Destroyer Flotilla – *Fregattenkapitän* (Frigate Captain) **Fritz Berger**

  Z2 *Georg Thiele* (Type 1934) – *Korvettenkapitän* (Corvette Captain) Max-Eckart Wolff

Second Destroyer Flotilla (part) – **Fregattenkapitän Erich Bey**

  Z9 *Wolfgang Zenker* (Type 1934A) – Fregattenkapitän Gottfried Pönitz

  Z11 *Bernd von Arnim* (Type 1934A) – Korvettenkapitän Curt Rechel

  Z12 *Erich Geise* (Type 1934A) – Korvettenkapitän Karl Smidt

  Z13 *Erich Koellner* (Type 1934A) – Fregattenkapitän Alfred Schulze-Hinrichs

Third Destroyer Flotilla – **Fregattenkapitän H.-J. Gadow**

  Z17 *Diether von Roeder* (Type 1936) – Korvettenkapitän Erich Holthof

  Z18 *Hans Lüdemann* (Type 1936) – Korvettenkapitän Herbert Friedrichs

  Z19 *Hermann Künne* (Type 1936) – Korvettenkapitän Friedrich Kothe

  Z21 *Wilhelm Heidkamp* (Type 1936) – Korvettenkapitän Hans Erdmenger

  Z22 *Anton Schmitt* (Type 1936) – Korvettenkapitän Friedrich Böhme

Cargo ships: *Bärenfels, Rauenfels, Alster*

Tankers: *Jan Wellem, Kattegat*

SECOND NAVAL GROUP – **KzS Hellmuth Heye (Trondheim)**

Heavy Cruiser *Admiral Hipper*, KzS Hellmuth Heye

Second Destroyer Flotilla (part) – **Fregattenkapitän Rudolf von Pufendorf**

  Z5 *Paul Jakobi* (Type 1934A) – Korvettenkapitän Hans-Georg Zimmer

  Z6 *Theodore Riedel* (Type 1934A) – Korvettenkapitän Gerhardt Böhmig

  Z8 *Bruno Heinemann* (Type 1934A) – Korvettenkapitän Hermann Alberts

  Z16 *Friedrich Eckoldt* (Type 1934A) – Korvettenkapitän Alfred Schemmel

Cargo Ships: *Sao Paulo, Levante, Main*

Tankers: *Skagerrak, Moonsund*

THIRD NAVAL GROUP – *Konteradmiral* (Rear Admiral) **Hubert Schmundt (Bergen)**

Light Cruiser *Köln* – KzS Ernst Kratzenberg

Light Cruiser *Königsberg* – KzS Heinrich Ruhfus

Gunnery Training Ship *Bremse* – Fregattenkapitän Jakob Förschner

Torpedo boat *Leopard* – *Kapitänleutnant* (Lieutenant-Commander) Hans Trummer

Torpedo boat *Wolf* – *Oberleutnant zur See (OzS)* (First Lieutenant) Broder Peters

Troop ship: *Rio de Janeiro*

Cargo ship: *Roda*

FOURTH NAVAL GROUP – **KzS Friedrich Rieve (Kristiansand, Arendal)**

Light Cruiser *Karlsruhe* – KzS Friedrich Rieve

Torpedo boat *Luchs* – KptLt Karl Kassbaum

Torpedo boat *Greif* – KptLt Wilhelm-Nikolaus Freiherr von Lyncker

Torpedo boat *Seeadler* – KptLt Franz Kohlauf

FIFTH NAVAL GROUP – *KAdm* Oskar Kummetz (Oslo, Oslofjord, Horten)

Heavy Cruiser *Blücher* – KzS Heinrich Woldag

Pocket Battleship *Lützow* – KzS August Thiele

Light Cruiser *Emden* – KzS Werner Lange

Torpedo boat *Möwe* – KptLt Helmut Neuss

Torpedo boat *Albatros* – KptLt Siegfried Strelow

Torpedo boat *Kondor* – KptLt Hans Wilcke

SIXTH NAVAL GROUP – **Korvettenkapitän Kurt Thoma**

2 Minehunting Flotilla

Minehunters *M-1, M-2, M-9, M-13*

SEVENTH NAVAL GROUP – **KzS Gustav Kleikamp (Korsör, Nyborg)**

Old Battleship *Schleswig-Holstein* – KzS Gustav Kleikamp

Mine Warfare Trial ships: *Claus von Bevern, Pelikan, Nautilus*

Cargo Ships: *Campinas, Cordoba*

EIGHTH NAVAL GROUP – Korvettenkapitän Wilhelm
  Schroeder (Copenhagen)
  Minelayer *Hansestadt Danzig* – Korvettenkapitän Wilhelm
    Schroeder
  Icebreaker *Stettin*

NINTH NAVAL GROUP – KzS Helmut Leissner (Middelfart, Belt
  Bridge)
  Cargo/Supply Ships: *Rugard, Arkona, Otto Braun, Cressida,*
    Silvia
  Minehunters: *M115, M129*
  Minesweepers: *R6, R7*

TENTH NAVAL GROUP – Kdr Friedrich Ruge (Esbjerg and
  Nordby)
  Patrol Craft: *Königin Luise*
12th Minehunter Flotilla – Korvettenkapitän Karl Marguth
  12 x minehunters
2nd Minesweeper Flotilla – Korvettenkapitän Gert von Kamptz
  8 x R-Boat minesweepers

NINTH NAVAL GROUP ELEVEN – Korvettenkapitän Walter
  Berger (Thyborön)
4th Minehunter Flotilla – Korvettenkapitän Walter Berger
  6 x minehunters
3rd Minesweeper Flotilla – KptLt Hagen Küster
  8 x minesweepers
  R boat tender *Von Der Groeben* – OzS Gustav Czycholl

U-BOAT FORCE – KAdm Karl Dönitz
U-Boat Groups One – Nine
  31 x U-Boats

LUFTWAFFE

Fliegerkorps X – GenLt Hans Ferdinand Geisler
Group I (*Gruppe* I), *Zerstörergeschwader* (Fighter-Destroyer
  Wing) 1
  Group I (*Gruppe* I), Zerstörergeschwader 76
  Group I (*Gruppe* I), *Jagdgeschwader* (Fighter Wing) 77
  Group I (*Gruppe* I), *Stukageschwader* (Dive Bomber Wing) 1
  Kampfgeschwader (Bomber Wing) 4
  Kampfgeschwader 26
  Kampfgeschwader 30
  Kampfgruppe (Bomber Group) 100
1(*Fern*)/*Aufklärungsgruppe* (1st (Long-range) Squadron,
  Reconnaissance Group) 120
  1(Fern)/Aufklärungsgruppe 122
2(*Heeres*)/*Aufklärungsgruppe* (2nd (Army Liaison) Squadron,
  Reconnaissance Group) 10
  KüstenFl.Gruppe (Coastal Flying Group) 506
  Kampfgeschwader zbV (Special Purpose Bomber Wing) 1

Lufttransportschef Land (Air Transport Command (Land)) –
  ObstLt Carl von Gablenz
  KGr zbV (Special Purpose Transport Wing) 101
  KGr zbV 102
  KGr zbV 103
  KGr zbV 104
  KGr zbV 105
  KGr zbV 106
  KGr zbV 107

Lufttransportschef See (Air Transport Command (Maritime))
  – *Hptm* (Capt) Förster
  KGr zbV (See) (Maritime Special Purpose Transport Wing)
  108

THE CAMPAIGN

The Opening German Moves (2–9 April 1940)

On the afternoon of 2 April, Hitler signed the operational order that demanded that Operation *Weserübung* be executed, setting into motion Großadmiral Raeder's grand scheme of invasion. For success to be achieved, he believed, the German

NAVAL OPERATIONS AND THE NORWEGIAN DEFENCES

The heavily outnumbered Kriegsmarine executed the audacious *Weserübung* plan. Committing virtually its entire surface fleet, it delivered thousands of soldiers to multiple port-cities. On 8 April, the *Admiral Hipper* sunk the destroyer HMS *Glowworm* and all German squadrons reached their destinations with minimal interference. But on the 9th, Allied attacks sank the light cruisers *Königsberg* and *Karlsruhe*. Worst, the Oscarborg fortress guarding Oslofjord sank the heavy cruiser *Blücher*.

At Narvik, engagements on the 10th and 13th of April sank all ten German destroyers for the loss of two British destroyers. When the Allies evacuated Trondheim in early May, the Luftwaffe sank two Allied destroyers. and on 8 June during the Narvik evacuation the returned German battle-cruisers sank the aircraft carrier HMS *Glorious* and two destroyers. Though the Kriegsmarine made a vital contribution to the operational success of *Weserübung*, the German naval losses crippled its surface fleet.

Upon hearing of the *Glowworm*'s fate in early April 1940, the battlecruiser HMS *Repulse* was sent north, pounding her way through heavy seas to join V Adm Whitworth's force tasked with hunting down and destroying the German squadron that had sunk the *Glowworm*. (© IWM, HU 54314)

forces needed to fully exploit the impacts of surprise, rapid action and audacity. Four nights later the German First Naval Group, consisting of Kdr Friedrich Bonte's ten destroyers, embarked 2,000 Gebirgsjäger from the 139th Regiment at Cuxhaven harbour. The destroyer flotilla joined the powerful German battle-cruiser squadron. This comprised *Gneisenau* and *Scharnhorst;* KzS Harald Netzbandt commanded the former, while the latter was under the control of KzS Kurt-Caesar Hoffmann.

These vessels were soon joined at Cuxhaven by the German Second Naval Group. This command deployed KzS Helmuth Heye's heavy cruiser *Admiral Hipper* together with four Type 1934A destroyers, which carried 1,700 Gebirgsjäger. This troop transportation force comprised the *Paul Jakobi* (Z5), the *Theodore Riedel* (Z6), the *Bruno Heinemann* (Z8), and the *Friedrich Eckoldt* (Z16). At midnight Central European Summer Time (GMT+1) the mighty force steamed out of the Schillig Roads. The fleet represented the largest German naval force assembled through the entire war. Steaming under a dark moonless sky the fleet headed north-north-west at the healthy speed of 26 knots. Recent RAF reconnaissance sorties had detected German warships gathering at North Sea ports, leading to suspicion that a major operation was under way. On 3 April, Coastal Command Lockheed Hudson aircraft sighted the armada. The RAF thus organised an ineffectual noontime attack by 18 Bristol Blenheim light bombers.

Off the German vessels' bows, at great range, three Royal Navy groups were already at sea. The largest was headed for the Vestfjord, the gateway to Narvik, with four mine-laden destroyers of the 2nd Destroyer Flotilla under the command of Capt Warburton-Lee. This force was screened by the British battle-cruiser HMS *Renown* and four destroyers under Vice Admiral William J. 'Jock' Whitworth. A smaller force, consisting of the minelayer HMS *Teviot Bank* and four more destroyers, was en route to mine the Inner Leads near Ålesund.

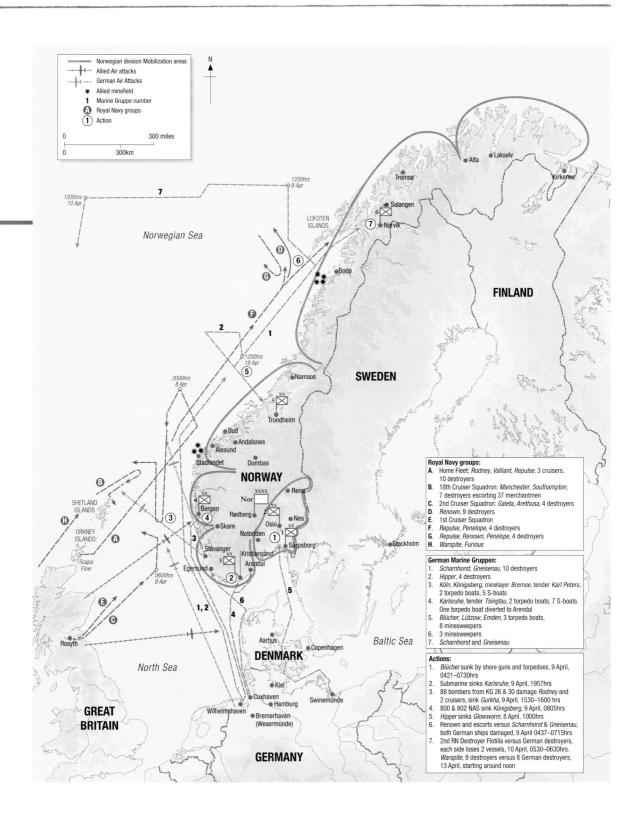

Norwegian division Mobilization areas
Allied Air attacks
German Air Attacks
＊ Allied minefield
1 Marine Gruppe number
Ⓐ Royal Navy groups
① Action

0   300 miles
0   300km

N

Norwegian Sea

1200hrs
9 Apr

1200hrs
10 Apr

LOFOTEN
ISLANDS

Tromsø

Alta   Lakselv

Kirkenes

Salangen

Narvik

Bodø

FINLAND

7

2   1

1200hrs
18 Apr

2000hrs
8 Apr

Namsos

SWEDEN

Trondheim

Bud
Andalsnes
Ålesund
Stadlandet
Dombas

NORWAY

Rena

Nor

Bergen
Rødberg
Skare
Notodden

Oslo

Nes

Sarpsborg

Stockholm

SHETLAND
ISLANDS

ORKNEY
ISLANDS

Scapa
Flow

Stavanger
Egersund
Kristiansand
Arendal

0600hrs
9 Apr

Rosyth

North Sea

Aarhus
Copenhagen

Baltic Sea

DENMARK

GREAT
BRITAIN

Kiel
Cuxhaven
Hamburg
Wilhelmshaven
Bremerhaven
(Wesermünde)

Swinemünde

GERMANY

Royal Navy groups:
A. Home Fleet: *Rodney, Valliant, Repulse,* 3 cruisers,
      10 destroyers
B. 18th Cruiser Squadron: *Manchester, Southampton,*
      7 destroyers escorting 37 merchantmen
C. 2nd Cruiser Squadron: *Galeta, Arethusa,* 4 destroyers
D. *Renown,* 9 destroyers
E. 1st Cruiser Squadron
F. *Repulse, Penelope,* 4 destroyers
G. *Repulse, Renown, Penelope,* 4 destroyers
H. *Warspite, Furious*

German Marine Gruppen:
1. *Scharnhorst, Gneisenau,* 10 destroyers
2. *Hipper,* 4 destroyers
3. *Köln, Königsberg,* minelayer *Bremse,* tender *Karl Peters,*
      2 torpedo boats, 5 S-boats
4. *Karlsruhe,* tender *Tsingtau,* 2 torpedo boats, 7 S-boats.
      One torpedo boat diverted to Arendal
5. *Blücher, Lützow, Emden,* 3 torpedo boats,
      8 minesweepers
6. 3 minesweepers
7. *Scharnhorst* and *Gneisenau*

Actions:
1. *Blücher* sunk by shore guns and torpedoes, 9 April,
      0421–0730hrs
2. Submarine sinks *Karlsruhe,* 9 April, 1957hrs
3. 88 bombers from KG 26 & 30 damage *Rodney* and
      2 cruisers, sink *Gurkha,* 9 April, 1530–1600 hrs
4. 800 & 802 NAS sink *Königsberg,* 9 April, 0805hrs
5. *Hipper* sinks *Glowworm,* 8 April, 1000hrs
6. Renown and escorts versus *Scharnhorst & Gneisenau,*
      both German ships damaged, 9 April 0437–0715hrs
7. 2nd RN Destroyer Flotilla versus German destroyers,
      each side loses 2 vessels, 10 April, 0530–0630hrs.
      Warspite, 9 destroyers versus 8 German destroyers,
      13 April, starting around noon

It began mining at 0500hrs on 8 April, accompanied by a public announcement of the operation and delivery of an explanatory note to the Norwegian government. Additionally, the Royal Navy's 18th Cruiser Division was escorting a convoy of merchant ships from the UK to Norway. Finally, on a sweep to round up enemy fishing trawlers in the North Sea were the cruiser HMS *Birmingham* and two more escorting destroyers.

That fateful morning the Royal Navy destroyer HMS *Glowworm* from the Vestfjord group had become separated. At dawn abeam Trondheim, it ran into the German squadron. VAdm Günther Lütjens ordered the heavy cruiser *Admiral Hipper* to sink the intruder. A one-sided duel ensued. The commander of HMS *Glowworm*, Lieutenant-Commander G. Broadmead Roope, initially attempted to flee and sent a contact report before mounting damage made escape impossible. Gallantly turning back, HMS *Glowworm* closed for a torpedo attack. His ship severely damaged, burning and sinking, Roope rammed the German heavy cruiser in the starboard bow, inflicting serious damage. The *Glowworm* sank, taking all but 38 men with her. Roope was posthumously awarded the coveted Victoria Cross for his outstanding heroism.

Though damaged by this ramming, *Admiral Hipper* managed to maintain position off Trondheim waiting for zero hour. At 1500hrs, however, KzS Heye's force was spotted by a British flying boat. This news energised the Admiralty who believed that the long-feared 'Atlantic breakout' of German surface raiders was under way. The *Teviot Bank* was ordered home and the minelaying destroyers were ordered to rejoin V Adm Whitworth.

Meanwhile the German Third Naval Group, led by KAdm Schmundt, departed the port of Wilhelmshaven shortly after midnight, bound for the Norwegian town of Bergen. Schmundt's command deployed the light cruisers *Köln* and *Königsberg*, the gunnery training ship *Bremse*, and the torpedo boats *Leopard* and *Wolf*, as well as supporting vessels.

At dawn KzS Rieve's German Fourth Naval Group departed from the port of Cuxhaven bound for Kristiansand. This force's main combat vessels included the light cruiser *Karlsruhe* and the torpedo boats *Luchs, Greif* and *Seeadler*. At around the same time Korvettenkapitän Thoma's Sixth Naval Group also departed from Cuxhaven on its mission to capture the port of Egersund. Thoma's group was built around the 2nd Minehunting Flotilla, which deployed four M-class minehunting vessels. Meanwhile, KAdm Oskar Kummetz's German Fifth Naval Group had also left German waters bound for the Norwegian capital, Oslo, with some 2,000 troops on board. This flotilla comprised the heavy cruiser *Blücher*, the heavy cruiser/pocket battleship *Lützow*, and the light cruiser *Emden*, together with torpedo boats *Möwe, Albatros* and *Kondor*.

Also, late in the afternoon of 8 April, 24 German He 111 bomber aircraft raided Scapa Flow to damage the Home Fleet as it prepared to sail, but they were too late – the Home Fleet had already left. However, Adm Forbes was steering to cut off a phantom 'Atlantic breakout'. At 2000hrs on 8 April 1940 the German First Naval Group arrived off the entrance to the Vestfjord and Kdr Bonte sheared off and headed up the long, deep fjord with nine troop-laden destroyers. VAdm Lütjens turned his two battle-cruisers to the north-west, waiting to rejoin the destroyers and head back to Germany. In that very direction, however, was Whitworth's force of HMS *Renown* and nine destroyers. During the night he had been ordered to prevent any German force proceeding to the port-town of Narvik.

At dawn, HMS *Renown* spotted the two German battle-cruisers and immediately intercepted them, and a heavy gun duel developed. The Royal Navy destroyers ineffectually fired at long distance, but their concerted action convinced Lütjens that he faced a superior force and that, coupled with significant damage to *Gneisenau*, prompted him to sheer away and at 0715hrs the enemy ships escaped.

Wesertag: The German Invasion of Denmark (9 April)

As *Kriegsmarine* vessels moved into their target harbours in Norway, at 0515hrs on Tuesday, 9 April 1940 – *Wesertag* (Weser Day) – the German Army launched one of the swiftest successful invasions in history. While the Danish Army had been forewarned, it was prohibited from deploying or from preparing defences because the government did not want to provoke a German invasion. The small, scattered frontier guard and the *Jutland* Division were mobilised at 0435hrs and mounted small delaying actions on the Jutland Peninsula. At 0615hrs German paratroopers jumped to secure the bridge connecting Falster to Zealand and to capture the nearby coastal fort at Vordingborg. This allowed a battalion of the German 198th Infantry Division to disembark at Gedser, on the southern coast of Falster, and race north to relieve the German assault forces unloading at Copenhagen.

Meanwhile, two naval groups landed more German 198th Division troops to secure the connections between Jutland and Zealand, capturing the Jutland–Funen Bridge spanning the Little Belt. At the eastern end of Funen, the German Seventh Naval Group landed 1,990 troops at Korsør and Nyborg to secure the ferry route across the Great Belt.

Copenhagen itself was taken by surprise by the German Eighth Naval Group. The auxiliary minelayer *Hansestadt Danzig*, the ice-breaker *Stettin* and two patrol boats audaciously steamed into the harbour at 0450hrs with their battle flags flying. The guns of Fort Middelgrund remained silent as the flotilla sailed past. Docking at a pier, the ships disgorged another battalion of the German 198th Infantry Division at 0518hrs. The German troops moved quickly to the Citadel – the ancient fortress that housed the Danish Army's headquarters. After quickly capturing the garrison, the invaders marched on to Amalienborg Palace, the residence of the Danish monarch, King Christian X, where they were opposed by the King's Lifeguard.

The primary instigator and the main driving force of Operation *Weserübung* was Großadmiral Erich Raeder, commander of the Kriegsmarine. He coveted Norwegian ports as powerful bases from which the German Navy could operate. (Photo by Keystone-France\Gamma-Rapho via Getty Images)

THE INVASION OF DENMARK

In February 1940, Gen von Falkenhorst added the capture of all Denmark to Operation *Weserübung* plan. Doing so would secure the sea and air lines of communication for the German conquest of Norway. It also allowed German air defences to be extended northward. The Danes stuck to their neutrality and sought not to provoke the Germans, though they did strengthen their defences. Two successful airborne landings preceded the ground invasion early in the morning of 9 April: at the Aalborg airfields and astride the bridge joining Falster and Zeeland. At Copenhagen, infantry landed and marched on the royal palace that was defended by the Royal Life Guards until King Christian X ordered Denmark's capitulation later that morning. Meanwhile, the 170th Infantry Division and 11th Motorised Rifle Brigade overran Jutland, encountering light delaying resistance.

While fighting proceded at the Amalienborg Palace, 28 Heinkel He 111 bombers roared over the city to intimidate the Danes into capitulation. The ploy worked: King Christian ordered a ceasefire. By 0834hrs Denmark had surrendered to Hitler's forces. Meanwhile at Værløse airfield, north of the city, as the first Danish Fokker C.V-E, took off, Messerschmitt Bf 110s strafed the airfield, shooting it down, and neutralizing 21 Danish aircraft. At 0700hrs a platoon of German Fallschirmjäger captured the two airfields at Ålborg. Then 53 Junkers Ju 52/3m transport planes air-landed a German infantry battalion, and within an hour the airfields were secured for use as staging bases against southern Norway.

The German Amphibious Landings in Norway (9 April)

As Denmark fell, six other German naval groups approached their Norwegian objectives to land their embarked assault forces. However, the element of surprise had been lost the evening before when a Norwegian submarine on patrol off Lillesand sank the German freighter *Rio de Janeiro*. Norwegian ships rescued the survivor, learning that the Germans were headed for Bergen to 'protect' it from the British! The local Kristiansand command immediately alerted the Norwegian Army HQ and the government. So now the conquest of Norway would depend on rapid action that was executed with boldness, tenacity, and great skill.

The Invasion of Oslo

During the early morning of 9 April 1940 KAdm Kummetz confidently led the German Fifth Naval Group up the narrowing foggy channel of the Oslofjord. Once past the shore batteries on Raøy and Bolærne Islands, at the mouth of the fjord, he landed two companies to take the Norwegian fortifications from the rear and sent another force to capture the naval base at Horton. The Norwegian minelayer *Olav Tryggvason* sank one mine-sweeper and damaged the German torpedo boat *Albatros*. The German force withdrew, landing the assault troops ashore further down the fjord. Marching overland, they overran the Horton naval base from landward.

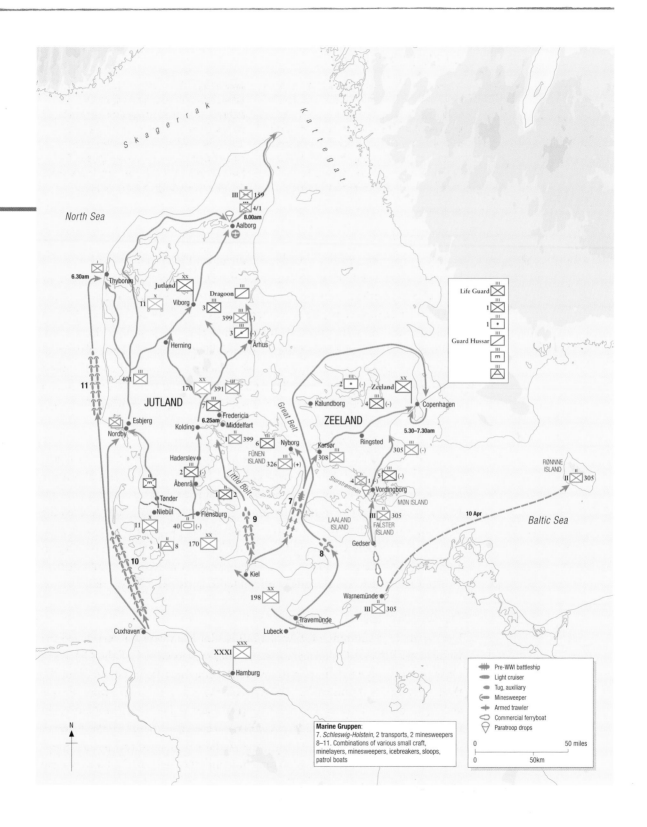

Skagerrak

Kattegat

North Sea

III ⊠ II 159
••• 4/1
8.00am
● Aalborg ⊽

6.30am ⊠ Thyborøn
XX
Jutland ⊠
X Viborg
11 ⊠
Dragoon ⊠ III
3 ⊠ III
399 ⊠ III (-)
● Herning 3 ⊠ III (-)
● Århus

401 ⊠ III

JUTLAND

170 XX ⊠ 391 ⊠ III
6.25am ⊠ ● Fredericia
● Kolding ● Middelfart
Esbjerg ⊠ I ⊠ 399
● Nordby 6 ⊠ 326 ● Nyborg
Haderslev ● FÜNEN 326 ⊠ (+)
2 ⊠ III (-) ISLAND
Åbenrå
I ⊠ 2
Tønder ●
Niebül ● ● Flensburg
11 ⊠ X 40 ⊟ (-)
I ⊠ 8 170 XX ⊠

10

9

7

8

Kiel ●
198 XX ⊠
● Travemünde
Lübeck ●
Cuxhaven ●

XXXI XXX ⊠
● Hamburg

N

Great Belt

● Kalundborg
2 ⊡ III (-) Zeeland XX ⊠
4 ⊠ III (-)
ZEELAND
● Copenhagen
5.30–7.30am
● Ringsted
Korsør ● 305 ⊠ III (-)
308 ⊠ III
Storstrømmen
4 ⊠ I 5 ⊠ III (-)
● Vordingborg
MØN ISLAND
LAALAND III ⊠ II 305
ISLAND FALSTER
ISLAND
● Gedser

10 Apr

Baltic Sea

RØNNNE
ISLAND
II ⊠ 305

● Warnemünde
III ⊠ II 305

Life Guard ⊠ III
1 ⊠ III
1 ⊡ •
Guard Hussar ⊠ III
⊟ m
⊠

Marine Gruppen:
7. *Schleswig-Holstein*, 2 transports, 2 minesweepers
8–11. Combinations of various small craft,
minelayers, minesweepers, icebreakers, sloops,
patrol boats

Pre-WWI battleship
Light cruiser
Tug, auxiliary
Minesweeper
Armed trawler
Commercial ferryboat
Paratroop drops

0   50 miles
0   50km

SEABORNE ATTACK IN OSLOFJORD, 9 APRIL 1940

Note: Gridlines are shown at intervals of 1km (1,093yds)

GERMAN UNITS

Marine Gruppe 5

1	Heavy cruiser *Blücher*
2	Armoured cruiser *Lützow*
3	Light cruiser *Emden*
4	Torpedo boat *Möwe*
5	Motor minesweepers *R.18* and *R.19*
6	Torpedo boat *Albatros*
7	Torpedo boat *Kondor*
8	Motor minesweepers *R.17* and *R.21*
9	Motor minesweepers *R.22* and *R.23*
10	Motor minesweepers *R.20* and *R.24*

German Army units

11	II/Infanterie Regiment 307
12	IV/Gebirgsjäger Regiment 139

▼ EVENTS

1. 0000HRS: Marine Gruppe 5 enters Outer Oslofjord.

0006–0015HRS: MG5 encounters Norwegian patrol boat *Pol III* and, following a confrontation, the German torpedo boat *Albatros* destroys it.

0010 AND 0025HRS: Norwegian patrol boats *Farm* and *Kjæk* sight and report MG5 passing.

0030–0040HRS: MG5 steams past Norwegian batteries at Bolærne and Rauøy Islands. Shots fired; no hits.

2. 0300HRS: Motor minesweepers *R.20* and *R.24* are loaded with 90 troops from *Emden* and sent south to capture the Rauøy Battery.

0330HRS: Other motor minesweepers are loaded with troops from *Emden* to assault Horton Naval Base; TBs *Albatros* and *Kondor* are detached for fire support. MG5 resumes steaming towards Oslo.

3. 0448HRS: Filtvet Naval Station sights MG5 and reports its passing; Norwegian minesweeper *Otra* identifies and reports them as German.

4. 0454HRS: Passing Norwegian merchant ship *Sørland*, motor minesweepers *R.18* and *R.19* attack it with gunfire, setting it ablaze.

5. 0521HRS: Oscarsborg Fortress opens fire – first salvo hits *Blücher*. Husvik Battery opens fire – multiple hits on *Blücher*. Torpedo battery fires two – both hit *Blücher*.

0530HRS: Oscarsborg Fortress shifts fire to the *Lützow*, achieving repeated hits, knocking out the ship's forward 28cm turret. KzS Thiele believes *Blücher* has run into minefield and orders 'full reverse' and to withdraw MG5 from the Narrows.

6. 0600HRS: *Blücher* halts out of arc of fire of Norwegian shore batteries, drops anchor and attempts to fight fires and control flooding.

0630HRS: Fires reach 10.5cm ammunition magazine; explosion dooms ship.

0700HRS: Abandon ship ordered.

0722HRS: *Blücher* capsizes and sinks.

7. 0535HRS: Torpedo boats *Albatros* and *Kondor* escort motor minesweepers *R.17* and *R.21* to Horton Naval Base. The torpedo boats remain outside harbour while the motor minesweepers go in. Norwegian minelayer *Olaf Tryggvason* stationed in harbour entrance and, unsure of the minesweepers' identity, initially lets them pass, but realizing the error, opens fire on *R.17* as it approaches quay, setting it on fire. Depth charges explode, sinking *R.17*. Norwegian minesweeper *Rauma* engages *R.21*, both ships hit and withdraw.

0730HRS: *Albatros* reattempts to enter Horton Harbour and is driven off, damaged, by *Olaf Tryggvason*.

8. 0700HRS: *Lützow*, *Emden*, *Möwe* and two MMS land troops at Son and Moss. Mountain troops (IV/GJR 138) advance on Drøbak while infantry (II/IR 307) march toward Oslo.

0800HRS: *Emden* moves over to Horton, putting more troops ashore to take the naval base from landward side.

0835HRS: Horton Naval Base surrenders to German troops.

9. 1417HRS: *Lützow* returns to entrance to Drøbak Narrows and begins bombarding Oscarsborg Fortress with aft 28cm turret at a range of 16,000–17,000m.

1900HRS: *Kondor* and two small vessels land troops in Drøbak. They advance to Husvik Battery and capture it at 1915hrs.

1925HRS: *Kondor* approaches Oscarsborg with white flag to begin surrender negotiations.

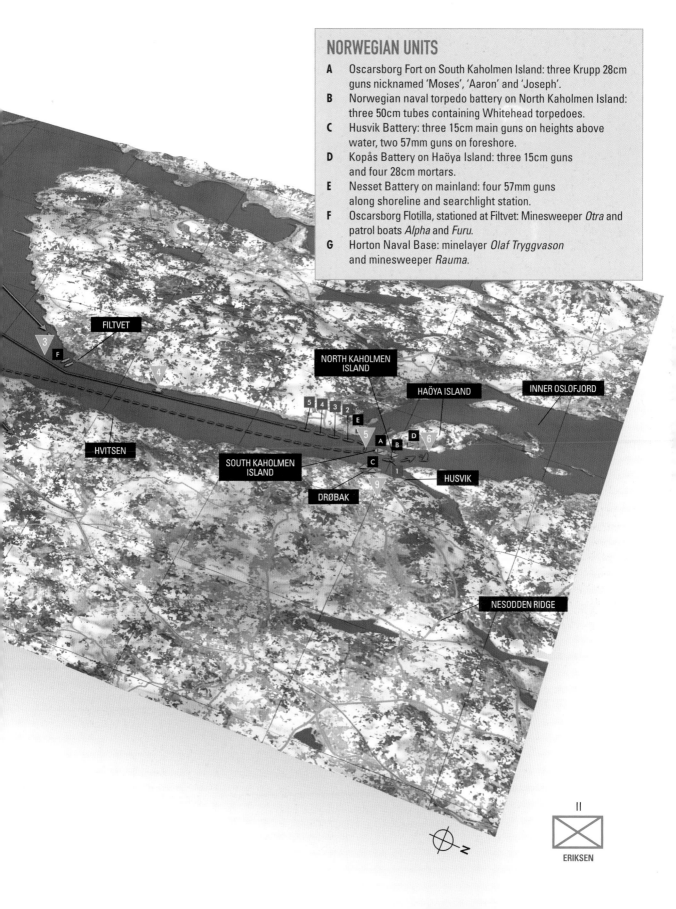

NORWEGIAN UNITS

A   Oscarsborg Fort on South Kaholmen Island: three Krupp 28cm guns nicknamed 'Moses', 'Aaron' and 'Joseph'.

B   Norwegian naval torpedo battery on North Kaholmen Island: three 50cm tubes containing Whitehead torpedoes.

C   Husvik Battery: three 15cm main guns on heights above water, two 57mm guns on foreshore.

D   Kopås Battery on Haöya Island: three 15cm guns and four 28cm mortars.

E   Nesset Battery on mainland: four 57mm guns along shoreline and searchlight station.

F   Oscarsborg Flotilla, stationed at Filtvet: Minesweeper *Otra* and patrol boats *Alpha* and *Furu*.

G   Horton Naval Base: minelayer *Olaf Tryggvason* and minesweeper *Rauma*.

FILTVET

NORTH KAHOLMEN ISLAND

HAÖYA ISLAND

INNER OSLOFJORD

HVITSEN

SOUTH KAHOLMEN ISLAND

HUSVIK

DRØBAK

NESODDEN RIDGE

II

ERIKSEN

OSLO AND CENTRAL NORWAY, 9–30 APRIL

The German assault on Oslo early on 9 April 1939 began disastrously. The Fifth Naval Group's sally up Oslofjord was thwarted by the Oscarsborg fort, which sank the cruiser *Blücher*, compelling landings at Son and Moss, 20 miles from Oslo. Meanwhile, paratroopers dropped and secured Fornebu airfield and air-landed reinforcements marched into Oslo. However, the time bought allowed King Håkon VII and his government to evacuate to Elverum. Within a couple days, the German 163rd and 198th Infantry Divisions began pushing the defenders back. The Norwegians conducted a fighting withdrawal towards Trondheim as the British 148th Infantry Brigade landed at Åndalsnes on the 18th (Sickleforce) and covered the Norwegian withdrawal from Lillehammer northwards. On a parallel route to the east, the Germans penetrated deeply to Tynset, over 160km (100 miles) north, on the 24th. By the end of the month, the Allies had evacuated the entire Åndalsnes venture. Meanwhile, to the west of Oslo, the German 163rd Infantry Division drove toward Bergen.

With surprise lost, KAdm Oskar Kummetz continued up the narrowing fjord towards Oslo. In clear daylight, the warships approached in full view of the two batteries guarding the narrow throat of the fjord: the eastern Husvik Battery and the western Oscarsborg Fortress at Kaholmen. As the Germans steamed brazenly between the forts, the Norwegians opened fire at point-blank range, hitting the heavy cruiser *Blücher* from both sides with devastating effect. Then two land-based torpedoes struck the ship port side, with the violent explosions disabling the main engines. The ship coasted out of Norwegian range and dropped anchor as the crew battled to save it from the terrible damage it had suffered.

Initially, the German heavy cruiser/pocket battleship *Lützow* followed the same course and received three hits. Quickly reversing, she retreated to the south and safety. Meanwhile, when the raging fires reached the *Blücher's* ammunition magazine, the latter exploded with extreme power. The stricken vessel rolled over and sank; 320 German sailors perished. The remaining German warships withdrew and deposited their two battalions on the east bank of the fjord at Son, some 32km (20 miles) short of their objective. They advanced to take the Drøbak Fortress from the rear, leaving it up to the German Air Force to take the Norwegian capital.

The German aerial onslaught on Oslo consisted of three waves. The first formation (consisting of 28 Heinkel He 111 bombers) was to intimidate the Norwegian government into capitulation; but this mission was delayed by bad weather. The second wave (some 29 Junkers Ju 52/3m transport aircraft) delivered German paratroopers of Fornebu airfield. Twenty minutes behind them 53 more transports brought in a German infantry battalion. Just after 0700hrs five Norwegian Gloster Gladiators launched from Fornebu airfield and engaged the German transport aircraft, shooting down two Messerschmitt Bf 110s for the loss of one of their

After the first two German attempts at assaulting Fornebu airfield were aborted, due to weather and Norwegian anti-aircraft fire, the third try succeeded. One vulnerable Junkers Ju 52/3m was lost to defensive anti-aircraft fire, but a staggering 240 others landed there on that first day. (© IWM, HU 93725)

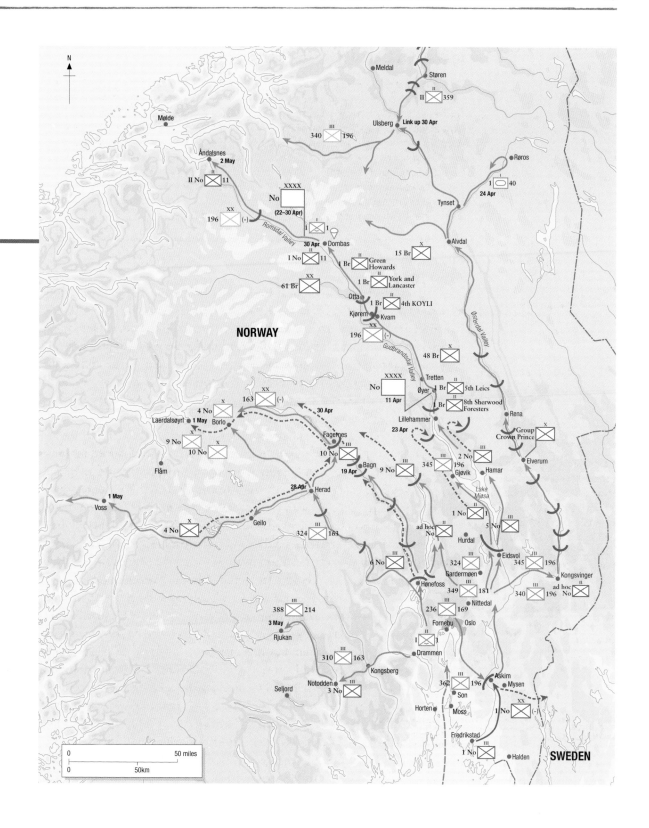

Once safely on the ground at Sola airfield, German infantry troops marched briskly to secure the nearby harbour at Stavanger, Norway, on 9 April 1940. (© IWM, HU 93732)

own. The German fighters continued to Fornebu airfield, strafed it, and forced the other pilots to land on frozen lakes. Only one Gloster survived the day.

Norwegian anti-aircraft guns thwarted the German transport aircrafts' initial attempts to land. Next, a damaged Messerschmitt Bf 110 fighter made a forced landing on the field. Almost out of fuel, the rest of his unit did the same, taxied to the corners of the airfield, and provided covering fire as the transport aircraft successfully landed. The fierce, if brief, resistance by the Norwegian forts, warships, Gladiator fighter aircraft, anti-aircraft guns, and ground crews gave the nation's government enough time to evacuate the capital. At 0830hrs on 9 April 1940 King Håkon VII, the Royal Family, the Cabinet, and the *Storting* (Norwegian Parliament) departed Oslo by train to Hamar, approximately 150km (93 miles) north of the capital.

Meanwhile, at Fornebu German infantry reinforced by two companies of paratroopers secured the airfield. Thereafter, 159 Junkers Ju 52/3m transport aircraft brought in more reinforcements, allowing the German air attaché, Hptm Eberhard Spiller, to organise six companies to march into the capital, Oslo.

By this time the Storting had heard the dismal news from each Norwegian city, and evacuated to Elverum, closer to the Swedish frontier. Fortunately, Oberst Ruge committed the 2nd Battalion Norwegian 5th Infantry Regiment to a blocking position between Hamar and Elverum. Once Spiller learned of the Norwegian government's location, he commandeered transportation to lift two paratrooper companies to raid Elverum and capture King Håkon VII. With a paltry force and without surprise, the Germans were halted by the hasty Norwegian defences and were sent reeling back to Oslo with Spiller mortally wounded. The German attempt to decapitate the Norwegian state had failed.

The Attacks at Stavanger and Sola

The riskiest operation was at Stavanger and its nearby Sola airfield, which were to be taken entirely by airborne assault. The forces involved consisted of one German Fallschirmjäger company delivered by 25 Junkers Ju 52/3ms and supported by a squadron of Heinkel He 111 bombers and followed by 104 Junkers Ju 52/3m transport aircraft bringing in additional infantry to consolidate the invaders' hold on the strategic port and airbase.

On the ground, the Norwegian bomber squadron – three Ca 310s and six C.V-E biplanes – were just preparing for take-off when the Germans struck. One Caproni burst into flames as the remaining Norwegian bombers narrowly escaped. Simultaneously, some 131 German Fallschirmjäger dropped in the vicinity and soon captured the airfield. The Junkers Ju 52/3ms then delivered two infantry battalions of the German 193rd Infantry Regiment on to the airbase without any enemy interference. These troops soon secured the port so that German merchant ships could bring in additional reinforcements. One of these vessels never arrived. As the port fell, the Norwegian destroyer *Æger* slipped out to sea and sank the German cargo merchantman *Roda* before being bombed and disabled itself in the Amøyfjord.

The German Assaults on Kristiansand, Arendal and Egersund

KzS Friedrich Rieve's German Fourth Naval Group arrived off Kristiansandfjord on schedule, but thick fog prevented an early approach up the fjord. At 0623hrs as the fog lifted the German light cruiser *Karlsruhe* approached, but was driven off by the Norwegian coastal fort on Odderøy. Rieve called for air support and three hours later 16 He 111 bombers silenced the Norwegian batteries. Rieve's assault troops landed and quickly stormed the fortifications. Soon afterwards the *Tsingtau* docked and unloaded elements of the German 310th Infantry Regiment, which quickly secured the city and its environs. The German torpedo boat *Greif* arrived off Arendal Harbour at 0850hrs with a bicycle squadron from GenMaj Hermann Tittel's German 69th Infantry Division. These troops came ashore unopposed and captured the telephone cable station. Similarly, at 0530hrs the three minesweepers of the German Sixth Naval Group arrived at Egersund with another company from the German 69th Division. They captured the cable station, severing telecommunications with Britain just when the Norwegian government needed them most.

German infantry head ashore at Narvik, protected by the powerful guns of the heavy cruiser *Admiral Hipper,* on 9 April 1940. The vessel was being repaired at the end of the war in the *Germaniawerft* dock facilities in Kiel harbour when on 3 May 1945 she was crippled by Allied bombing; her crew scuttled the vessel the next day. (© IWM, HU 93731)

German Operations at Bergen and Trondheim

The German Third Naval Group similarly arrived off Bergen on schedule. There the cruisers transferred their troops to smaller vessels for the amphibious assaults on the coastal fortifications. KAdm Schmundt landed troops to capture the shore batteries at Kvarven and Sandviken and steamed his larger warships into the channel towards the port. Alerted, Kvarven's guns hit the German light cruiser *Königsberg* three times, causing significant damage, flooding and fires. The German ship had to drop anchor to prevent drifting aground and returned fire with its aft guns as damage control parties fought the internal fires. The Luftwaffe was called in and at 0706hrs Heinkel He 111 bombers arrived and quickly silenced the Norwegian forts. Soon afterwards the Gunnery Training Ship *Bremse* docked and landed the headquarters staff of GenMaj Tittel's German 69th Infantry Division. This vessel also landed two battalions of the German 159th Infantry Regiment, which immediately secured Norway's second largest city.

Trondheim proved easiest to secure. The German Second Naval Group also reached its objective on time and KzS Heye's vessels steamed into the fjord, pretending to be British warships to pass right by the harbour defences. Realizing the ruse too late, the Norwegian Hysnes Battery opened fire as the warships sped past. At 0530hrs the German heavy cruiser *Admiral Hipper* anchored and the Gebirgsjäger it had transported dashed ashore: Trondheim surrendered without a fight. After noon German Heinkel He 115 torpedo-bombers arrived to begin searching for the warships of the British Home Fleet. For German land-based aircraft an ice air strip was hastily improvised and that afternoon six four-engined transport aircraft brought in German reinforcements to Trondheim.

Once the defending Norwegian warships had been eliminated, the German Gebirgsjäger could offload their equipment from the crowded destroyers in relative safety. Here the destroyer *Hans Lüdemann* (Z-18) is unloaded at the Post Pier in Narvik harbour on 9 April 1940. (© IWM, HU 93722)

The Bitter Encounters at Narvik

Early on 9 April, nine of Bonte's destroyers arrived safely at the entrance of the Vestfjord and at 0300hrs entered the Ofotfjord. Two German destroyers landed companies of Gebirgsjäger at Ramnes and Hamnes to secure the coastal batteries thought to be guarding the narrows. Approaching Narvik through mist and patchy fog, three destroyers moved off north into the Herjangsfjord to land a battalion at Bjerkvik. These troops quickly captured the Norwegians' Elvegårdsmoen ordnance depot.

The group flagship, the Type 1936 destroyer *Wilhelm Heidkamp* (Z21) arrived off Narvik at 0415hrs in thick fog and confronted the Norwegian coastal defence ship *Eidsvold*. The latter fired a warning shot across its bow and Bonte immediately sent an officer by boat to demand their surrender. As the parlay progressed, Korvettenkapitän Rechel steered the destroyer *Bernd von Arnim* (Z11) past the two warships toward the Post Pier. The *Norge* spotted the *Bernd von Arnim* and trained its guns on the intruder. When negotiations finally failed, the *Wilhelm Heidkamp* fired four torpedoes, and sank the *Eidsvold*, killing 262 Norwegian sailors. *Norge* then opened fire on the *Bernd von Arnim* and Rechel in return fired all of his vessel's torpedoes. These hit the *Norge,* which promptly rolled over and sank, killing 173 Norwegian naval personnel.

Seizing this fleeting opportunity, the German Gebirgsjäger leapt ashore and quickly secured their objectives around the harbour in the face of light resistance. Finally, the *Wilhelm Heidkamp* docked on the harbour-side and disembarked

GenLt Dietl and more German troops. Dietl moved immediately to the local Norwegian military headquarters where Oberst Konrad Sundlo, commander of the Narvik garrison, quickly surrendered the town. Two Norwegian companies escaped, travelling up the ore railway towards the Swedish border, to establish a blocking position between the two locations.

Waiting to refuel the near-empty German destroyers was the 11,766-ton *Jan Wellem*, a converted whaling ship that had arrived from Murmansk. Unfortunately, the big ship lacked the fuel to completely refill the ten destroyers and had very slow pumps. The other crucial German tanker, the 6,031-ton *Kattegat*, had almost made it to Narvik when it was challenged by the 266-ton Norwegian naval auxiliary *Nordkapp* and was scuttled in panic by its crew. Despite his tactical success, however, Bonte found himself unable to head for home due to lack of fuel. It would take 36 hours before his force was ready to run back to Germany.

The Royal Navy Responds (7–12 April)

Attempting to prevent the Atlantic breakout, the Royal Navy's Home Fleet departed Scapa Flow at 2115hrs on 7 April and headed north-east. Simultaneously, V Adm Edward-Collins' 2nd Cruiser Squadron departed Rosyth and steered to intercept 130km (81 miles) off Stavanger. HMS *Glowworm*'s chance encounter with the enemy led Adm Forbes north-eastwards to intercept the enemy squadron. When a RAF Sunderland aircraft located Heye's ships, Forbes steered north-west to intercept.

By this time, the Admiralty had abandoned Plan R.4. The troops and their equipment were disembarked at Rosyth and V Adm Cunningham's 1st Cruiser Squadron put to sea immediately and headed north to join the Home Fleet. Confusing and contradictory reports flooded the Admiralty: most alarming was the British Naval Attaché's report from Copenhagen that the German Fifth Naval Group had passed northwards through the Great Belt and into the Kattegat.

Admiral Forbes knew he had one German force north of him, last reported headed west, and another equally powerful force in the Kattegat perhaps coming out. He split his own force, sending HMS *Repulse*, one cruiser and four destroyers northwards to join Whitworth's squadron to engage the first enemy formation. Meanwhile, he turned south with his remaining warships to rendezvous with the British 2nd Cruiser Squadron and attack the second.

A view of Narvik Harbour following the first destroyer battle. Moored to the left side of the Post Pier is the German destroyer *Hans Lüdemann* and to the right is the *Hermann Künne* (Z-19), both badly damaged in the attack. (Photo by ullstein bild/ullstein bild via Getty Images)

Destroyer Battle in Narvik Harbour, 10 April 1940

A few moments after dawn – at high tide and through intermittent light snow squalls – Capt Bernard Warburton-Lee steered his flagship, HMS *Hardy* (1), into Narvik harbour and slowly turned about to come broadside to the two German destroyers visible in the hazy morning twilight. Beyond the screen of merchant shipping crowding the harbour the enemy flagship, *Wilhelm Heidkamp* (2), could be plainly seen and Flotilla Torpedo Officer Lt G. R. Heppel gasped, 'There's a torpedo target such as I've never seen in my life!' Capt Warburton-Lee responded with 'Well, get on with it then.' After a touch of engine revolutions to bring the *Hardy* about into a perfect beam firing position, Heppel unleashed three torpedoes from the forward tubes; all ran hot, straight and true, with the centre 'fish' hitting the aft quarter of its target. Immediately Warburton-Lee ordered revolutions for 20 knots and turned farther port towards the harbour entrance. As the *Hardy* moved and the view through the screen of merchant shipping changed, additional German destroyers were revealed. Heppel immediately ordered the aft tubes (3) swung to starboard and the crew tried frantically – against the slippery footing of the icy deck and the increased resistance of the cold mounting pivot – to move the 10-ton weapon into firing position. Meanwhile, in the distance, the morning calm was shattered by the explosion of the *Heidkamp*'s aft ammunition magazine, killing Kdr Bonte and 80 other German sailors and throwing the ship's aft three 12.7cm gun turrets into the air. The destruction of the German destroyer squadron at Narvik had begun. (Artwork by John White, © Osprey Publishing)

Farther south the British 1st and 18th Cruiser Squadrons combined under the command of V Adm Layton. German intentions became clear at 2355hrs, when Forbes received word that the Polish submarine *Orzel* had sunk the German transport vessel *Rio de Janeiro* in the Skagerrak much earlier that day. Unfortunately, the three Royal Navy armadas were too far off the Norwegian coast to intervene on 9 April.

At first light, the Luftwaffe's coastal reconnaissance planes located two major enemy surface groups: two battleships, six cruisers and a large destroyer screen northwest of Bergen (the Home Fleet) and nine cruisers and 11 destroyers to the port's west-south-west (the Cruiser Force). With this knowledge, the German Fliegerkorps X mounted a large anti-shipping strike that day with 41 He 111 and 47 Junkers Ju 88 bombers. The Ju 88s found the cruiser force, sunk the destroyer HMS *Gurkha* and damaged both the light cruisers HMS *Southampton* and HMS *Galatea*. Further German bombers attacked the British Home Fleet, hitting the flagship. Forbes prudently retired out of range of the aircraft of German Fliegerkorps X.

Meanwhile at Narvik, Bonte's force had settled into the task of refuelling as Whitworth's force unexpectedly arrived off the entrance to the Vestfjord. Believing only one German destroyer to be at Narvik, the Admiralty ordered Capt Warburton-Lee to proceed to Narvik and sink or capture the enemy ship. On this faulty intelligence, that afternoon Warburton-Lee led his 2nd Destroyer Flotilla, increased to five ships by the arrival of HMS *Hostile,* up the passage to Narvik to attack at dawn. At Narvik, Bonte dispersed his flotilla among adjacent feeder fjords and posted U-boats in the Vestfjord as sentries. However, the passing snow squalls concealed the British destroyers' approach. At 0510hrs, as dawn began to break, Warburton-Lee's flagship manoeuvred quietly in the snowy, early morning gloom, into an excellent firing position.

At 0530hrs HMS *Hardy* unleashed its torpedoes which hit and blew up the German flagship destroyer, *Wilhelm Heidkamp* (Z21). The sinking caused the death of 81 German sailors, including Bonte. The Type 1936 destroyer *Diether von Roeder* (Z17) was also hit repeatedly and set on fire. HMS *Hunter* also hit the *Anton Schmitt* (Z22) with two torpedoes; the vessel broke in half and sank at once, killing 50 of the crew. The German destroyers *Hans Lüdemann* (Z18) and *Hermann Künne* (Z19) – both then engaged in refuelling from a tanker vessel – slipped their cables and went into action. Unready for battle, their fire was inaccurate, and they took repeated hits from the British destroyers.

After a second British attack accomplished little due to the mist thickening and obscuring the possible targets, Warburton-Lee turned his destroyers around and headed back towards the entrance to the Ofotfjord. Suddenly from starboard three German destroyers emerged from the Herjangsfjord. A running gun battle erupted before Frigattenkapitän Erich Bey quickly broke off the chase due to lack of fuel. However, 16km (ten miles) down the Ofotfjord two more German destroyers – the *Georg Thiele* (Z2) and the *Bernd von Arnim* (Z11) – suddenly loomed out of the Ballangenfjord, crossing the *Hardy*'s bow firing full broadsides. This deluge of fire swept the *Hardy*'s bridge, incapacitating everyone, including

Blackburn Skuas preparing for take-off from RNAS Hatston in the Orkney Islands. Flying at the absolute limit of their operating range, the Fleet Air Arm became the first air force to sink a major enemy warship by dive-bombing during World War II, sinking the German light cruiser *Königsberg* off Bergen on 10 April 1940. (© IWM, A 8218)

The battleship HMS *Warspite* steaming into Ofotfjord behind its screen of nine destroyers on 13 April 1940, at the start of the Second Battle of Narvik. This photograph was taken from *Warspite*'s Swordfish floatplane, which sank the German submarine *U-64* during this mission.

Warburton-Lee. The shattered British destroyer swerved out of line and beached herself on the shore in an attempt to stop herself from sinking.

Next, HMS *Hunter* drew the enemy's accurate fire and, soon ablaze and out of control, inadvertently collided with HMS *Hotspur*. The *Havock* and *Hostile* then swerved around the two locked British destroyers and passed alongside the Type 1934 destroyer *Georg Thiele* (Z2) and the Type 1934A *Bernd von Arnim* (Z11) at point-blank range, exchanging furious salvoes of fire. Finally, the battered HMS *Hotspur* extricated herself from the clutches of the sinking HMS *Hunter* and escaped after the other two vessels. Returning to the entrance of the Vestfjord, the three British destroyers encountered and sank the German supply ship *Rauenfels,* which had been carrying key cargo – most of General Dietl's heavy weapons, including many of his mountain artillery guns.

Warburton-Lee's bold initiative and resolute determination won the First Battle of Narvik for the British, but at a heavy cost: 147 men killed and two destroyers sunk, with a third badly damaged. For his courageous leadership and ultimate sacrifice, Warburton-Lee was posthumously awarded the coveted award for gallantry, the Victoria Cross. This victory set the stage for a series of crippling punishments for the Kriegsmarine's audacious attempt to invade Norway.

The first setback was provided by the Fleet Air Arm. At 0515hrs on 10 April, some 16 Blackburn B-24 Skua dive-bombers headed for Bergen, the extreme limit of their operational range. Their target was the damaged German light cruiser *Königsberg*. The Blackburn Skuas scored three hits: the *Königsberg* burned for two hours before an internal explosion blew her apart. Fifteen Skuas made it back. Meanwhile, the other German warships were returning individually to their home bases.

To catch them, V Adm Horton sensibly spread 18 Allied submarines across the waters of the Kattegat and Skagerrak. On 9 April, the German light cruiser *Karlsruhe* was crippled by the T-class submarine HMS *Truant*, and then scuttled by the Germans. Similarly, the following night, the heavy cruiser/pocket battleship *Lützow* was also torpedoed by a Royal Navy submarine, in this case HMS *Spearfish*. Towed to Kiel harbour, *Lützow* was out of the war for 12 months while extensive repairs were completed. Additionally, during the next week British submarines also sank eight German merchant vessels returning to Germany from Norway. Two British submarines were lost in these efforts.

Meanwhile VAdm Lütjens steamed the German battle-cruisers *Gneisenau* and *Scharnhorst* well to the west, headed generally southwards. On 12 April 1940 the heavy cruiser *Admiral Hipper* joined for the final dash home. Finally, Forbes headed north to join Whitworth off Narvik, which became the sole objective of the British response.

Forbes had been joined on 10 April by the aircraft carrier HMS *Furious*, embarking 18 Fairey Swordfish TSR biplanes, and by the battleship HMS *Warspite*. The following day HMS *Furious* delivered the first ever British carrier-launched air attack. Her 18 Swordfish aircraft attacked with torpedoes two German destroyers located in the Trondheimfjord. Fortunately for the Germans, no hits were scored because the torpedoes grounded in the shallow anchorage.

At Narvik, Frigattenkapitän Bey planned his scheme of defence. The German Type 1936 destroyer *Diether von Roeder* (Z17) had been damaged and immobilised in the first battle. Subsequently, its crew moored the vessel to the Post Pier to act as a static harbour defence platform. Meanwhile, the Type 1934A destroyer *Erich Koellner* (Z13) had been irreparably damaged after running aground in Narvik harbour. Similarly, the Germans turned this vessel into a static floating battery at the entrance to the Ofotfjord. Bey planned on deploying the other six destroyers in his group into the side fjords upon receiving word of the approaching enemy. From these locations he hoped his vessels could take the British vessels by surprise.

At 0830hrs the next morning Whitworth headed up the Vestfjord with the battleship HMS *Warspite* and no fewer than nine destroyers. This represented a powerful striking force. Warned of their approach at 1010hrs, Bey deployed his ships according to his previous plans. Next, the *Warspite*'s floatplane sighted the German submarine *U-64* on the surface, recharging its batteries in the Herjangsfjord, and sank it. Three British destroyers then battered the *Erich Koellner* (Z13) into a burning hulk before the main guns from HMS *Warspite* sunk the hapless German destroyer. Subsequently, as the British entered the Ofotfjord, four German destroyers emerged from Narvik and attacked, but they were driven off. In an hour of hard fighting the Germans were forced into the end of the fjord, running out of ammunition as well as manoeuvring room.

The German destroyer *Georg Thiele* (Z-2) fought valiantly at Narvik and, once all rounds were expended, Korvettenkäpitan Max-Eckart Wolff ran her aground on 13 April, thus saving the surviving crew. Some 14 sailors died and 28 were wounded. (© IWM, A 24)

At the harbour entrance the German Type 1934A destroyer *Erich Geise* (Z12) made a dramatic last stand and battered and drove away HMS *Punjabi*. The *Erich Geise* was in turn blasted into a drifting, burning wreck by the destroyer HMS *Bedouin* and the mighty battleship HMS *Warspite*. The entrance open, HMS *Cossack* then steamed in to eliminate the immobile Type 1936 destroyer *Diether von Roeder*. However, the latter pummelled the former and drove HMS *Cossack* aground at Ankenes. Finally, when completely out of ammunition, the crew of the *Diether von Roeder* (Z17) abandoned her and set off explosives to destroy the vessel.

Meanwhile, the German Type 1936 destroyer *Hermann Künne* (Z19) – undamaged but now completely out of ammunition – beached herself in the Herjangsfjord and was abandoned and blown up. Four other German destroyers fled into the Rombaksfjord, three of them continuing to the very end of the fjord where they were beached, with the crews escaping on to the rocky shore. The *Georg Thiele* (Z2) made a desperate last stand and, though hit repeatedly by her pursuers, blew the bow off HMS *Eskimo* with her last torpedo. Once the last round had been fired, the ship was run hard aground. The crew escaped ashore to join their naval comrades and the now isolated German mountain troops. The following day Whitworth departed the Ofotfjord, informing the Admiralty that the Germans ashore appeared stunned and disorganised. He recommended a landing force be sent to occupy the town without delay.

The German Advance through Central Norway (10–21 April)

On 10 April 1940, with the Oslofjord area occupied, GenMaj Erwin Engelbrecht moved his German 163rd Infantry Division out of Oslo to overrun the scattered and slowly reacting elements of the 1st Norwegian Division. To begin the offensive drive northwards into central Norway, GenLt Pellengahr's German 196th Infantry Division arrived on 11 April and mounted the advance towards Trondheim.

The German forces operating in Norway were well equipped with artillery. One such weapon was the 10.5cm le FH 18 light field howitzer, like this one with the 233rd Artillery Regiment seen heading north out of Oslo for the front line. (© IWM, HU 93720)

The narrow valleys, deep snows and sparse roads leading northwards from Oslo limited the advance to two independent fronts. Battle Group Pellengahr (formed around the German 324th and 345th Infantry Regiments), began pushing up the Gudbrandsdalen valley towards Hamar. Meanwhile, another task force, formed around 340th Infantry Regiment under the command of Obst Fischer, advanced up the Østerdal valley to Elverum.

That same day Oberst Ruge assumed command of the Norwegian Army. However, he found he possessed effective control only over the Norwegian 2nd Infantry Division. This formation, mobilised under great difficulty, fielded only two infantry battalions, a dragoon regiment, and three 75mm gun artillery batteries. Initially it held the line between Hurdal and Eidsvoll. But, handicapped by poor communications, it relinquished this excellent defensive position following light German probing attacks.

The Germans coordinated their various combined-arms attacks very well. Before an assault somewhere in Norway, an infantry platoon commander confers with his armour support leader in a light armoured command tank. (© IWM, MH 2621)

The Norwegians' one bright spot was the defeat and capture of a company of German paratroopers at Dombås, where the rail line up the Gudbrandsdalen split off to Trondheim. On 14 April, 162 German paratroopers jumped into an enemy stronghold. The Norwegians had heavily defended the strategic railway intersection and took most of the company prisoner. The remaining 34 men held out for four days and surrendered only when all their food and ammunition was exhausted.

Despite this setback, by the evening of 19 April Norwegian withdrawals had allowed Pellengahr to take both Hamar and Elverum in his two-pronged advance. He was aided by the arrival of the 1st Company of the 40th Special-Purpose Armoured Battalion; on 17 April three experimental prewar German NbFz B heavy tanks were unloaded at Oslo to join Pellengahr's battle group.

When the Germans attacked Elverum, the king – who had refused to accept a government led by Quisling – with his family and members of the Norwegian Storting escaped, first to Molde, then eventually to Tromsø, from where they were able to travel to England and set up a government in exile.

Meanwhile, GenMaj Woytasch's German 181st Infantry Division had also unloaded at Oslo's docks. Elements from this formation were swiftly airlifted to Trondheim from 18 April. Subsequently, one German merchantman and two submarines also ran the British naval blockade to reinforce the Germans forces there. By 21 April 1940, moreover, sufficient German infantry were at Trondheim to allow Obst Weiss' Gebirgsjäger to drive northwards to relieve Dietl's beleaguered regiment.

The Allied Ground Intervention Forces Arrive (14–25 April)

Recognizing that his only hope was to delay the German advance towards Trondheim long enough for Allied forces to arrive, the recently-promoted Generalmajor Ruge demanded British reinforcements. The only forces available were already on their way to Narvik: the 24th (Guards) Brigade and the British 146th (Territorial) Brigade. In London the euphoria of V Adm Whitworth's victory over the German destroyers at Narvik misdirected the War Cabinet. Believing that Narvik could be captured by a single brigade landed directly into the town, on 14 April they ordered Lord Cork to do so and diverted the British 146th Brigade to Namsos to retake Trondheim from the north. The British 24th Brigade, continuing to Narvik, became the basis for Rupertforce. And the British 146th Brigade became the basis for Mauriceforce. But by splitting the force originally intended for Narvik, the British dissipated their strength and left neither force strong enough to take its objective.

The British 146th Brigade unloaded over the next two days. Its commander, Maj Gen Carton de Wiart, arrived on 15 April. Unloading his poorly-equipped and inexperienced British troops the next day, he immediately set them on the road to Trondheim. On 19 April, the French 5e Demi-Brigade Chasseurs Alpins also arrived. But, lacking motor transport, they were left behind while the British forces moved to Steinkjer (at the head of the Beitstadfjord). Having joined with a Norwegian battalion, the British deployed into defensive positions around Vist, where they were immediately engaged by the Gebirgsjäger advancing out of Trondheim.

In skirmishes over 21–22 April, the Gebirgsjäger drove the British back while another German mountain-troop battalion landed on their flank at Kirkenes. Meanwhile the German Air Force pounded Steinkjer and Namsos, ensuring complete defeat. The route to Trondheim blocked, his forces in danger of encirclement and his supply base under merciless aerial attack, Carton de Wiart withdrew to extricate his troops from the closing trap.

To form the southern arm of the pincer to retake Trondheim, the British 148th Infantry Brigade was loaded aboard V Adm Edward-Collins' ships and transported across the North Sea on 17 April. This became the core element of Sickleforce. This contingent, under the command of Brig Harold Morgan, unloaded during 18–19 April at Åndalsnes. Two companies moved by train to Dombås to secure the important road/rail junction, arriving the

Soldiers of the British 146th Brigade crowd the deck of SS *Oronsay* as the troops of Mauriceforce steams into Namsos Harbour during mid-April 1940. The F-class destroyer HMS *Fury* provides close escort. (© IWM, N 42)

day the German paratroopers surrendered. In response to Ruge's request, Morgan's small force was diverted from its original mission. Abandoning the planned envelopment of Trondheim, two companies travelled by train to just north of Lillehammer where Morgan established his brigade HQ.

By the time the British arrived at the front, however, the Norwegians had pulled back along both shores of frozen Lake Mjøsa. On the east side, the Norwegian 5th Infantry Regiment held out at Strandlykkja for two days until a German battalion outflanked them by marching across the frozen lake. Surprised and panicked, the Norwegian troops retreated precipitously, abandoning the next two defensive positions. On the west, the single battalion of the Norwegian 4th Infantry Regiment retreated as well, to Gjøvik. The first two British companies deployed to the west shore reinforced this battered battalion at the hamlet of Biri. Meanwhile the other two British companies relieved the Norwegian troops deployed in front of the town of Lillehammer.

Approaching them, GenLt Pellengahr's two spearhead battalions pushed northwards up the shorelines of Lake Mjøsa. These units were supported by engineer parties and several motorised machine-gun platoons, as well as six light tanks and two experimental German NbFz B heavy tanks. Additionally, unchallenged, eight German Heinkel He 111 bombers aggressively attacked on 21 April, with Pellengahr launching his ground assault at 1400hrs, just as the British were relieving the Norwegians in the forward positions.

Unseasoned, having limited ammunition, and with no available artillery, Morgan's men held out most of the day but withdrew to Fåberg during the night. The next morning the Germans renewed their assaults with air, artillery, and tank support, easily outflanked the British and drove them back in disarray. One last stand was made at Tretten Gorge on 23 April, the most defensible position in the Gudbrandsdalen valley.

Pellengahr used his artillery with great skill. Shortly after noon two light tanks broke through the main British position while infantry infiltrated from the flank. Soon a large part of the British force was cut off while the Luftwaffe strafed those attempting to retreat. After nightfall exhausted remnants finally escaped to the north, leaving 706 officers and men killed, missing, or captured. The British 148th Brigade had ceased to exist.

To reinforce Sickleforce, the British 15th Brigade was detached from the 5th Infantry Division in the BEF located in northern France and embarked for Norway on 15 April. Originally intended to be used in the direct amphibious assault on Trondheim, this force consisted of three battalions and only one anti-tank gun company – because a German U-boat sank the brigade's motor transport and artillery en route. The brigade arrived at Åndalsnes on 23 April and headed south, passing the remains of the 148th Brigade and the 2nd Norwegian Infantry Division, to establish a defensive position at Kvam, 55km (34 miles) south of

BATTLES AROUND LILLEHAMMER, 20–24 APRIL 1940

Note: Gridlines are shown at intervals
of 1km (1,093yds)

148th

MORGAN

SLAGBRENNA

MESNA

ÖYER

BALBERGKAMP

LILLEHAMMER

BRØTTUM

FÅBERG

TRETTEN

GAUSDAL

FRYDENLUND

▼ EVENTS

1. 20 APRIL: Norwegian
infantry (II/IR 5) and dragoons
(DR 2), under Oberst Jørgen Jensen,
hold firm on the south slope of the Lundehögde
against artillery bombardments and infantry attacks by
IR 345 throughout the day. GenLt Pellengahr is reinforced by
a motorised machine-gun battalion and prepares to renew the
assaults the following day.

2. 20 APRIL: The first British unit to arrive and detrain at Fåberg,
a half-battalion of 1st/8th Sherwood Foresters (A and D Coy, under
Maj J. K. L. Roberts), bivouac at Nykirke before deploying to defend
the Bråstad Bridge, relieving the exhausted Norwegian I/IR 4. Two
battalions of IR 324, with supporting troops, face them. Overall Allied
commander is Oberst Thor A. Dahl.

3. 21 APRIL: Following bombing attacks by eight He 111s (II/KG 54) in
the morning and heavy artillery bombardment (AR 223), at 1400hrs the
German infantry attacks the Norwegian dragoons while Gebirgsjäger
(IV/GJR 138) climb the heights to the east and infiltrate the flanks. DR 2
is forced back upon the British half-battalion (1st/5th Royal
Leicestershire) as they attempt to relieve the Norwegians in position.
Meanwhile, on the shoreline road, the motorised machine-gun
battalion almost cuts off the Allied retreat.

4. 2000HRS, 21 APRIL: The Royal Leicestershire half-battalion
establishes a new line behind Åsmarka and DR 2 withdraws through
this line and safely evacuates to Lillehammer. The British follow at
midnight but the rearguard is overrun by German armoured cars on
the south edges of Lillehammer and captured. The half-battalion of
Sherwood Foresters withdraw via an alternate route.

5. 22 APRIL: Now in command of his units
and the Allied defensive positions north of
Lillehammer, Brig H. de R. Morgan deploys the
half-battalion of Sherwood Foresters between the shoreline
and the steep face of Balberg with the battered companies of the
Royal Leicestershires as a second line of defence. The lines are
hastily improvised and were attacked at midday along the shore
road while German mountain troops scale the heights of the Balberg
and fall upon the British flank and rear at 1530hrs, even attacking the
148th Bde HQ, precipitating a further retreat up the valley.

6. EVENING, 22 APRIL: To prevent being cut off from the east, Maj
Roberts withdraws his half-battalion of Sherwood Foresters, leading
them on an arduous retreat north into the Gausdal Valley, where they
hide from the Luftwaffe during the day. Resuming their journey at
0300hrs the next day, they arrive at Tretten by 0700hrs. Oberst Dahl,
having begun his retreat earlier, crosses the river upstream and moved
further to Fåvang to set up the next blocking position.

7. 1030HRS, 23 APRIL: Brig Morgan's 148th Bde makes its last stand south of Tretten Gorge. Two companies of Foresters and one of Leicesters cover the oblique shore road supported by the remaining Norwegian dragoons on the left flank. Maj Robert's half-battalion protects the bridge and provides – along with the remaining Leicesters – the reserve. Following the successful format of previous engagements, at 1300hrs the Germans begin probing with infantry and bombarding with artillery while three tanks (1./Pz.-Abt. zbV 40) penetrate the British lines along the road. This threatens to close the British avenue of retreat.

8. 1800HRS, 23 APRIL: German mountain troops, having scaled the heights to the east, descend behind the Norwegian dragoons attacking 148th Bde support troops in the rear. At 1900hrs a retreat is initiated but is hampered by air attacks, allowing German troops to close upon the forward British forces from all sides. A fighting withdrawal is attempted, but communication problems result in some units not disengaging, while others are caught on the road by pursuing German armoured cars. Only 30 per cent of the 148th Bde escapes destruction – most being captured – while the Norwegian infantry (I/IR 4) establishes a temporary blocking position at Fåvang.

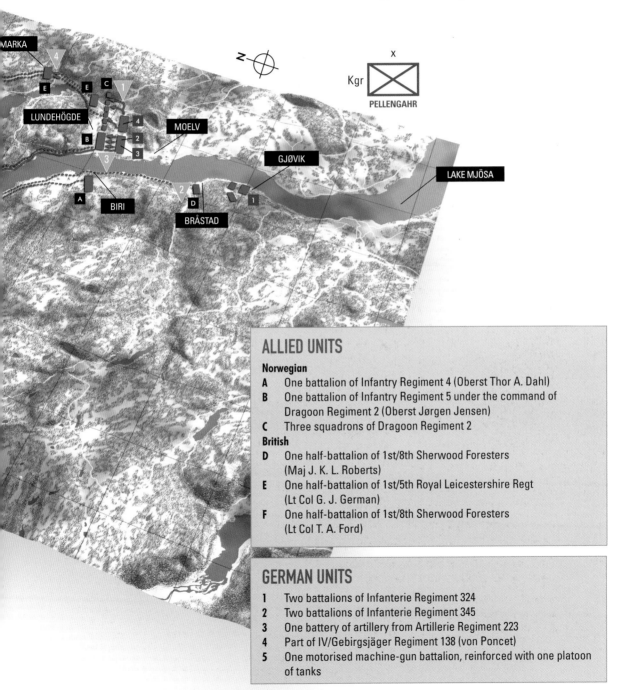

ALLIED UNITS

Norwegian
A One battalion of Infantry Regiment 4 (Oberst Thor A. Dahl)
B One battalion of Infantry Regiment 5 under the command of Dragoon Regiment 2 (Oberst Jørgen Jensen)
C Three squadrons of Dragoon Regiment 2

British
D One half-battalion of 1st/8th Sherwood Foresters (Maj J. K. L. Roberts)
E One half-battalion of 1st/5th Royal Leicestershire Regt (Lt Col G. J. German)
F One half-battalion of 1st/8th Sherwood Foresters (Lt Col T. A. Ford)

GERMAN UNITS

1 Two battalions of Infanterie Regiment 324
2 Two battalions of Infanterie Regiment 345
3 One battery of artillery from Artillerie Regiment 223
4 Part of IV/Gebirgsjäger Regiment 138 (von Poncet)
5 One motorised machine-gun battalion, reinforced with one platoon of tanks

NbFz B Heavy Tank in the Battle of Kvam, 25 April 1940

Having practically destroyed the British 148th Brigade in the battles around Lillehammer and swept away the weak Norwegian forces at Fåvang and Ringebu, GenLt Pellengahr's column marched north through the Gudbrandsdalen as if on parade. Leading the procession was one of the three operational NbFz B (also known as PzKpfw VI) heavy tanks in the German Army **(1)**. Specifically designed as an infantry support vehicle, the 35-ton 'land battleship' sported three turrets – the main turret carrying coaxially mounted 37mm and 75mm guns along with a small machine-gun turret fore and aft for close-in defence. Supporting this behemoth was a single PzKpfw II light tank **(2)** and an SdKfz 231 armoured car **(3)**. Behind this vanguard came the procession of lorried infantry, truck-towed artillery and marching troops. On 25 April, as the column emerged from the narrower defiles of the River Lågen **(4)** they saw the valley open up into gently sloping farmlands sweeping up the sides of the evergreen-capped ridge on the right and the broad, flat Viksöy Island, fringed with willows, on the left. Hidden in the trees on both flanks – with excellent fields of fire

covering the roadway – were A and B Companies of 1st Bn, KOYLI, each with a Hotchkiss 25mm A/T gun **(5)**. When the leading vehicles of the German column came inside a quarter mile, A Coy unleashed the first shot from their concealed position on Viksöy Island, disabling the NbFz B with a hit on its running gear. The escorting PzKpfw II manoeuvred around the disabled heavy tank only to be knocked out by the second round from A Coy's gun. The SdKfz 231 beat a hasty retreat and the column behind came to a halt. Though immobilized the NbFz B fought on, using its 37mm and 75mm guns against A Coy on Viksöy Island while behind it the Germans unloaded from their lorries, unlimbered their artillery and deployed for a more traditional advance and assaults. Using artillery barrages and flanking manoeuvres they attacked British positions throughout the rest of the day. The KOYLI fought doggedly and, withdrawing slowly and begrudgingly, they held up Pellengahr's advance for two full days, finally vacating the field at 1800hrs on 26 April. (Artwork by John White, © Osprey Publishing)

Dombås. Sent to lead the enlarged Sickleforce was Maj Gen Paget, commander of the British 18th Infantry Division.

Hardly had the British deployed into position when Pellengahr's spearhead – led by a solitary NbFz B heavy tank – attacked. The brigade's Hotchkiss 25mm anti-tank guns knocked out the NbFz B and the initial attacks were repulsed. Despite heavy artillery bombardment and flank infiltration, the British held for two days. Threatened with encirclement, the battered British troops finally

In contrast to the well-equipped Germans, British forces had often to rely on local Norwegian generosity; Mr Sellæg's horses are seen here towing a British 40mm Bofors medium anti-aircraft gun into position at Hæknes. (© IWM, N 77)

retreated and fell back through Kjørem, where they prepared their next defensive stand. After multiple hard-fought engagements, each ending in retreat, Paget concluded that further defence in central Norway was untenable in the face of the Luftwaffe's air supremacy. He called for air support since the entire length of his supply line, as well as his base at Åndalsnes, was now under constant air attack. Although RAF fighters were on the way, they would not be enough.

The Luftwaffe Rules Both the Air and the Waves (12 April–3 May)

Continued Norwegian resistance and the vigorous British response resulted in stepped up German Air Force operations. Therefore, the German Luftflotte V (Fifth Air Fleet) was formed on 12 April under the command of the Luftwaffe GenObst Milch. Subordinated to it was the German Fliegerkorps X, which provided area defence from Sola with Messerschmitt Bf 110 and Junkers Ju 88C platforms. Subsequently, GenLt Geisler's German Fliegerkorps X moved numerous Messerschmitt Bf 109Es to Kjevik airfield to protect Oslo Harbour and Fornebu from RAF bomber raids. Junkers Ju 87 Stuka dive-bombers and Heinkel He 111 medium bombers mounted anti-shipping strikes from Sola while other supported Pellengahr's advance northwards. In addition, further reinforcements in mid-April included two groups of Junkers Ju 88As, two of Heinkel He 111 bombers and one squadron of four-engine Focke-Wulf FW 200C maritime patrol bombers to curb Royal Navy operations.

The British response was underwhelming. RAF Bomber Command attempted to neutralise Sola and Fornebu airfields by unescorted air attacks, which were inevitably decimated by German fighters and flak; the British lost 31 bombers in 576 sorties. In a desperate effort to close Sola's operations, the Home Fleet sent the heavy cruiser HMS *Suffolk* and four destroyers to bombard the airfield.

Early on 17 April, the heavy cruiser launched its Walrus seaplane to illuminate the target, but a Junkers Ju 88C shot it down. Consequently, the bombardment was inaccurate and ineffectual; in response, the Luftwaffe launched 82 bomber sorties, hitting HMS *Suffolk* twice. The crippled vessel limped home, barely reaching Scapa Flow.

The only way to counter the threat posed by the Luftwaffe was to base RAF fighters in Norway. But this effort was so pitifully small it was doomed to fail. Since no airfields existed in the region, the frozen Lake Lesjaskog was selected. The RAF's No 263 Squadron, comprising 18 Gloster Gladiator IIs, sailed from Orkney on 20 April aboard HMS *Glorious* and, arrived four days later. They operated in severely primitive conditions and with an almost total absence of support. The Luftwaffe quickly located the base and bombed it repeatedly. On 25 April, renewed German Air Force raids destroyed all but five Gladiators and the base became untenable. With their fuel exhausted, the last three Gladiators were burned the next day and the personnel evacuated.

For anti-aircraft defence the Royal Navy put its faith in anti-aircraft guns: high-angle 3.7in. for barrage fire against level bombers and quad-mounted 0.5in. machine guns for close-in defence against dive-bombers. However, against dive-bombers the machine guns' lethal envelope was too small. In the air-sea battles in the Åndalsnes and Namsos fjords, the planes emerged triumphant. Once the Luftwaffe discovered Allied use of the two small ports, they were mercilessly bombed, despite the dedicated anti-aircraft (AA) ships stationed in them. HMS *Bittern* at Namsos

ABOVE HMS *Suffolk*'s bombardment of Sola airfield had no effect on the anti-shipping abilities of Fliegerkorps X. Hit twice amid 82 aerial attacks, the stricken cruiser limped back into Scapa Flow on the morning of 18 April 1940, her quarterdeck awash. The heavy cruiser had to be beached to prevent her sinking. (© IWM, HU 49670)

RIGHT British anti-aircraft cruisers and sloops attempted to defend Allied ports of embarkation, and frequently took the brunt of the air attacks themselves. Here the anti-aircraft sloop HMS *Bittern* burns following a Stuka strike on Namsos harbour, on 30 April 1940. (© IWM, N 64)

was damaged so badly on 30 April that she had to be sunk. Two other anti-aircraft (AA) sloops and one anti-aircraft cruiser were so damaged they had to leave. During the 1,050 bombing sorties flown against the two ports, anti-aircraft fire shot down only nine German bombers.

Meanwhile, British 15th Brigade again attempted to stop the determined German advance at Kjørem. The Germans attacked on 27 April 1940 and, after holding out for a day, the British were forced to retire to Otta, 20km (12 miles) to the rear. There, the following day, the Green Howards made a determined stand, inflicting heavy casualties. When they withdrew that evening, Pellengahr made no move to pursue. Meanwhile in Østerdal, Obst Fischer's battle group had made steady progress against weak Norwegian resistance and, on 26 April, was at Alvdal, some 96km (60 miles) north-east of Dombås, threatening the Allied rear. Three days later Fischer linked up with forces from Trondheim, making the outcome obvious.

With Sickleforce unprotected against Luftwaffe air attacks, threatened from the rear, and hopelessly outgunned at the front, on 28 April 1940 the War Cabinet finally ordered the British expeditionary forces to be evacuated, leaving the Norwegians devastated and demoralised. Despite constant air pounding, Maj Gen Paget successfully extricated his forces from a hopeless tactical situation, re-embarking between 30 April and 2 May. King Håkon, Genermajor Ruge, and the Norwegian government evacuated from Mølde – bound for Tromsø in the far north. Unable to follow them, Genermajor Hvinden Haug surrendered the Norwegian 2nd Infantry Division on 3 May. Sickleforce had lost 1,301 men killed, missing, or captured in ground combat, yet miraculously 5,084 were safely evacuated back to the United Kingdom.

Mauriceforce, evacuating Namsos on much the same schedule, was not so lucky. Following the withdrawal from Steinkjer, the British fell back towards the port and established a defence in depth. The Germans, however, satisfied that they had sealed off the northern threat to Trondheim, dug in around Steinkjer. Mauriceforce's evacuation was thus impeded only by weather. Fog in the fjord limited the first night's embarkation to only a single battalion so the remaining 5,350 troops were loaded the second night, 2–3 May. The rearguard boarded the Tribal class destroyer HMS *Afridi* at 0430hrs, as the sun rose. At 1145hrs Heinkel He 111 and Junkers Ju 88 bombers so wrecked the French destroyer *Bison* that it had to be abandoned. German Junkers Ju 87 *Stuka* dive-bombers arrived soon after and repeatedly hit HMS *Afridi*. She too was abandoned with the loss of 100 men. Critically, the two British forces, totalling more than a division, had been beaten and driven out, largely by the German monopoly of air power. The German Air Force was indeed decisive in determining the outcome of the fighting for central Norway.

At Otta, Battle Group Pellengahr prepares for the final push to oust Sickleforce from central Norway, during 27–28 April 1940. Beyond this German mortar team position, one can observe the terrain in which the British set up their defensive positions. (© IWM, HU 93717)

THE BATTLE FOR NARVIK: LATER STAGES, 9 MAY–10 JUNE 1940

As Dietl considered withdrawing to Sweden and internment, everything changed. On 10 May, Hitler invaded the West and suddenly Narvik mattered much less. Général Béthouart's attacks north of Bjerkvik forced Dietl to evacuate the front he had long held. On the 11th and 12th, warships bombarded Ofotfjord, and Allied mountain troops plus Norwegians assaulted on a wide front. Auchinleck replaced Mackesy on the 13th but left the Narvik attacks to Béthouart to concentrate on slowing the German advance from Trondheim. Béthouart shoved the Germans back along the Rombaksfjord, and by the 21st, the German lodgement north of Narvik had largely been lost. On 28 May, Allied troops launched overland and amphibious assaults which took the town of Narvik. However, on 31 May, Churchill ordered the troops home because of the dire situation in France. Allied ships evacuated Narvik on 7 June. A week later, the first of the German volunteer relief force from Trondheim linked up with Dietl's men.

The Ground Battle for Narvik (14 April–31 May)

As German forces overwhelmed Allied efforts in central Norway, the Allies closed in on Narvik. The British 24th Brigade began landing at Harstad, some 55km (34 miles) from Narvik, on 14 April. Initially, the brigade relieved Norwegian units, freeing them to fight the Germans. Maj Gen Mackesy faithfully fulfilled his orders to establish a base from which to launch an advance upon Narvik. Unfortunately, this contravened Whitehall's, and the overall commander's, desire for an immediate amphibious landing at Narvik. Consequently, GenLt Dietl was given plenty of time to incorporate 1,600 sailors, organise his defences, and be reinforced by air. Dietl defended a long perimeter with two battalions along the northern front and the third defending along the shores of the Ofotfjord and the Beisfjord. The naval regiment, armed with Norwegian weapons captured at Elvegårdsmoen, guarded the fjord shorelines as well as the railway line along the south shore of the Rombaksfjord from Narvik to Sildvik.

Within this perimeter was the frozen Lake Hartvigvatn. On 13 April ten German Junkers Ju 52/3m transport aircraft landed on the lake, bringing in four 75mm mountain guns. However, only one transport returned. In addition, 85 Junkers Ju 52/3ms based at Trondheim's Værnes airfield flew 387 airlift sorties, dropping 528 troops, including a battalion of German Fallschirmjäger fresh from combat in Holland as well as 66 Gebirgsjäger who had completed a ten-day parachuting course. Thirteen transport aircraft were lost during the airlift operation.

On 23 April, the Norwegians attacked to retake Narvik. While their assault at Lapphaug Pass was repulsed, another battalion crossed the western mountain range and captured Gratangsbotn. However, a snowstorm suspended the attack, allowing the Germans to reinforce and retake Gratangsbotn. Thereafter a stalemate ensued. Lord Cork flirted with a direct assault on Narvik. On 24 April, HMS *Warspite*, three cruisers and a destroyer bombarded the town to provide a diversion

SWEDEN

Olsborg

6 No

XX

No 16

6 No

XX

Fossbakken

Lapphaug

Salangsdalen

Gratangsbotn

Gratangen

Labergdal

Ose

No 14

9–10 Jun

Schleebrugge

139

25 Jun

139

139

139

139

9–10 Jun

Lake Hartvatn

Elvegård

Bjerkvik

Fr

Fr

Fr

Herjangsfjord

Rombaksfjord

Narvik

13 Fr.

13 May

20–21 May

28 May

Irish Guards

Bogen

Bogen Inlet

14 May to Bodø

Skånland

RN Anchorage

Ofotfjord

Ankenes

Håkvik

2nd South Wales Borderers

28 May

Beisfjord

9 Jun

139

139

31 May

29–30 May

Lake Storvatn

Podhale Pol

Ballangen

Bjørnfjell

Fjøm Norddalen 31 May

10 Jun

Sildvik

Northern Command Br

XXX

Harstad

Bodø

Front line 21 May
Front line 30 May
Front line 1 June
Front line 2 June
Swedish (neutral)

5 miles

5km

0
0

for the Norwegian offensive in Lapphaug Pass. In case the opportunity arose Mackesy had embarked the Irish Guards on the repair ship *Vindictive* to go ashore and secure the port. In snowy, tempestuous conditions the bombardment had little effect and German surrender did not occur. Landing troops from open boats and advancing uphill in hip-deep snow was deemed to be suicidal.

Despite their victories at Lapphaug and Gratangsbotn, the Germans evacuated both positions on 26–27 April to shorten their lines. The same day the British finally moved against the enemy, the 2nd South Wales Borderers sailing to Ballangen on the south side of the Ofotfjord. Three days later they travelled by water to Håkvik and advanced along the shore road to Båtberget where they were halted by the Germans.

On 28 April the French 27e Demi-Brigade Chasseurs Alpins arrived and manned an outpost line from Håkvik to Lake Storvatn to protect the British flank. The energetic, dynamic, and aggressive Général de Brigade Béthouart was eager immediately to engage the enemy. His other two battalions joined the Norwegians in the north and attacked Labergdal Pass on 4 May and the Germans finally gave up the position six days later.

By this time, the German subjugation of central Norway was complete and the German Fliegerkorps X moved its forces to Værnes to resume the battle between bombers and ships. The first unit based there was the German path-finding Bomber Wing (*Kampfgeschwader*) KG 100, which sank the Polish destroyer *Grom* at Narvik. Two groups of Heinkel 111 bombers and one of Junkers Ju 87 Stuka dive-bombers soon followed to arrive at Værnes. However, these could not stop the continued flow of Allied troops and on 6 May the 13e Légion Étrangère Demi-Brigade arrived, followed three days later by the 1st Polish Carpathian *Podhale* Mountain Brigade. The Poles took up positions at Båtberget, facing the Germans at Ankenes, while the legionnaires at Ballangen prepared for the Allies' first real amphibious wartime assault.

Béthouart's plan was first to occupy the northern shore of the Ofotfjord, opposite Narvik, and subsequently launch a cross-fjord assault into the town of Narvik itself. Beginning at midnight – still daylight at that latitude – on 12–13 May the battleship HMS *Resolution*, two cruisers and five destroyers shelled the area west of Bjerkvik. Then a small amphibious flotilla landed two companies and a Hotchkiss H-39 light tank. Reinforced by two more companies an hour later, the legionnaires silenced the German resistance along the shore and advanced upon Bjerkvik from the west.

The second wave, the French 2nd Legionnaire Battalion, landed at 0300hrs approximately 600m south of Bjerkvik, forming the southern arm of a pincer movement against the German stronghold. The battalion's assaults soon recaptured Elvegårdsmoen and Øyjord. From there they could look across the Ofotfjord and see the town of Narvik.

On 13 May, meanwhile, Maj Gen Auchinleck had arrived to replace Mackesy. Based on the latter's dispositions, however, Auchinleck could find no way to accelerate the Allied advance on Narvik. Additionally, there was the worrisome news of the advance of German Gebirgsjäger; these were now reinforced by the 2nd Mountain Infantry Division recently landed at Trondheim and approaching from the south to relieve Dietl's forces. Turning the Narvik enterprise over to Bèthouart, Auchinleck moved the British 24th Brigade south to Bodø to stem the advancing Germans.

This operation was plagued with misfortune. On 15 May, the troopship HMS *Chrobry* carrying the 1st Irish Guards was sunk by six Heinkel He 111s, killing the battalion commander and losing the only three Vickers Mark VI light tanks the British would have had in Norway. Similarly, the heavy cruiser HMS *Effingham* ran hard aground and had to be abandoned. Meanwhile the approaching Germans used the same tactics they had perfected in central Norway to drive back the British troops in engagement after engagement. The British finally evacuated Bodø on 31 May 1940.

Meanwhile north of Narvik, the fall of Bjerkvik collapsed the German perimeter. The Norwegians, supported by Fokker C.V-D light bombers, had been attacking for two days, pushing up the north slope of the Kuberg Plateau in deep snow. The German outpost line was driven back. In concert with the landings on the 13th, the French 27e Demi-Brigade and Norwegian troops attacked south of Labergdal Pass. The German units finally gave way when it was learned that the Allies had taken Bjerkvik in their rear; thus, the Gebirgsjäger withdrew to the south-east, allowing the Chasseurs Alpins to link up with the legionnaires the following morning.

As Bèthouart consolidated on the north shore of the Ofotfjord, he prepared for a cross-fjord assault to retake the town of Narvik. After 21 May, the air situation improved because the RAF No 263 Squadron returned to Norway with another 18 Gloster Gladiator IIs augmented by No 46 Squadron with 18 Hawker Hurricane Is, both units being based at Bardufoss. Yet the battle between German bombers and Allied ships raged on in the Ofotfjord: on 26 May the anti-aircraft cruiser HMS *Curlew* was sunk at Skånland. At 2340hrs on 27 May, four Royal Navy destroyers in Rombaksfjord shelled the assault area just east of Narvik, while two French and one Norwegian 75mm gun batteries bombarded from Øyjord.

From the bridge of HMS *Cairo*, the French Général de Brigade Béthouart monitors the progress of the assault on Narvik. He proved the most aggressive of the Allied commanders. (© IWM, HU 93730)

At midnight – but in broad daylight – 290 French Legionnaires and two H-39 light tanks landed ashore. The legionnaires pushed doggedly uphill as the next wave, the 2nd Battalion, 15th Norwegian Infantry Regiment landed and captured the high ground covering the eastern approaches. By 0400hrs the Allied beachhead was secured, but the Norwegians and legionnaires were heavily engaged in a see-saw battle with the enemy. Barrages from the destroyer HMS *Beagle* and the field guns at Øyjord finally broke German resistance.

Meanwhile Luftwaffe air attacks forced the British warships to discontinue their bombardment of the German positions: HMS *Cairo* being hit twice. The raids also delayed the landing of the 2nd Legionnaire Battalion, allowing Dietl's troops to escape eastwards, retiring up the ore railway towards Bjornfjell. At 1700hrs the Allies entered the city. Graciously, Béthouart allowed the Norwegians, led by Generalmajor Carl Fleischer, the honour of entering Narvik first.

The Final Act – the Allies Depart and Operation *Juno* (14 May–13 June)

Since the Luftwaffe could not prevent the Allies from recapturing Narvik and pressing Dietl's forces back toward the Swedish frontier, Großadmiral Raeder hoped that the remaining heavy warships of his Kriegsmarine could. Thus, Operation *Weserübung* ended as it began, with a German naval foray, codenamed Operation *Juno*.

As early as 14 May, the Kriegsmarine had proposed to sortie the battle-cruisers *Gneisenau* and *Scharnhorst*, as well as the heavy cruiser *Admiral Hipper*, to attack British shipping off Harstad. A week later Raeder suggested the concept to Hitler as a means of relieving the pressure on Narvik. By this time, the evacuation of the British Expeditionary Force from the town of Dunkirk, was in full cry. Emboldened by the German forces' amazing accomplishments in the Western campaign, Hitler consented, and the sortie was scheduled for 4 June 1940.

The precipitous collapse of the Western Front had a decisive effect on the Allies as well. On 24 May 1940 the British War Cabinet, now headed by Winston Churchill as Prime Minister, decided to abandon Norway. Lord Cork, Auchinleck and Béthouart were informed. Béthouart bravely elected to continue the final move to recapture Narvik, despite the ongoing agony of his country's defeat. However, as soon as Narvik was secure and Dietl's troops were driven back into a perimeter around Bjornfjell, the

BELOW Although the Luftwaffe continued to raid Allied shipping near Narvik – as seen here with HMS *Vindictive* under attack – they failed to notice that a full-scale Allied evacuation was well under way. (© IWM, N 248)

BOTTOM The empty British troopship *Orama* goes down as the Kriegsmarine destroyer *Hans Lody* stands close by ready to rescue the survivors. (Photo by Popperfoto via Getty Images/ Getty Images)

evacuation of 24,500 Allied troops began, organised into three convoys.

The first convoy steamed out of the Andfjord on 6 June with around 15,000 Allied troops aboard, followed the next day by a slow convoy. Adm Forbes dispatched the battleship HMS *Valiant* and four destroyers to shepherd these two convoys across the North Sea. The surplus-to-requirements liner *Orama* was sent home unescorted with the hospital ship *Atlantis*. The two RAF squadrons at Bardufoss were evacuated as well. They had flown 638 sorties and shot down 14 enemy aircraft. HMS *Glorious* arrived offshore with a reduced air group so it could accommodate all twenty surviving RAF planes. Immediately they were retrieved, the carrier, escorted by two destroyers, headed for Scapa Flow.

The main batteries of the battle-cruisers *Gneisenau* and *Scharnhorst* open fire on the Royal Navy aircraft carrier HMS *Glorious*, during 8 June 1940. (© IWM, HU 3287)

Amazingly, the Allied evacuation escaped the Germans' notice. Because the ongoing evacuation was unknown when *Adm* Marschall sailed from Kiel on 4 June 1940, he was ordered to attack Allied shipping at Harstad. His force consisted of the two battle-cruisers, one heavy cruiser, four destroyers and two torpedo boats. They slipped out of the Skaggerak and steamed northwards, unseen by the RAF. That same day Luftwaffe reconnaissance discovered the first group of troopships, but this convoy was thought to be empty hulls returning to the UK.

The next morning Marschall's force encountered the tanker *Oil Pioneer* steaming from Tromsø with only one trawler as an escort. Both were quickly sunk with only 29 survivors. Shortly afterwards the *Scharnhorst*'s floatplane discovered the *Orama* and *Atlantis* to the north and the heavy cruiser *Admiral Hipper* and the destroyers were dispatched to intercept them. The *Orama* was sunk, but because the *Atlantis* obeyed the rules of war, and sent no warning signals, it remained unmolested. It rescued 275 survivors from *Orama*. Just as the Narvik evacuation went undetected by the Luftwaffe, the presence of Adm Marschall's squadron was still unknown to the British. After two months of German naval inactivity, complacency had settled in. The *Glorious* steamed homewards sedately, with no aircraft armed or launched for scouting. Thus, the carrier was surprised at 1600hrs when the two German battle-cruisers bore down on it.

The destroyers HMS *Ardent* and HMS *Acasta* made smoke, but within minutes hits blasted the carrier and soon the ship was a blazing hulk, dead in the water and listing heavily. Hurriedly abandoned, she capsized and sank at 1740hrs The *Ardent* attacked, punching through the smokescreen to close and launch torpedoes. The battle-cruisers blasted it into a blazing wreck that rolled over and sank at 1728hrs. HMS *Acasta* attacked too and torpedoed *Scharnhorst*, but *Acasta* did not survive the attack. She sank 40 minutes later. Of the 1,559 British personnel involved in this action, tragically only 40 survived.

ALLIED FORCES IN THE RECAPTURE OF NARVIK, 12–28 MAY 1940

Note: Gridlines are shown at intervals of 1km (1,093yds)

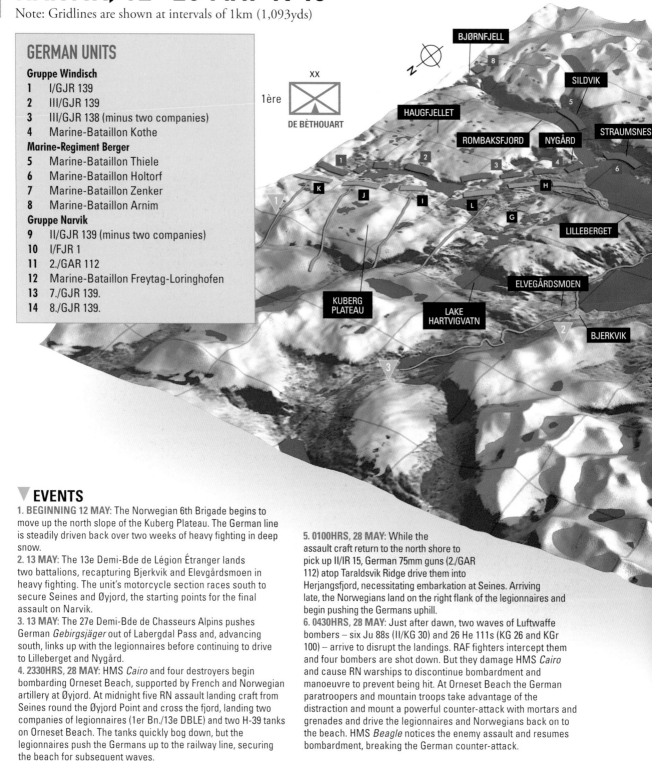

GERMAN UNITS

Gruppe Windisch
1. I/GJR 139
2. III/GJR 139
3. III/GJR 138 (minus two companies)
4. Marine-Bataillon Kothe

Marine-Regiment Berger
5. Marine-Bataillon Thiele
6. Marine-Bataillon Holtorf
7. Marine-Bataillon Zenker
8. Marine-Bataillon Arnim

Gruppe Narvik
9. II/GJR 139 (minus two companies)
10. I/FJR 1
11. 2./GAR 112
12. Marine-Bataillon Freytag-Loringhofen
13. 7./GJR 139.
14. 8./GJR 139.

1ère DE BÈTHOUART

BJØRNFJELL
SILDVIK
HAUGFJELLET
STRAUMSNES
ROMBAKSFJORD
NYGÅRD
LILLEBERGET
ELVEGÅRDSMOEN
KUBERG PLATEAU
LAKE HARTVIGVATN
BJERKVIK

▼ EVENTS

1. BEGINNING 12 MAY: The Norwegian 6th Brigade begins to move up the north slope of the Kuberg Plateau. The German line is steadily driven back over two weeks of heavy fighting in deep snow.

2. 13 MAY: The 13e Demi-Bde de Légion Étranger lands two battalions, recapturing Bjerkvik and Elevgårdsmoen in heavy fighting. The unit's motorcycle section races south to secure Seines and Øyjord, the starting points for the final assault on Narvik.

3. 13 MAY: The 27e Demi-Bde de Chasseurs Alpins pushes German *Gebirgsjäger* out of Labergdal Pass and, advancing south, links up with the legionnaires before continuing to drive to Lilleberget and Nygård.

4. 2330HRS, 28 MAY: HMS *Cairo* and four destroyers begin bombarding Orneset Beach, supported by French and Norwegian artillery at Øyjord. At midnight five RN assault landing craft from Seines round the Øyjord Point and cross the fjord, landing two companies of legionnaires (1er Bn./13e DBLE) and two H-39 tanks on Orneset Beach. The tanks quickly bog down, but the legionnaires push the Germans up to the railway line, securing the beach for subsequent waves.

5. 0100HRS, 28 MAY: While the assault craft return to the north shore to pick up II/IR 15, German 75mm guns (2./GAR 112) atop Taraldsvik Ridge drive them into Herjangsfjord, necessitating embarkation at Seines. Arriving late, the Norwegians land on the right flank of the legionnaires and begin pushing the Germans uphill.

6. 0430HRS, 28 MAY: Just after dawn, two waves of Luftwaffe bombers – six Ju 88s (II/KG 30) and 26 He 111s (KG 26 and KGr 100) – arrive to disrupt the landings. RAF fighters intercept them and four bombers are shot down. But they damage HMS *Cairo* and cause RN warships to discontinue bombardment and manoeuvre to prevent being hit. At Orneset Beach the German paratroopers and mountain troops take advantage of the distraction and mount a powerful counter-attack with mortars and grenades and drive the legionnaires and Norwegians back on to the beach. HMS *Beagle* notices the enemy assault and resumes bombardment, breaking the German counter-attack.

7. 0000HRS, 27/28 MAY: At Ankenes the Polish 2e Bn. attacks, supported by two H-39 tanks, RA 25-pdrs and HMS *Southampton's* gunfire. Despite the support, the attack is repulsed and a seesaw battle develops with a ferocious German counter-attack at 0700hrs. However, by noon the Poles have stabilised the situation and as the heights above the town are taken the Germans retreat to Nyborg and evacuate in small boats. The Poles' 1er Bn pushes down the ridgeline and descended upon Beisfjord village to cut off the German escape route.

8. 0700HRS, 28 MAY: After the Luftwaffe air attacks, the legionnaires' 2e Bn and three more H-39s are landed on the right flank of Orneset Beach and begin pushing towards Narvik, about midday taking the northern heights overlooking the railway station. After a day of hard fighting, Maj Haussels decides the town can no longer be defended and orders the German units to retreat overland to the east. At 1700hrs the Norwegian troops enter Narvik. Meanwhile the legionnaires' motorcycle section races down to Beisfjord village to link up with the advancing Polish Brigade.

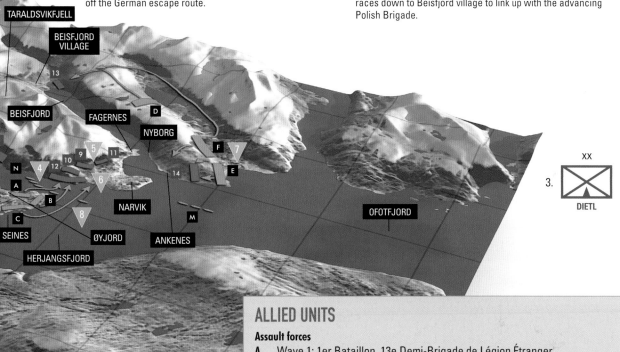

ALLIED UNITS

Assault forces

A   Wave 1: 1er Bataillon, 13e Demi-Brigade de Légion Étranger

B   Wave. 2: II/Infantry Regiment 15, Norwegian 6th Infantry Brigade

C   Wave 3: 2e Bataillon, 13e Demi-Brigade de Légion Étranger
Supporting units: Two batteries 2e Groupe Autonome d'Artillerie Coloniale and Norwegian 10th Motorised Artillery Battery; 342e Compagnie Autonome de Chars de Combat (platoons assigned to various infantry units)

Polish Podhale Bde

D   1er Bataillon

E   2e Bataillon

F   4e Bataillon

French 27e Demi-Brigade Chasseurs Alpins

G   6e Bataillon

H   14e Bataillon
Supporting units: 2e Groupe Autonome d'Artillerie Coloniale

Norwegian units

I   I/IR 14

J   II/IR 16

K   I/IR 16

L   Alta Battalion

Royal Naval units

M   Zone 1 (off Ankenes): Light cruiser HMS *Southampton*, anti-aircraft (AA) cruiser HMS *Coventry*, destroyer HMS *Firedrake*

N   Zone 2 (off Narvik and Orneset Beach) AA Cruiser HMS *Cairo* (flagship), destroyers HMS *Beagle*, HMS *Fame*, HMS *Havelock* and HMS *Walker*, AA sloop *Stork*

FAA Skua Attack on the *Scharnhorst* in Trondheimfjord, 13 June 1940

In an effort to extract some retribution for the loss of HMS *Glorious*, and to attempt a repeat of the FAA's brilliant dive-bombing victory over the *Königsberg* at Bergen two months prior, at 0100hrs on 13 June 1940 HMS *Ark Royal* launched 15 Blackburn Skua dive-bombers **(1)** to attack the Kriegsmarine's battle squadron while it rode peacefully at anchor at Trondheim Harbour following Operation *Juno*. Led by Lt Cdr John Casson, the formation approached from the north at 0243hrs, in clear skies and broad daylight typical of the northerly latitude and time of year. Alerted by the premature arrival of RAF Beauforts attacking Værnes airfield, Messerschmitts were airborne and attacked the incoming raiders over the fjord, forcing a confusing series of defensive reactions. Approaching the target – the battlecruiser *Scharnhorst* **(2)** – Casson led No 803 NAS in their diving attacks first and lost four aircraft, including his

own, shot down. Capt R. T. Partridge followed with No 800 NAS, diving into a maelstrom of flak from the ship below. His bomb missed, but his wingman, Lt Kenneth Spurway, followed suit and placed his 500lb SAP bomb **(3)** on the starboard side abaft the funnel. Unfortunately, it failed to detonate. Capt Partridge was shot down during egress, to become a POW for the rest of the war. Spurway and the second wingman, PO (Airman) H. A. Monk, escaped seawards, but the next three Skuas were all shot down, bringing the total to eight aircraft lost and no damaging hits achieved. For the Blackburn Skua, this was its last hurrah. Because of high attrition rates, it was withdrawn from frontline service shortly afterwards. (Artwork by John White, © Osprey Publishing)

As Marschall sailed his two capital ships toward Trondheim, the second group of Allied troopships departed the Andfjord. This evacuation force carried some 10,000 troops, escorted by the anti-aircraft cruiser HMS *Coventry* and two destroyers. They were joined by HMS *Ark Royal*, HMS *Southampton* and three destroyers. Aboard the cruiser were Lord Cork, Auchinleck and Béthouart. From Tromsø the cruiser HMS *Devonshire* sailed on its own with King Håkon, his government and Genermajor Carl Fleischer aboard. Incredibly, it was not until

HMS *Valiant* met *Atlantis* the next day that the Royal Navy realised Marschall's squadron had been at large in the area. That day Genermajor Ruge disbanded the Norwegian Army and reluctantly began negotiations to surrender his nation to the Germans.

There was still one air operation to be played out before the campaign ended. With the two German battle-cruisers anchored in the Trondheimfjord, the Royal Navy hoped to repeat its initial success against berthed warships by sending in its Blackburn B-24 Skua dive-bombers to inflict hopefully crippling damage. On 13 June, the Home Fleet steamed within attack range and HMS *Ark Royal* launched 15 Blackburn B-24 Skuas. This time, however, none of the advantages possessed two months before existed. A pre-emptive attack on Værnes by RAF Beaufort twin-engine fighter-bombers only alerted the Germans. In response Messerschmitt Bf 109Es and Bf 110s scrambled. Meanwhile the two British Fleet Air Arm squadrons encountered heavy anti-aircraft fire and were savaged by Messerschmitts, with eight B-24 Skuas shot down. Only one bomb hit the *Scharnhorst* and it failed to explode.

The various Allied amphibious assaults and ground advances were assisted by a company of 15 Hotchkiss H-39 French light tanks. Seen here, one is ready for evacuation after the battle. (© IWM, N 228)

THE AFTERMATH

By 28 July 1940, the battered operational remnants of the German battle fleet – just one battle-cruiser, one heavy cruiser, a light cruiser and four destroyers – arrived back at Kiel harbour. Some 15 of the 22 major German warships committed to the invasion of Norway had failed to return. Großadmiral Raeder had previously asserted that the capture of Norway's key port facilities was worth the loss of half his fleet: the cost was even more than that! Operation *Weserübung* certainly was a German operational success: Denmark and Norway were absorbed into the Third Reich's empire of occupation. German military efficiency and superiority, in all but the navy, conquered Norway in only 60 days despite brave Norwegian resistance, the efforts of the Royal Navy, and the commitment of the first Allied expeditionary force of World War II.

But the Kriegsmarine was crippled during its Norwegian adventure, losing one (of two) heavy cruisers, two (of six) light cruisers, ten (of 20) destroyers and six U-boats. It would never recover the operational strength that it possed prior to the execution of Operation *Weserübung*. On the return to Kiel harbour on 20 June 1940, the *Gneisenau* was torpedoed and, like her sister *Scharnhorst*, this put her in dry dock for the rest of 1940. Consequently, the Kriegsmarine was reduced to a solitary heavy cruiser, two light cruisers and four destroyers being in an operational state. Crucially the heavy losses incurred during the execution of Operation *Weserübung* rendered impossible the contemplated German September 1940 cross-Channel invasion of England.

Nevertheless, the Germans reaped some significant operational advantages from securing Norway: safe deep anchorages for their few remaining capital ships, from which they could threaten the Allied convoy route to the USSR during the dark days of 1942–43. The Germans also obtained excellently located U-Boat bases. Yet, the campaign accelerated the demise of the German surface fleet. From the seeds sown in the crippling losses of Operation *Weserübung*, Hitler gradually lost faith in the navy's surface fleet and from January 1943 he placed his faith in unrestricted submarine warfare. This left Raeder superfluous and on 30 January 1943 Großadmiral Karl Dönitz, head of the U-boat arm, replaced him as leader of the Kriegsmarine.

On land the price of holding their conquests proved costlier than the acquisition. Most of Gen d.Inf von Falkenhorst's divisions remained in Norway to protect the precious prize right through until the war's end in May 1945. In Denmark, the Nazi's supposed 'model protectorate', much of the population actively opposed the German occupation. By August 1943 the activities of the Danish resistance provoked a severe crackdown from the approximately 170,000 German occupation troops located in the country.

On the other hand, the British showing in their first face-to-face combat with the Germans was dismal. Taken by surprise, the British handed the initiative to a determined enemy. The British forces were hamstrung by slipshod operational planning and ineffective command arrangements. The Germans defeated them in detail on the ground, and the British proved incapable of countering the Luftwaffe in the air. Indeed, despite some promising examples of courageous valour on land, in the air and at sea, the spring 1940 Norwegian campaign painfully revealed that the British had a lot to learn about modern warfare.

The Allied surface warship losses incurred – one heavy cruiser, one anti-aircraft cruiser, ten destroyers and sloops, and five submarines – could be sustained. But the loss of HMS *Glorious* – one of only four Royal Navy carriers in service – was a particularly hard blow. The lack of carrier-based fighters and the ineffectiveness of shipboard anti-aircraft guns proved to be the foremost maritime lessons. These would take years – and much American materiel – to correct.

In the final analysis Operation *Weserübung* was a costly enterprise that benefitted the victor to only a modest degree. But as a joint campaign it set the standard for all other air-land-sea offensives that followed it, including the Allies' successful return to the European Continent in D-Day's Operation *Neptune/ Overlord*. Thus, while Operation *Weserübung* may have cost a lot and benefitted Germany only modestly, it taught valuable lessons to Hitler's adversaries, lessons that were eventually used to break the Nazi grip on Western Europe.

THE BATTLEFIELD TODAY

On the battlefields of Norway and Denmark little evidence remains today of the tumultuous struggle that occurred there some 70 years ago. This is principally because of the post-war growth of the cities and towns at which these bitter clashes occurred. As a result, since 1945 there has been considerable development of businesses and urban neighbourhoods across the battlefields where these tactical actions took place. For example, the pivotal location at Fornebu Airport, close to the Norwegian capital, Oslo, was closed in 1998 and is now an extensive business park.

There are exceptions to this general rule, however. Because of its isolation, the town of Narvik provides the battlefields most unchanged by the expanse of human progress in the 70 years since these actions raged. For example, the Post Pier, the site of the initial landings of the Gebirgsjäger, still stands, minus one of its buildings destroyed by an errant British torpedo on 13 April 1940. The most significant original structure in the town is the ore railway power station, which is little changed in its form since 1940, except for its new roof. Orneset Beach, just to the east of town, where the Légion Étrangère and the Norwegian 15th Infantry Regiment came ashore to recapture Narvik, is largely unchanged.

Farther to the east, at the village of Sildvik on the south shore of Rombakfjord, the rusted prow of the last remaining operational German destroyer – the valiant *Georg Thiele* (Z2) – can be viewed jutting from the water where it was run ashore ending the desperate battle of 13 April. Finally, a solitary Hotchkiss H-39 tank – among other artefacts from the conflict – can be viewed in Narvik at the Nordland Red Cross War Museum, which is well worth a visit.

Most resilient to post-1945 change have been the concrete bunkers and gun emplacements that formed part of the Norwegian coastal artillery fort network. For example, at Oscarsborg the embrasures and ancient 28cm guns that helped sink the German heavy cruiser *Blücher* can still be seen. However, the fortress remains in use as a training centre, so access is limited and must be coordinated in advance.

Some of the most significant elements of the campaign have been preserved in museums. The most important of these establishments is the *Forsvarsmuseet* (the Norwegian Armed Forces Historical Museum). This is located at the old Fort Akershus, the ancient bastion that guarded Oslo's inner harbour, which also served as the depot base of the Norwegian 1st Infantry Division back in spring 1940. Norwegian army and naval armaments from 1940, and even some German equipment such as an Enigma machine and a Henschel Hs 293 guided missile can be seen there. The *Forsvarsmuseet*'s historical aircraft collection is located at Gardermoen. This airfield was the former depot station of the Norwegian 2nd Infantry Division, and now it has become Oslo's commercial airport.

3

THE SPRING 1940 WESTERN CAMPAIGN

PHASE ONE:
THE CHARGE TO THE SEA (10–20 MAY 1940)

THE ORIGINS OF THE CAMPAIGN

After the Germans invaded Poland on 1 September, two days later France and Britain declared war on the Third Reich. Next, from 7 to 12 September the French Army mounted a half-hearted offensive into the German Saar region, to distract the Germans from completing their crushing campaign in Poland. This had little effect, and the Germans achieved stunning initial success in their war against Poland. Indeed, just hours after the Polish Army besieged in Warsaw surrendered on 27 September 1939, Adolf Hitler announced to his senior commanders his intent to invade France via the territory of Belgium and the Dutch salient of Maastricht. His aim was to reach the Channel coast and thus inflict strategic defeat on France, which could also serve as a foundation for a possible future invasion of the United Kingdom. He wished to end the war in the West decisively, so that he could turn his thoughts to conquering the Soviet Union.

Concerned about Western Allied rearmament, on 9 October Hitler directed the three service chiefs to plan a pre-emptive invasion to be launched as soon as possible and in the greatest possible strength. On 19 October 1939, the OKH (Army High Command) chief of staff Gen d.Art (later GenObst) Halder presented the *Fall Gelb* (Case Yellow) plan. Slated to commence in November, the hasty plan envisaged a direct frontal attack by the 56 German infantry divisions forces then stationed in the west and reinforced by nine newly arrived or recently formed Panzer (armoured) divisions.

OPPOSITE After the Germans had successfully smashed through the defences at Sedan, large numbers of French soldiers were taken prisoner. Here some of these are seen marching eastward toward a German assembly camp on 14 May 1940. (Photo by ullstein bild/ ullstein bild via Getty Images)

The initial versions of the plan envisaged the main thrust was to be through central Belgium with armoured, motorised troops on the northern wing, mountain troops advancing through the Ardennes region on the southern flank, and airborne forces landing in the rear. In the north, GenObst von Bock's Army Group B (some 43 divisions in four armies, plus two air-delivered divisions) was to cross the Maas/ Meuse between Nijmegen and Namur and drive to the Channel coast. Dutch neutrality was to be respected, except for the necessity of transiting the 'Maastricht Appendix' (a sliver of the Netherlands on the east bank of the Maas descending south between Belgium and Germany), which GenObst von Reichenau's Sixth Army had to cross in order to bypass the Liège fortresses to the north, while GenObst von Kluge's Fourth Army skirted Liège to the south. These two armies – including nine Panzer and four motorised divisions – would link up west of Liège and advance together through Brussels and Charleroi to Calais and Boulogne in France.

In the German centre, GenObst von Rundstedt's Army Group A (22 divisions in the Twelfth and Sixteenth Armies) was to protect Bock's left flank from French attacks from the south-west. In the south, facing the indomitable Maginot Line, the role of GenObst Ritter von Leeb's Army Group C was primarily defensive, holding the Rhine and preventing a more determined replay of the French offensive into the Saar. In addition, by mounting a feint threat against the powerful French forces deployed along the Maginot Line, Army Group C prevented the French from redeploying forces to halt Gen d.Kav von Kleist's armoured assault through the Allied centre. Leeb's command fielded the 25 divisions of the German First and Seventh Armies. Dedicated air support for the planned German ground offensive would be provided by Luftflotten 1, 2 and 3.

None of the participants – the OKH, the Luftwaffe, the army group commanders, nor even Hitler – were particularly content with the plan as then conceived. GenLt von Manstein gennant Lewinski, Rundstedt's Chief of Staff, criticised the extant plan as a crude frontal attack to gain territory that lacked both the intent and the appropriate dispositions to deliver decisive strategic victory. Rundstedt agreed with these views and both senior officers pressed the OKH for a change in the plan. They urged a shift of the *Schwerpunkt* (Main Effort) of the invasion to the offensive's southern wing – where, coincidentally, their area of operations was situated.

Subsequently, during November 1939 Hitler too began tinkering with the original plans. He suggested adding a two-division mechanised corps to Army Group A to make a penetration via Arlon, Belgium, cross the River Meuse at Sedan, and attack towards the town of Laon; this would facilitate Army Group B's

The Nazi leader Adolf Hitler was the driving force behind the 1940 invasion of the West. He believed that Blitzkrieg was an effective way to realise his aggressive foreign policy of territorial conquest. Here the Führer is seen making an impassioned speech in the late 1930s. (Photo courtesy of the Libraries and Archives Canada, PA-130023)

advance beyond Liège. This led the OKH to allocate Gen d.Pztr Guderian's XIX Corps (Motorised) to Army Group A. Guderian's role in the assault was added to *Fall Gelb* as an amendment.

Subsequently, Guderian, Rundstedt and Manstein all badgered the OKH to assign a third, heavily-armoured, army to their Army Group A. The OKH, however, felt that a large body of mobile forces could not move through the icy, snow-clogged, narrow and winding roads of the Ardennes region during winter. Next, in January 1940 the aircraft carrying *Maj* Reinberger mistakenly made an emergency landing at Mechelen, on the Belgian frontier. Belgian police arrested Reinberger before he could destroy the plans he carried detailing the Luftwaffe's part in *Fall Gelb*. Despite the compromising of their plans, the continuing concerns about the impassability of the Ardennes in winter led the OKH to continue sticking with the original plan.

However, the Chief of the German General Staff, GenObst Halder, remained gravely concerned about the vulnerable southern flank of the offensive. Likewise, Hitler feared that the Panzers' advance would be stopped by the Allies along the River Maas and around the Liège fortified region. The Führer predicted that these armoured formations would be much better employed in the area around the town of Sedan, where the enemy would least expect them.

Subsequently, during February the OKH developed Manstein's envisaged *Sichelschnitt* (Cut of the Scythe) plan into a new version, finalised by 24 February 1940. This made Rundstedt's Army Group A in the German centre the point of main effort. This command's operations were to be spearheaded by Panzer Group Kleist – an army-level formation controlling no fewer than five Panzer and three motorised infantry divisions. Army Group B's powerful secondary effort into northern Belgium and the Netherlands would trigger France's defensive Dyle Plan, pulling France's strategic reserves into the north and fixing them there. Meanwhile, Army Group C's feints against the Maginot Line would keep these powerful French forces in the south. Then the Germans would make the killer blow in the centre; Kleist's armoured army would infiltrate through the weakly-defended Ardennes, smash across the River Meuse and race toward the Channel coast.

Erich von Manstein is credited as being one of the chief architects of the final, revised *Fall Gelb* plans. In his subsequent career he had outstanding successes on the Eastern Front before his subordinate commands became caught in the winter 1942–43 setbacks at Stalingrad and in the Donbass. (Photo by Photo12/Universal Images Group via Getty Images)

CHRONOLOGY: 1940 WESTERN CAMPAIGN (PHASE ONE: *FALL GELB*)

1939

1 September	Germany invades Poland, starting World War II in Europe.
3 September	Britain and France declare war on Germany.
10 September	The BEF begins arriving in France.
27 September	OKW initial planning conference for the assault on the West.

9 October	Hitler's *Weisung* (War Directive) Nr. 6 orders the OKH to begin planning for the invasion of northern France and the Low Countries.
19–29 October	OKH produces the original and revised *Fall Gelb* plan for the future Western offensive.
24 October	Army Group A headquarters established at Koblenz.
31 October	Army Group A memorandum sent to OKH urging a complete change in the concept of operations of the *Fall Gelb* plan – it is rejected.
14 November	The OKW directs the OKH to include the conquest of Holland in *Fall Gelb* plan, amplified the following day with amending directive specifying an offensive up to the Dutch Grebbe Line.
15 November	Général d'Armée Maurice Gamelin, the Supreme Commander of Allied Armies, adopts the Dyle Plan designed to meet the German invasion in Belgium while the Maginot Line holds the French frontier.
20 November	Hitler's Weisung Nr. 8 orders the OKH planning to be flexible enough to shift the *Schwerpunkt* (Main Effort) if the opportunity for greater success in the south presents itself.
1940	
10 January	A German courier aircraft mistakenly lands near Mechelen, Belgium, and copies of the airborne portion of the *Fall Gelb* plan are captured.

The German invasion of the Netherlands was spearheaded by the Luftwaffe's Fallschirmjäger (paratroopers) and Luftlandetruppen (air-landing troops). These forces seized key depth targets well behind the front line. (© IWM, MH 8059)

25 January	The *Fall Gelb* plan is revised to include the occupation of Holland.
7, 14 February	The German Army Group A's 'war games' convince OKH Chief of Staff, Halder, that a major revision of the *Fall Gelb* plan is necessary.
17 February	At a luncheon Hitler hears Manstein's recommendation to shift the *Schwerpunkt* of *Fall Gelb* to Army Group A.
18 February	Halder delivers to Hitler a rewritten draft of the OKH *Fall Gelb* plan, which places the *Schwerpunkt* of the attack through the Ardennes – Hitler orders the *Fall Gelb* directive to be changed accordingly.
24 February	Hitler signs the *Aufmarschanweisung Nr 4 Fall Gelb* (Campaign Instruction No 4, Case Yellow) deployment order.
20 March	Général Gamelin adopts the Dyle (Breda Variant) Plan, designed to meet the German invasion in Belgium while the Maginot Line holds the French frontier.
9 April	German naval units, army divisions, and Luftwaffe squadrons begin the invasion of Denmark and Norway.
10 May	*Fall Gelb* – German invasion of the West – begins.
11 May	The BEF and French 1ère Armée (First Army) begin to arrive at their intended positions on the Dyle Line.
12–13 May	The Battle of Gembloux, focusing Allied attention in the north while German Panzers approach through the Ardennes region in the south.
12–14 May	The Battle of Dinant – Rommel crosses the Meuse against a disorganised French defence.
13–14 May	The Battle of Sedan – Guderian's Panzer divisions overwhelm the unprepared French defences. Général d'Armée Huntziger's forces withdraw southward; Guderian's forces break out toward the west.
14–15 May	Reinhardt's forces cross the River Meuse at Monthermé and advance to the town of Montcornet; the German breakout from the Meuse bridgeheads begins.
16 May	Rundstedt's first *Haltbefehl* (Halt Order) is issued; this is ignored by Guderian's spearhead Panzer units.
17, 19 May	De Gaulle's armoured counter-attacks have no effect on the German advances.
18 May	Following a crisis in command, Guderian is allowed to continue a 'reconnaissance in force'. BEF orders non-essential personnel evacuated from the port towns of Boulogne, Calais and Dunkirk.

19 May	Gamelin is replaced by Général Weygand. Kleist's Panzers are released from the *Haltbefehl* to continue advance toward the coast. The BEF, the French 1ère Armée, and the Belgian Army establish a new defensive line on the Scheldt/ Escaut river. The BEF's Air Component (BEF-AC) evacuates to England.
20 May	The forward detachments of Guderian's Panzers reach the English Channel near Abbeville, cutting off all Allied forces north of the River Somme.

THE OPPOSING COMMANDERS

The German Commanders

GenObst Gerd von Rundstedt commanded Army Group A during the 1940 campaign. Born in 1875 into the military aristocracy, he served as an infantry company commander and a corps' chief of staff during the Great War. After a short retirement from 1938 to 1939, he was recalled to command an army group in the Polish campaign. Despite his age, Rundstedt was a resourceful and widely-respected commander. A military traditionalist, he remained suspicious of the subsequently termed Blitzkrieg armoured tactics. Thus, when the OKH grouped five Panzer and three motorised infantry divisions into one armoured phalanx under his command, it also searched for a more traditional commander who could rein in the aggressive young Panzer generals.

This the OKH found in **Gen d.Kav Ewald von Kleist**, who had retired in 1938. The scion of a famous *Junker* (aristocractic) military family, he rose to command a cavalry regiment during World War I. Recalled to duty, during the 1939 Polish campaign he commanded the German XXII Corps, which fielded two mobile divisions. Experienced in handling armour but considered tactically conservative, he had the balance that the OKH thought necessary to control a difficult subordinate like Heinz Guderian.

Aggressive and temperamental, **Gen d.Pztr Heinz Guderian** was commissioned in 1908. During World War I he commanded a cavalry signals company and was then appointed to the elite Greater General Staff. In 1922 he joined the Reichwehr's Army Troop Bureau as a staff officer in the Inspectorate of Transportation Troops. Enthused by mobile warfare tactics, during 1931 he took command of the Reichwehr's experimental motorised battalion. He promoted his radical theories of deep penetrating armoured thrusts in his book *Achtung – Panzer!* (1937). By then he and others had developed decisive armoured attack tactics: massed tank assaults penetrating deep into the enemy's rear areas to paralyze their command and control, using air attacks as 'flying artillery' and accompanied by motorised infantry. During the 1939 Polish campaign his XIX Corps (Motorised) daringly executed a deep and wide envelopment of the enemy's Northern Front.

GenMaj Erwin Johannes Eugen Rommel performed superbly as an audacious armoured commander during the 1940 campaign. Originally an infantry officer, his aggressive leadership during the World War I Battle of Caporetto on the Italian Front won him the coveted *Pour le Mérite*. His proximity to Hitler from 1937 to 1939 benefitted his career; he commanded the Führer Headquarters Escort Battalion. As a reward, Hitler subsequently appointed Rommel as commander of the coveted 7th Panzer Division in Gen d.Inf Hermann Hoth's XV Corps (Motorised).

The 60-year-old **GenObst Fedor von Bock** commanded Army Group B during the Western campaign. Born into the Prussian military aristocracy in 1880, he was commissioned in 1898, and won the *Pour le Mérite* leading a battalion in World War I. Promoted to Generaloberst in 1938, he commanded Army Group North during the 1939 Polish campaign.

Serving in GenObst Walter von Reichenau's Sixth Army, **Gen d.Kav Erich Hoepner** had commanded the German XVI Corps (Motorised) during the autumn 1939 invasion of Poland. Born in 1886, Hoepner was a career cavalry officer who became an early supporter of the Nazi movement. An early advocate of mechanisation, Hoepner proved a successful commander during both the 1939 Polish and 1940 Western campaigns.

Luftwaffe GenLt Kurt Student controlled the airborne forces that spearheaded Army Group B's operations in the Netherlands. Born on 12 May 1890, he was commissioned as an infantry lieutenant, but soon joined the fledgling Imperial German Flying Corps. During the Weimar years he became an avid military glider enthusiast. After joining the newly-established German Air Force in 1934, he spearheaded the development of Germany's embryonic parachute, glider, and air-landing troops. From 1939 to 1940 GenMaj Kurt Student first assumed command of 7th *Flieger* (Flyers) Division and then subsequently became the Inspector of Parachute and Air-landing Forces.

ABOVE Erwin Rommel was a very ambitious commander who exploited his personal relationship with Hitler to get a coveted Panzer division command for the 1940 campaign. During these battles his fast-paced, audacious, and risk-embracing command style did much to realise the vision of Blitzkrieg. (Photo by Albert Harlingue/ Roger Viollet via Getty Images)

The Allied Commanders

The French Commanders

Général d'Armée Maurice Gamelin was France's Chief of the General Staff and the Allied Supreme land forces commander. Commissioned in 1891, he became in 1916 France's youngest and most capable divisional commander. Steeped in the Great War's successful – though costly – defensive tactics, he was uninterested in technology and thus failed to assimilate the mobile warfare concepts that emerged during the next two decades. Gamelin was a politically adroit,

In this image the Allied Supreme Commander, the French Général d'Armée Maurice Gamelin, inspects the formed-up ranks of a Francophone Canadian infantry battalion, the Royal 22e Régiment, at their barracks in Aldershot in the UK, on 28 March 1940. (Photo courtesy of the Libraries and Archives Canada, PA-034157)

intellectually superior and professionally detached officer. Not a leader of men, he preferred to be thought of as a 'philosopher general' who managed resources and composed plans. Ensconced in his HQ on Paris's eastern outskirts – close to political power – he eschewed radios for fear that the Germans could locate his HQ by their transmissions. Instead he relied on the slower national telephone and telegraph network and motorcycle dispatch-riders to communicate with his *Grand Quartier Général* (GQG).

Général d'Armée Alphonse-Joseph Georges was the French commander responsible for conducting the ground war. As commander of *Théâtre d'Opérations du Nord-Est* (TONE) he coordinated the operations of the three groups of armies that controlled the entire front from the Channel coast to the Swiss border. Général Georges had risen through professional merit and many considered him to be France's finest soldier. Temperamentally different to Gamelin, Georges served on Foch's staff during World War I. During the 1930s, however, the Foch-Georges relationship significantly deteriorated.

Général d'Armée Gaston-Henri Billotte commanded the Groupe d'Armées 1. This command controlled four subordinate French armies plus the BEF, arrayed to the critical front between the towns of Lille and Longuyon. He focused on commanding the two French armies and BEF that were advancing into Belgium and southern Holland; he thus neglected the Second and Ninth Armies that held the front along the River Meuse.

Commanding the French 2e Armée (Second Army) – at the hinge of the French line swinging into Belgium – was **Général d'Armée Charles Huntziger**.

Commissioned in 1901, Huntziger had significant combat experience both before and during World War I. Considered another brilliant intellect, Huntziger secured rapid promotion. He was also arrogant and complacent and thus lacked interest in considering alternatives to the 'proven' concept of unbroken linear defence.

Commanding the French 9e Armée (Ninth Army) – which was to move into southern Belgium and defend the River Meuse – was **Général d'Armée André Georges Corap**, a 62-year-old Norman who had spent most of his career serving in North Africa. He graduated first of his intake from Saint-Cyr in 1898 and served in the Great War as a staff officer. During the late 1930s Corap headed the somnolent 2e *Région Militaire* around Amiens and in September 1939 he was assigned the supposedly peripheral Ardennes sector. Ignorant of modern mechanised warfare, he failed to anticipate the sheer speed and combat power that Kleist's Panzers would unleash upon his sluggish, largely reservist infantry formations.

Commanding France's strongest military formation – the highly mobile 1ère Armée (First Army) – was **Général d'Armée Jean Georges Blanchard**. A career artillerist, during World War I he served in frontline positions before being assigned to Marshal Joffre's staff. Promoted rapidly through the general officer ranks in the 1930s, Blanchard was a smart, astute, and studious leader with a scientific approach to solving military problems.

The French senior commander who later replaced Jean Georges Blanchard as commander of the 1ère Armée was **Général de Corps René Jacques Adolphe Prioux**. He was a career cavalryman in the truest, most traditional sense of the word. But once acceptance of motorised and mechanised vehicles could no longer be avoided, Prioux became one of France's most talented and resourceful cavalry commanders during the interwar period. In 1940 he was the logical choice to direct the French Army's elite *Corps de Cavalerie* (the Cavalry Corps). This command consisted of the the 2e and 3e *Divisions Légères Mécaniques* (or DLM, 2nd and 3rd Light Mechanised (Armoured Cavalry) Divisions). In effect, René

BELOW LEFT During May 1940 Général Alphonse-Joseph Georges commanded the French North-eastern Theatre Headquarters. Here, on 18 August 1939, Georges (right) has returned to Paris with British Prime Minister Winston Churchill after a tour of the Maginot Line. (Photo by Topical Press Agency/Hulton Archive/Getty Images)

BELOW RIGHT Général d'Armée Gaston-Henri Gustave Billotte commanded the Groupe d'Armées 1, which felt the full force of the German invasion. His actions failed to prevent the Panzer wedge that had got across the River Meuse from charging west to reach the Channel coast on the 20th; the next day he was tragically killed in a road accident. (Photo by Keystone/Stringer/Hulton Archive/Getty Images)

British General Lord Gort (left) commanded with skill the operations of the BEF in France. The surprising triumph of the evacuation from Dunkirk (26 May–4 June) saved his command from annihilation. Here he is seen conversing with General Dill (centre) and his corps commander Alan Brooke (right). (© IWM, F 2027)

Prioux's command operated as France's only permanently-established armoured corps. Adhering completely to the cavalry side of the French Army's bifurcated armour doctrine, however, René Prioux used his tanks as he had horse-mounted cavalry – as screens, for reconnaissance, and in mounted charges.

The British Commanders

Born in Ireland in 1886, **Lord Gort** (the 6th Viscount Gort of Limerick) commanded the British forces in France. After completing his education at Harrow school, in 1905 he was commissioned into the Grenadier Guards. During the Great War, as a battalion commander, he was wounded four times, being awarded the Victoria Cross and two Distinguished Service Orders. A large, burly man, Lord Gort was the inspiring vision of a born fighter and was selected as the new Chief of the Imperial General Staff (CIGS), having jumped over several more senior generals in doing so. Once World War II began, he was given the coveted command of the BEF that had been deployed to France. Lord Gort proved to be a decisive leader of the BEF.

The Belgian Commanders

The Belgian Army Chief of the General Staff (CGS) from 1935 to 1939, *Lieutenant-Général* (**Lt Gen**) **Édouard Van den Bergen** was responsible for defence planning up through the Mechelen Incident. During this episode he brought the army to full alert, recalled around 80,000 troops from winter leave through radio broadcasts, and opened the French border to allow the Allies unimpeded entry – all without the consent of the Belgian monarch, King Léopold III. As the army's official Commander-in-Chief, the king took umbrage at this and in January 1940 he demoted Bergen merely to command V Corps.

Lieutenant-Général Raoul van Overstraeten was King Léopold's aide-de-camp (ADC) and chief military advisor in 1940. He attended the *École Royale Militaire* (the Belgian Royal Military Academy) in 1902 and graduated into the horse artillery branch. At the start of the Great War, Overstraeten had a Cavalry Division staff officer appointment and was involved in the Belgian resistance against the German invasion. Later in that global conflict he served in the successful Allied East African campaign. Subsequently, he rose to command the Belgian Horse Artillery branch, became the ADC for the Belgian Minister of Defence, and commanded the *École de Guerre* (War College) before being selected as King Léopold's ADC.

The Belgian king, **Léopold III,** had been educated in the United Kingdom at Eton College, and then had gone on to study at Ghent University. By 1940 he had been on the throne only six years. Although he had seen action as a private soldier in the Belgian 12e Régiment during the Great War, he could hardly be considered experienced in military matters. Despite this, constitutionally he remained the Commander-in-Chief of the Belgian Armed Forces.

The Dutch Commanders

As the war-clouds gathered over Europe during August 1939, the Dutch Armed Forces began their general mobilisation. This process required the reactivation of the office of the Supreme Commander of the Royal Dutch Armed Forces. Being a woman, the 60-year-old monarch, Queen Wilhelmina, constitutionally could not assume this office. Consequently, this responsibility was then invested in the Chief of the Dutch General Staff, *Generaal* (Gen) **Izaak H. Reijnders**. However, six months later Reijnders resigned. The Dutch government disagreed with his attempts to establish a continuous defensive line by extending the southern flank to join the Belgians. The government also refused funding for his construction of modern fortifications in both the main and secondary defensive lines. After his resignation, his roles were taken over by Generaal Henri Winkelman.

In May 1940 the 64-year-old formerly retired **Generaal Henri Winkelman** was Chief of the Dutch General Staff (CGS) and the Supreme Commander of the Royal Dutch Armed Forces. An infantry officer commissioned in 1896, during the mid-1930s Winkelman commanded 4e Divisie before retiring when he was passed over for the CGS position. Elderly and conventional, Winkelman based his defence on the traditional Dutch system of static positions behind rivers, canals, and inundations.

Léopold III, King of the Belgians, was officially the Commander-in-Chief of the Belgian Armed Forces. He had served briefly as an Other Rank in the Great War, but was hardly a military expert. He keenly defended his titular authority, however, demoting Lieutnant-General Van den Bergen in early 1940 when the latter mobilised without gaining the King's consent. (© IWM, HU 48971)

THE OPPOSING GROUND PLANS

The German *Fall Gelb* Plan

The German *Fall Gelb* plan was a detailed deployment order designed to launch the initial phase of Nazi Germany's campaign to eliminate the Western democracies from the European conflict. It was the first of two intended operations – the second one being *Fall Rot* – that between them would conquer France, Belgium, Luxembourg and the Netherlands; the Italian invasion of south-eastern France, designated *Fall Braun* (Case Brown), would assist *Fall Rot*. *Fall Gelb* envisaged operations that would overwhelm the entire northern half of the Western Front; thus it aimed to capture all of Dutch and Belgian territory, as well as most of northern France.

Indeed, the *Fall Gelb* invasion plan consisted of four parallel simultaneous elements. Firstly, GenObst Ritter von Leeb's German Army Group C would stage a powerful feint, backed by limited attacks, against the Maginot Line fortifications to pin the 24 divisions of French interval troops to their positions,

THE EVOLUTION OF THE FINAL GERMAN *FALL GELB* INVASION PLAN

After going through three major adjustments, the final version of the *Fall Gelb* plan for the invasion of the West, finalised in late February 1940, has become known as *Sichelschnitt* (Cut of the Scythe). It comprised four key elements: (1) Army Group B's northern forces would mount a combined air assault and ground invasion of the Netherlands. (2) This command's southern forces would charge into central Belgium and smash into the advancing British and French forces then executing the Dyle-Breda Plan. (3) Simultaneously, Army Group C would mount an offensive feint against the Maginot Line in Alsace-Lorraine. (4) Finally, Army Group A – forming the German covert main effort – would attack southern Belgian and the Ardennes region around the French-Belgian-Luxembourg border region.

and thus prevent them being able to counter-attack the southern flank of the German breakthrough in the Ardennes region. Second, there would be an airborne invasion of the Netherlands by the Luftwaffe's *Luftlandekorps* (Airborne Corps), with ground relief provided by Gen d.Art von Küchler's Eighteenth Army (from Bock's Army Group B). Third, there would be a strong advance through central Belgium spearheaded by GenObst von Reichenau's Sixth Army (again from Army Group B), which was designed to convince the Allied command that it was the German main thrust. Fourth and last, there would be an advance – as the covert German main effort – through Luxembourg and southern Belgium by the armoured formations of GenObst von Rundstedt's

The German invasion plan envisaged that Army Group C would only mount a feint attack against the powerful French Maginot Line fortifications, fixing considerable French troops in the south of the theatre of operations. Indeed, only well into the follow-up assault, *Fall Rot*, did German forces actually attacked the Maginot Line en masse. Here a German assault team attacks a Maginot Line bunker with a flame-thrower in mid-June 1940. (DE AGOSTINI PICTURE LIBRARY via Getty Images)

Fortified lines
Maginot Line
Lesser defensive lines
Case Yellow, 19 October 1939
Case Yellow, 29 October 1939
Case Yellow, 30 January 1940
Case Yellow, 24 February 1940

0   50 miles
0   50km

N

NETHERLANDS

Emden

Groningen

Kornwederzand Wons Line

Meppel

IJsselmeer

Amsterdam

IJssel

Gronau

North Sea

NL   I   IV   X

The Hague   Lek   II   Grebe Line

Arnhem

Rotterdam   *Waal*   *Maas*   XXVI

Moerdijk Bridges   III   Peel Line   Rhine   18   XXII

Breda   IX   XI

GERMANY

Bruges   Antwerp   V   Albert Canal   XVI   Düsseldorf

Ghent   IV   II   I   XIX

BELGIUM   Be   Cologne

Dunkirk   Dyle   XXVII   XIV

Louvain   Maastricht

I   H Res Br   Lille   VI Res   Brussels   Fort Eben Emael   XVI

Aachen

Gembloux   Liège   V   XV   XXI   A

16   Lijs   Escaut   VII   III   Meuse   VIII   II   XVIII   XIX   Koblenz

I Br   Sambre   Namur   Ourthe   XLI   12   Mosel

III Res Br   Arras   3   Dinant   III   XIV

Cav   Maubeuge   Givet   ChA   VII

Cambrai   4   5   Monthermé   *Ardennes Forest*   LUX.   XIII   XXXXX   C

Abbeville   11   *Semoise*   Trier   XXIII   1

Amiens   41   Sedan   10   18   Longwy   XXX

Somme   24   Saarbrücken

Compiègne   *Aisne*   Verdun   42   Co   III   XXIV

FRANCE   Reims   Metz   6

Seine   9   20

La Ferté-sous-Jouarre   *Marne*   *Meuse*

Paris   Nancy

Strasbourg

Oise   *Semoise*   *Moselle*   *Saar*

Army Group A; these were grouped together as Panzer Group Kleist. This element's aim was to achieve a major breakthrough between the town of Sedan, in France, and that of Dinant, in Belgium. The effectiveness of this fourth element depended on how convincing the third facet was.

In addition, Army Group B's 'Matador's Cloak' – the second facet – was a separate entity designated Operation *F*. This effort to eliminate the Dutch swiftly from the Allies' war effort involved 6,500 troops from the 22nd *Luftlande* (Air-landing) Division securing three key airfields around The Hague; they would then storm the Dutch capital to capture the government and the High Command, thereby securing a prompt Dutch capitulation. Meanwhile, additional troops from Luftwaffe GenLt Kurt Student's 7th Flieger Division would secure the bridges spanning the rivers that formed the south side of 'Fortress Holland', as well as an airfield at Rotterdam. This would open the way for a motorised corps to relieve the lightly-armed air assault forces. In short, the Germans intended to conquer Holland using the largest airborne assault thus far in the history of warfare.

This Matador's Cloak envisaged that GenObst von Reichenau's Sixth Army would overrun the Belgian defences deployed along the River Maas. To achieve this Reichenau's army command controlled no less than five subordinate commands: The three infantry divisions of GenLt von Both's I Corps; the one Panzer formation and the two infantry divisions of Gen d.Inf von Schwedler's IV Corps; Gen d.Inf Geyer's IX Corps, with a further three divisions under command; GenLt von Kortzfleisch's XI Corps with three divisions; and finally the two divisions of XXVII Corps, led by Genl d.Inf Wäger.

This German assault on the Belgian defences would be facilitated by glider-borne forces seizing three bridges near Maastricht as well as neutralising the powerful Belgian fortress of Fort Eben Emael. Once this 'door' had been 'kicked in', the Sixth Army's final subordinate command – Gen d.Kav Hoepner's XVI Corps (Motorised) – would drive deep into central Belgium. The Panzers would charge for the open space between the Dyle and Meuse rivers – the Gembloux Gap. If the Allies took the bait, the Panzers and the trailing infantry corps would be met by the Allies' best mobile forces – the BEF and the French 1ère Armée. These forces would thus be fixed in this contact battle, and would not be able to redeploy to block Army Group A's Panzer divisions as they approached the River Meuse around Sedan after infiltrating through the thickly forested, hilly and winding roads of the Ardennes.

Army Group A's massed armour – controlled by Panzer Group Kleist – was to advance through the Ardennes region's difficult terrain and then assault the Meuse river defences. Once across, the Panzers would daringly charge westward toward the Channel coast. This rapid exploitation would encircle the French Groupe d'Armées 1 in the north and pin them against the coastline. This Panzer envelopment would thus create a *Kesselschlacht* (Cauldron Battle) which would lead to the capitulation of the entire Allied north. Army Group A's following-up infantry formations would secure the Panzer advance's southern flank by assuming defensive positions along the Aisne and Somme rivers.

Panzer Group Kleist fielded two Panzer and one motorised corps, advancing in file through the Ardennes terrain, one corps after another. Guderian's XIX Corps (Motorised), consisting of three Panzer divisions, spearheaded the German attack. The Corps' operational mantra became: 'It will take us three days to the River Meuse, and on the fourth day we will be across the Meuse.' Next in the line of advance came GenLt Reinhardt's XLI Corps (Motorised) with two Panzer and a motorised infantry division. Security for the Panzers' left (southern) flank was provided by the two motorised infantry divisions fielded by Gen d.Inf von Wietersheim's XIV Corps (Motorised). This armoured blow was aimed at the hinge point between Général d'Armée Huntziger's relatively-static French 2e Armée and Général Corap's forward-deploying French 9e Armée, much of which had to move across southern Belgium to occupy defensive positions along the Meuse.

Following the Panzers came Army Group A's marching infantry formations. These formations hustled forward to prevent gaps from forming behind the advancing Panzers, and deployed to the left, first along the River Aisne, then later the River Somme, to protect the southern flank of the armoured thrust.

As soon as the Germans attacked on 10 May, the BEF advanced north to the River Dyle in Belgium as planned. Here a British Universal Carrier, towing an Ordnance QF 2-pdr Mk IX anti-tank gun, is being welcomed by a group of Belgian civilians. The British troops are driving through Herseaux on their way to the Dyle. (© IWM, F 4345)

Three German higher commands controlled these 22 divisions: GenObst List's German Twelfth Army, Gen d.Inf Busch's Sixteenth Army, and GenObst von Kluge's Fourth Army. In addition, a further 45 divisions remained in the OKH reserve. On Guderian's right (northern) flank the two Panzer divisions of Hoth's XV Corps (Motorised) were to advance. This move by elements of the Fourth Army ensured that the Allied mobile forces in Belgium could not strike the Panzer spearhead's northern flank.

The French Dyle Plan

French perception was that if a German invasion did ever occur, it would be in the north, into neutral Belgium and northern France, since the Maginot Line fortifications were perceived invincible. The French Plan D, therefore, envisaged the best Allied formations racing north into Belgium as soon as the invasion commenced. From his secret cursory November 1939 contacts with the neutral Belgian Army staff, Gamelin knew that their planned defence line was along the Albert Canal and River Maas, extending in a salient from Antwerp to Liège to Namur. However, Gamelin knew that his mobile forces could not reach this line before German mobile units overwhelmed the defending Belgians. Therefore Gamelin decided on a shorter and straighter defensive line. This ran from the port city of Antwerp through the towns of Louvain and Wavre on to Namur, Givet, and Sedan. He calculated that two of his three motorised armies (the French 1ère Armée and the BEF) could reach this line and establish a defence if the Belgians held the Germans along the Albert and Maas lines for up to seven days. The Louvain–Wavre sector was anchored on the Dyle river, and thus this deployment order became Plan D.

However, in the early springtime Gamelin became worried that the Allied plan needlessly sacrificed the Netherlands. Believing that including the small Dutch Army in the Allies' overall defensive array would force the Germans to divert forces to their northern flank, Gamelin detailed his mobile reserve to link up with the Dutch north-east of Antwerp, at Breda. Consequently, Général d'Armée Giraud's Seventh Army was transferred to the far north end of the Allied line, a position from which it would race to Breda. This change rendered it unavailable to counter any German breakthroughs, wherever they might occur. On 20 March this revised Dyle (Breda Variant) Plan was issued.

From the line of the Dyle–Meuse rivers Gamelin intended to employ the French Army doctrine of the Methodical Battle whereby the defender's advantages, especially in firepower (artillery and machine guns), coupled with an involved 'deliberate planning' process, were expected to halt the German advance. In case of a breach in the continuous line of battle his riposte was the plugging of the gap by moving reserves into the path of the enemy breakthrough.

THE OPPOSING FORCES

The German Forces

German Ground Forces

The German ground forces that executed the 1940 invasion of the West were divided into three army group commands. From north to south these were GenObst von Bock's Army Group B, GenObst von Rundstedt's Army Group A and GenObst Ritter von Leeb's Army Group C. Army Group B was deployed against the Dutch border and the northern half of the Belgian border. Army Group A was concentrated in the central sector against southern Belgium and Luxembourg. Finally, Leeb's Army Group C was deployed opposite the Maginot Line fortifications from Luxembourg down to the Swiss border.

The invasion of the Netherlands and northern Belgium was Bock's Army Group B's responsibility. Across the northern flank the Luftwaffe's 7th Flieger Division spearheaded operations. This formation's *Gruppe Nord* (Group North) was to parachute on to the three airfields around The Hague and secure them for the arrival of elements from GenLt von Sponeck's 22nd *Luftlande* (Air-landing) Division. Meanwhile, the German *Gruppe Süd* (Group South) was to secure the river bridges at Moerdijk, Dordrecht, and Rotterdam, as well as seize an airfield near Rotterdam. At the same time, GenLt Wobig's XXVI Corps would cross the Maas between Nijmegen and Maastricht and penetrate the Peel Line. This would open up the way for GenLt Dr Alfred Ritter von Hubicki's 9th Panzer Division to race westwards to the relieve the paratroopers holding the bridges leading to Rotterdam.

As the 'Matador's Cloak', GenObst von Reichenau's Sixth Army executed a fundamentally separate mission. The Sixth Army was organised into five corps commands that between them contained two Panzer and 18 infantry divisions. GenLt Stever's 4th Panzer Division would make the breakthrough thrust at Maastricht and across the Albert Canal. Once the door to Belgium had been 'kicked in' through this attack, Gen d.Kav Hoepner's XVI Corps (Motorised) would move forward and charge westward, thus realising the planned diversionary thrust into central Belgium.

Hoepner's corps command controlled GenMaj Stumpff's 3rd Panzer Division as well as GenLt von Wiktorin's 20th Motorised Infantry Division. Between them the Sixth Army's spearhead – the 3rd and 4th Panzer Divisions – fielded a total of 606 tanks. This mass of armour included 252

Although the under-gunned and poorly-armoured PzKpfw II light tank was barely fit for combat by 1940, the Wehrmacht still employed them in large numbers for scouting, screening and reconnaissance duties. By 1944 only a handful remained, like this one seen in France, mainly in command tank variants. (Photo courtesy of the Libraries and Archives Canada, PA-115750)

A German tank column advances through a northern Belgian village during May 1940. The unit seen here would seem to be following up behind the spearheads; the crews apparently perceive that the enemy threat level is relatively low, as they are not battened down in their hatches. (LAPI/Roger Viollet via Getty Images)

obsolete machine-gun armed PzKpfw I tanks, 234 PzKpfw II old light tanks, 80 PzKpfw III medium tanks and 48 heavy PzKpfw IVs. The rapid advance of these two Panzer formations was perfect for creating the impression of a major mechanised offensive into the Belgian plain.

The German central sector was controlled by Army Group A. This command controlled the campaign's main effort, spearheaded by Panzer Group Kleist. This powerful army-level concentration of five Panzer and three motorised infantry divisions controlled three mobile corps. Each of these three corps advanced through the Ardennes region in file ahead, with Guderian's XIX Corps (Motorised) leading the way. Guderian's three Panzer divisions between them fielded 745 armoured fighting vehicles, of which 174 were PzKpfw III medium tanks. While the PzKpfw III Ausf. E and Ausf. Fs were technically slightly inferior to equivalent French tanks, tactically they proved more effective. German tanks possessed commanders who were situated high in the turret, with a dedicated optical system for greater situational awareness; a dedicated two-man gun crew; an internal intercom system to control the vehicle; and a radio to manoeuvre with other tanks in his unit. Additionally, the PzKpfw III's electrical system, gunsight, speed and manoeuvrability were all superior to its French adversary. Guderian's forces were augmented by 104 PzKpfw IV fire-support tanks and by 467 PzKpfw I and II light tanks, fit only for screening duties.

Behind Guderian's spearhead divisions came the second echelon – the 6th and 8th Panzer Divisions of GenLt Reinhardt's XLI Corps. These two formations were equipped with 234 Czech-built PzKpfw 35(t) and 38(t) tanks. These 10-ton vehicles were classified as light tanks, but their 30mm armour and 3.7cm main guns made them the combat equivalent of the PzKpfw III. They were augmented by 120 PzKpfw Is and IIs, as well as by 47 PzKpfw IV heavy tanks.

Echeloned to the north of Guderian's spearhead was Gen d.Inf Hoth's XV Corps (Motorised). This command fielded GenLt von Hartlieb gennant Walsporn's 5th Panzer Division and GenMaj Rommel's 7th Panzer Division. Between them these two potent mobile formations fielded a total of 462 tanks. This included 52 PzKpfw III medium, 91 PzKpfw 38(t) medium and PzKpfw IV heavy tanks, as well as 319 semi-obsolete PzKpfw I and II light tanks. As a result, Kleist's five Panzer and three motorised infantry divisions created a densely packed 80km (50 mile) wide armoured wedge that fielded no less than 1,664 tanks. This total included 906 light, 551 medium and 207 heavy tanks. This mighty German armoured phalanx formed the greatest concentration of mechanised forces yet seen in warfare.

Finally, across the southern sector were deployed the 25 infantry divisions of Leeb's Army Group C. This command controlled the front that stretched from Luxembourg down to the Swiss border. The command's mission was to mount a feigned threat against the Maginot Line fortifications. This would fix the powerful French forces located both in the Maginot Line and behind it, thus preventing them being redeployed to threaten the German southern flank as the Panzers raced westward to the Channel coast.

The Luftwaffe

An entire Luftwaffe Luftflotte provided dedicated support to the two spearhead German army groups. Gen d.Flg Kesselring's Luftflotte 2 assisted the operations mounted by Bock's Army Group B across the Netherlands and northern Belgium. Meanwhile, Gen d.Flg Sperrle's Luftflotte 3 supported Army Group A. Kesselring's Luftflotte 2 comprised four subordinate commands: 2nd Fighter Command; *Fliegerkorps* zbV (the Special-Purpose Air Corps), Fliegerkorps IV; and Fliegerkorps VIII. The 233 Messerschmitt Bf 109 and 92 Messerschmitt Bf 110 fighters of *Jagdfliegerführer* 2 (JFF 2, the 2nd Fighter Command) were to provide air cover for the air landing missions. Similarly, supporting these air-assault sorties, the Fliegerkorps zbV fielded 149 combat-ready Heinkel 111 and 21 Junkers Ju 88 bombers, together with some 37 Junkers Ju 87 Stuka dive-bombers. General Kesselring's two other Fliegerkorps supported Reichenau's advance into central Belgium. The 135 He 111Hs and Ps, as well as 86 Junkers Ju 88A bombers of Fliegerkorps IV attacked distant Allied airfields, depots and railways. Meanwhile, the 198 Junkers Ju 87B, 38 Henschel Hs 123A and 83 Do 17Z bombers, plus the 115 Messerschmitt Bf 109Es fighters, of Fliegerkorps VIII provided battlefield interdiction and close air support for the ground advance.

Luftflotte 3 consisted of Jagdfliegerführer 3 (JFF 3, the 3rd Fighter Command) and three bomber Fliegerkorps (Flying Corps). On 10 May 1940 Luftflotte 3 fielded 482 serviceable Messerschmitt Bf 109E single-engine fighters and 74 Bf 110C/Ds twin-engine heavy ones. In addition, it also fielded 72 reconnaissance aircraft and 302 Heinkel He 111, 22 Junkers Ju 88A and 264 Dornier Do-17 bombers, plus 103 Junkers Ju 87B Stuka dive-bombers. Do 17Z crews exploited the platform's exceptional manoeuvrability to execute ultra-low level 1,000kg bomb strikes on enemy airfields, command centres, troop concentrations and motorised columns. Delivering its five bombs with deadly precision, the Stuka psychologically terrorised enemy personnel.

The Allied Forces

GenObst von Bock's Army Group B faced two French infantry-based formations – the French 1ère and 7e Armées (First and Seventh Armies), together with the BEF, and the hitherto neutral Belgian and Dutch Armies. Unlike the two French armies defending the River Meuse south of Namur, the 1ère and 7e Armées were the most mobile commands within the French land forces. Jean Georges Blanchard's First Army consisted of seven active-duty infantry divisions, including motorised and Colonial formations. They would be screened by the rapid forward deployment of the Corps de Cavalerie. Consisting of the cavalry branch's 2e and 3e Divisions Légères Mécaniques, or DLMs, this was the only Allied command that resembled a German Panzer corps.

The French had two distinct armoured formations and doctrines: the heavy, slow, infantry-supporting *Divisions Cuirassées* (DCr, or armoured divisions) and the cavalry arm's well-balanced, fast, and powerful Divisions Légères Mécaniques. All three DLMs fielded an armoured brigade (two tank regiments plus motorised infantry, reconnaissance, and artillery regiments), plus the usual supporting units. A typical French armoured regiment consisted of 84 tanks, including 44 S35 cavalry tanks as well as 44 Hotchkiss H35 and H39 light infantry-support tanks.

ABOVE During the 1940 campaign, General der Flieger Hugo Sperrle commanded Luftflotte 3, which supported Army Group A's ground operations. Subsequently, in the rank of Generalfeldmarschall, his Luftflotte 3 defended Germany from the Allied Strategic Bomber Offensive and attempted to repel the 1944 Normandy landings. In autumn 1944 he was dismissed and put on the Führer reserve. (Photo by PhotoQuest/Getty Images)

RIGHT Each of the three regular French Divisions Cuirassée (DCr) – heavy infantry-support armoured divisions – fielded 68 Char Renault B1 bis heavy tanks. This Char B1 bis is seen moving up towards the front line in mid-May 1940. (Photo by Keystone-France/Gamma-Keystone via Getty Images)

The SOMUA S35 was a fast, long-ranged and powerfully armed, well-armoured tank able to deliver the cavalry arm's traditional roles of reconnaissance, screening, and mounted charges. Powered by a 190hp petrol engine, the 21.4-ton vehicle could travel 230km (143 miles) at up to a maximum speed of 40km/h (25 mph). It mounted an excellent high-velocity 47mm SA-35 L/34 turret cannon and coaxial 7.5mm M31 machine gun. It was protected by 35–55mm (1.37–1.97in.) armour. However, the otherwise superior design was hamstrung by the lack of radios at the platoon level.

Each French mechanised light division fielded 88 SOMUA S35s as well as 87 Hotchkiss H35 and H39 tanks in its combat brigade, as well as a reconnaissance regiment. Each division also had a motorised infantry regiment of 3,088 truck-mounted troops backed by 63 Renault AMR 33 and AMR 35 tankettes or Hotchkiss H35 and H39 infantry-support tanks, and 12 25mm anti-tank guns. The unit's reinforced motorised artillery provided 24 light (75mm) and 24 medium (105mm) guns, eight 47mm anti-tank guns and a small battery of 25mm anti-aircraft guns. Altogether, the Corps de Cavalerie was more than a match for Hoepner's XVI Corps (Motorised).

Général d'Armée Giraud's Seventh Army had the separate mission of linking up with the Dutch forces at Breda. It was a smaller version of the 1ère Armée, consisting of Général Picard's 1ère Division Légère Mécanique and the 9e, 21e and 25e *Divisions d'Infanterie Motorisée* (DIM, or motorised infantry divisions), together with two marching infantry divisions.

The contribution of the BEF to Plan D was for its seven infantry divisions to establish a defensive line between Louvain and Wavre in central Belgium. The British 1st Army Tank Brigade, as well as two mechanised reconnaissance brigades, remained in reserve. Two British Territorial (reservist) divisions and three lines of communications divisions would be left in France. Each of the BEF's three corps

The British 1st Army Tank Brigade deployed 77 machine gun-armed Matilda I infantry tanks. Here two Matilda Is of the 4th Battalion, the Royal Tank Regiment are undergoing maintenance, seemingly for the benefit of the photographer. (© IWM, O 747)

had sufficient motor transport to move one division each day. Each corps fielded an impressive 2,472 artillery pieces, though few of these were modern. The BEF's two light armoured reconnaissance brigades each fielded 56 machine-gun-armed Vickers Mk VIb tankettes and 88 Universal Carriers. Meanwhile, the 1st Army Tank Brigade deployed 77 Matilda I and 23 Matilda II infantry-support tanks. Whereas the Mk Is merely carried machine guns, the 26.5-ton Matilda Mk IIs mounted a 2-pounder (40mm) gun and sported 75mm-thick armour plate.

Général d'Armée Huntziger's 2e Armée and Général Corap's 9e Armée defended the western bank of the River Meuse, facing the assault of Rundstedt's Panzer spearheads. Confident that the Ardennes' forests, hills, ravines and narrow winding roads fundamentally hampered a large-scale mechanised invasion, the French frontier fortifications from La Ferté to Givet along Belgium's south-western border were the weakest. This was the very sector where these two infantry-based armies were stationed.

The westward continuation of the Maginot Line fortifications along the Meuse's western bank comprised a string of concrete blockhouses each manned by an infantry section from the Montmédy Fortified Sector; these well-trained fortress troops possessed high morale. In the sector adjacent to the town of Sedan the French 147th Régiment d'Infanterie de Forteresse manned eight blockhouses and 46 pillboxes. Behind them, on the La Marfée heights another 16 casemates were under construction to create defensive depth. Part of Huntziger's French 2e Armée, Général Lafontaine's French 55th Infantry Division defended the Sedan sector. Meanwhile, screening to the east, along the Semois river and into the forested and hilly Ardennes region, were two French *Divisions Légères de Cavalerie* (DLCs, light cavalry divisions). In reserve, Huntziger had three battalions of Renault R-35 light infantry-support tanks and a horse-mounted cavalry brigade.

Corap's Ninth Army, which was to advance across south-western Belgium to occupy its positions on the River Meuse, was of similar composition. The command fielded two regular and four reservist infantry divisions, one fortress division and two motorised-cavalry divisions, plus a North African *Spahis* horse-mounted brigade. His reserves consisted of two Renault R-35 tank battalions and an FT-equipped light tank battalion. Corap's front-line troops were generously supported with artillery, including 300 75mm light field guns, as well as 108 105mm pieces and 192 155mm guns; most of these, however, were horse-drawn. Corap's front-line infantry, moreover, were supported by 243 Renault R-35 and FCM-36 light infantry-support tanks. These modern 10.43/ 12.15-ton vehicles sported a 37mm cannon and a single 7.5mm coaxial machine-gun. The French attached three-tank platoons of these tanks to infantry battalions, which the massed Panzer columns easily overwhelmed.

The French GQG's strategic reserve of 13 infantry divisions were spread out behind the front, as were three Divisions Cuirassées of *Groupement Cuirassé* 'K' (the Armoured Group Keller). Each DCr comprised 68 Char B1 bis heavy tanks, 90 Hotchkiss H-39 light tanks, a truck-mounted infantry battalion, and a tractor-towed artillery regiment. The 31-ton Char B1 bis was the French infantry's primary weapon for counter-attacking enemy breakthroughs. This heavily armoured tank sported a hull-mounted, short-barrelled 75mm bunker-busting howitzer, and a turret-mounted 47mm tank-killing cannon. However, the Char B1 bis was hampered because it was slow, possessed limited operational range, used high-octane aviation gasoline, and had archaic gunsights.

The Allied Air Forces

Within the *Armée de l'Air* (AdA, French Air Force), FACNE (the Air Forces for Cooperation with the North-eastern Front) provided aerial cover for Général Georges' TONE armies. Within FACNE, ZOAN (*Zone d'Operations Aériennes Nord* or North Air Operations Zone) fielded 1,250 French and British aircraft. However, ZOAN's 11 fighter squadrons were distributed right across the front.

Fielding 50 Morane Saulnier MS-406s, 25 Curtiss H75s and 10 Potez 631s, Groupement de Chasse No 23 supported Huntziger's and Corap's armies. Moreover, ZOAN's 1st Air Division controlled most of the AdA's meagre available bomber force; it fielded just 14 LeO 451, 17 obsolete Amiot, and 25 Breguet 693 aircraft. Some 20 of the AdA's 33 bomber groups, however, remained unavailable to support TONE's armies as they were re-equipping in southern France. The RAF's

During the campaign the French Groupement de Chasse No 23 deployed 50 Morane Saulnier MS-406 aircraft. Entering service in 1939, the MS-406 was a highly manoeuvrable and robust design. That said, it was under-gunned and under-powered in comparison with the Messerschmitt Bf 109e, which outclassed it. German fighters destroyed 122 MS-406s in air-to-air combat. (Photo by ullstein bild/ullstein bild via Getty Images)

Advanced Air Striking Force (AASF), based at airfields around the city of Reims, provided additional Allied offensive bomber capability. It fielded 110 Fairey Battle Mk I and 24 Bristol Blenheim Mk IV light bombers, together with 54 Hawker Hurricane Mk I fighter-escorts.

The Neutral Forces

In peacetime the defensively-orientated Belgian Army comprised 126,800 troops, organised into six infantry, two cavalry and four reserve divisions, two bicycle-mounted *Chasseurs Ardennais* (ChA) light infantry divisions, and the Liège and Namur Fortress Commands. After mobilisation in August 1939, the army swelled by May 1940 to 22 divisions with around 600,000 troops, although over half of these were still in training. Belgian infantry divisions fielded 24 Schneider 105mm and Ehrhardt 75mm field guns, 36 artillery pieces and 12 47mm FRC anti-tank guns. However, the infantry lacked motor transport and the artillery was horse-drawn. The two cavalry divisions were more mobile, comprising eight motorcycle-mounted and two lorried regiments, with two regiments of (24 each) truck-towed Mle06 75mm field guns. The Belgian Army attached a 12-strong unit of 47mm-gunned T-13 tank destroyers to each of its nine infantry divisions, while each of its two cavalry divisions fielded 18 T-13s alongside 18 T-15 tankettes. During April 1940, moreover, the Belgians concentrated 90 T-13s and T-15s into an ad hoc armoured brigade that was attached to the *Groepering Keyaerts* (K-Grp) in the Ardennes region. Held in reserve at Brussels, the Tank Squadron of the Belgian Corps de Cavalerie fielded eight Renault ACG-1 14.3-ton light tanks.

During early 1940 the French Armée de l'Air squadrons deployed across northern France lacked sufficient bomber aircraft capability. To compensate for this the British Royal Air Force formed the Advanced Air Striking Force (AASF). This command, deployed on French soil, fielded eight squadrons of short-range light bombers. The slow, poorly protected, and inadequately defended Fairey Battle aircraft performed disappointingly in this role. These examples are seen in flight on 1 September 1939 somewhere over England. (Photo by Fox Photos/ Stringer/ Hulton Archive/ Getty Images)

The Belgian Air Force deployed several squadrons of the out-moded Fairey Fox fighter biplane. This Belgian Air Force Fox VIc aircraft was seen at Zurich during July 1937. (Photo by Charles E. Brown/Royal Air Force Museum/Getty Images)

Organised into three regiments, the Belgian Air Force was tailored to support army operations, but primarily fielded obsolete biplanes. The 41 ancient Fairey Fox and 21 obsolescent Renard R.31 aircraft of the 1st Air Regiment provided battlefield observation. The 2nd Air Regiment's fighter aircraft included 39 Gloster Gladiators and Fiat CR.42s, 29 ancient Fox VI/ VIIIs, and 11 Hawker Hurricanes. The tactical bombers of the Belgian 3e Régiment d'Aéronautique included 37 obsolete Fox biplanes and operational Fairey Battle monoplanes.

After mobilisation in August 1939, the defensively-orientated 114,000-man *Koninklijke Landmacht* (Royal Netherlands Army) fielded eight infantry divisions and one light (cyclist) division, as well as two brigade groups; additionally, there were 24 frontier battalions and 16 blocking battalions. The 10,000-man Dutch infantry division lacked significant combat power, particularly as the entire army only fielded 310 outdated Krupp 75mm field guns and 52 Bofors 105mm howitzers, as well as 386 Böhler 47mm anti-tank guns. Moreover, the 8,500-man Light Division, the army's only mobile formation, lacked the hitting power needed to deal with mechanised units.

The Dutch Army's *Luchtvaartbrigade* (Military Aviation command) fielded 126 aircraft organised in the 1st and 2nd Aviation Regiments. The 1st Regiment's fighter force included 20 obsolete Fokker D.21s and 23 twin-engine G.1 *Jachtkruisers*. Its *Strategischegroep* (Strategic Group) deployed nine obsolescent Fokker T.5 twin-engine bombers and 10 obsolete Fokker C.10 reconnaissance biplanes. Assigned to support the army, the 2nd Aviation Regiment fielded 30 ancient Fokker C.5/C.10s, 15 Koolhoven F.K.51 observation biplanes, eight Fokker D.21s and 11 Douglas DB-8/3N two-seat attack aircraft.

THE ORDERS OF BATTLE: THE GROUND FORCES

THE GERMAN ORDER OF BATTLE (10 MAY 1940)

Army Group B – GenObst Fedor von Bock (Northern Sector)

Luftlandekorps (Luftwaffe) – GenLt Kurt Student

7th Flieger Division – (GenLt Kurt Student)

22nd Air-landing Infantry Division – (GenLt Hans von Sponeck)

SIXTH ARMY – GenObst Walter von Reichenau

I Corps – GenLt von Both

1st Infantry Division – GenMaj Philipp Kleffel

11th Infantry Division – GenLt Herbert von Böckmann

223rd Infantry Division – GenLt Paul-Willi Körner

IV Corps – Gen d.Inf Viktor von Schwedler

4th Panzer (Armoured) Division – GenLt Johann Joachim Stever

18th Infantry Division – GenLt Friedrich-Carl Cranz

35th Infantry Division – GenLt Hans Wolfgang Reinhard

IX Corps – Gen d.Inf Hermann Geyer

19th Infantry Division – GenMaj Otto von Knobelsdorff

30th Infantry Division – GenLt Kurt von Briesen

56th Infantry Division – GenMaj Karl Kriebel

XI Corps – GenLt Joachim von Kortzfleisch

7th Infantry Division – GenLt Eccard Freiherr von Gablenz

14th Infantry Division – GenLt Peter Weyer

31st Infantry Division – GenLt Rudolf Kämpfe

XVI Corps (Motorised) – Gen d.Kav Erich Hoepner

3rd Panzer (Armoured) Division – GenMaj Horst Stumpff

20th Motorised Infantry Division – Gen d.Inf Mauritz von Wiktorin

XXVII Corps – Gen d.Inf Alfred Wäger

253rd Infantry Division – GenLt Fritz Kühne

269th Infantry Division – GenMaj Ernst-Eberhard Hell

The Army Reserve:

61st Infantry Division

216th Infantry Division

255th Infantry Division

EIGHTEENTH ARMY – Gen d.Art Georg von Küchler

XXXIX Corps – GenLt Rudolf Schmidt

208th Infantry Division – GenLt Moritz Andreas

225th Infantry Division – GenLt Ernst Schaumburg

X Corps – GenLt Hansen

1st Kavallerie (Cavalry) Division – GenMaj Kurt Feldt

207th Infantry Division – GenLt Carl von Tiedemann

227th Infantry Division – GenLt Friedrich Zickwolff

Leibstandarte-SS Adolf Hitler

SS-Standarte *Der Führer*

XXVI Corps – GenLt Albert Wobig

9th Panzer (Armoured) Division – GenLt Dr Alfred Ritter von Hubicki

254th Infantry Division – GenLt Walter Behschnitt

256th Infantry Division – GenLt Gerhard Kauffmann

SS-Verfügungsdivision (Motorised) – SS-*Gruppenführer* (SS Lt Gen) Paul Hausser

ARMY GROUP A – GenObst Gerd von Rundstedt (Central Sector)

PANZER GROUP KLEIST – Gen d.Kav Ewald von Kleist

XIX Corps (Motorised) – Gen d.Pztr Heinz Guderian

1st Panzer (Armoured) Division – GenLt Friedrich Kirchner

2nd Panzer (Armoured) Division – GenLt Rudolf Veiel

10th Panzer (Armoured) Division – GenLt Ferdinand Schaal

XLI Corps (Motorised) – GenLt Georg-Hans Reinhardt

6th Panzer (Armoured) Division – GenMaj Kempf

8th Panzer (Armoured) Division – GenLt Kuntzen

2nd Motorised Infantry Division – GenLt Bader

XIV Corps (Motorised) – Gen d.Inf Wietersheim

13th Motorised Infantry Division – GenLt Rotkirch-Panthen

29th Motorised Infantry Division – GenLt Lemelsen

FOURTH ARMY – GenObst Günther von Kluge

II Corps – Gen d.Inf Strauß

12th Infantry Division – GenMaj Seydlitz-Kurzbach

32nd Infantry Division – GenLt F. Böhme

V Corps – Gen d.Inf Ruoff

251st Infantry Division – GenLt Kratzert

267th Infantry Division – Gen d.Pztr Feßmann

VIII Corps – Gen d.Art Heitz

8th Infantry Division – GenLt Koch-Erpach

28th Infantry Division – GenLt Obstfelder

XV Corps (Motorised) – Gen d.Inf Hermann Hoth

5th Panzer (Armoured) Division – GenLt Max von Hartlieb gennant Walsporn

7th Panzer (Armoured) Division – GenMaj Erwin Rommel

62nd Infantry Division – GenMaj Keiner

The Army Reserve:

4th Infantry Division

87th Infantry Division

211th Infantry Division

263rd Infantry Division

TWELFTH ARMY – GenObst Sigmund Wilhelm List

III Corps – Gen d.Art Haase

3th Infantry Division – GenLt Lichel

23th Infantry Division – GenLt Brockdorff-Ahlefeldt

VI Corps – *General der Pioniere* (General of Engineers) Förster

16th Infantry Division – GenLt Krampf

24th Infantry Division – GenMaj Tettau

XVIII Corps – Gen d.Inf Beyer

5th Infantry Division – GenLt Fahrmbacher

21st Infantry Division – GenMaj Sponheimer

25th Infantry Division – GenLt Clößner

1st Gebirgsjäger Division – GenLt Kübler

The Army Reserve:

9th Infantry Division

27th Infantry Division

SIXTEENTH ARMY – Gen d.Inf Ernst Busch

VII Corps – GenObst Eugen Ritter von Schobert

36th Infantry Division – GenLt Lindemann

68th Infantry Division – GenMaj Braun

III Corps – GenLt Heinrich von Vietinghoff gennant Scheel

17th Infantry Division – GenLt Loch

34th Infantry Division – GenLt Sanne

XXIII Corps – GenLt Schubert

58th Infantry Division – GenMaj Heunert

76th Infantry Division – GenMaj de Angelis

The Army Reserve:

6th Infantry Division

15th Infantry Division

26th Infantry Division

33th Infantry Division

52nd Infantry Division

71st Infantry Division

73rd Infantry Division

ARMY GROUP C – GenObst Wilhelm Ritter von Leeb (Southern Sector)

FIRST ARMY – GenObst Erwin von Witzleben

Higher Command XXXVII – GenLt Böhm-Tettelbach

246th Infantry Division

215th Infantry Division

262nd Infantry Division

257th Infantry Division

XXIV Corps – Gen d.Pztr Leo Freiherr Geyr von Schweppenburg

60th Infantry Division

252nd Infantry Division

168th Infantry Division

XII Corps – GenObst Gotthard Heinrici

268th Infantry Division

198th Infantry Division

XXX Corps – Gen d.Art Otto Hartmann

258th Infantry Division

93rd Infantry Division

79th Infantry Division

Higher Command XXXXV – Gen d.Inf Kurt von Greiff

95th Infantry Division

167th Infantry Division

The Army Reserve:

197th Infantry Division

SEVENTH ARMY – GenObst Friedrich Dollmann

Higher Command XXXIII – Gen d.Kav Georg Brandt

213th Infantry Division

554th Infantry Division

556th Infantry Division
239th Infantry Division
XXV Corps – Gen d.Inf Karl Ritter von Prager
557th Infantry Division
555th Infantry Division
6th Gebirgsjäger Division
The Army Reserve:
218th Infantry Division
221st Infantry Division

THE ALLIED AND NEUTRAL ORDER OF BATTLE

THE ROYAL NETHERLANDS GROUND FORCES (NEUTRAL)

KONINKLIJKE LANDMACHT (THE ROYAL NETHERLANDS
ARMY) – *GENERAAL* (GEN) HENRI WINKELMAN

VELDLEGER (THE FIELD ARMY) – *Luitenant-Generaal*
(Lt Gen) Jan Baron van Voorst tot Voors
I Legerkorps (Army Reserve) – *Generaal-Majoor*
(Maj Gen) Carstens
1e Divisie
3e Divisie
II Legerkorps – Generaal-Majoor Herberts
2e Divisie
4e Divisie
III Legerkorps – Generaal-Majoor Nijnatten
5e Divisie
6e Divisie
Lichte Divisie
IV Legerkorps – Generaal-Majoor van der Bent
7e Divisie
8e Divisie
Vesting Holland (Fortress Holland) – Luitenant-Generaal
van Andel
Grebbe Line
Peel Division
Meuse-Lek River Defence Sector
Frontier Troops Command

**ITALIAN ARMY GROUP WEST – Luogotenente Generale
del Regno D'Itali**
First Army – Generale Designato D'armata Pintor
2nd Corps – Generale di Corpo D'armata Bertini
3rd Corps – General Designato D'armata Arisio
15th Corps – General di Corpo D'armata Gambara
Fourth Army – Generale Alfredo Guzzoni
1st Corps – General di Corpo D'armata Vecchiarelli
4th Corps – General di Corpo D'armata Mercalli

THE BELGIAN GROUND FORCES (NEUTRAL)

ARMÉE BELGE (BELGIAN ARMY) – King Léopold III
Ier Corps – *Lieutenant-Général* (Lt Gen) Vanderveken
4e Division d'Infanterie
7e Division d'Infanterie
IIe Corps – Lieutenant-Général Michem
6e Division d'Infanterie
9e Division d'Infanterie
IIIe Corps – Lieutenant-Général de Krahe
2e Division d'Infanterie
3e Division d'Infanterie
Brigade Cycliste Frontiere
Forteresse de Liège
IVe Corps – Lieutenant-Général Bogaerts
11e Division d'Infanterie
12e Division d'Infanterie
15e Division d'Infanterie
18e Division d'Infanterie
Ve Corps – Lieutenant-Général Vandenbergen
13e Division d'Infanterie
17e Division d'Infanterie
VIIe Corps – Lieutenant-Général Deffontaine
2e Division Chasseurs Ardennais (ChA)
8e Division d'Infanterie
Forteresse de Namur
Corps de Cavalerie – Lieutenant-Général de Neve de Roden
1ère Division d'Infanterie
14e Division d'Infanterie

2e Division de Cavalerie

Groepering-K – Lieutenant-Général Kayerts

1ère Division de Cavalerie

1ère Division Chasseurs Ardennais

Réserve d'Armée:

VIe Corps – Lieutenant-Général Vaerstraete

5e Division d'Infanterie

10e Division d'Infanterie

FRENCH ARMY – Général d'Armée Maurice Gamelin, Commandant Suprême des Armées Alliées

THÉÂTRE D'OPÉRATIONS DU NORD-EST [TONE] – Général d'Armée Alphonse-Joseph Georges

GROUPE D'ARMÉES 1 (FIRST FRENCH ARMY GROUP) – Général d'Armée Gaston-Henri Billotte

1ÈRE ARMÉE – Général d'Armée Jean Georges Blanchard

Corps de Cavalerie – *Général de Corps* René Prioux

2e Division Légère Mécanique (2e DLM) – Général de Brigade Bougrain

3e Division Légère Mécanique (3e DLM) – Général Langlois

3e Corps Armée – Général de Corps Benoît-Léon de La Laurencie

1ère Division d'Infanterie Motorisée (1ère DIM)

2e Division d'Infanterie Nord Africaine

4e Corps Armée – Général de Corps Henri Aymes

15e Division d'Infanterie Motorisée (15e DIM)

1ère Division d'Infanterie Marocaine

5e Corps Armée – Général de Corps Altmayer

12e Division d'Infanterie Motorisée

5e Division d'Infanterie Nord-Africaine

101e Division d'Infanterie de Forteresse

Réserve d'Armée:

32e Division d'Infanterie

7E ARMÉE – Général d'Armée Henry Honoré Giraud

1er Corps Armée – Général de Corps Théodore-Marcel Sciard

25e Division d'Infanterie Motorisée (25e DIM)

16e Corps Armée – Général de Corps Marie-Bertrand-Alfred Fagalde

9e Division d'Infanterie Motorisée (9e DIM)

Secteur Fortifié (SF, Fortification Sector) des Flandres

Réserve d'Armée:

1ère Division Légère Mecanique (1ère DLM) – Général Picard

6e Division d'Infanterie

21e Division d'Infanterie

68e Division d'Infanterie

2E ARMÉE – Général d'Armée Charles Huntziger

10e Corps Armée – Général de Corps Grandsard

55e Division d'Infanterie – Général Lafontaine

3e Division d'Infanterie Nord-Africaine

18e Corps Armée – *Général de Corps* Rochard

41e Division d'Infanterie

1ère Division d'Infanterie Coloniale

3e Division d'Infanterie Coloniale

Réserve d'Armée:

2e Division Légère de Cavalerie (2e DLC)

5e Division Légère de Cavalerie (5e DLC)

1ère Brigade de Chasseurs

Secteur Fortifié (SF) de Montmédy

71e Division d'Infanterie

9e ARMÉE – Général d'Armée André Georges Corap

1ère Division Légère de Cavalerie (1ère DLC)

4e Division Légère de Cavalerie (4e DLC)

3e *Spahis* Brigade

2e Corps Armée – Général de Corps Bouffet

5e Division d'Infanterie Motorisée (5e DIM)

11e Corps Armée – Général de Corps Martin

18e Division d'Infanterie

22e Division d'Infanterie

41e Corps Armée de Forteresse – Général de Corps Libaud

61e Division d'Infanterie

102e Division d'Infanterie de Forteresse

Réserve d'Armée:

4e Division d'Infanterie Nord-Africaine

53e Division d'Infanterie

GROUPE D'ARMÉES 2 (SECOND FRENCH ARMY GROUP) –
Général d'Armée Ándre-Gaston Prételat

3e ARMÉE – Général d'Armée Condé
Directly reporting:
  3e Light Mechanised Division
  6e Division d'Infanterie
  6e Division d'Infanterie Nord-Africaine
  6e Division d'Infanterie Coloniale
  7e Division d'Infanterie
  8e Division d'Infanterie
Corps Colonial
  2e Division d'Infanterie – Général Klopfenstein
  British 51st (Highland) Infantry Division – Maj Gen Victor
    Fortune
  56e Division d'Infanterie
6e Corps Armée
  26e Division d'Infanterie
  42e Division d'Infanterie
24e Corps Armée – Général de Corps Fougère
  51e Division d'Infanterie Boell
42e Corps Armée – Général de Corps Sivot
  20e Division d'Infanterie Corbe
  58e Division d'Infanterie Perraud

4e ARMÉE – Général d'Armée Edouard Réquin
Directly reporting:
  Polish 1st Infantry Division
  45e Division d'Infanterie
9e Corps Armée – Général de Corps Laure
  11e Division d'Infanterie
  47e Division d'Infanterie – Général Mendras
20e Corps Armée – Général de Corps Hubert
  52e Division d'Infanterie
  82e African Division d'Infanterie

5e ARMÉE – Général d'Armée Victor Bourret
Directly reporting:
  44e Division d'Infanterie
8e Corps Armée
  24e Division d'Infanterie

  31e Division d'Infanterie
12e Corps Armée
  16e Division d'Infanterie
  35e Division d'Infanterie
  70e Division d'Infanterie
17e Corps Armée
  62e Division d'Infanterie
  103e Division d'Infanterie
43e Corps Armée
  30e Division d'Infanterie

GROUPE D'ARMÉES 3 (THIRD FRENCH ARMY GROUP) –
Général d'Armée Antoine Marie Benoît Besson (Maginot
Line)
8e Armée – Général d'Armée Marcel Garchery
7e Corps Armée
  13e Division d'Infanterie
  27e Division d'Infanterie
13e Corps Armée
  19e Division d'Infanterie
  54e Division d'Infanterie
  104e Division d'Infanterie
  105e Division d'Infanterie
44e Corps Armée
  67e Division d'Infanterie
45e Corps Armée
  57e Division d'Infanterie
  63e Division d'Infanterie
  Polish 2nd Infantry – Fusiliers Division

ARMÉE DES ALPES Général d'Armée René Olry
  3 x Divisions Infanterie (Reserve Type B)
  14e Corps Armée HQ
  15e Corps Armée HQ
  Secteurs Fortifié: Dauphiné, Savoie, Alpes Maritimes
  Secteurs Défense (SD, Defence Sectors): Rhône, Nice

GRAND QUARTIER GÉNÉRAL (GQG) RÉSERVES
Groupement Cuirassée – Général Keller
  1ère Division Cuirassée – Général Bruneau (1ère DCr)
  2e Division Cuirassée – Général Bruché (2e DCr)

3e Division Cuirassée – Général Brocard (3e DCr)

HQ, 21e Corps Armée – Général Flavigny

HQ, 23e Corps Armée – Général Touchon

10e Division d'Infanterie

14e Division d'Infanterie

23e Division d'Infanterie

28e Division d'Infanterie

29e Division d'Infanterie

36e Division d'Infanterie

43e Division d'Infanterie

3e Division d'Infanterie Motorisée (3e DIM)

THE BRITISH GROUND FORCES

BRITISH EXPEDITIONARY FORCE (BEF) – General Lord Gort

I Corps – Lt Gen Michael Barker

1st Division – Maj Gen Harold Alexander

2nd Division – Maj Gen Henry Loyd

48th (South Midland) Division – Maj Gen Andrew Thorne

II Corps – Lt Gen Alan Brooke

3rd Division – Maj Gen Bernard Montgomery

4th Division – Maj Gen Dudley Johnson

50th Division – Maj Gen Giffard Martel

III Corps – Lt Gen Ronald Adam

42nd (East Lancashire) Division – Maj Gen William Holmes

44th (Home Counties) Division – Maj Gen Edmund Osborne

Line of Communications Troops

12th (Eastern) Division – Maj Gen Roderic Petre

23rd (Northumbrian) Division – Maj Gen Arthur Herbert

46th (North Midland and West Riding) Division – Maj Gen Henry Curtis

General Headquarters (GHQ) Forces

5th Division – Maj Gen Franklyn

1st Army Tank Brigade

2 x Armoured Reconnaissance Brigades

51st (Highland) Division: attached French 3e Armée (behind Maginot Line)

4 x field artillery regiments, Royal Artillery (RA)

8 x medium artillery regiments, Royal Artillery

3 x heavy artillery regiments, Royal Artillery

3 x super-heavy artillery regiments, Royal Artillery

THE AIR FORCES

THE LUFTWAFFE – *Generalfeldmarschall* Herman Göring

Luftflotte 2 – Gen d.Flg Albert Kesselring (Supporting Army Group B)

Fliegerkorps zbV – GenMaj Richard Putzier

Fliegerkorps IV – Gen d.Flg Alfred Keller

Fliegerkorps VIII – GenMaj Wolfram von Richthofen

Jagdfliegerführer 1 (Jafü 'Deutsche Bucht') – ObstLt Carl Schumacher

Jagdfliegerführer 2 – GenMaj Hans von Döring

Flakkorps II – GenLt Otto Dessloch

Luftflotte 3 – Gen d.Flg Hugo Sperrle (Supporting Army Group B)

Fliegerkorps I – Gen d.Flg Ulrich Grauert

Fliegerkorps II – GenLt Bruno Loerzer

Fliegerkorps V – GenLt Robert Ritter von Greim

Jagdfliegerführer 3 – Obst Gerd von Massow

Flakkorps I – *General der Flakartillerie* (General of

Anti-aircraft Artillery) Herbert Weise

THE DUTCH AIR FORCES

***LUCHTVAARTBRIGADE* (ROYAL NETHERLANDS ARMY AVIATION BRIGADE) – LUITENANT-GENERAAL PETRUS BEST**

1e Luchtvaart Regiment (1st Army Aviation Regiment)

Ie Groep [Strategischegroep] (Strategic Group)

StratVer Vliegerskader (Strategic Reconnaissance Squadron)

Bom Vliegerskader (Bombing Squadron)

IIe Groep [Jachtgroep] (Fighter Group)

1. Jacht Vliegerskader (JaVA)

2. Jacht Vliegerskader

3. Jacht Vliegerskader

4. Jacht Vliegerskader

2e Luchtvaart Regiment

Ie Verkenningsgroep (Reconnaissance Group)

IIe Verkenningsgroep

IIIe Verkenningsgroep

IVe Verkenningsgroep

Jachtgroep, 2e Luchtvaart Regiment:

1-V- 2.LvR

3-V- 2.LvR

3e Luchtvaart Regiment

Elementary Training School   (At Vlissingen)

Advanced Training School   (At Haamstede)

Operational Training School   (At De Vlijt, Texel Island)

THE BELGIAN AIR FORCES

DÉFENCE AÉRIENNE DU TERRITOIRE (AERIAL DEFENCE COMMAND) – LIEUTENANT-GÉNÉRAL EMILE DUVIVIER

AÉRONAUTIQUE MILITAIRE BELGE (THE BELGIAN AIR FORCE) – *GÉNÉRAL-MAJOR* (MAJ GEN) HIERNAUX

1ère Régiment d'Aéronautique (Observation & Army Cooperation) – *Colonel* Foidart

Escadrille (Squadron) 1/I/1

Escadrille 3/II/1

Escadrille 5/III/1

Escadrille 7/IV/1

Escadrille 9/V/1

Escadrille 11/VI/1

2e Régiment d'Aéronautique (Fighters) – Colonel de Woelmont

Escadrille 1/I/2

Escadrille 2/I/2

Escadrille 3/II/2

Escadrille 4/II/2

Escadrille 5/III/2

Escadrille 6/III/2

3e Régiment d'Aéronautique (Reconnaissance & Bombers) – Colonel Hugon

Escadrille 1/I/3

Escadrille 3/I/3

Escadrille 5/III/3

Escadrille 7/III/3

DÉFENSE TERRESTRE CONTRE AÉRONEFS, DTCA (BELGIAN AIR DEFENCE COMMAND) – *GÉNÉRAL DE BRIGADE* (BRIG) FRÈRE

1ère Régiment d'DTCA

2e Régiment d'DTCA

ARMÉE DE L'AIR, AdA (THE FRENCH AIR FORCE) – Général Joseph Vuillemin

Forces Aériennes de Coopération du Front Nord-Est, FACNE (The Air Forces for Cooperation with the North-eastern Front) – Général Marcel Têtu

Zone d'Operations Aériennes Nord, ZOAN – Général François d'Astier de La Vigerie

Fighters

Groupement de Chasse No 23 – Général Jean Romatet

Escadrille (Squadron) GC II/2   22 x MS 406s (as of 10 May) (Allocated to 9e Armée)

Escadrille GC III/2 28 x MS 406s (Allocated to 1ère Armée)

Escadrille GC III/3   23 x MS 406s (Arrived 10 May)

Groupement de Chasse No 25 – Colonel de Moussac

Escadrille GC III/1   20 x MS 406s (Allocated to 7e Armèe)

Escadrille GC I/4   26 x H-75s (Arrived 10 May)

Escadrille GC II/8   11 x MB 152s (Coastal air defence)

Bombers:

1ère Division Aérienne – Général Escudier

Escadrille GR II/33   6 x Bloch 174s

Escadrille GR I/52   10 x Potez 637s

Groupement de Bombardement du Jour No 6 – Général Lefort

Escadrille GB I/12   7 x LeO 451s

Escadrille GB II/12   7 x LeO 451s

Groupement de Bombardement du Jour No 9 – Colonel François

Escadrille GB I/34   8 x Amiot 143s

Escadrille GB II/34   9 x Amiot 143s

Groupement de Bombardement d'Assaut No 18 – Général Girier

GBA I/54   13 x Breguet 693s

GBA II/54   12 x Breguet 693s

Strategic Reconnaissance:

Escadrille GR II/33 13 x Potez 637/63-11s and 6 x Bloch 174s

Tactical Reconnaissance:

Escadrille GR I/14 Potez 63-11 Assigned to 1ère Armèe

Escadrille GR I/35 Potez 63-11 Assigned to 7e Armèe

Escadrille GR II/22

Escadrille GR II/52

AÉRONAUTIQUE NAVALE (FRENCH NAVAL AIR SERVICE):

F1C	Flotille de Chasse
AC 1 and AC 2	24 x Potez 631s (Calais-Marck)
F1A	Flotilla du Béarn
AB 2	12 x LN 401s (Berck-sur-Mer)
AB 3	12 x Vought 156Fs (Boulogne-Alprech)

THE NAVAL FORCES

KONINKLIJKE MARINE (THE ROYAL NETHERLANDS NAVY) – VICE-ADMIRAAL (V ADM) JOHANNES FÜRSTNER

The Coastal Squadron

Light cruiser *Sumatra*

Destroyer *Van Galen*

3 x coastal submarines

2 x gunboats

5 x torpedo boats

1 x motor torpedo boats

8 x minelayers

1 x mine-sweeper

The IJsselmeer Squadron

3 x gunboats

1 x torpedo boat

3 x minesweepers

THE BRITISH FORCES

THE ROYAL AIR FORCE (RAF)

The British Air Forces in France (BAFF) – Air Marshal Arthur Barratt

The Advanced Air Striking Force (AASF) – Air Vice Marshal Playfair

The British Expeditionary Force Air Component (BEF-AC) – AVM Charles Blount

50 (Army Cooperation) Wing – Gp Capt Churchman

51 (Army Cooperation) Wing – Wg Cdr Eccles

60 (Fighter) Wing – Wg Cdr Boret

61 (Fighter) Wing – Wg Cdr Eccles

63 (Fighter) Wing – Wg Cdr Finch (deployed 10 May 1940)

67 (Fighter) Wing – Wg Cdr Walter

70 (Reconnaissance) Wing – Wg Cdr Opie

71 (Bomber) Wing – Air Commodore Field

75 (Bomber) Wing – Gp Capt Wann

76 (Bomber) Wing – Gp Capt Kerby

MARINE LUCHTVAARTDIENST (THE ROYAL NETHERLANDS NAVAL AVIATION SERVICE)

GVT 2 and 4	7 x T.8Ws
Six other GVTs	25 x reconnaissance floatplanes
Elementary Training School	De Kooy airfield
Floatplane Training School	De Mok, Texel Island

KORPS MARINERS (THE ROYAL NETHERLANDS NAVAL MARINE CORPS) – KOLONEL (COL) VON FRIJTAG DRABBE

Rotterdam Garrison

Den Helder Depot

The Luftwaffe Strikes: Bergen Airfield, 0520hrs, 10 May 1940

Hauptmann Blödorn led his five Ju 88A-5s of 7./KG 4, approaching Bergen airfield from the north-east, while the Heinkels came in from the North Sea. Arriving overhead at 0540hrs, from 9,844ft (3,000m) Blödorn hurtled down towards his target: the twelve Fokker G.1s of 4e *Jachtvliegtuig Afdeling* (4e JaVA) arranged in three rows on the newly completed concrete platform. Blödorn **(1)** planted his two SC 500 1,102lb bombs in front of Hangar 6 **(2)**, destroying one G.1 and damaging the ones around it. His wingmen **(3)** bombed hangars 5 and 6, destroying two more G.1s. The Heinkels struck next, littering the hangars and platforms with smaller SC 50 bombs, destroying the buildings and damaging seven G.1s. Only one Dutch Jachtkruiser aircraft **(4)** was able to scramble. The only AA weapons on the field itself were two 7.92mm Spandau M.25 machine guns in the control tower **(5)**. These slightly damaged three He 111s as they made their bomb runs. Eventually, the 4e JaVA was decimated. (Artwork by Peter Dennis, © Osprey Publishing)

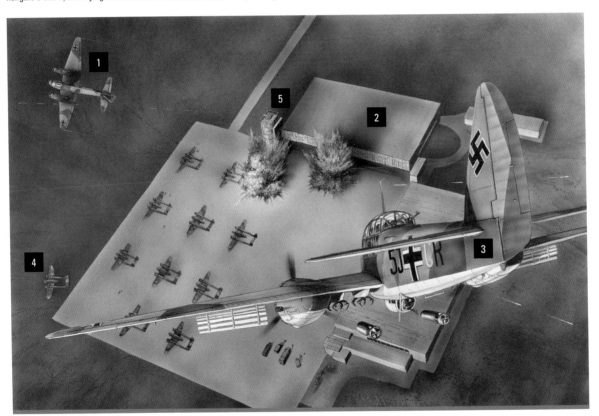

THE CAMPAIGN

The Initial Luftwaffe Air Strikes (10–12 May 1940)

Between the hours of 0400 and 0600 (Central European Summer Time, that is UTC+2 or GMT+2), 500 Luftwaffe twin-engine bombers, organised in two waves, initiated the German campaign by launching surprise attacks on 72 French, Belgian and Dutch airfields. In the north, Luftflotte 2 (supporting the imminent assault of GenObst von Bock's Army Group B) mounted effective attacks that destroyed 190 French, Belgian and Dutch aircraft. Indeed, these sorties decimated the small Dutch air force, leaving it with just 12 operational fighters and five bombers. In the centre, in Army Group A's sector, Luftflotte 3's attacks on airfields secured more modest success, destroying 31 Allied aircraft for the loss of 40 bombers. That afternoon a third German wave of 500 bombers struck 88 rail centres, factories, communications centres and headquarters.

Just behind these first two waves, German transport aircraft delivered thousands of airborne troops on to their targets in Holland and at the Belgian fortress of Eben Emael. Simultaneously, in Operation *NiWi*, 98 light aircraft attempted to deliver two companies from ObstLt Schwerin's elite Infantry Regiment 'Großdeutschland' to seize the key crossroads at Nives and Witry; this mission would facilitate the Panzer columns' infiltration through the Ardennes region. As Ewald von Kleist's armour moved into the Ardennes during 10 May, moreover, German fighters mounted standing patrols in the skies above them to prevent Allied reconnaissance detecting their advance. Throughout 10 May the German Air Force lost 88 twin-engine bombers plus many others damaged or inoperable, so from 11 to 14 May daily bomber sorties fell to under 1,000. Most of these sorties attacked Allied lines of communications to a depth of 80km (50 miles) beyond the River Meuse, to slow Général Alphonse-Joseph Georges' units' movement toward the front line in Belgium. In addition, from 11 to 12 May Luftflotte 3's aircraft attacked no fewer than 34 French airfields. Overall, between 11 and 15 May Luftwaffe operations destroyed a further 147 Allied fighters. These losses, and the damage inflicted to airfields, restricted the Allies to just 595 daily fighter sorties on average from 11 to 15 May. The Jagdwaffe's daily average of 1,500 sorties enabled the Germans to secure aerial superiority, taking a heavy toll on any Allied daylight bombing missions.

The German Air Assault on Holland (10–11 May)

The German invasion of the Netherlands mounted by GenObst von Bock's Army Group B was spearheaded by massed air assaults deep into Dutch territory. First, paratrooper and air-landed troops of Gruppe Nord from GenLt von Sponeck's 22nd Air-Landing Division were to seize three airfields surrounding The Hague, and then storm the Dutch capital. Second, 6,500 German paratroopers and air-landed troops from GenLt Kurt Student's 7th Flieger Division were to be inserted around Rotterdam and three sets of key bridges.

At 0510hrs some 197 German Junkers Ju 52/3m transport planes took off from their airbases heading toward Rotterdam. At 0540hrs the formation split, with one group angling off north-west towards The Hague while the others fanned out to the west and south-west. Around 0625, these groups arrived over their drop

ABOVE Luftflotte 2, commanded by Gen d.Flg Albert Kesselring, supported the invasion of the Netherlands and northern Belgium mounted by GenObst von Bock's Army Group B. Kesselring went on to be a successful ground forces commander. (Photo by ullstein bild/ullstein bild via Getty Images)

BELOW Immediately following the initial Luftwaffe bombing attacks on Dutch airfields, some 197 Ju 52/3m tri-motor transports arrived over Rotterdam, two key Dutch bridges, and the three airfields around The Hague. They delivered paratroopers from the 7th Fliegerdivision on to their objectives.

THE AIRBORNE COUP DE MAIN ATTEMPT AGAINST THE HAGUE, 10 MAY 1940

The German Gruppe Nord conducts airborne assaults on three airfields around The Hague (Valkenburg, Ypenburg, and Ockenburg). However, Dutch counter-attacks manage to recapture the airfields.

Note: Gridlines are shown at intervals of 5km (3.1 miles)

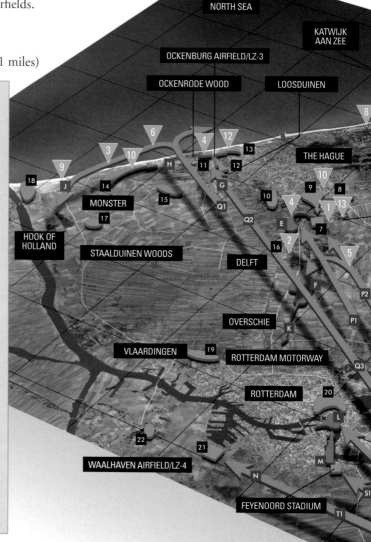

DUTCH UNITS

1. III Bataljon/4e Regiment Infanterrie (III-4e RI)
2. I-4e RI
3. II-4e RI
4. III Bataljon/2e Regiment Artillerie (III-2e RA)
5. 1e Regiment Huzaren Motorrijders (1e RHM)
6. 22e Depotbataljon/2e Depot de Infanterie
7. III Bataljon/Regiment Grenadiers (plus two platoons of 1e Esk Paw armoured cars)
8. 14e Depotbataljon/6e Depot de Infanterie
9. II Bataljon/Regiment Grenadiers (plus elements of Border Bataljon and 4e Depotbataljon)
10. II Bataljon/2e Regiment Artillerie (II-2e RA)
11. 22e Depotcompagnie Bewakingstroepen.
12. Grenadier Regiment staff, 1e Compagnie, and MG, A/T and mortar companies
13. I Bataljon/Regiment Grenadiers (minus 1e Compagnie)
14. I Bataljon/Regiment Jagers
15. I Bataljon/2e Regiment Artillerie (I-2e RA)
16. Delft Technische Institut Compagnie (university cadets)
17. II Bataljon/Regiment Jagers
18. II-39e RI (reinforced)
19. I Bataljon/10e Regiment Artillerie (I-10e RA)
20. Korpsmariners bataljon and III-39e RI (-)
21. III Bataljon/Regiment Jagers
22. 1-III-39e RI
23. 3e Halfregiment Huzaren

▼ EVENTS

1. 0628HRS: LZ-2 – disrupted by intense AA fire, IV./KGzbV 1 scatters I./FJR 2 in five groups, mostly to the south and west of Ypenburg.

2. 0630HRS: Delft – three Ju 52/3ms from 4./KGrzbV 172 drop one platoon of 6./FJR 2 south of Delft to secure section of Delft–Rotterdam motorway as an emergency landing strip. 'Gruppe Gunkelmann' annihilated by local Dutch recruits and university cadets.

3. 0635HRS: LZ-1 – seven Ju 52/3ms (two others shot down by T.5s) from 4./KGrzbV 172 overshoot DZ and drop half of 6./FJR 2 on beaches west of Valkenburg. LZ-3 – 12 Ju 52/3ms (one other shot down by AA) from 16./KGzbV 1 overshoot DZ and drop one platoon of 3./FJR 2 on beach south-west of Ockenburg, and another on Hook of Holland. Others fly north and drop the rest of 3./FJR 2 on beach west of Valkenburg.

4. 0700–0720HRS: LZ-1 – KGrzbV 11 lands III./IR 47 on Valkenburg, defeating defenders and securing the airfield, Oude Rijn bridges, and Leiden–The Hague motorway. LZ-2 – KGrzbV 12 (minus) is repulsed with severe losses; ten Ju 52/3ms land elements of 6. and 8./IR 65 on The Hague–Rotterdam motorway south-east of Delft. Two hours later I./FJR 2 and II./IR 65 complete the capture of Ypenburg airfield. LZ-3 – 3./KGrzbV 12 lands 5./IR 65 on Ockenburg, securing the airfield.

5. 0745HRS: LZ-3 – 1./KGrzbV 9 delivers Radf-Schw 2/AR 22 (two platoons). LZ-2 – KGrzbV 9 (minus) driven off with heavy losses, 23 Ju 52/3ms land south-east of Delft, delivering 22. Inf-Div staff, signals, pioneers and 13./IR 47. Joining survivors of 6. and 8./IR 65, this force advances north, helping paratroopers capture Ypenburg airfield.

6. 0835–0842HRS: LZ-3 – ten Ju 52/3ms from 3./KGrzbV 9 diverting from Ypenburg land Gen Sponeck and 22. Inf-Div staff on to beaches and fields south-west of Ockenburg.

7. 0940HRS: LZ-1 – 1e RHM drives elements of III./IR 47 off the Leiden–The Hague motorway and back to Valkenburg airfield.

8. 1105–1135HRS: LZ-1 – 16 Ju 52/3ms from I./KGzbV 1 land 236 infantry of II./IR 47 on beaches west of Valkenburg, augmenting 60 paratroopers from 3./FJR 2 dropped in error near Katwijk.

9. 1140–1300HRS: Hook of Holland – ten Ju 52/3ms diverting from Ypenburg land parts of three companies of IR 65; 89 men withdraw into Staalduinen Wood, forming 'Gruppe Martin'.

10. 1240HRS: LZ-3 – after repulsing German attempts to enter The Hague and to capture Loosduinen, supported by I-2e RA, I-Grenadiers attack Ockenburg airfield and I-Jagers attack Ockenrode Wood. LZ-2 – supported by II-2e RA, II-Grenadiers (reinforced) attack towards Ypenburg airfield.

11. 1400HRS: LZ-1 – two battalions of 4e RI, supported by III-2e RA, attack the north-west side of Valkenburg airfield, driving III./IR 47 into Valkenburg village.

12. 1600HRS: LZ-3 – Ockenburg airfield is recaptured; 'Gruppe Sponeck' concentrates 360 survivors in Ockenrode Wood.

13. 1630HRS: LZ-2 – Ypenburg airfield is recaptured; 1,295 survivors of 'Gruppe Friemel' are captured; 200 survivors form 'Gruppe Wischhusen' and escape to the south-east.

14. 1900HRS: LZ-1 – Valkenburg airfield is recaptured.

Fortress Holland XXX
VAN ANDEL

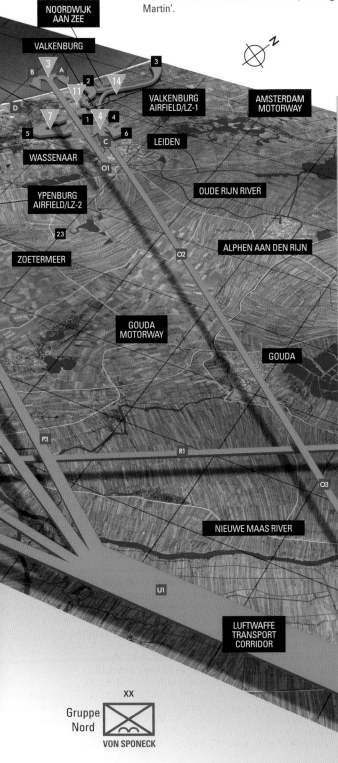

NOORDWIJK AAN ZEE

VALKENBURG

VALKENBURG AIRFIELD/LZ-1

AMSTERDAM MOTORWAY

LEIDEN

WASSENAAR

YPENBURG AIRFIELD/LZ-2

OUDE RIJN RIVER

ZOETERMEER

ALPHEN AAN DEN RIJN

GOUDA MOTORWAY

GOUDA

NIEUWE MAAS RIVER

LUFTWAFFE TRANSPORT CORRIDOR

Gruppe Nord XX
VON SPONECK

GERMAN UNITS

A. 'Gruppe Voigt' – 3. Kompanie/FJR 2 (two platoons from Ockenburg misdropped) plus 86 men from 6./IR 47 that landed on the beach

B. 'Gruppe Erdmann' – 6./FJR 2 (three platoons) plus 117 men from 5./IR 47 landed on the beach.

C. III./IR 47 plus 88 men from 6. and 8./IR 47

D. 'Gruppe Müller' and 'Gruppe Jennefeld' – 90 men from 6. and 7./IR 47 landed on the beaches

E. I./FJR 2 (minus 3. Kompanie)

F. 'Gruppe Friemel' – II./IR 65, reinforced with pioneer, signals, and ordnance troops and surviving elements of I./FJR 2

G. 5./IR 47 and Radfahr-Schwadron 2/AR 22 (Radf-Sch 2/AR 22)

H. 'Gruppe Sponeck' – various elements of 22. Inf-Div staff, military police, pioneers, II Bataillon and 2. Artillerie Batterie staffs, plus one platoon from 3/FJR 2

J. 'Gruppe Martin' – 89 members of 2., 3., and 7./IR 65 landed by IV./KGzbV 1

K. 'Gruppe Wischhusen' – 200 survivors from IR 65

L. 'Gruppe Schrader' – 11./IR 16 (reinforced)

M. 'Gruppe Kerfin' – 11./FJR 1

N. III./FJR 1 (minus 11. Kompanie)

LUFTWAFFE FLIGHT PATHS

O1. To LZ-1. Paratroopers: 4./KGzbV 172 carrying 6./FJR 2

O2. To LZ-1. First wave: KGrzbV 11 carrying III./IR 47

O3. To LZ-1. Second wave: I./KGzbV 1 carrying II./IR 47

P1. To LZ-2. Paratroopers: IV./KGzbV 1(-) carrying I./FJR 2(-)

P2. To LZ-2. First wave: KGrzbV 12(-) carrying 6. and 8./IR 65

P3. To LZ-2. Second wave: KGrzbV 9(-) carrying 22. Inf-Div Stab and 13./IR 47

Q1. To LZ-3. Paratroopers: 16./KGzbV 1 carrying 3./FJR 2

Q2. To LZ-3. First wave: 3./KGrzbV 12 carrying 5./IR 65

Q3. To LZ-3. Second wave: 1./KGrzbV 9 carrying Rad-Schw 2/AR 22

R1. To Rotterdam/Noordereiland: 'Staffel Schwilden' carrying 11./IR 16

S1. To Rotterdam/Feyenoord stadium: 7./KGzbV 1 carrying 11./FJR 1

T1. To LZ-4. Paratroopers: II./KGzbV 1(-) carrying III./FJR 1(-)

U1. To LZ-4. First wave: III./KGzbV 11 carrying III./IR 16 Stab, 9./IR 16 and 2./Pion-Btl 22

The He 111 medium bomber played a key role in the missions mounted by Luftflotten 2 and 3 in support of the 1940 invasion. In an attempt to secure air superiority, in the war's first few days the Luftwaffe executed numerous bombing strikes against French, Belgian, and Dutch airfields. Kesselring's Luftflotte 2 destroyed half the Dutch air force, decimated the Belgian air arm, and eliminated several French squadrons.

zones close to the airfields of Ypenburg, Valkenburg and Ockenburg and began dropping their paratrooper 'sticks'. The Junkers attempted to drop 435 paratroopers on to Ypenburg airfield. However, intense Dutch flak fire shot down four transport aircraft, shattered the formations, and scattered the descending paratroopers in a wide area around the aerodrome. This scattering, plus the stubborn resistance offered by the defending two Dutch infantry companies, prevented the paras seizing the airfield. Thus, when at 0711hrs some 36 Junkers Ju 52s attempted to assault land 429 troops, 13 planes were shot down, 17 diverted elsewhere and many others crash-landed on the airfield.

Consequently, of the 40 Junkers Ju 52s transport aircraft of the second wave, carrying Sponeck and 508 infantrymen, some 18 landed along The Hague–Rotterdam motorway, while 12 others diverted to Ockenburg airfield. During the late morning the 785 German troops now assembled at Ypenburg airbase captured all but the north corner of the airfield. Next, the German infantry advanced to the south-east edge of The Hague. Surprisingly, a swiftly mobilised force of untrained Dutch recruits drove the Germans back towards the airfield. Subsequently, Dutch reinforcements recaptured the aerodrome and took 1,295 German prisoners.

A second formation of transport aircraft meanwhile attempted to drop 61 German Fallschirmjäger on to Valkenburg airfield. However, the pilots miscalculated and mistakenly deposited their two paratrooper platoons on to the beaches either side of the aerodrome at 0625hrs. Just 25 minutes later the first of 53 Junkers transport planes began to land on the airfield, delivering some 783 infantrymen. Most of the 50 Luftwaffe transport aircraft landed safely, but some got bogged in the soft grassy ground, preventing further landings. That morning the 857 assembled invaders captured the airfield and began advancing southwards towards the city of The Hague. The Dutch 1st Hussar Motorcycle Regiment quickly counter-attacked, however, forcing the Germans to withdraw into a defensive perimeter around the airfield. From 1345hrs a more powerful Dutch ground attack eventually recaptured the airfield and later surrounded the 670 remaining German troops in the adjacent village.

Meanwhile, further German Junkers transport aircraft attempted to drop 148 German Fallschirmjäger on to Ockenburg airfield, but only 40 landed near the airfield. Over the next 75 minutes 27 Junkers Ju 52 transport planes laden with 221 German infanteers and 121 bicycle reconnaissance troops landed on Ockenburg airfield. After further combat, at 0930hrs, the Germans captured the entire aerodrome. By early afternoon, however, a powerful Dutch counter-strike had retaken the airfield.

During that morning, therefore, a total of 3,550 Gruppe Nord troops had reached their objectives, out of a force of 6,500 that had set out. By late afternoon, however, just 1,650 German troops remained fit for action. The German High Command now realised that the initial objectives of Gruppe Nord's assault around The Hague were beyond reach. It ordered the scattered units to fall back towards the bridgehead in Rotterdam. There they would dig in and hold while awaiting relief by the Panzers approaching from the east. Under the leadership of Sponeck, the German 22nd Air-Landing Division's mission had largely been a failure.

Simultaneously, three other transport plane formations began to deliver some 4,300 troops of the German 7th Flieger Division in aerial assaults intended to secure three pairs of bridges that would permit the Panzers to enter *Vesting Holland* through the weak southern 'back door'. These bridge-pairs were located at Moerdijk (spanning the wide Hollandsch Diep estuary), at Dordrecht (over the Oude Maas river) and at Waalhaven (for the nearby crossing of the Nieuwe Maas in Rotterdam).

At 0620 two German Fallschirmjäger companies landed on either side of the estuary and quickly seized both ends of both the Moerdijk bridges. The Dutch forces reacted strongly but eventually, after a six-hour pitched battle, the paratroopers overcame the defenders. Meanwhile, at 0625hrs, a dozen Junkers had dropped one company of paratroopers at Dordrecht. One German platoon quickly seized the western ends of the road and railway bridges that spanned the Oude Maas. However, a swift Dutch riposte managed to bottle up the paratroopers on the river's western bank. A further two paratrooper companies that had been dropped between Dordrecht and Moerdijk then fought their way to the Dordrecht bridges.

Meanwhile, from 0630hrs some 106 Junkers Ju 52 transport aircraft landed on Waalhaven airfield near Rotterdam, delivering 1,295 paratroopers into action. The Germans overwhelmed the three defending Dutch *Jäger* (light infantry)

Two companies of the II Battalion of Fallschirmjägerregiment 1 landed at either end of the key Moerdijk railroad and highway bridges spanning the kilometre-wide Hollandsch Diep estuary. In this Nazi propaganda re-enactment, the Moerdijk railway bridge is visible in the left background. (© IWM, HU 31441)

ARMY GROUP B'S INVASION OF THE NETHERLANDS AND NORTHERN BELGIUM, 10–12 MAY

In the north of the theatre the German Army Group B invaded the Netherlands and northern Belgium. On its northern flank, Luftwaffe air assault forces daringly attempted to seize numerous depth targets around The Hague, Rotterdam and Moerdijk, while Eighteenth Army's ground forces overwhelmed the initial Dutch defences. Further south the German Sixth Army smashed its way through the Dutch Peel Line defences and secured the fortified region around Maastricht, including the Eben Emael fortress. Meanwhile, the Allied western flank executed the Dyle-Breda Plan. While the French 7e Armée charged to Antwerp, the BEF and the French 1ère Armée advanced north-east to take up their planned defensive positions along the River Dyle in central Belgium.

Some 86 Junkers Ju 88A medium bombers served with the Fliegerkorps IV within Kesselring's Luftflotte 2, together with a further 21 platforms in the Fliegerkorps zbV. These bombers helped spearhead the German 'Counter-Air Campaign', seeking to win local aerial superiority by attacking enemy airbases, and the aircraft parked on them. (© IWM, MH 6115)

companies and subsequently advanced towards the two bridges spanning the Nieuwe Maas river. At 0610hrs the bridges – that connected the Northern Island to either bank – had been seized by 90 Germans troops who had been flown into Rotterdam by 12 elderly float biplanes. The local Dutch forces mounted several spirited counter-attacks but failed to dislodge the invaders.

Meanwhile further transport aircraft had landed 1,180 additional German troops at Waalhaven airfield. Indeed, by the end of the day Gruppe Süd had massed around 3,700 troops at Rotterdam. These forces fanned out, reinforcing the garrisons now holding the six bridges, in readiness for the anticipated larger-scale Dutch Army counter-measures. It was anticipated that it would take the advancing Panzer divisions three more days to arrive, but only if they were not delayed by the spearheads of Giraud's approaching French 7e Armée. The German 7th Flieger Division's operation had been partially successful, but it had been won at the painful price of 256 transport planes either destroyed, abandoned, or deemed unserviceable.

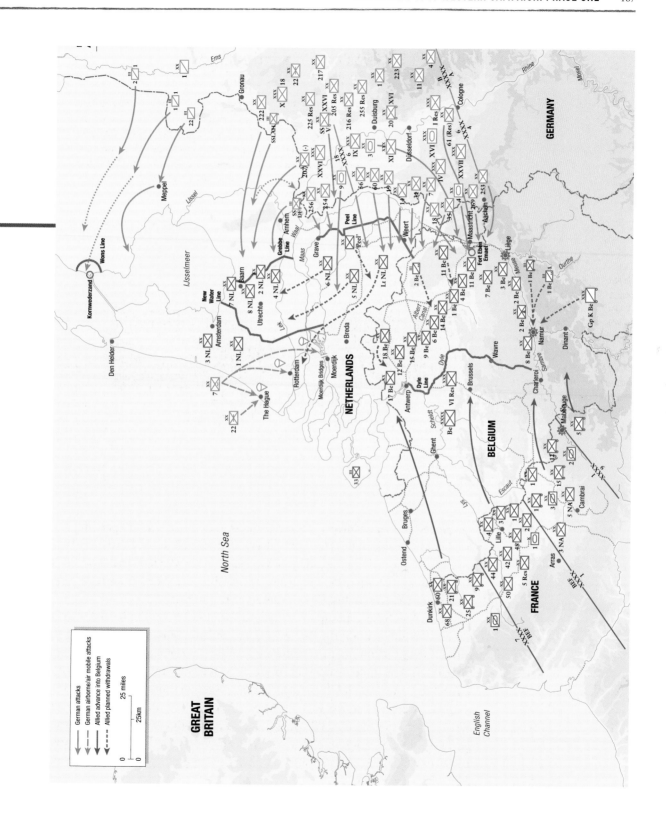

Army Group B's Ground Invasion of the Netherlands and Northern Belgium (10–12 May)

While the Luftwaffe strikes, and airborne operations, unfolded across the Netherlands and northern Belgium, Army Group B's ground invasion also commenced. On the extreme northern flank of Küchler's Eighteenth Army sector, Feldt's 1st Kavallerie Division smashed through the weak Dutch border defences and charged west toward the IJsselmeer's north-eastern shores. By 11 May the German cavalry formation had reached the inland sea's eastern shores and on the 12th it assaulted the Dutch Wons Line defences. These fortifications protected the road-bridge that formed the northern boundary of the IJsselmeer inland sea.

Further south, two infantry divisions from Ulex's German X Corps easily broke through the meagre border defences. Subsequently they advanced west to push aside five infantry battalions defending the River IJssel's right bank; the Germans soon secured bridgeheads across it at Doesburg and Zutphen, north-east of Arnhem, that afternoon. By 11 May these formations had charged further west to reach the powerful Dutch Grebbe Line defences that ran south from the Isselmeer to the River Waal. The next day they assaulted the line and made some penetrations of it. During the 13th, with the Grebbe Line crumbling, the Dutch withdrew to the secondary defensive line that screened Fortress Holland: this ran south from east of Amsterdam down to Utrecht.

Meanwhile, on Eighteenth Army's southern flank, three divisions from Wobig's XXVI Corps charged west from the Maas between Nijmegen and Gennep to penetrate the northern flank of the Peel Line's defences. This opened the way

Once the German invasion had commenced, massed French forces advanced north-east as planned into central Belgium. Here a French motorised anti-tank unit passes through a Belgian village on the way to Gembloux. (© IWM, F 4548)

for Hubicki's 9th Panzer Division, on the Eighteenth Army's extreme southern flank, to race westwards to Breda; from there it would head north across the paratrooper-held Moerdijk bridges and seize Rotterdam. By nightfall, the 9th Panzer Division had advanced some 15km (nine miles) to reach Mill. The next day it charged an astonishing 50km (31 miles) westward, sweeping aside the battered Peel Division, to capture the town of Tilburg.

Further south, the three infantry corps deployed on the northern and central sectors of Reichenau's Sixth Army frontage smashed through the Maas river defences between Venlo and Maastricht. The next day they penetrated the Peel Line defences, forcing the ad hoc Peel Division to retreat behind the Zuid-Willemsvaart Canal; its mission was to delay the Germans long enough for Lieutenant-Général de Krahe's Belgian IIIe Corps to withdraw. These advances were facilitated by German glider-borne forces seizing three bridges near Maastricht as well as neutralizing the formidable Belgian Eben Emael fortress.

As soon as the German infantry assault had created some manoeuvre space, the two mobile divisions of Hoepner's XVI Corps (Motorised) charged full-pelt into central Belgium. The Panzers raced through the Gembloux Gap – the large open space between the Dyle and Meuse rivers – toward the town of Gembloux. Here, on the 12th, they joined a meeting engagement with the north-easterly moving elements of the French 1ère Armée. The Allies had taken the bait: with the most mobile Allied divisions now locked in a contact battle with Army Group B's southern forces, they could not easily redeploy to counter the daring German infiltration through the Ardennes region.

During 11 May, meanwhile, the spearheads of the 7e Armée also began to arrive at their agreed objectives around Breda and Central Belgium. The French 1er Corps deployed on a defensive line south from Breda toward Antwerp, which was covered by Général de Corps Fagalde's French 16e Corps. Further south still, the British Expeditionary Force's spearheads were arriving on a north-south line from Louvain.

The Dyle Manoeuvre and Army Group B's Advance into Southern Belgium (10–13 May)

Between 10 and 12 May, Gamelin's Dyle Plan deployment unfolded as intended with few disruptions, except for the Breda extension. As the BEF's three British divisions and the 1ère Armée's six French divisions began arriving at their designated positions – and the Belgian Army withdrew to the Koningshooikt-Wavre (K-W) Line – it became obvious that a new formal command structure was needed to direct the disparate elements of these three Allied armies.

Thus, on 12 May the French, British and Belgium commanders met near the city of Mons. Despite the unsettling tactical reverses in southern Holland and on the Albert Canal, prospects for a successful defence in central Belgium seemed

PANZERS TO THE RESCUE, 12–14 MAY 1940

On 12 May 1940 the Dutch Lichte Divisie (Light Division) attempted to dislodge the German paratroopers' hold on the Dordrecht bridges, but was defeated by a timely flanking counter-attack. The following morning leading elements of the 9th Panzer Division arrived, eliminating the threat at Dordrecht, and made contact with Student's forces at Rotterdam. A Luftwaffe air attack on 14 May ended all resistance; Rotterdam surrendered, and shortly after the Dutch capitulated.

Note: Gridlines are shown at intervals of 5km (3.1miles)

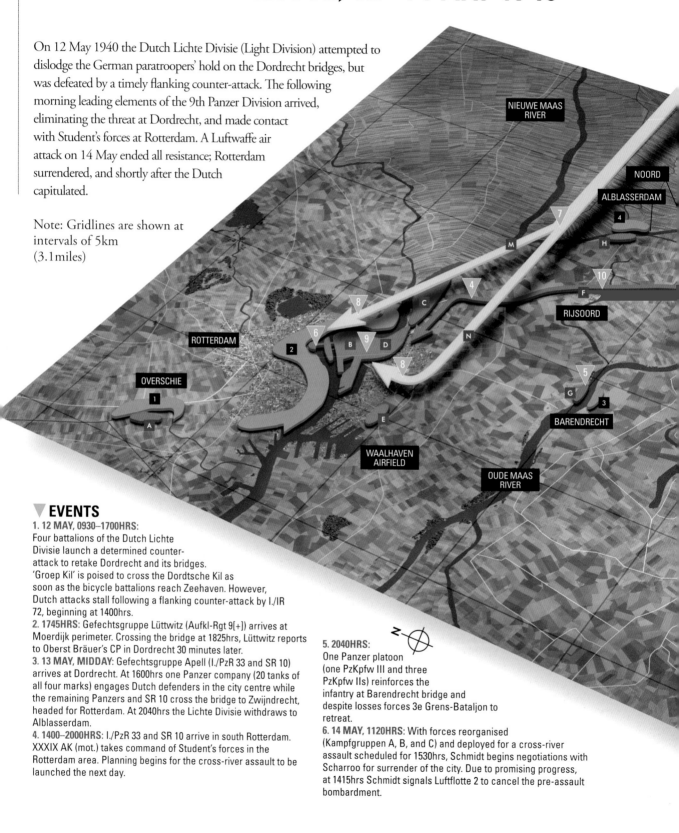

NIEUWE MAAS RIVER

NOORD

ALBLASSERDAM

RIJSOORD

ROTTERDAM

OVERSCHIE

BARENDRECHT

WAALHAVEN AIRFIELD

OUDE MAAS RIVER

▼ EVENTS

1. 12 MAY, 0930–1700HRS:
Four battalions of the Dutch Lichte Divisie launch a determined counter-attack to retake Dordrecht and its bridges. 'Groep Kil' is poised to cross the Dordtsche Kil as soon as the bicycle battalions reach Zeehaven. However, Dutch attacks stall following a flanking counter-attack by I./IR 72, beginning at 1400hrs.

2. 1745HRS: Gefechtsgruppe Lüttwitz (Aufkl-Rgt 9[+]) arrives at Moerdijk perimeter. Crossing the bridge at 1825hrs, Lüttwitz reports to Oberst Bräuer's CP in Dordrecht 30 minutes later.

3. 13 MAY, MIDDAY: Gefechtsgruppe Apell (I./PzR 33 and SR 10) arrives at Dordrecht. At 1600hrs one Panzer company (20 tanks of all four marks) engages Dutch defenders in the city centre while the remaining Panzers and SR 10 cross the bridge to Zwijndrecht, headed for Rotterdam. At 2040hrs the Lichte Divisie withdraws to Alblasserdam.

4. 1400–2000HRS: I./PzR 33 and SR 10 arrive in south Rotterdam. XXXIX AK (mot.) takes command of Student's forces in the Rotterdam area. Planning begins for the cross-river assault to be launched the next day.

5. 2040HRS:
One Panzer platoon (one PzKpfw III and three PzKpfw IIs) reinforces the infantry at Barendrecht bridge and despite losses forces 3e Grens-Bataljon to retreat.

6. 14 MAY, 1120HRS: With forces reorganised (Kampfgruppen A, B, and C) and deployed for a cross-river assault scheduled for 1530hrs, Schmidt begins negotiations with Scharroo for surrender of the city. Due to promising progress, at 1415hrs Schmidt signals Luftflotte 2 to cancel the pre-assault bombardment.

7. 1430HRS: Unaware of Kesselring's 'abort attack' order, KG 54 approaches from the east and splits into two attack groups. Initially, red flares fired from the bridges – signalling abort the attack – are not seen.

8. 1440HRS: KG 54's main group attacks as planned. I./KG 54 sees the red flares and aborts its attack; only three aircraft release bombs.

9. 1730HRS: Scharroo surrenders the city, PzR 33 and SS-LAH cross the bridges into Rotterdam. Shortly afterwards Student is wounded by friendly fire from an SS motorcycle battalion.

10. 15 MAY, 1145HRS: At Schmidt's HQ in Rijsoord, Winkelman and Küchler sign the armistice, Winkelman surrendering all Dutch forces under his command.

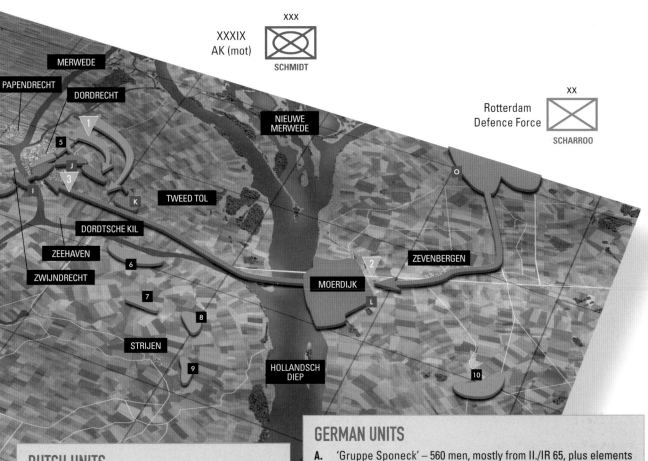

DUTCH UNITS

1. Overschie Attack Force – II-RGr, II-12e RI and III-9e RI with II-2e RA
2. Rotterdam Defence Force (front rank) – II-RJ, IV-10e RI, I-11e RI, IV-15e RI, III- and IV-21e RI, II-25e RI, II-32e RI, III-39e RI and Korpsmarinersbatalijon with I-10e RA
3. 3e Grens-Bataljon
4. I Bataljon/1e Regiment Wielrijders (I-1e RW) and I Bataljon/Korps Rijdende Artillerie (I-KRA)
5. II-1e RW and 2e RW with II-KRA
6. 'Groep Kil' – I-34e RI and remnants of 28e RI
7. I-23e RA
8. 25e Bataljon Artillerie
9. II-23e RA
10. 6e Grens-Bataljon

GERMAN UNITS

A. 'Gruppe Sponeck' – 560 men, mostly from II./IR 65, plus elements of various 22. Inf-Div units
B. 'Kampfgruppe A' – III./IR 16, I./PzR 33 (-) and Pion.-Bat. 22 (-)
C. 'Kampfgruppe B' – I./IR 16 and 1./Pion.-Bat. 22
D. 'Kampfgruppe C' – SS-LAH and 1./PzR 33
E. Stab, 5. and 6./AR 22
F. HQ XXXIX AK (mot.)
G. 5. and 6./IR 16
H. 4. and 7./IR 65
I. 7./IR 16
J. 'Gruppe Bräuer' – two companies each from I./FJR 1, III./FJR 1 and II./FJR 2
K. I./IR 72 (-)
L. II./FJR 1 (-)
M. KG 54 (-)
N. I./KG 54
O. 254th Infanterie Division

favourable, provided a proper command structure could be established. Since Gamelin had effectively abdicated control of events, Général d'Armée Georges decided that Général d'Armée Billotte should direct the Belgian Army and BEF in addition to placing a fourth French army (Giraud's) under his command.

Late on 12 May the BEF's three divisions arrived along a 27km (17 mile) wide sector of the Dyle river, between the towns of Louvain and Wavre. To the British left (north), eight Belgian infantry divisions withdrew to a 50km (31 mile) wide frontage along the K-W Line, with three more formations in reserve; two other Belgian divisions held the Willebroek Canal. By 14 May, moreover, on the northern flank, Giraud's 7e Armée had withdrawn to defend the Scheldt Estuary.

On General Gort's right (south), Général d'Armée Blanchard's elite 1ère Armée established a defence-in-depth supported by massed artillery along the line from Wavre to Gembloux to the Namur railroad, where the embankments offered a strong natural defence. In contrast, the Belgians, hamstrung by the lack of pre-campaign coordination, had expected the French to advance to and hold the line that stretched from Wavre through Perwez on to the town of Namur and had built the *barrage de Cointet* fence accordingly. On the Allied southern flank – originally manned by de Krahe's Belgian IIIe Corps around the city of Liège – the French withdrew back to Namur, leaving the 12 forts (six small and six large, that ringed Liège at a distance of 7–9km (4–6 miles) from the city) to their respective fates. The Belgians had constructed these 12 forts, which formed the *Position Fortifiée de Liège*, during 1888–91, to block the traditional westward movement corridor from Germany. Around Namur they were joined by Groepering-K, arriving from the Ardennes region, and reinforced by the French 12e DIM.

By 12 May the Allies had 22 divisions on the River Dyle Line, with another 12 in reserve. They faced the 16 infantry divisions of Reichenau's Sixth Army. In the north Wobig's XXVI Corps pushed Giraud's forward divisions back to the city of Antwerp in some disorder. Meanwhile Geyer's IX Corps assaulted the defensive positions along the K-W Line manned by Bogaerts' Belgian IVe Corps. Showing operational acumen, Reichenau attempted to penetrate the Allied line at the seams between its disparate armies. At Louvain the German XI Corps unsuccessfully attempted a breakthrough of the BEF's positions. Simultaneously, IV Corps attacked at Wavre, driving de La Laurencie's French 3e Corps back to the Lasne river before Blanchard's

At 1400 hours on 10 May the 12th Battalion, the Royal Lancers, crossed the Franco-Belgian border. The unit's vehicles raced ahead of Gort's three British infantry divisions. The unit was equipped with 60 Morris CS9 armoured cars, like these, seen here on manoeuvres. (© IWM, O 594)

reserves restored the line. Meanwhile, Namur – the fortified southern anchor to the Dyle Line – held stoutly against assaults by the German XXVII Corps.

But by 12 May, the French Groupe d'Armées 1 commander Général d'Armée Billotte had more to worry about than the Allied conglomerate holding the Dyle river line. He had learned from French aerial reconnaissance that large German armoured columns were then driving through the difficult terrain of the Ardennes toward the River Meuse adjacent to the towns of Dinant, Givet, and Bouillon. Initially, Billotte – like all the French Army generals – dismissed these enemy actions in the Ardennes as a minor secondary effort about which he need not be overly concerned.

Yet during the 13th Rommel's units had forced a crossing of the River Meuse at Dinant, Kempf's troops had assaulted Monthermé, and Guderian's soldiers were across the river at Sedan. The French High Command reacted strongly, dispatching all three of its armoured divisions southward to reinforce the Second and Ninth Armies. But the day was filled with disasters; after his centre was overrun by Rommel's spearheads, Général Corap ordered his Ninth Army to withdraw to the French frontier. To maintain the integrity of his front, Billotte recommended that Corap instead hold an intermediate stop-line located between the towns of Charleroi and Rethel. Accordingly, at 1900hrs Billotte ordered Blanchard to withdraw the 1ère Armée to the Charleroi Canal, connecting Tubize (near Waterloo) with the Sambre river.

By then, however, the spearheads of the German 3rd and 4th Panzer Divisions – controlled by Hoepner's XVI Corps (Motorised) – had advanced south-west through the hamlets of Waremme, Avennes and Braives. Finally, at the village of Crehen they approached the Gembloux Gap, the infamous movement corridor through central Belgium. Here, Hoepner's Panzer spearheads encountered the eastward advance of Général de Corps Prioux's elite French Corps de Cavalerie. His headquarters controlled two powerful subordinate formations – 2e and 3e Divisions Légères Mécaniques. During the battles at Hannut and Gembloux, which raged between 13 and 15 May, Prioux's two DLM formations halted the hitherto headlong westward advance of the two Panzer divisions controlled by Hoepner's XVI Corps (Motorised).

Army Group A's Assault against the Allied Centre (10–12 May)

During 10 May, as Army Group B's assault on the Netherlands and northern Belgium unfolded, Army Group A's attack commenced across the central sector of the front – on southern Belgium, Luxembourg and north-eastern France. Across the army group's northern flank, Fourth Army's three infantry corps smashed through the weak Belgian defences and marched westward toward the southerly course of the River Ourthe as it rose into the northern Ardennes. Manoeuvring behind this infantry-led break-in, Rommel's 7th Panzer Division – the spearhead

The mission allocated to Gen d.Kav Erich Hoepner's XVI Corps (Motorised) was to charge deep into central Belgium into the Gembloux Gap and fix the best Allied mobile forces in a contact battle, while to the south Kleist's massed armour infiltrated through the Ardennes. (Photo by Keystone/Stringer/Hulton Archive/ Getty Images)

The BEF's advance into central Belgium during 10–12 May was facilitated by the fact that its spearhead divisions were largely motorised. Here a convoy of lorries loaded with British troops make their way through a Belgian town during their retreat from the Dyle Line. (© IWM, F 4396)

of Hoth's XV Corps (Motorised) – advanced through St Vith to Chabrehez, with Walsporn's 5th Panzer Division following. Commanded by Strauß, the advancing German II Corps also moved forward to protect Hoth's exposed southern flank.

To the south, the German Twelfth Army and Panzer Group Kleist spearheaded the German infiltration through south-eastern Belgium and the northern half of Luxembourg into the hilly, forested Ardennes region. Across the Twelfth Army's northern sector, the German III, XVIII and VI Corps attacked into northern Luxembourg to cover the Panzers' advance. Also on 10 May, across the Army's southern flank, Panzer Group Kleist's armour burst through central Luxembourg. Indeed, during that morning the spearhead of Panzer Group Kleist's 41,140 motorised vehicles raced through central Luxembourg. Organised into two armour-heavy mobile corps and a motorised infantry corps, the five Panzer and three motorised infantry divisions of Panzer Group Kleist operated along three axes of advance (*Rollbahnen*) – the northern, central and southern. With thousands of vehicles winding their way along narrow roads on a one-tank frontage, the Panzer columns stretched a staggering 180km (112 miles) back deep into German territory. Guderian's XIX Corps (Motorised) lead the assault, with each of his three divisions allocated to one of the three Rollbahnen; behind these forces, the two Panzer and one motorised infantry divisions of GenLt Reinhardt's XLI Corps (Motorised) waited to join the fray.

On Guderian's central route of advance through the Sûre river valley GenLt Kirchner's 1st Panzer Division easily swept aside a company from the First Regiment of Belgian Chasseurs Ardennais. Next, by 1900hrs it had overwhelmed the defence of Bodange, mounted by another Chasseur company. Meanwhile, along the northern Rollbahn, GenLt Veiel's 2nd Panzer Division pushed through Nives as Chasseur Ardennais units staged a fighting withdrawal westward towards Namur, where they rejoined the Belgians' main line of defence. Finally, on the southern Rollbahn near Arlon the German 10th Panzer Division overwhelmed elements of the French 2e DLC that had advanced north-eastward from the French border area of Montmédy; subsequently, the French withdrew to the south behind the River Semois.

During 11 May 1940 along the central Rollbahn Kirchner's 1st Panzer Division smashed through the 32km (20 mile) wide screen established by the French 5e DLC between Libramont and Rossignol, forcing it to retreat to the Semois. The southward withdrawal of the cavalry divisions from Huntziger's Second Army now left the horse-mounted 3e Spahis Brigade (from Corap's Ninth Army) isolated in the Ardennes region. Upon discovering this the brigade withdrew westward to the Meuse, creating the first crack between the French 2e and 9e Armées; into this gap Kirchner's 1st Panzer Division advanced to the River Semois. By now French reconnaissance sorties had reported back that the enemy was making an important drive westward in the Ardennes. With Gamelin, Georges, Billotte, and the other Allied army commanders overwhelmingly focused on the titanic tank clash then developing on the north Belgium plain, they discounted these reports, believing that they only indicated a minor German feint.

Early on 12 May the 1st and 10th Panzer Divisions captured the town of Bouillon and established crossings over the Semois. When Georges heard of this setback he gave the Second Army top priority for Allied air support, but Huntziger failed to order any sorties. Subsequently, the two Panzer formations advanced west toward the town of Sedan, and by nightfall their leading elements occupied portions of the River Meuse's eastern bank. Despite the fact that Guderian's XIX Corps (Motorised) had advanced to the River Meuse in just three days, due to the chaotic, 250km (156 mile) long traffic jams on the northern Rollbahn, Reinhardt's two divisions had been seriously delayed.

Late on 12 May, when Georges had learned that the Panzers were approaching Sedan, he transferred the 21e Corps Armée HQ from GQG reserve to Huntziger's Army. He assigned to this new Corps HQ both Général Brocard's French 3e DCr and 3e DCM. Between them these two formations were to form the doctrinal 'plug' behind Sedan, in case the Germans broke through. The French expected these forces to be ready on 14 May, well in advance of the expected German assault that was anticipated on the 16th. But the German Panzer commanders – the impatient zealots of Blitzkrieg – had no intention of waging the struggle at the same slow tempo as did their enemies.

Kleist's Panzers Assault across the River Meuse (13–14 May)

During 12 May the mass of German armour that had infiltrated through the Ardennes was charging toward the Meuse on a 64km (40 mile) frontage. On the northern axis GenLt von Walsporn's 5th and Rommel's 7th Panzer Divisions from Hoth's XV Corps (Motorised) were closing in on the town of Dinant. On their southern flank, the 32nd Division (from XII Corps) was trying not to fall to far behind on its advance from west of Marche toward the town of Givet. Meanwhile, in the centre, Reinhardt's XLI Corps (Motorised)

THE INFILTRATION OF PANZER GROUP KLEIST'S PANZER WEDGE THROUGH THE ARDENNES, 10–12 MAY 1940

During 10–12 May Army Group B's charge into central Belgium fixed the most effective Allied forces into a contact battle there; simultaneously powerful French forces remained self-fixed in defence of the Maginot Line to the south. Meanwhile, fielding some 1,664 tanks, Panzer Group Kleist's five Panzer and three motorised infantry divisions covertly drove through the difficult forested, hilly terrain of the Ardennes in the weakly defended Allied centre. By the 12th this powerful 80km (50 mile) wide armoured wedge had successfully traversed the Ardennes and was disgorging onto the approaches to the River Meuse. Once across, this force – the largest mechanised phalanx yet seen in history – represented a titanic threat; it was about to charge to the Channel coast and split the Allied forces in half.

was heading west-southwest toward the town of Monthermé. On its northern flank, the four infantry divisions of Gen d.Art Haase's III Corps and Gen d.Art Heitz's VIII Corps were marching west to the portion of the River Meuse that stretched south from Givet. Finally, on the southern axis, Guderian's 2nd, 1st and 10th Panzer Divisions were advancing across a 16km (ten mile) frontage toward the town of Sedan, where the River Meuse flowed first north-west then west to Flize. The most climactic encounters of the campaign were about to occur.

As described, on 10 May, across the northern Ardennes, Hoth's XV Corps (Motorised) had closed on Chabrehez. Meanwhile, from the west, Corap's 1ère DLC and 4e DLC advanced across the River Meuse and pushed on to the River Ourthe. The next morning Rommel's 7th Panzer Division secured Chabrehez and raced to the Ourthe. There on the 12th it swiftly shattered the French 4e DLC, the remnants of which fled into the forests in disorder. Rommel's two main battle groups then charged west to reach the River Meuse at Dinant and Yvoir during the mid-afternoon of 12 May.

At his HQ in Vervins, Corap was alarmed by aerial reconnaissance reports of a powerful motorised enemy approaching Marche and of the collapse of his cavalry screen. In response, he ordered the 1ère DLC and 4e DLC to withdraw behind the River Meuse and for all the bridges between Dinant and the Bar river to be destroyed. Additionally, he sent a battalion from the 5e DIM to the French 11e Corps to cover the gap between Yvoir and Dinant. The French also hurried four infantry battalions to the town of Dinant. The exhausted infantrymen arrived at 1600hrs that afternoon, just as Rommel's motorised forces lined the opposite bank of the river, looking intently for a way across. Finally, at shortly before midnight on the 12th, Rommel's motorcycle recce troops found an undefended crossing point across the River Meuse between Yvoir and Dinant, at Houx, and established a bridgehead on the opposite shore.

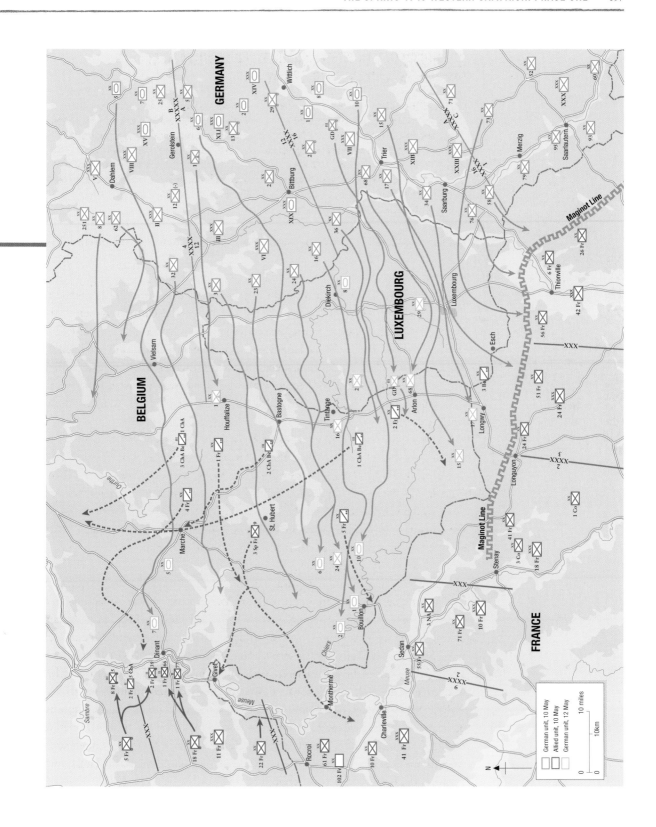

ROMMEL CROSSES THE MEUSE AT DINANT, 12–14 MAY 1940

The crossing of the River Meuse by Rommel at Houx and Dinant.

Note: Gridlines are shown at intervals of 2km (1.24 miles)

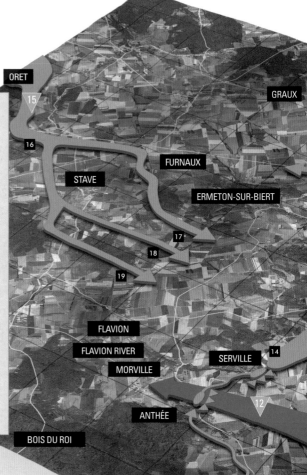

FRENCH AND BELGIAN UNITS

1. 8e Régiment d'Infanterie/5e Division d'Infanterie Motorisée)
2. Belgian II Bn/5e Régiment de Chasseurs Ardennais
3. Remnants of 4e DLC (withdrawing to the west)
4. II Bn/14e Dragons-portes Régiment
5. 1er GRDI/5e DIM
6. II Bn/129e Régiment d'Infanterie Motorisée
7. 39e RIM (minus II Bn)/5e DIM
8. 129e RIM (minus II Bn)/5e DIM
9. II Bn/39e Régiment d'Infanterie Motorisée
10. 1ère Cie/1er RAM and 3e Esc/6e BCC
11. 66e Régiment d'Infanterie/18e DI
12. 77e Régiment d'Infanterie/18e DI
13. 125e Régiment d'Infanterie/18e DI
14. 19e RAD, 111e RALHC, and 219e RALD (artillery)
15. 30e GRDI/18e DI and ad hoc units defending the Flavion River position
16. 1ère Division Cuirassée
17. 37e BCC/1ère DCr (Char B1 bis)
18. 26e BCC/1ère DCr (H-39s)
19. 28e BCC/1ère DCr (Char B1 bis)

▼ EVENTS

1. 12 MAY, 1600HRS: The last of 9e Armée's cavalry units withdraw across the River Meuse and the bridges are blown, effectively halting the pursuing Panzers.

2. 2100HRS: Motorcycle infantry of 3./Aufkl.-Abt. 8 successfully infiltrate across the river at Houx and establish a foothold, quickly being reinforced by Rommel's Kradsch. Bat. 7, and expand the bridgehead towards La Grange.

3. 13 MAY, 0600HRS: Rommel attempts assaults across the Meuse near Yvoir (Schützen-Rgt. 6) and Dinant (Schützen-Rgt. 7), but both are repulsed with heavy losses.

4. MORNING: The motorcycle infantry drive the II/39e RIM from La Grange and clear the Bois de Surinvaux, allowing Schützen-Rgt. 14 to begin crossing the Meuse.

5. 1000HRS: With direct fire support from PzKpfw IVs (3./Panzer-Rgt. 25), the crossings north of Dinant resume and Bouvignes is occupied, clearing the 66e RI from its riverbank positions.

6. MIDDAY: Schützen-Rgt. 14 drives westward towards Haut-le-Wastia, securing the plateau above Anhée, while I./Schutzen-Rgt 13 crosses the Meuse and begins pushing the 129e RIM back across the River Molignée.

7. AFTERNOON: Général Boucher orders a counter-attack against the Haut-le-Wastia salient using II/129e RIM and the 1er GRDI's motorcycle infantry and machinegun carriers. However, a Stuka strike (III./StG 51) disrupts the infantry approach march, dispersing them into the Bois de Ronquière, so the attack is postponed and subsequently cancelled.

8. 2000HRS: Général Martin orders a counter-attack against the Bois de Surinvaux, but the infantry (I and III/39e RIM) fail to arrive at the start line in time, so the tanks (3e/6e BCC) drive to Bois de Surinvaux without support, and subsequently return to Bois de Foy.

9. AFTERNOON: Schützen-Rgt. 7 wheels south to envelop and destroy most of the 66e RI, the remnant of which retreats north-west to near Sommières. Threatened, 77e RI withdraws to defend Onhaye. With the bridgehead secured, the Panzer-Rgt. 25 begins ferrying tanks across on pontoon barges.

10. OVERNIGHT: A pontoon bridge is completed at Houx and the Panzer-Rgt. 31 crosses, driving to Sommières and destroying the remnant of the 66e RI.

11. 14 MAY, DAYBREAK: Schützen-Rgt. 7 advances to Onhaye and, supported by five tanks, begins to clear the town. At 0900hrs, Panzer-Rgt. 25 follows with approximately 25 tanks, sweeping around the town to the north to block the defenders' retreat, annihilating them.

12. AFTERNOON: Panzer-Rgt. 25 continues west through Anthée, destroying the scattered defenders in detail, until darkness forces Rommel's Panzers to halt at Morville.

13. AFTERNOON: Panzer-Rgt. 31 attacks to the west, resulting in a see-saw battle with the 18e DI's reserves, reconnaissance group and other ad hoc units attempting to hold along the River Flavion. The Panzers eventually reach Falaën by nightfall, after which the defenders withdraw in disorder.

14. EVENING: The 8. Infanterie-Division crosses the Meuse behind the 5th Panzer-Division, pushes across the Molignée, and attacks through Warnant to Bioul, pushing back the 5e DIM and covering the Panzer's right flank.

15. EVENING: Driving all night, the 1ère DCr (1st Armoured Division) arrives from Charleroi the next morning. With their fuel exhausted the division's three tank battalions deploy in fields to await the arrival of their refuelling vehicles.

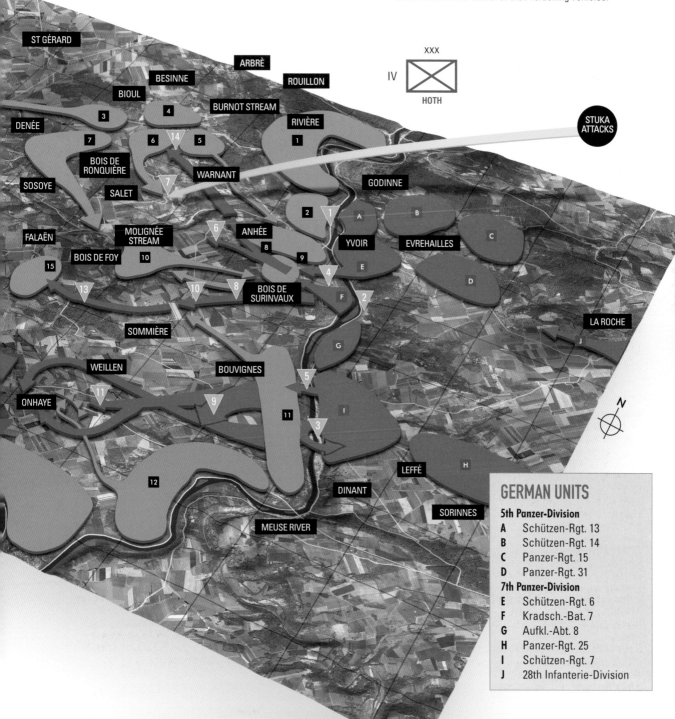

GERMAN UNITS

5th Panzer-Division

A	Schützen-Rgt. 13
B	Schützen-Rgt. 14
C	Panzer-Rgt. 15
D	Panzer-Rgt. 31

7th Panzer-Division

E	Schützen-Rgt. 6
F	Kradsch.-Bat. 7
G	Aufkl.-Abt. 8
H	Panzer-Rgt. 25
I	Schützen-Rgt. 7
J	28th Infanterie-Division

Having successfully infiltrated through the Ardennes, the main challenge facing the Panzer divisions was to get across the obstacle of the River Meuse swiftly. Here German landing forces prepare to cross the Meuse at Montherme. (DE AGOSTINI PICTURE LIBRARY via Getty Images)

On 13 May, after early morning Luftwaffe attacks, Rommel's assaults across the River Meuse began. Beneath an artillery barrage his combat engineers and riflemen crossed the 250ft-wide river in rubber boats. The French fought back tenaciously, and only a few troops made it to the opposite shore. After resuming the crossings at 1100hrs Rommel's troops gradually secured the western bank and cleared Bouvignes. Meanwhile, at Houx the 5th Panzer Division's repeated assaults expanded its bridgehead, despite facing several spirited French counter-attacks. At 1930hrs, moreover, two French infantry battalions counter-attacked Rommel's main bridgehead at Dinant, but failed to stem the German expansion, both there and further south around Bouvignes.

Early on 14 May 1940 Rommel's spearheads successfully advanced 5km (three miles) to Onhaye and by nightfall they had advanced on to Morville, clearing enough room west of Dinant for the entire division to assemble and continue the advance the next day. With GenLt von Walsporn's 5th Panzer Division established west of Houx, both Panzer divisions were now poised for a major thrust towards the town of Philippeville. During the two-day battle, the Germans had decimated the equivalent of an entire French division. Reacting to this defeat, Corap rushed the 4th Colonial Infantry Division from Trilon to Florennes, while Georges redirected Général Bruneau's 1ère DCr to the town of Flavion, to plug the gap in the French line that Rommel's advance had created.

Just before midnight on 12 May, as Rommel's motorcyclists crossed the River Meuse at Houx and Guderian's staff planned their assault at Sedan, the spearhead of Reinhardt' XLI Corps – 6th Panzer Division – arrived on the River Meuse at Monthermé, located 18km (11 miles) north-northwest of Sedan and 36km (22 miles) south-southwest of Houx. Here the River Meuse cut through the Ardennes ridge via a deep gorge. Colonial elements of the French 102e Division d'Infanterie de Forteresse defended the town from well-prepared positions. With Kempf's artillery still ensnarled in traffic jams to the east, 360 bomber and 90 Stuka sorties supported his assault river-crossing. Despite the air attacks the first attempted crossing, upstream from the destroyed bridge, was repulsed with heavy losses. Next, Kempf's engineers attached rafts to the twisted metal of the destroyed bridge to make a rickety footbridge. Next, after dusk riflemen began crossing and by midnight had established a small, tenuous battalion-size bridgehead. South of Kempf's bridgehead, the 3rd Infantry Division (from III Corps) arrived at the town of Nouzonville on 13 May and on the third attempt successfully established a bridgehead. Meanwhile, to the north, at Givet – between Kempf's and Rommel's bridgeheads – GenLt Böhme's 32nd Infantry Division also successfully established a bridgehead across the river.

The French 11e Corps attempted to form a defensive line south of Florennes and astride the road to Philippeville. However, with his army unravelling before him, Corap decided to withdraw en masse 24km (15 miles) to prepared positions lining the French frontier, and duly informed Billotte. The latter agreed but recommended an intermediate stop-line between Charleroi and Rethel. With three different proposed defensive lines, orders to the retreating units became hopelessly confused. With communications broken by movement and spotty receipt of orders, the elements of three divisions became scattered on the way back to the French frontier.

Into this chaos was sent France's premier armoured formation, Général Bruneau's 1ère DCr. Initially moved to Charleroi, Billotte held this division in reserve awaiting the outcome of the clash in the Gembloux Gap. Realizing, too late, the magnitude of the disaster at Dinant, he assigned it to Corap early on 14 May to counter-attack the Dinant bridgehead. The division's armour, followed by the motorised infantry and artillery, struggled forward just 37km (23 miles) overnight along bomb-blasted and refugee-clogged roads to assemble near Flavion early on 15 May. Because of the slow pace, the 65 char B1 bis and 40 Hotchkiss H-39 tanks used all their fuel and had to await replenishment before attacking.

Early on 13 May the right flank of Général d'Armée Huntziger's 2e Armée remained off-balance, and unprepared to meet the horrendous assault Guderian's forces were about to unleash upon them. Général Lafontaine's 55th Infantry Division was shuffling its

Although still employed by the German Panzer divisions for scouting duties during the 1940 Western campaign, the woefully under-gunned and under-protected Pzkpfw I light training tank was obsolescent. Some 216 Pzkpfw I Ausf B chassis were used to create the 15cm sIG 33 (sf) heavy self-propelled howitzer. A 36-strong detachment of these served with the 5th Panzer Division in France. (Photo by Michael Nicholson/Corbis via Getty Images)

ABOVE During the battle of Sedan, Guderian's Panzer divisions were out-gunned by the defending French artillery. To compensate for this, German aircraft – including Dornier Do 17s like this one – played a key role providing reinforcing fire support. (Photo by ullstein bild/ullstein bild via Getty Images)

RIGHT A stick of the much-dreaded Ju 87 Stuka dive-bombers peel off into a steep dive in late May 1940. Although these planes inflicted significant lethal and psychological damage, these assets were only available in relatively limited numbers. (© IWM, HU 58529)

forward companies westward, building defence in depth behind the fortress-infantry units that manned the blockhouses and pillboxes in this sector. This allowed the exhausted troops of the 71st Infantry Division, after a staggering 61km (38 mile) forced night march, to move into positions south-east of Sedan. In addition, the arrival of reinforcements meant that the Sedan sector now had 152 artillery pieces supporting its defence.

During that morning of 13 May, across the river Guderian's troops were preparing for their afternoon assault. The 1st Panzer Division and the elite Infantry Regiment 'Großdeutschland' were to launch the main attack in the centre, crossing the river just north of the city of Sedan. Subsequently, this central assault would be covered by the time-phased crossings of Schaal's 10th Panzer Division to the south-east at Wadelincourt and 2nd Panzer Division to the west at Donchery. Supporting the main attack Guderian concentrated 96 artillery barrels. To compensate for their modest ammunition stocks, the assault relied heavily on the aerial bombardment provided by II Fliegerkorps. At midday 90 Junkers Ju 87 Stuka dive-bombers struck the French artillery emplacements, followed by 310 Do-17 sorties that bombed French riverside positions and communication routes. Subsequently, 180 Stuka sorties dive-bombed the riverbank casemates.

As the last Stuka dive-bombers left the battlefield, Guderian's 96 guns unleashed a 50-minute barrage pinning down French front-line troops, cutting off reinforcements and silencing the surviving French artillery; simultaneously, 36 8.8cm Flak 36/37s guns and 16 PzKpfw IVs engaged the French casemates with direct fire. Next, from 1600hrs, four combat-engineer battalions crossed the 65-yard-wide river in heavy kapok rafts. Though dazed by the bombardments, the surviving French fortress troops manned their weapons, sweeping the river with machine-gun fire. Despite suffering heavy casualties from the hail of French fire, and indeed several repulsed crossing attempts, that afternoon the 1st Panzer Division's assault forces managed to establish small bridgeheads on the French side of the river. Meanwhile from 1730hrs Veiel's 2nd Panzer Division – deployed on Guderian's right flank – successfully assaulted across the River Meuse at Donchery.

The German spearhead units continued to press forward, expanding the bridgeheads. By the evening, however, the French defence began to crumble. Consequently, by midnight the four motorised infantry battalions established across the river had managed to expand the bridgeheads into one continuous 8km (five mile) deep salient that stretched for 13km (eight miles) from west of Donchery eastwards to Wadelincourt. And crucially for the defenders, that evening the Germans managed to seize the crucial terrain of the La Marfée heights virtually uncontested. This was the result of a fully fledged French fiasco. The fortress infantry defending the heights' eastern slope north-east of Bulson reported approaching Panzers. The word spread to the 55th Division's artillery units, who made the premature decision to retreat. Soon the news that Panzers were at Bulson spread like a wildfire and whole units turned and fled in disorder: the developing defeat now became a rout.

By the morning of 14 May Guderian's engineers had finished building their first pontoon bridge, and the 1st Panzer Division's tanks began crossing the river at 0720hrs. He quickly sent them south to take the Bulson Ridge, the next high ground beyond La Marfée heights. Subsequently, a French counter-attack force of 40 slow FCM-36 infantry-support tanks and an infantry battalion moved in two groups from Chémery towards the Bulson ridge. After a bitter engagement, German ripostes drove both French columns from the ridge back into Chémery, with only ten tanks surviving the battle. Meanwhile, in the centre ObstLt Schwerin's elite Infantry Regiment 'Großdeutschland' continued its advance southwards, capturing Villers and Maisoncelle, where they found 40 abandoned artillery pieces.

By 1300hrs the last line of defence manned by Lafontaine's battered 55e Division had been overrun by the German assaults; its shattered remnants withdrew in disarray southwards to Roucourt Bois to join Flavigny's 21e Corps. That same

During the morning of 14 May the Allies conducted a maximum aerial effort to destroy the pontoon bridges that the Germans had constructed across the River Meuse at Sedan during the previous night. Some of these sorties were executed by RAF Bristol Blenheim bombers like these. (Photo by Central Press/Stringer/Hulton Archive/Getty Images)

GUDERIAN CROSSES THE MEUSE AT SEDAN, 13–14 MAY 1940

The crossing of the River Meuse by Guderian's XIX Corps at Sedan.

Note: Gridlines are shown at intervals of 2km (1.24 miles)

XXX
XIX ⊠
GUDERIAN

▼ EVENTS

1. 13 MAY, 1200–1600HRS: After two hours of small harassing attacks, Fliegerkorps II launches the largest, most concentrated bombing assaults flown by the Luftwaffe during World War II. Stukas hit artillery emplacements and riverside bunkers, while Do 17Zs bomb the front-line positions and interdict the reinforcements' routes of march.

2. 1600HRS: Following a 50-minute artillery barrage three battalions of SR (mot.) 1 with Kradsch. Bat. 1 and Pion.-Bat. (mot.) 37 make simultaneous crossings at four points north of Sedan against feeble opposition. Most of the reservists flee before the attackers, allowing SR (mot.) 1 to reach the railway line by 1730hrs. At Sedan, II./IRGD and Sturm-Pion.-Bat. (mot.) 43 cross at two places in the face of fierce machine-gun fire from II/147e RIF.

3. 1600HRS: Simultaneously 10. Panzer-Division attempts two crossings south-east of Sedan. The one at Bazeilles by SR (mot.) 69 and Pion.-Bat. (mot.) 49 is repulsed by I/147e RIF with heavy losses. At Wadelincourt, SR (mot.) 86 and Pion.-Bat. (mot.) 41 are driven back before they can get their rafts into the water.

4. 1730HRS: I. and II./SR (mot.) 2 with Pion.-Bat. (mot.) 49 attack at Donchery against stiff resistance by III/147e RIF. On the east side, II. Bat. gains a foothold and begins to eliminate the defenders along the riverbank, allowing I. Bat. to cross at 2000hrs. The riflemen then advance south securing the wooded heights of Croix Piot by midnight.

5. 1830HRS: II. and III./SR (mot.) 1 attack the western end of the blockhouse/pillbox line of II/147e RIF, overcoming tenacious French defence in battle lasting an hour and a half, and push through Frénois.

6. 2100HRS: SR (mot.) 1 continues its advance towards Cheveuges. Without orders I/331e RI withdraws southwest, but III/295e RI hastily deploys and temporarily halts SR (mot.) 1's advance. After a sharp action, around midnight this unit, too, evacuates the area allowing SR (mot.) 1 to capture Chéhéry unchallenged.

7. EVENING: SR (mot.) 86 finally establishes a bridgehead at Wadelincourt.

8. 14 MAY, 0100HRS: Pion.-Bat. (mot.) 37 completes its pontoon bridge at Gaulier and Aufkl.-Abt. (mot.) 4's armoured cars begin crossing at 0300hrs, followed by the vehicles of SR (mot.) 1. Tanks of II./Pz.-Rgt. 2 begin crossing at 0720hrs.

9. EARLY MORNING: Pion.-Bat. (mot.) 41 builds the second pontoon bridge across the river at Wadelincourt, and once I/147e RIF vacates its southern positions, Pion.-Bat. (mot.) 49 builds one near Bazeilles.

10. 0600HRS: SR (mot.) 1 begins a powerful drive southwards, against very little opposition. II./SR (mot.) 1 splits off to the west, capturing the bridge at Omicourt at 0730hrs. IRGD splits off to attack the remnants of French units at Bulson at 0900hrs.

11. 0600HRS: II./SR (mot.) 69 attacks II/147e RIF positions while I./SR (mot.) 86 attacks II/295e RI. This opens the way for Aufkl.-Abt. (mot.) 4 to drive to Chaumont, cutting off the French retreat and guarding the flank of IRGD as they attack Bulson.

12. 0700HRS: The left wing of the French counter-attack begins its drive to retake Chéhéry and secure Bulson; 7e BCC is followed 20 minutes later by 213e RI. At Bulson, they encounter 4./Pz.-Rgt. 2. Additional Panzer companies join the battle and by 1000hrs, the French are defeated and withdraw to Chémery.

13. 1045HRS: The right wing of French counter-attack is finally organised, but Lafontaine cancels it, ordering the 4e BCC and 205e RI to withdraw into Bois de Raucourt.

14. MIDDAY: II./Pz.-Rgt. 2 and StPion.-Bat. (mot.) 43 attack Chémery, capturing the city and its bridge to Malmy by 1300hrs.

15. AFTERNOON: IRGD advances south, and secures Maisoncelle and Villers.

16. 1400HRS: Guderian orders Kirchner to wheel 1. Panzer-Division right and drive to the west as far as possible before sunset.

17. 1500HRS: After beating off feeble counter-attacks by 3e Spahis Bde., III./SR (mot.) 1 drives west six miles to capture Signy, signalling the breakout of Guderian's Panzers.

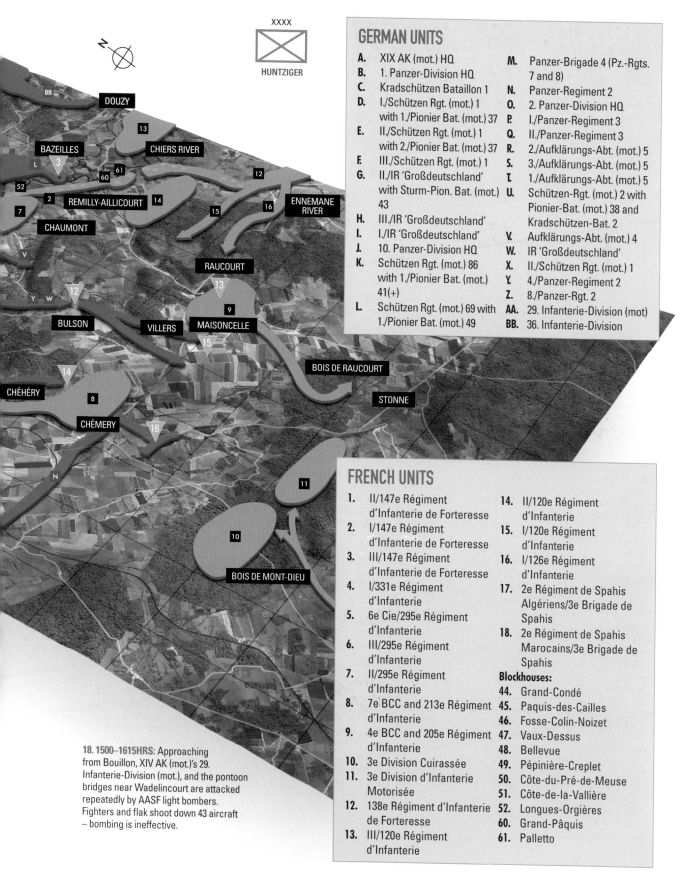

XXXX
HUNTZIGER

GERMAN UNITS

A. XIX AK (mot.) HQ
B. 1. Panzer-Division HQ
C. Kradschützen Bataillon 1
D. I./Schützen Rgt. (mot.) 1 with 1./Pionier Bat. (mot.) 37
E. II./Schützen Rgt. (mot.) 1 with 2./Pionier Bat. (mot.) 37
F. III./Schützen Rgt. (mot.) 1
G. II./IR 'Großdeutschland' with Sturm-Pion. Bat. (mot.) 43
H. III./IR 'Großdeutschland'
I. I./IR 'Großdeutschland'
J. 10. Panzer-Division HQ
K. Schützen Rgt. (mot.) 86 with 1./Pionier Bat. (mot.) 41(+)
L. Schützen Rgt. (mot.) 69 with 1./Pionier Bat. (mot.) 49

M. Panzer-Brigade 4 (Pz.-Rgts. 7 and 8)
N. Panzer-Regiment 2
O. 2. Panzer-Division HQ
P. I./Panzer-Regiment 3
Q. II./Panzer-Regiment 3
R. 2./Aufklärungs-Abt. (mot.) 5
S. 3./Aufklärungs-Abt. (mot.) 5
T. 1./Aufklärungs-Abt. (mot.) 5
U. Schützen-Rgt. (mot.) 2 with Pionier-Bat. (mot.) 38 and Kradschützen-Bat. 2
V. Aufklärungs-Abt. (mot.) 4
W. IR 'Großdeutschland'
X. II./Schützen Rgt. (mot.) 1
Y. 4./Panzer-Regiment 2
Z. 8./Panzer-Rgt. 2
AA. 29. Infanterie-Division (mot)
BB. 36. Infanterie-Division

FRENCH UNITS

1. II/147e Régiment d'Infanterie de Forteresse
2. I/147e Régiment d'Infanterie de Forteresse
3. III/147e Régiment d'Infanterie de Forteresse
4. I/331e Régiment d'Infanterie
5. 6e Cie/295e Régiment d'Infanterie
6. III/295e Régiment d'Infanterie
7. II/295e Régiment d'Infanterie
8. 7e BCC and 213e Régiment d'Infanterie
9. 4e BCC and 205e Régiment d'Infanterie
10. 3e Division Cuirassée
11. 3e Division d'Infanterie Motorisée
12. 138e Régiment d'Infanterie de Forteresse
13. III/120e Régiment d'Infanterie

14. II/120e Régiment d'Infanterie
15. I/120e Régiment d'Infanterie
16. I/126e Régiment d'Infanterie
17. 2e Régiment de Spahis Algériens/3e Brigade de Spahis
18. 2e Régiment de Spahis Marocains/3e Brigade de Spahis

Blockhouses:
44. Grand-Condé
45. Paquis-des-Cailles
46. Fosse-Colin-Noizet
47. Vaux-Dessus
48. Bellevue
49. Pépinière-Creplet
50. Côte-du-Pré-de-Meuse
51. Côte-de-la-Vallière
52. Longues-Orgières
60. Grand-Pâquis
61. Palletto

18. 1500–1615HRS: Approaching from Bouillon, XIV AK (mot.)'s 29. Infanterie-Division (mot.), and the pontoon bridges near Wadelincourt are attacked repeatedly by AASF light bombers. Fighters and flak shoot down 43 aircraft – bombing is ineffective.

DOUZY
BAZEILLES
CHIERS RIVER
REMILLY-AILLICOURT
CHAUMONT
ENNEMANE RIVER
RAUCOURT
BULSON
VILLERS
MAISONCELLE
BOIS DE RAUCOURT
STONNE
CHÉHÉRY
CHÉMERY
BOIS DE MONT-DIEU

'Victory or Defeat Will Depend on those Bridges'

At 0100hrs on 14 May, Guderian's Pioneer-Bataillon (mot.) 505 completed constructing a 16-tonne Brückengerät B across the River Meuse, connecting the villages of Gaulier and Glaire. At midday, with 2nd Panzer Division's Pioneer-Bataillon (mot.) 38 still working to finish their own pontoon bridge at Vrigne-Meuse, Guderian ordered that division to send its Panzers and self-propelled anti-tank guns across the Meuse using the Gaulier–Glaire bridge. Seen here is the last PzKpfw III Ausf. E tank **(1)** of Panzer Regiment 3's 4. Kompanie crossing the bridge while the first Panzerjäger I of Panzerjäger-Abteilung (mot.) 38 waits its turn to cross. **(2)** Tank number '435' was the fifth tank of 4. Kompanie's 3rd platoon, as its number coding indicates. The yellow unit marking – including 2. Panzer-Division's 'two-dot' symbol – and white 'K' for 'Gruppe Kleist' are carried on the upper glacis of the hull, while the yellow triangle stencil on the turret indicates the 3rd Platoon. Realizing the danger, the AdA and AASF mounted a maximum effort to destroy the bridges. After an initial misdirected effort by ten RAF Fairey Battles – the two morning raids attacked bridges upstream from Sedan, well inside friendly lines – the French launched mid-morning strikes by Bre 693 assault aircraft, followed by modern LeO 451

and ancient Am 143M bombers at midday. These attacked the 10th Panzer Division's pontoon bridge at Wadelincourt and the mechanised columns queued up to cross it. In the mid-afternoon the AASF sent 45 Battles and eight Blenheims also against pontoon bridges east of Sedan and the vehicles queuing up for them, followed by 29 Blenheims from Bomber Command that attacked troop concentrations and vehicle columns from Givonne to Bouillon. The Gaulier–Glaire bridge was not attacked all day. However, flying to attack the eastern bridges and vehicle columns, the RAF bombers frequently overflew the Gaulier–Glaire bridge – such as the 'vic' of three Fairey Battles **(3)** shown here – en route to their targets. Guderian's bridges were defended by the respective Panzer division's attached Luftwaffe flak battalions, such as the two 2.0cm FlaK 30s **(4)** seen here from Flak-Abteilung (mot.) 83, as well as elements of the corps-level 102. FlakRegiment (mot). The Luftwaffe anti-aircraft guns shot down 19 Battles, while defending Messerschmitts destroyed another 11 Battles and 13 Blenheims. An additional ten Fairey Battles were so badly damaged they were abandoned on their airfields during the ensuing retreat. (Artwork by Peter Dennis, © Osprey Publishing)

morning the reinforcing 3e DCr and 3e Division Motorisée reached Le Chesne. Huntziger ordered these forces to deploy around the Bois de Mont-Dieu to contain the enemy, and then to launch a counter-attack as soon as possible in the direction of the sector that stretched from Maisoncelle through Bulson to Sedan.

Meanwhile, the Germans had completed another pontoon bridge over the Meuse during the night at Wadelincourt, allowing Schaal's 10th Panzer Division to move its heavy vehicles towards the battlefront, and a third bridge went up north-west of the villages of Remilly and Aillicourt. Belatedly realising the danger to his far right flank, Billotte ordered a maximum aerial effort to destroy the pontoon bridges. In the late morning 39 Allied aircraft attacked the pontoons, followed by a midday strike by 16 French bombers. Finally, during the mid-afternoon eight AASF Blenheims and 63 Battles attacked the two eastern German pontoon bridges and the columns of armoured vehicles queuing up for them. Enemy fighter and dense flak accounted for a staggering 53 aircraft – the highest losses of any day in the RAF's history thus far.

With his lines of communication across the River Meuse secure and his opponent reeling southwards in disarray, at 1400hrs on 14 May 1940 Guderian made the seminal decision upon which the entire *Fall Gelb* campaign turned. Guderian ordered the 1st Panzer Division to wheel west and advance as rapidly as possible across the Bar river and Ardennes Canal. Consequently, at 1500hrs its spearheads struck out to the west from Omicourt, advancing 10km (six miles) to reach the village of Signy by midnight. The unrelenting Panzer charge westward had just begun. During an intense two-day battle on 13–14 May Guderian's XIX Corps had established a large bridgehead beyond Sedan for the tolerable price of 120 men killed and 400 wounded. In so doing Guderian's forces had destroyed both the French 55e and 71e Infantry Divisions.

By 14 May, the French Second Army, led by Général d'Armée Charles Huntziger, had been decimated by the German armoured advance. Subsequently Huntziger was given the painful mission of supervising the humiliating French capitulation at Compiègne on 22 June. (Photo by Hulton-Deutsch/Hulton-Deutsch Collection/Corbis via Getty Images)

The German Breakout from the Meuse Bridgehead (15–17 May)

By the morning of 15 May Rundstedt's units were piling into the 79km (49 mile) wide by 14km (nine mile) deep bridgehead that the German forces had established across the River Meuse. The westward-facing edge of this salient stretched north-to-south along a line that lay east of the vector from Maubeuge in the north down to Rethel and Stonne in the south-east. Some seven Panzer, three motorised and nine marching infantry divisions were already well on the way to completing their assembling in this bridgehead. Opposing them, Corap's battered Ninth Army could muster five mechanised, three motorised and ten marching infantry divisions against the invaders, but all these formations had already suffered significant casualties.

The mortal threat the Panzers posed, almost certainly itching to burst west out of this bridgehead, was by now abundantly clear to the Allied high command. Indeed, that morning the demoralised French Prime Minister Paul Reynaud

Most of the artillery that equipped Germany's numerous infantry divisions was horse-drawn, rather than self-propelled or towed by tracked, half-tracked or wheeled vehicles (that is, it was not motorised). In this image GenObst von Bock inspects a parade formed by a horse-drawn artillery column close to the Etoile, Paris, in late June 1940. (Photo by Universal History Archive/ Universal Images Group via Getty Images)

telephoned his British counterpart, Winston Churchill. Reynaud exclaimed that since a torrent of enemy tanks was already bursting through the central sector, the Allies effectively had already been defeated. The successful German surprise infiltration of Kleist's armoured wedge through the supposedly impassable Ardennes had clearly inflicted an extraordinarily powerful psychological blow on the French high command. The Allied forces now certainly needed to prevent the Panzers from breaking out, if the Allies were to have any chance of wresting back the strategic initiative from the invading German forces.

During the morning of 15 May, along the northern axis of the German breakthrough beyond the Meuse, the 5th and 7th Panzer Divisions (from Hoth's XV Corps) charged west toward Philippeville, sweeping aside several weak detachments from the French 1ère DCr and 4e Division d'Infanterie Nord-Africaine while inflicting heavy losses on them. By noon Rommel's Panzers had cleared Philippeville and during the afternoon they pushed a further 10km (six miles) westward, piercing the two designated French rearward defensive lines. In the German central sector, the units of the 41e Corps Armée de Forteresse began to fall back toward Corap's designated rearward defensive line. Simultaneously, GenMaj Kempf's 6th Panzer Division broke out into open country. Meanwhile, at Nouzonville the 102e Division d'Infanterie de Forteresse tried to fall back. However, its mainly non-motorised units were swiftly overtaken by units of both Kempf's 6th Panzer Division and GenLt Kuntzen's 8th Panzer Division, and were promptly decimated; a similar fate befell the 61e Division d'Infanterie to the north of Monthermé. Consequently, by that evening, the 6th Panzer Division had reached Hirson, just 16km (ten miles) shy of the HQ of 9e Armée at Vervins. By midnight on the 15th, therefore, the German forces had decimated the French 41e Corps, creating a vacuum in front of GenLt Reinhardt's XLI Corps.

Into this empty void stumbled the various detachments of the French 2e Division Cuirassée, which had redeployed south by train to Hirson, having just raced north-east to Charleroi on 14 May. The crumbling French sector between

THE SPRING 1940 WESTERN CAMPAIGN: PHASE ONE

Huntziger and Corap's armies was now taken over by a new command, Army Detachment Toulon, that reported directly to Georges' TONE HQ. Toulon took control over the remnants of the 41e Corps, the 2e Division Cuirassée, and the 3e Spahis, as well as the 14e and 36e Divisions d'Infanterie that were arriving from the south. All French tactical manoeuvre, however, was now hampered by the fact that every road in the region was now clogged with thousands of frightened refugees fleeing the fighting. As this large irregular stream of French 2e Division vehicles, men and units – spread across some 40km (25 miles) – moved eastwards, the 6th Panzer Division's vanguards slashed through them like a sabre, scattering them widely between Hirson and Saint-Quentin. This success enabled Kuntzen's 8th Panzer Division to dash toward Hirson, while 6th Panzer Division charged south-west toward the town of Montcornet, which it reached by midnight; here it bumped into recce units from Guderian's 2nd Panzer Division, which that day had charged westward from the north-eastern face of the Sedan bridgehead. Of course, Georges needed a scapegoat for the calamity that had occurred across the front of the French 9e Armée that day. Therefore that evening he sacked Corap and replaced him with Général Giraud.

On the 15th, across the southern axis, Guderian's three Panzer divisions were also anxious to make similar progress westward, but they were in places stymied by the last vestiges of French resistance. On Guderian's extreme northern flank, the 2nd Panzer Division made reasonable progress toward Montcornet, but were slowed by the 3e Spahis. Likewise, to the south, Kirchner's 1st Panzer Division struck west, but was held up by the 3e Spahis' tenacious defence of La Horgne and the resistance offered at Bouvellemont by elements of the newly-arriving French 14e Division d'Infanterie. Concerned about the weakness of the southern flank of the Sedan bridgehead in the face of newly-arriving French reinforcements, Gen d.Kav von Kleist now wanted Guderian merely to consolidate the bridgehead and build a defence along the southern perimeter. But after a heated discussion, he reluctantly granted the XIX Corps (Motorised) commander his requested freedom to exploit westward. Guderian did leave Schaal's 10th Panzer Division and the elite Infantry Regiment 'Großdeutschland' behind with Gen d.Inf von Wietersheim's XIV Corps (Motorised) to defend the south flank of the Sedan bridgehead around the village of Stonne. This proved prudent, as these forces were available to repulse the counter-attack mounted by the French 3e DCr – part of the newly arriving 21e Corps Armée HQ – that day. Although the French heavy tanks made some progress, by the afternoon the 10th Panzer Division and the Infantry Regiment 'Großdeutschland' had stabilised this threatening tactical situation.

During the early hours of 16 May, the Army Group A headquarters learned to its surprise that the 6th Panzer Division had reached the town of Montcornet during the night. Rundstedt now became concerned that the south-eastern face of his three-corps Panzer-wedge was now dangerously stretched across 89km (55 miles) from Montcornet to Stonne; he worried that only the 19km (12 mile) front around Stonne, south of Sedan, was properly defended. He thus ordered all units to halt along the north-south line that ran from Beaumont through Hirson and Montcornet on to Guignicourt. He excepted from this prohibition any advanced recce units that were permitted to continue 49km (30 miles) further west to the River Oise to seize bridgeheads between Guise and La Fère; but an advance beyond the Oise was not be permitted until 18 May. This delay would enable the German Twelfth Army's infantry divisions to reach and cover the exposed German southern flank, making it more secure from French counter-attacks. OKH Commander-in-Chief GenObst von Brauchitsch had been similarly concerned about the exposed southern flank and was thus relieved to learn of Rundstedt's decision to halt the Panzers. That evening he endorsed Army Group A's *Haltbefehl* (halt order).

On the morning of 16 May Guderian's 1st and 2nd Panzer Divisions bypassed the town of Rethel and surged westward. In a stunning advance they charged 64km (40 miles) west across open French countryside, and swiftly dispersed the French 3e DLC. By midnight the 2nd Panzer Division's advanced recce spearheads had arrived at the town of Montcornet, where they met the vanguard detachments of Kempf's 6th Panzer Division. Indeed, during 16 May the divisions of Hoth's, Reinhardt's and Guderian's Panzer-heavy corps had raced forward on a 56km (35 mile) wide front from Beaumont to Hirson and Montcornet. These actions caused the French 9e Armée, cut off from its neighbours to the north and south, to disintegrate rapidly. In response, its new commander, Général Giraud, ordered the battered remnants of the 2e DCr to counter-attack toward Montcornet. Subsequently, he amended his orders to this division, instead ordering a defensive mission, much to the frustration of the French tankers.

Early on the 17th, Guderian met the 6th Panzer Division commander Kempf – a subordinate of Hoth XV's Corps – at Montcornet. Since Kleist's delineation of corps boundaries only went as far as Rundstedt's stop line, on which the two men now stood, Guderian swiftly took charge of the situation. He ordered the 6th, 1st and 2nd Panzer Divisions to charge west, respectively to Guise, to Origny and to Ribemont and Moy, to secure crossings over the River Oise. Blatantly disregarding his superiors' orders to halt, he ordered all three divisions – not just their advanced units – to keep driving west to the Oise until the last drop of petrol was gone. Guderian was determined to realise his vision of audacious risk-embracing fast-paced Blitzkrieg operations – a vision that almost terrified his more tactically conservative superior officers.

That afternoon Général d'Armée Georges spread the scattered tank companies of the French 2e DCr across numerous crossing points along the western bank of the Oise. These small defensive 'corks' were both leaderless – the formation's command post was moving from Rethel to Guiscard – and lacking adequate artillery and infantry support. The 6th Panzer Division attacked forcefully at

1900hrs, crushing the four tank companies deployed at Guise and Proix. By nightfall on 17 May the 6th Panzer Division had secured two bridgeheads across the River Oise to the south-east of the town of St Quentin.

Early on the 17th Rundstedt became increasingly anxious about the ever-extending southern flank, especially in the Laon area, where the French 4e DCr had just begun to arrive. He now ordered that the Oise and Sambre rivers were to not be passed without his express authorisation. Rundstedt, the conservative commander steeped in the methodical ways of World War I, had been astonished by the speed of Guderian's advances. Hitler, too, was agitated over the apparent vulnerability of the extended Panzer thrust and so he confirmed Rundstedt's *Haltbefehl*. The Fuhrer also peremptorily ordered OKH Commander-in-Chief von Brauchitsch to adopt the measures necessary to rectify this vulnerability. Meanwhile, unaware of their superiors' mounting fears, by 0900hrs Veiel's 2nd Panzer Division had charged through Origny and Kirchner's 1st Panzer Division had reached Ribemont and Moy; Bruché's three surviving tank companies withdrew their H-39s to the south-west.

Meanwhile, the German 1st Panzer Division was charging toward the Serre river. Now, however, it faced a hastily launched French counter-attack against its exposed southern rear flank that threatened its lines of communication. For from the area north-east of Laon the newly arrived French 4e DCr surged 11km (seven miles) into the undefended German flank. The French formation was an untrained and improvised grouping commanded by Colonel de Gaulle. However, with the help of close air support from Stuka dive-bombers, the threat was brushed aside by afternoon, and the Panzers continued driving west while De Gaulle's unit retired to the south-west.

At 0700hrs Kleist – who was extremely angry that Guderian had exceeded his remit – had ordered an immediate halt and flew to Guderian's HQ near Soize near the town of Montcornet to enforce this halt. During a violent reprimand, Kleist accused Guderian of outright disobedience. This violent altercation prompted the volatile Guderian to resign. He telephoned to recall 2nd Panzer Division commander Veiel to take charge of the XIX Corps (Motorised), and angrily informed Rundstedt of his decision. Can a frontline commander in contact with the enemy resign? The army group commander immediately ordered Twelfth Army commander GenObst List to go to Guderian's HQ to defuse this bitter row. If command squabbles such as this escalated further, they might be a greater detriment to German progress than that being generated by the defending Allied forces. During the afternoon's somewhat calmer meeting List informed Guderian that he had no choice but to remain in command of XIX Corps (Motorised). List also told him that the OKH-sanctioned halt order must be obeyed. However, with Rundstedt's approval, List fashioned a clever compromise whereby Guderian was allowed to undertake reconnaissance-in-force to the west, but with the proviso that he had to keep his HQ at Soize.

Général Charles de Gaulle commanded the improvised 4e Division Cuirassée during late May and early June 1940, using it to counter-attack aggressively. During his subsequent exile in the UK he served as the Free French Minister of War and national leader. (Photo by Hulton Archive/ Getty Images)

That evening, Guderian's actions showed that he in effect had immediately torn up this carefully brokered compromise agreement. He ordered all his four subordinate formations – the 1st and 2nd Panzer Divisions had now been reinforced by Schaal's 10th Panzer Division and Schwerin's elite Infantry Regiment 'Großdeutschland' – to continue advancing westwards that evening. This was not what had been agreed. Leaving his HQ at Soize, Guderian followed the Panzer spearheads with his advanced tactical HQ. His staff even went to the length of laying miles of telephone wire from his main HQ at Soize, so that the Wehrmacht's wireless intercept units could not monitor his communications or learn of his true location. This was insubordination on an epic scale. To maintain the pace of his high-tempo, risk-embracing, Blitzkrieg-style onslaught, Guderian found himself fighting both the Allied enemy and his own more tactically conservative superiors!

By midnight on the 17th, meanwhile, Hoth's subordinate 5th Panzer Division had reached the Sambre, 14km (nine miles) south-west of Maubeuge, while Rommel's 7th Panzer Division had crossed that river and was headed for the town of Cambrai. In the centre, GenLt Reinhardt's subordinate 8th Division had crossed the River Oise near Hirson and was headed west, while the 6th Panzer Division was a further 24km (15 miles) west, having crossed the Oise, and was racing northwest toward Cambrai. Finally, Guderian's 1st, 2nd and 10th Panzer Divisions all reached the River Oise and established bridgeheads across it. Along the exposed southern flank, the motorised infantry formations of Wietersheim's XIV Corps (Motorised) were thinly stretched on the west-east facing front from Rethel back to Stonne near Sedan.

Army Group B's Tank Battles at Hannut & Gembloux (13–15 May)

While Kleist's massed armour was crossing the River Meuse and establishing a large salient on the western hinterland during 13–15 May, the German operations in the north had unfolded. The key component of the German plan was the rapid advance of the Panzer elements south-westward. Their rapid progress would lock the wheeling French 1ère and 7e Armées, and the BEF, into a bitter contact battle in central Belgium. This would prevent these, the most mobile Allied formations, from redeploying to counter-attack the Panzer advance westward toward the coast.

During the morning of 12 May, as described, the spearheads of the 3rd and 4th Panzer Divisions – from Hoepner's XVI Corps (Motorised) – had advanced south-west through the villages of Waremme, Avennes and Braives. Upon arrival at Crehen they clashed with elements of the newly-arriving 3e DLM, part of Prioux's elite Corps de Cavalerie. Its sister formation, the 2e DLM, was then locked in battle with German infantry formations to the north. A bitter see-saw battle for Crehen and Thisnes unfolded throughout the day, with the former being recaptured by the French. During the evening, however, Hoepner concentrated all his corps' armour on a narrow front north and south of Hannut, in preparation for a renewed, concerted attack the next day. The 3e DLC, meanwhile, braced itself for the next day's attacks. Four of its battalions defended the line of the Petite Gette stream and the string of hamlets west of Hannut, while the 87 tanks of its immediate armoured reserve waited near Jauche; a further depth reserve of 78 tanks remained at Merdorp and Jandrenouille.

On 13 May 1940 the 256 operational tanks of GenLt Stever's 4th Panzer Division attacked the French forces at Hannut while GenMaj Stumpff's as yet unbloodied 3rd Panzer Division assaulted the French line along the Petite Gette. After intense preliminary artillery and Stuka strikes, Hoepner's attacks began at 1230hrs. His spearhead infantry units assaulted the Hannut area while the Panzers roared south towards Merdorp and Wasseignes. In the north, however, fierce French resistance held the German attempts to capture bridges across the Petite Gette. After a later successful crossing the German Panzers were met by vigorous French mechanised counter-attacks. At Merdorp, meanwhile, the 3e DLM repulsed the initial German assaults in heavy fighting, and a complex battle ensued for much of the day. However, by mid-afternoon, the assaults forced the remaining 12 surviving French tanks to break out to the village of Jandrenouille. ObstLt Eberbach exploited this with armoured attacks toward Jandrain, which eventually broke French resistance.

With his line pierced at Jauche-Jandrain, Prioux now ordered a general retreat. During that evening the 3e DLM withdrew its battered remnants to Prioux's intermediate stop line, 9km (six miles) ahead of Général d'Armée Blanchard's designated main defence line; it had lost 106 tanks within 48 hours. Still fighting off German infantry, the neighbouring 2e DLM did not retreat until after dark. Although retiring over refugee-clogged roads was difficult, by morning both divisions were positioned in a coherent defence behind the Belgian serrated-steel anti-tank fence that ran from the village of Beauvechain via Perwez to Fort Marchovelette.

Hoepner's armour commenced its advance at 0600hrs on 14 May. It smashed through the fence at Perwez and became embroiled in fierce fighting there and at Grand Leez. The German units made slow progress against stubborn French resistance until at midday they were halted by tank-supported Moroccan infantry at the village of Ernage, just north of the town of Gembloux. Meanwhile, the Panzers had broken through at Thorembais, but at Walhain they were repulsed by SOMUA tanks before the French finally withdrew.

Having successfully fulfilled his mission of delaying Hoepner's Panzers, that evening Prioux withdrew his two mechanised-cavalry divisions through Blanchard's lines, having lost 134 tanks in the hard-fought three-day battle. The next day Hoepner attempted to force his way through the French 1ère Armée positions north of Gembloux, but was unable to make a successful penetration. By the time his corps was withdrawn from the battle on 16 May, his two divisions had lost 48 tanks destroyed, while another 174 were unserviceable. This successful

The Tank Battle at Hannut – Defending Jandrain, 1420hrs, 13 May 1940

S/Lt le Bel, a platoon commander in Capt Lizeray's 13e Escadron, 11e RDP, recalls the battle of Jandrain. 'Lizeray's 12 Hotchkiss H39 tanks, as well as most of Capt Laffargue's mounted infantry (dragoons) and a battery of four 25mm anti-tank guns, defended Jandrain village. The neighbouring village of Jauche was defended by the SOMUAs of the 1ère Cuirassiers. Jandrain and Jauche formed the linchpin connecting the two wings of Général Langlois's defensive line. The Panzers began their advance at midday, first attacking Orp-le-Petit, the next village to the north, before shifting south; 2. Kompanie/PzR 6 – about 20 PzKpfw I/IIs accompanied by two PzKpfw IVs – attacked the northern outskirts of Jandrain an hour later. The defenders included S/Lt Jolibois's **(1)** platoon of five H39s supported by the 3e Escadron of dragoons, dragoons **(2)**, and a 25mm A/T gun **(3)**. Sgt Morel's A/T gun crew quickly knocked out a PzKpfw I

(4), and the remaining light tanks retreated westward **(5)**, leaving the heavier PzKpfw IVs **(6)** bombarding the French positions. Jolibois and five dragoons were killed. By 1500hrs elements of II./PzR 6 arrived, PzKpfw IIIs engaging in a slugging contest that destroyed half of Lizeray's H39s as the Panzers penetrated into the village from the north and west. Laffargue ordered Lizeray to withdraw his remaining H39s and form a 'last square' in the village centre. Battling tenaciously for another hour, with the 6./PzR 35 closing in from the south and engaging the SOMUAs at Jauche, de Vernejoul ordered Laffargue to withdraw his dragoons. But with the village invested from three sides, and the fourth under constant fire, only le Bel – leading four other H39s – was able to escape.' (Artwork by Peter Dennis, © Osprey Publishing)

French action debunks the myth that the German Blitzkrieg of 1940 was unstoppable. However, once Prioux's divisions were back in Blanchard's main line, he reassigned each of their tank battalions to one of his division and corps commanders as a mobile 'plug' to counter local breakthroughs. In triggering Blanchard's assignment, Hoepner, Reichenau, and Bock's aggressive offensive had nonetheless fulfilled Army Group B's mission to divert to itself the strongest possible Anglo-French forces, thus facilitating the Panzer breakout in the centre.

With Guderian's and Rommel's dual successes on the River Meuse, on 14 May Blanchard's two armoured divisions were hurriedly reassigned to Général d'Armée Corap's shattered Ninth Army. Both of these powerful formations, however, would be destroyed before they could make a difference. Général Bruneau's 1ère DCr was swiftly crushed by Walsporn's 5th Panzer Division while de-training near Dinant. Meanwhile, Général Bruché's 2e DCr was badly mauled by Kempf's 6th Panzer Division while en route to the city of Sedan. Finally, on 18 May Hoepner's XVI Corps (Motorised) was reassigned to Rundstedt's Army Group A. It thus withdrew from combat and headed south-west to reinforce the Panzers' headlong charge to the Channel coast, and thus help encircle the Allied armies in Belgium.

The Panzers Charge West and the French Riposte (17–19 May)

On 15 May Général d'Armée Georges had sacked Corap as commander of the disintegrating Ninth Army, replacing him with the energetic Giraud, who had led the French 7e Armée into southern Holland. Georges also took direct control of both Giraud's command and Huntziger's French 2e Armée. Next, on the evening of the 16th Georges ordered Giraud and Général Touchon to attempt a mechanised counter-breakthrough to be executed north of the River Aisne in the area that stretched from Attigny through Rethel and on to Château Porcien.

To this end Bruneau's 1ère DCr redeployed to the Avesnes–La Capelle area to counter-attack the northern flank of Guderian's salient. Passing through Avesnes around midnight, the French armour unexpectedly blundered into elements of Rommel's 7th Panzer Division. In a brief but intense encounter, Bruneau's command was driven back with heavy losses, eventually retreating north to the

During the Panzer charge west toward the English Channel, Erwin Rommel's Tactical Headquarters had swiftly to ascertain the best routes of advance. Here Rommel and his key staff officers plan the future advance in a field next to his command armoured half-track. (Photo © CORBIS/ Historical/ Corbis via Getty Images)

On 19 May Général Aubert Frère was given the task of reconstituting the devastated French 7e Armée with drafts drawn from the Maginot Line. Here he is seen (on the right) talking to Maréchal Pétain during 1940. (Photo by KEYSTONE-FRANCE/Gamma-Rapho via Getty Images)

town of Maubeuge. Rommel daringly exploited this success, reaching Le Câteau at 0615hrs the next day. The 7th Panzer Division had advanced a staggering 80km (50 miles) in just 48 hours, passing Rundstedt's Halt Line in the process. Next, during the morning of 17 May, as Walsporn's 5th Panzer Division crossed the Sambre at Berlaimont, it was stung by a counter-attack from Général Picard's 1ère DLM, which had just arrived from northern Belgium. This riposte failed to destroy the Panzers' bridgehead and the French formation retired to Le Quesnoy at dusk after suffering heavy losses.

On the south side of the Panzer salient, the only forces Touchon had available to execute Georges' ordered breakthrough operation was De Gaulle's 4e DCr, a hurriedly-assembled assortment of mechanised units gathering around the town of Laon. His mission was to defend the Rethel–La Fère area against a possible Panzer thrust towards Paris and gain time for the recently-reformed French 6e Armée (formerly the Army Detachment Touchon) to establish itself along the Aisne and Ailette rivers. To do so, the aggressive De Gaulle determined to secure bridgeheads on the Serre river at Saint-Pierremont and Montcornet, defend there and engage the German columns moving westwards through Marle.

The next morning, 140 French tanks and a battalion of bus-borne infantry gathered just east of Laon, and at daybreak they set out in two columns headed north-east. Crossing the Canal de Desschement at Chivres, they overran elements of the 1st Panzer Division' reconnaissance battalion. Subsequently, the French Char B1s and D2 tanks advanced towards Saint-Pierremont while the Renaults continued towards Montcornet. At Saint-Pierremont, the Char tanks battled their way across the Serre bridges. However, a German motorised infantry battalion counter-attacked the small French bridgeheads, forcing the enemy to withdraw. Meanwhile, at Montcornet, 25 R-35s threatened the 1st Panzer Division HQ, but were finally repulsed.

On the morning of 19 May, the Panzer divisions' reconnaissances in force surged forward across the River Oise and Sambre Canal. The 2nd Panzer Division seized Saint-Quentin that morning, while the 1st Panzer Division captured the town of Péronne and secured its key bridges across the River Somme by mid-afternoon. Meanwhile, Rommel's armour surged forward to Cambrai, while the 6th Panzer Division both destroyed the last remnants of the French 2e DCr at Le Catelet and captured the headquarters of 9e Armée just before midnight; army commander Giraud was captured the next morning. Army Group A's Panzers had thus annihilated the French 9e Armée, in the process destroying the two most powerful French armoured divisions and outmanoeuvring the third. It was a desperate blow to French hopes of halting the Panzer onslaught.

By 19 May Général d'Armée Billotte had fully realised the extreme gravity of the debacle to the south. He thus began planning for the eventuality that the Allied forces in the north might become separated from those south of the Panzer thrust toward the coast. His group of armies was already conducting a three-phase withdrawal – from the River Dyle to the River Senne, then to the River Dendre and then to the River Escaut over a four-night period. This withdrawal was intended to prevent the rampaging Panzers from curling in behind his right flank. Général d'Armée Georges, meanwhile, extended the southern defensive line from La Fère, along canals connecting the River Oise to the River Somme and following the Somme to the sea. He also moved several divisions from behind the Maginot Line fortifications to form a new French 7e Armée under the command of Général d'Armée Frère.

That same day Gamelin – who had done nothing significant to impact the unfolding battle until now – assumed direct command of the *Théâtre d'Opérations du Nord-Est* (North-East Theatre of Operations HQ) from Georges. Subsequently, he learned from limited aerial reconnaissance that there was a vacuum of enemy forces in the triangle that lay between Laon and Montcornet and Neufchâtel. Gamelin thus ordered Georges to throw his mobile forces against the rear of the Panzer divisions into this apparent vacuum. No sooner had this order been issued, than Gamelin was sacked by French Prime Minister Paul Reynaud, who replaced him with the 73-year-old Général d'Armée Weygand. Reynaud suspended all counter-offensive operations for two full days until the new Commander-in-Chief determined the French Army's next move.

The Destruction of RAF No 114 Squadron at Condé-Vraux Airfield, 11 May 1940

One German airfield-strike mission undertaken at the start of the campaign ably illustrates the nature of the German counter-air efforts in the campaign. Taking off at dawn from Aschaffenburg airfield, 25 miles southeast of Frankfurt, Oblt Oskar Reimers, commander of 4. Staffel/KG 2, led his nine Dornier Do 17Z-2s at very low altitude, heading west. Crossing the French frontier south of Sedan, the formation of three Ketten (three-aircraft 'vics') flew down the Aisne valley, passing to the north of Reims, before swinging round to the left at the Aisne–Marne Canal to approach their target from the north-west. Their target was Condé-Vraux, an RAF Advanced Air Striking Force (AASF) airfield approximately 25 miles south-west of Reims, where 11 Bristol Blenheims of No 114 Squadron were ranged upon the aerodrome, armed and fuelled, waiting for their aircrews who were just finishing their morning mission briefing. Ordered to attack the bridges spanning the Albert Canal in Belgium, take-offs were scheduled for 0600hrs. At 0545hrs, Oblt Reimers, flying Do 17Z-2 U5+LM (1), approached Condé-Vraux at church-steeple height, achieving complete surprise.

Reimers and his two wingmen each released ten 50kg fragmentation bombs, followed by six other bombers. The second Kette (2) followed about 20 seconds behind the leaders, offset to one side to attack the Blenheims not targeted by the leaders. The third Kette (3) followed 20 seconds later, hitting the squadron fuel dump. The entire attack lasted 45 seconds. The RAF ground crewmen dived for cover as the Dorniers crossed the airfield boundary, roaring in at low level and high speed. The small bombs erupted amongst the parked Blenheims (4), blowing up one after another. The attack was so sudden that the base's anti-aircraft gunners had no time to react: a solitary Vickers .303in. machine gun opened fire as the last Dornier egressed to the east. Six Blenheims were destroyed in the attack. The remaining five were all damaged to some extent and, when 114 Squadron evacuated the Condé-Vraux seven days later, they were all abandoned. No RAF aircrews were lost and only two ground crewmen were slightly wounded in the surprise attack. (Artwork by Peter Dennis, © Osprey Publishing)

A Change in the Skies (15–24 May)

By 15 May 1940 – the day the Panzers broke out of their three Meuse bridgeheads – the Luftwaffe was now operating with near impunity in the skies above the unfolding ground offensives. During the next 48 hours the German Luftflotten 2 and 3 switched back to airfield attacks, bombing 17 bases and destroying over 40 Allied aircraft. Consequently, on the 16th the Armée de l'Air (AdA) could only manage 153 fighter sorties, down two-thirds from the daily average of 470 sorties during the campaign's first week.

Further base raids on the 19th left the French Groupement 6 with only ten serviceable bombers. Such losses, when combined with the fear that the rapidly advancing Panzers would overrun the airfields of the RAF's Advanced Air Striking Force (AASF) en route next triggered a wholesale evacuation of Allied air forces from the battle area. The aircraft were withdrawn to various locations, including Paris, Troyes and – for the AASF – back to England. These withdrawals significantly hampered the effect that Allied air power could exert on Kleist's Panzers as they charged toward the Channel coast.

During 13–24 May, moreover, the offensive efforts of the German Luftflotten 2 and 3 – in the face merely of sporadic and ineffective Allied opposition – slowly shifted to transportation interdiction, including the bombing of 198 railway marshalling yards and stations. These devastating strikes slowed Allied redeployments by rail and stymied timely counter-attacks. Meanwhile, Kleist's thrust to the English Channel continued to be directly supported by Fliegerkorps II, with in addition Fliegerkorps VIII supporting Guderian's XIX Corps (Motorised) from 19 May.

ABOVE After pioneering air-ground cooperation during the 1939 Poland war, GenMaj Wolfram von Richthofen commanded Air Corps VIII in the 1940 Western campaign. From 19 May his command focussed on supporting the ground advance of Guderian's armoured divisions. (© IWM, HU 55040)

LEFT The principal aerial platform that the German ground forces relied upon to break up local Allied counter-strikes was the Ju 87 Stuka. But the Henschel Hs 123 ground-attack biplane also played a key role in such responses. At Cambrai on 22 May, for example, Hs 123s inflicted heavy losses on the 2e DLM. (Photo by ullstein bild/ullstein bild via Getty Images)

THE PANZER CHARGE TO THE SEA, 16–20 MAY

After the successful German breakout from the Meuse bridgehead, on 16–19 May the Panzers charged westward, brushing aside Allied local counter-attacks. By the 20th, the southernmost formation of Guderian's corps, the 10th Panzer Division, had captured the key town of Amiens. Further north, the 6th Panzer Division had captured Doullens, and the 2nd Panzer Division had passed to the south of that town. That evening the 2nd Division's forward detachment charged, heedless of any flank threats, toward the Channel coast astride the Somme estuary north-east of Abbeville. Shortly before midnight on the 20th, its spearhead tanks reached the English Channel. The dire Allied strategic situation now became cataclysmic. The tip of the German Panzer wedge had reached the sea, thus cutting the Allied north from the rest of the forces deployed in central France.

Crucially, German Junkers Ju 87 Stuka dive-bombers and Dornier bombers effectively covered Guderian's exposed southern flank, attacking French armoured columns around Montdidier. When the 4e DCr counter-attacked Schaal's 10th Panzer Division from the area of Laon on 19 May, the French tanks were forced to withdraw by four hours of Stuka bombardments. Similarly, when on 22 May the French 2e DLM's counter-attack neared Cambrai, Hs 123 assault biplanes relentlessly attacked it, knocking out 15 tanks. By this point the Luftwaffe's main problem was not the Allies' air defence but the pace of the advance. Although the very efficient, radio-equipped forward air signals liaison detachments attached to each Panzer division enabled Stuka dive-bombers to attack targets within 45–75 minutes of notification, their capabilities were limited by the ability of the Junkers Ju 52 transport units (decimated in the initial airborne assaults in Holland) to keep the advanced aerial units supplied with fuel and bombs.

The Panzer Charge to the Sea (19–20 May)

On the same day that Giraud was captured and Gamelin was fired – 19 May – the ban on Guderian's units making reconnaissances-in-force was lifted. Early that morning the 1st Panzer Division forced a bridgehead across the Somme at Péronne while Reinhardt's spearheads drove west from Le Catelet. Général d'Armée Georges now recognised that he had little left to block the Panzers' westward charge to the sea; once there, the lines of communications with Billotte's Groupe d'Armées 1 to the north would be severed.

Only one water barrier now remained across Kleist's path: the unfinished Canal du Nord, stretching from Péronne on the Somme to Douai on the Scarpe. Having no more French units with which to defend this line, Georges directed the British 23rd (Northumbrian) Division to secure the canal crossings. But the 23rd Division was an untrained and understrength Territorial Army formation lacking adequate artillery and anti-tank capabilities. During the 20th the division deployed along the Canal's northern sector. This position was immediately compromised by the 1st Panzer Division through its capture of the town of

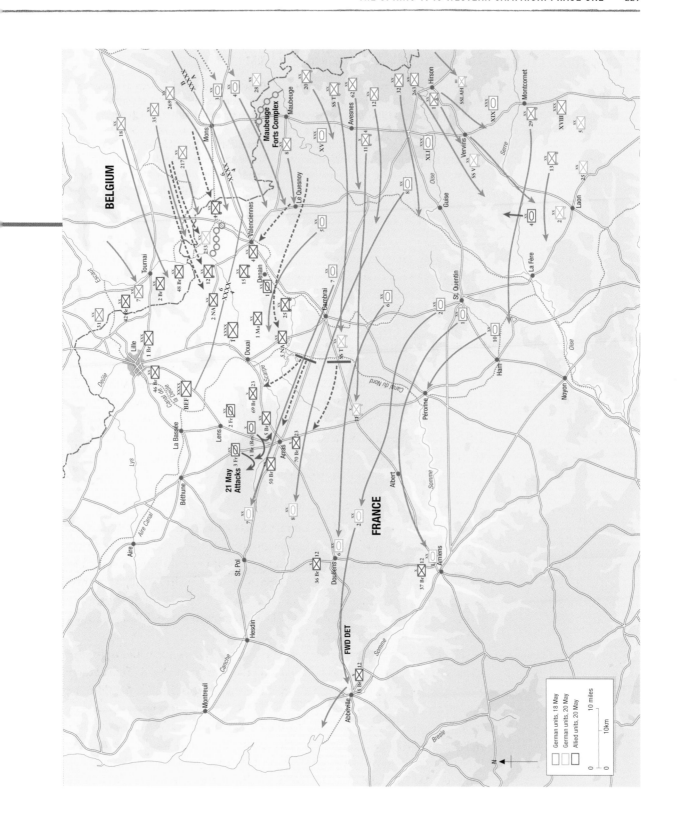

BELGIUM

Maubeuge
Forts Complex

Maubeuge

Mons

Le Quesnoy

Valenciennes

Tournai

Denain

48 Br

2 Br

Lille

BEF

1 Br

2 Fr

Lens

La Bassée

Béthune

Aire

Douai

Cambrai

Avesnes

Hirson

Montcornet

Vervins

Guise

La Fère

Laon

St. Quentin

Ham

Noyon

Péronne

Albert

Amiens

Arras

21 May
Attacks

St. Pol

Douliens

FRANCE

Hesdin

Montreuil

FWD DET

Abbéville

German units, 18 May
German units, 20 May
Allied units, 20 May

10 miles

10km

N

Krisis Arras: 'I Personally Gave Each Gun its Target'

GenMaj Erwin Rommel's attack west of Arras, intending to surround the city from that direction, was still being organised when the defending British launched a spoiling attack designed to clear the southern approaches to the city of Rommel's forces, and thus delay his attack. At the head of Schützen-Regiment (mot.) 6, the 7th Panzer-Division commander was hustling to rejoin Panzer-Regiment 25 when his column came under heavy shellfire from the north, driving his motorised riflemen into defensive positions behind the River Crinchon near the village of Wailly. There, Rommel found his advanced battery of howitzers, 3./ Artillerie-Regiment (mot.) 78, being attacked from the west by British tanks (7th Bn. Royal Tank Regiment). Defending the rather exposed battery of four 10.5 cm leFH 18 field howitzers were a troop of three half-track mounted 2.0cm FlaK 30 anti-aircraft guns **(1)** from 2./leichte Flak-Abteilung (mot.) 59 and a battery of 3.7cm PaK 35/36 anti-tank guns **(2)** from Panzerjäger-Abteilung (mot.) 42, covering the western approaches to the howitzers from their left flank. As Rommel later related: 'After notifying the divisional staff of the critical situation in and around Wailly we drove off to a hill 1,000 yards west of the village, where we found a light anti-aircraft troop and several anti-tank guns located in hollows and a small wood, most of them totally under cover. About 1,200 yards west of our position, the leading enemy tanks, among them one heavy, had already crossed the Arras-Beaumetz railway and shot up one of our Panzer IIIs (out of view to the left/west). At the same time several enemy tanks **(3)** were advancing down the road from Bac du Nord and across the railway line towards Wailly **(4)**. It was an extremely tight spot, for there were several enemy tanks very close to Wailly on its northern side. The crews of a howitzer battery **(5)**, some distance away, now left their guns … I brought every available gun into action at top speed against the [enemy] tanks. Every gun, both anti-tank and anti-aircraft, was ordered to open rapid fire immediately and I personally gave each gun its target. With the enemy tanks so perilously close, only rapid fire from every gun could save the situation. We ran from gun to gun. The objection of the gun commanders that the range was still too great to engage tanks effectively was overruled. All I cared about was to halt the enemy tanks by heavy gunfire. Soon we succeeded in putting the leading enemy tanks out of action. Over by the howitzer battery also – despite a range of 1,200 to 1,500 yards – the rapid fire of our anti-tank and our 8.8cm anti-aircraft guns succeeded in bringing the enemy to a halt and forcing some of them to turn away.' (Artwork by Peter Dennis, © Osprey Publishing)

Péronne; early on 20 May, moreover, the 2nd Panzer Division arrived at Combles, turning the British Division's other flank. Abandoning the canal line, the division split into two. Subsequently, GenLt Kuntzen's 8th Panzer Division crossed the Canal at Inchy-en-Artois and overran the retreating British units.

Meanwhile Rommel's 7th Panzer Division advanced on the town of Arras and attacked the city while the newly-arrived SS-Motorised Division *Totenkopf* passed to the north to encircle from the west. To buy time to allow the numerous British support elements in Arras to evacuate, BEF Commander Lord Gort created *Frankforce*, a temporary counter-offensive grouping led by Maj Gen Franklyn. This formation controlled Franklyn's own British 5th Division as well as Maj Gen Martel's 50th Division and the 1st Army Tank Brigade. Prioux added his now-depleted 3e DLM as a flank guard for the British right wing.

From 1430hrs on the 21st, two British combined-arms columns – built around the 1st Brigade's 88 tanks – advanced to cross the Scarpe river 8km (five miles) west of the town of Arras, then swept around the city's outskirts in a counter-clockwise flow until the Cojeul river was reached. Simultaneously, the 3e DLM's 60 tanks engaged Rommel's armour south of the Scarpe. After advancing to the Arras–Doullens road, the right-hand British column was eventually halted at Wailly by German 88mm flak guns delivering massed direct fires. The left column, meanwhile, had overrun the German positions around Agny and Beaurains. Eventually, however, German 10.5cm howitzers and 8.8cm flak guns halted the riposte, destroying 36 British tanks. Subsequent German counter-thrusts drove the attackers back to their starting points. Although the riposte had shocked the Germans, eventually it was totally defeated, with the British losing 46 tanks. The Panzer charge west could thus now continue.

Meanwhile, on the 20th, VI Corps guarded the Stonne sector south of Sedan while III Corps faced Touchon's newly formed French 6e Armée on the River Aisne and Général de Corps Rochard's French 18e Corps filled in along the Ailette. This freed up XIV Corps' motorised infantry divisions to move westwards and cover the La Fère-Ham sector. Once Schaal's 10th

The widely-respected Général Henri Giraud (centre) commanded the French 7e Armée, slated to charge north to Breda. However, when by 16 May Général Corap's 9e Armée had all but disintegrated, Giraud was ordered to assume command of it. But he could not save this army and on the 19th was himself captured. (Photo by KEYSTONE-FRANCE/ Gamma-Rapho via Getty Images)

Panzer Division rejoined Guderian's Corps, it covered the exposed southern flank, permitting the other two divisions to charge westward for the Channel coast. The only thing standing in their way were the British 12th (Eastern) Division's three widely-scattered brigades that each held a vital road/railroad intersection.

Early on 20 May 1940, Kirchner's 1st Panzer Division drove through Albert, destroyed the British 37th Brigade at Amiens, and established a 6km (four mile) deep bridgehead. The 2nd Panzer Division meanwhile raced to Abbeville, destroying the British 35th Brigade. Throwing all caution to the wind, its reconnaissance battalion recklessly raced west, arriving at the English Channel shore north-west of Abbeville by sunset. Simultaneously, the 6th Panzer Division (from Reinhardt's XLI Corps) captured Doullens and annihilated the British 36th Brigade. In just one day three Panzer divisions had eliminated an entire British infantry division and decisively altered the Allies' situation. The Allied north had been cut off from the forces defending France to the south: in ten momentous days, *Fall Gelb* had achieved a decisive strategic victory in the north of the Western theatre. The scale of the triumph left Adolf Hitler beside himself with joy; equally, it shattered the morale of the defending Allied forces.

The Allied North Falls Back (16–20 May)

Following the successful defence of the sector that stretched between the town of Hannut and Gembloux from 13 to 15 May, Général d'Armée Blanchard ordered his 1ère Armée formations to retire that night, so as to be in place along the Charleroi Canal by the morning of the 17th. The retreat was conducted in an orderly fashion, but its urgency caused much equipment, artillery, and anti-tank weaponry to be abandoned. The rapid breakout of the Panzers from the River Meuse bridgeheads between 13 and 16 May now threatened to turn the southern flank of Billotte's Groupe d'Armées 1. However, the excessive demands of coordinating the operations of six Allied armies became all too apparent at this stage. Indeed, Billotte's overworked staff was only finally able to devise a fighting retreat to the River Escaut and issue instructions to the BEF and Belgian Army on the morning of the 16th. The Groupe d'Armées 1 was to withdraw westward in three phases: to the River Senne on the night of 16/17 May, to the River Dendre on 17/18, and the Escaut on 18/19 May.

The BEF's withdrawal, if somewhat confused by conflicting information received from its flanks, was conducted in good order and the Germans did not vigorously pursue its units as they retreated back to the Escaut. Taking its positions between Audenarde and Maulde, by 21 May the BEF manned a strong defensive position, having suffered only about 500 combat casualties thus far. For the Belgians, however, the westward retreat was an especially bitter pill. Having thrown their lot in with the Allies, they discovered that the greater part of their country – including the cities of Brussels, Antwerp, and Namur – was being abandoned to the Germans. On the K-W Line, the Belgian IVe Corps held up IX Corps while the Belgian II and VI Corps withdrew to the Willebroek Canal on 16 May. During the 17th all four Belgian corps retired to the River Dendre while King Léopold's GHQ relocated to Ghent.

During 17 May, to replace Giraud's 7e Armée, then being dismantled to provide forces for stemming the Panzer breakthrough to the south, the Belgian Corps de Cavalerie regrouped west of Antwerp. These Belgian cavalry units mounted spirited counter-attacks led by their few light tanks; surprisingly, these local ripostes managed successfully to check the advance of GenLt Wobig's German XXVI Corps. Under the cover of these delaying actions, the Belgian Army withdrew in good order. Its formations redeployed behind the River Escaut from Terneuzen in the north down to Audenarde. The next day Giraud's 7e Armée was disbanded, its remaining 16e Corps Armée being attached to the Belgian Army.

The BEFs' infantry was supported by six battalions of divisional cavalry. These units fielded Vickers Mark VIb tankettes as well as Universal Carriers. The British employed these vehicles in local counter-attacks, especially along the River Escaut in Belgium. However, these lightly protected, machine gun-armed, armoured vehicles suffered heavy casualties in these ripostes. (© IWM, O 681)

That same day Billotte sent the French 9e DIM to guard the River Oise between Hirson and Guise. As soon as it arrived in this area it was swiftly engaged by Kuntzen's 8th Panzer Division, and quickly decimated. Meanwhile Picard's 1ère DLM and the 25e DIM were dispatched to join the shattered French 9e Armée. Three days prior Giraud had replaced Corap as its commander, but the tactical situation was already well beyond salvaging. Giraud could not prevent the Panzer onslaught completely overrunning his new command by 18 May; the next day the German advance captured Giraud himself.

During 20 May 1940 the Allies' strategic situation degenerated from very bad to terrible when Guderian's Panzers reached the English Channel shore to the north-west of Abbeville. It was perhaps the defining moment of the campaign. The Panzer charge to the sea had sealed the BEF, the French 1ère and 7e Armées, and what remained of the Belgian Army in a boot-shaped pocket defined by the towns of Ghent, Dunkirk, and Lille: some 600,000 troops were deployed in this encircled *Kessel* (cauldron).

The day before Gamelin had been sacked, and 73-year-old Weygand, recalled from Syria, became the new Allied Supreme Commander. A breath of fresh air, Weygand had a plan to cut off the over-extended Panzers and ordered the air force to fly him to Calais, from where he would travel to Ypres to discuss his ideas with Billotte, King Léopold, and the BEF commander, Lord Gort. The furious battle to save the Allied northern forces from destruction was about to begin – a struggle that to a large degree could determine the fate of the rest of France.

As the 1940 campaign unfolded, the German advance disrupted Allied aerial operations. In the face of growing Luftwaffe aerial superiority, Allied fighters struggled to exert much impact. This deterioration was slightly offset in late May when a new RAF asset, the Supermarine Spitfire, began operating over the Dunkirk pocket. While technically a match for the Messerschmitt Bf 109E, the Spitfire's performance was limited by the RAF's restrictive formations, rigid tactics and pilot inexperience. (Photo by Fg. Off. B J Daventry/ Imperial War Museums via Getty Images)

PHASE TWO:
END-GAME IN THE WEST (21 MAY–25 JUNE 1940)

THE ORIGINS OF THE CAMPAIGN'S SECOND PHASE

From 10 to 20 May 1940 – a paltry period of just 11 days (or some 260 hours) – the military invasion of the West that the German Wehrmacht had unleashed had utterly stunned the watching world. France, perceived by many commentators as the strongest military power in Europe, had suffered a crippling strategic blow. Hitler's Wehrmacht had achieved in under a fortnight a more significant strategic success than that they achieved during four years of war waged by the Imperial German Armed Forces during the Great War. Belgium, the Netherlands and Luxembourg had all been swiftly defeated by Germany's raw military power; northern France had also been overrun and the BEF had been ignominiously driven back to the United Kingdom.

Aided by a clever strategic plan, the German operations had exploited the expected Allied strategy. Army Group B's secondary effort into the Netherlands and northern Belgium sucked the powerful Allied forces committed to the Dyle (Breda Variant) Plan into a bitter contact battle waged in central Belgium. Meanwhile, GenObst Ritter von Leeb's Army Group C sat poised to assault the potent French Maginot Line fortifications, thus fixing the powerful forces of the Groupe d'Armées 2 within these fortifications along the France-German border in Alsace-Lorraine.

With the Allies sucked into the north and south, the German main effort surprisingly came through the dreadful tank country of the Ardennes region. Moving as best they could along narrow winding roads in forested river-swept terrain, Gen d.Kav von Kleist's Panzers managed to infiltrate through this weak Allied centre and mount a sudden assault crossing of the River Meuse. Once achieved, Kleist's mobile divisions surged west to reach the English Channel on 20 June and cut off the Allied forces in the north from those in the rest of France. The Germans first had to liquidate the enemy forces trapped in the Dunkirk–Lille pocket, and then turn their attention to *Fall Rot* – the invasion of the rest of France.

CHRONOLOGY: 1940 WESTERN CAMPAIGN
(PHASE TWO: *FALL ROT*)

1940

21 May   BEF spoiling attack at Arras stuns German Army leaders. Weygand meets with Billotte and King Léopold; Billotte is fatally injured in a car crash.

ABOVE The British V Adm Bertram Ramsay successfully directed the execution of Operation *Dynamo*. Subsequently, during summer 1944 Ramsay was the Naval Commander-in-Chief of the Allied Expeditionary Forces for the Normandy campaign. Sadly he was killed on 2 January 1945, when the aircraft in which he was travelling crashed. (Photo by Hulton Archive/ Stringer/ Getty Images)

22 May	German Panzer formations invest the French ports of Calais and Boulogne.
23 May	Lord Gort orders the BEF to withdraw to the town of Dunkirk.
24 May	Because of fears about the exposed southern flank of the Panzer corridors' advance toward the Channel coast, Rundstedt again orders the Panzers to halt – Hitler affirms decision with the OKW-directed *Haltbefehl*.
26 May	Operation *Dynamo* – the naval evacuation of BEF from France – begins; Hitler rescinds the *Haltbefehl*.
28 May	Belgian Army surrenders.
31 May	French 1ère Armée surrenders at Lille; around 35,000 troops are captured
4 June	Evacuation of Allied forces from Dunkirk ends. The remaining 34,000 French troops defending Dunkirk surrender. Operation *Dynamo* and the evacuations preceding it rescue some 221,504 British and 170,475 French troops.
5 June	*Fall Rot* – final Wehrmacht conquest of France – begins with GenObst von Bock's Army Group B initiating its offensive against the western end of the French Weygand Line defences on the Somme and Aisne rivers.
6–7 June	During the night Général d'Armée Besson's Groupe d'Armées 3 abandons the River Somme position (the Weygand Line) and withdraws to the south.
9 June	Rundstedt's Army Group A joins the unfolding *Fall Rot* offensive against the Weygand Line defences along the River Aisne.

RIGHT An armada of 'little ships' – civilian vessels of all shapes and sizes – directly helped to bring home an additional 28,708 troops, as well as assisting in ferrying soldiers from the shore to the naval vessels anchored in deeper waters. Here a drifter, dangerously overloaded with many soldiers, heads back toward the English Coast while in the background the oil refinery in Dunkirk continues to burn. (© IWM, HU 2108)

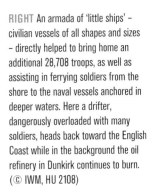

10 June	Germany's Axis partner, Mussolini's Fascist Italy, declares war on the Allies and prepares its invasion of south-eastern France.
14 June	The French capital, Paris, capitulates to the German forces. The German First Army (from GenObst Ritter von Leeb's Army Group C) initiates Operation *Tiger* against the Maginot Line defences in the Faulquemont–Saarguemines sector.
15 June	The German Seventh Army (from Army Group C) initiates Operation *Bear,* its offensive across the Rhine against the Maginot Line.
16 June	Prime Minister Paul Reynaud forced to resign; the new, anti-war, government led by Philippe Pétain takes power.
17 June	The spearheads of Panzer Group Guderian reach the town of Pontarlier on the Swiss border, encircling Général d'Armée Prételat's Groupe d'Armées 2 along and behind the Maginot Line fortifications in Alsace-Lorraine. Pétain's government opens ceasefire feelers with Germany.
19 June	Rommel's 7th Panzer Division races through Normandy, the Cotentin Peninsula and into Brittany to capture Cherbourg and St Malo.
20 June	The 400,000 troops of the Italian Army Group West invade south-eastern France.
21 June	The dozen German marching infantry divisions of the German Fourth and Eighteenth Armies cross the River Loire on the 330km (205 mile) front between the cities of Nantes and Orléans.
22 June	At 1836hrs France signs armistice with Germany. Signing takes place in the same train wagon located at Compiègne that was used when Imperial Germany signed the November 1918 Armistice that ended the Great War.
25 June	At 0035hrs the ceasefire ending the Franco-German Conflict takes effect.

GenObst Wilhelm Ritter von Leeb commanded the German Army Group C that mounted the threat of direct assault against the Maginot Line. In July 1940 Hitler promoted Leeb, as well as his fellow army group commanders Bock and Rundstedt, to the lofty rank of field marshal as reward for the amazing success achieved by the German invasion. (Photo by Heinrich Hoffmann/ullstein bild via Getty Images)

THE CAMPAIGN

The First Battle of the Ports (20–24 May)

During 21 May the OKH restructured Army Group A in preparation for the next phase of *Fall Gelb*. To fight on two diametrically opposed fronts, Rundstedt's command was split: List's Twelfth Army was to defend the southern (Aisne–Ailette–Somme) side of the corridor while GenObst von Kluge's Fourth Army

Men of a Waffen-SS light machine-gun team make their way through thick underbrush near Watten. They operate a 7.92mm MG 26(t) (the Czech-built ZB vz.26 weapon). Because OKH's 'go' order was received too late in the day to resume Panzer operations on 26 May, Guderian's motorised infantry units went into action without armoured support. (© IWM, MH 1923)

was to continue offensive operations to the north. Kleist's group, minus the German XIV Corps, was transferred to Kluge's army. In addition, within the Fourth Army Hoth's command was upgraded to a Panzer group with the arrival of two motorised corps – the XVI and XXXIX – from Bock's Army Group B. The latter corps, consisting of GenLt von Wiktorin's 20th Motorised Infantry Division and the independent 11th Motor-Rifle Brigade, was assigned to the Arras sector, allowing the Panzers to swing round to the west to envelop the city.

German offensive operations resumed on 22 May, with Rommel's 7th Panzer Division crossing the River Scarpe west of the town of Arras. This advance was once again halted by a French mechanised spoiling attack, at Mont-Saint-Éloi. Only when GenLt von Walsporn's 5th Panzer Division arrived the next morning could Rommel outflank the French resistance by moving to the north. Early on 24 May the Allies abandoned the town of Arras and withdrew behind the Canal Line (which ran along the Aa, the Aire and the La Bassée Canals). Initially Kleist held Guderian's Corps on the River Somme to guard against any counter-offensive by the newly forming French 7e Armée; on the north side he deployed Reinhardt's XLI Corps (Motorised) west of the town of Arras. To safeguard against any further surprise Allied ripostes, Kleist held Schaal's 10th Panzer Division at Doullens as his main reserve force.

Early on 22 May Guderian's armour headed north to take the coastal towns of Boulogne and Calais while Reinhardt covered his inland flank by advancing towards Saint-Omer. At 0800hrs Guderian's two Panzer divisions and the Infantry Regiment 'Großdeutschland' launched northwards to besiege the two Channel ports. That morning, while the French 21e Division d'Infanterie was rushed across Flanders to block the Panzers south of the town of Boulogne, its vanguards were overrun by Kirchner's 1st Panzer Division while still on their trains. Meanwhile the two French fortress battalions defending the town of Boulogne were reinforced by the seaborne arrival of the British 20th Guards Brigade. Throughout the 23rd the 2nd Panzer Division's attack into the town's suburbs progressed slowly in the face of fierce Allied resistance. That afternoon, however, the War Office ordered the British brigade evacuated, and that evening seven Royal Navy destroyers evacuated 4,368 troops from the town. Despite their exasperation at their allies' precipitous departure, the French defenders fought tenaciously for another 36 hours until finally surrendering at noon on 25 May. Back on the 23rd, meanwhile, the 1st Panzer Division had laid siege to Calais, defended by three French battalions and the British 30th Brigade.

Once Kleist realised that the Arras attack was a one-off event, however, he released Schaal's 10th Panzer Division to move to Calais, while the 1st Panzer Division charged north-north-east towards the town of Dunkirk. The 10th Panzer Division invested Calais early on 24 May and throughout the next 72 hours an intense urban battle raged; the German assaults finally overwhelmed the last defenders late on the 26th May.

While these sieges progressed, the Allied spoiling attack near the town of Arras had meanwhile caused great anxiety among senior German commanders. Kleist worried about another Allied riposte, noting his own rising losses, reducing his five divisions' strength to only 1,220 tanks. Consequently, late on the 23rd Rundstedt decreed that the Fourth Army would not advance on 24 May, to allow the lagging infantry to close with the lead Panzers. That day Hitler visited Rundstedt to discuss the situation, the elimination of the Allied pocket, and the impact on the follow-on *Fall Rot* plan to conquer the rest of France. Hitler worried that the Panzers would bog down in Flanders and not be available for the *coup de grâce* against France. Additionally, for political reasons he wanted Bock's Army Group B to push the Allied forces out of Belgium, and against the Panzers soon to be arrayed along the Canal Line, so that their final surrender would occur on French – rather than neutral – soil. Consequently, Hitler issued a *Haltbefehl* instructing the Panzers merely to hold the favourable defensive line Lens–Béthune–Aire–St Omer–Gravelines and allow the enemy to attack it. The Panzer formations were to be husbanded for future, more important, tasks in *Fall Rot*.

The Führer's *Haltbefehl* (Halt Order) Rescinded (26–28 May)

From 24 to 25 May 1940 Hitler's hoped-for south-westward movement of the Allied armies into France from Belgium did not materialise. Instead, the Allies continued tenaciously to resist Bock's Army Group B in Belgium. Along the Canal Line scattered Allied units were digging in, and between the two fronts, the southernmost BEF units and French 1ère Armée were withdrawing northwards towards Dunkirk. Consequently, at 1530hrs on 26 May Hitler directed Army Group A to resume its offensive with a forward thrust toward Tournai, Cassel and Dunkirk. However, it took over 12 hours for the Panzer formations within Kluge's Fourth Army to deploy, so their assaults could not begin until the next morning, 27 May. Guderian's motorised infantry started their attacks immediately, but at Bourbourg the French defenders repulsed the highly-trained troops of the Infantry Regiment 'Großdeutschland' with heavy casualties. At the village of Watten the newly-arrived *Leibstandarte-SS Adolf Hitler* (the Führer Bodyguard) crossed the Aa Canal and subsequently made good progress until French reinforcements halted it at Bollezeele. The 2nd Panzer Division overran the defenders, forcing them to withdraw to Drincham, while the 1st Panzer Division broke through the Allied defensive to reach Gravelines.

The 3rd Grenadier Guards Counter-attack, 2000hrs, 27 May 1940

Lt Col Franklin Lushington of the 97th (Kent Yeomanry) Artillery Regiment RA recalls the 3rd Grenadier Guards counter-attack. 'Pulling back from the French frontier defences at Roubaix the day before, the battalions of Maj Gen Alexander's 1st Division were ordered to march to Dunkirk where they would be the first to man the port's perimeter. The retreat corridor was held open by the 5th Division, with the 143rd Brigade attached. Filling in behind the battered Belgian Army, which was forced to withdraw northwards from the River Lys, the 143rd Brigade deployed along the Ypres Canal north of Comines with two 5th Division brigades extending the line to Ypres. Attacked violently throughout the day by the German 61st Infantry Division, these Territorials gave ground grudgingly, suffering heavy casualties, prompting Lt Gen Alan Brooke, commanding II Corps, to detach three 1st Division battalions to help stiffen the defence of the retreat corridor. Despite having marched 20 miles during the night, Maj Allan Adair led the tired Tommies of the 3rd Battalion The Grenadier Guards to the Bois de Ploegsteert where he received his orders – counter-attack eastwards until reaching the Comines–Ypres Canal – directly from Franklyn. After a brief rest, that afternoon Adair deployed his battalion in two ranks of two companies, line abreast with a section of Vickers Universal machine gun carriers on each flank, and advanced eastwards with fixed bayonets. The guardsmen began their attack just after 2000hrs, supported by barrages from five artillery regiments. However, soon they were subjected to heavy artillery and mortar fire themselves and were slowed by the cumbersome crossing of a deep, five-foot wide stream and 'innumerable fences'. The battalion's carrier platoon **(1)** engaged enemy machine gun nests concealed in a copse of trees – 'the whole front was lit up by the enemy's tracer ammunition' – while there was 'a farm blazing directly in front of . . . 2 Company's line of advance' **(2)**. As the dusk twilight faded into darkness, Maj Adair **(3)** followed with 3 and 4 Company; 'the leading sections were silhouetted in the flames as they went forward towards the canal bank'. By the time 1 and 2 Companies reached the canal, they had suffered such horrendous casualties they were unable to hold the line and fell back a quarter of a mile to where 3 and 4 Companies had dug in – using their bayonets as picks and shovels – in a long field ditch. The battalion held out against German shelling and attacks through the night and all the next day. At 2200hrs Adair and the surviving nine officers and 270 other ranks (from the estimated 412 men that began the assault) withdrew back towards Dunkirk.' (Artwork by Peter Dennis, © Osprey Publishing)

Early on the 27th, across the southern end of the battle-line, three Panzer divisions and the SS-*Totenkopf* (Death's Head) and SS-*Verfügungs* (At Readiness) motorised formations assaulted the 32km (20 mile) canal frontage from Aire to La Bassée held by Maj Gen Loyd's British 2nd Division. With no anti-tank guns and little artillery, the British were overrun at every point. On the north flank, the British 6th Brigade was wiped out by Stumpff's 3rd Panzer Division, while in the centre the 4th Brigade was destroyed by Stever's 4th Panzer Division and the SS-Totenkopf. To the south the British 5th Brigade was beaten back by Rommel's 7th Panzer Division, which subsequently drove an armoured wedge towards Armentières. The British 2nd Division's sacrifice allowed General Gort to transport four formations out of the Lille end of the pocket, withdrawing towards the town of Dunkirk. The French 1ère Armée – now commanded by Prioux – followed; marching on foot, exhausted and hungry, most of the French units could not keep up with the British withdrawal. While Général de Corps de La Laurencie's French 3e Corps followed the British divisions north of Lille and established a defence along the River Lys, the 4e Corps only made it to Seclin, while the French 5e Corps continued to disintegrate. The next morning (28 May) the Luftwaffe, after three days devastating Dunkirk's port facilities, attacked Prioux's exhausted units. Completely bereft of air cover, the French 4e and 5e Corps were pounded mercilessly, stopping all movement; just a few remnants of 5e Corps managed to escape.

On the morning of 27 May, after the *Haltbefehl* had been rescinded, the Panzer divisions resumed their westward advance. Here Pzkpfw II light tanks from Rommel's 7th Panzer Division cross the La Bassée Canal via a pontoon bridge. The lead tank is from the 25th Panzer Regiment's headquarters staff troop.

The Battle for Cassel, 28 May 1940

The town of Cassel is strategically located atop a 176m-high (577ft) sugarloaf-shaped hill 30km (19 miles) due south of Dunkirk, and is the junction of five major roads through the area. This medieval walled city was defended by two of the 145th Brigade's infantry battalions, its company of nine 25mm Hotchkiss anti-tank guns, the 209th Battery (reinforced), the Worcestershire Yeomanry (53rd Anti-tank Regt) with 15 2-pdrs and a battery of four 18-pdrs from 5th Regiment, Royal Horse Artillery. In the previous two days the defenders had transformed Cassel into a fortress by loopholing the outer walls for the artillery and anti-tank guns and building barricades in the narrow streets. The infantry, 2nd Bn, the Gloucestershire Regt (2nd Glosters) and the 4th Bn, the Oxfordshire and Buckinghamshire Regt (4th Ox and Bucks) – established a defence in depth. Once the Panzer offensive resumed Kampfgruppe Koll, built around ObstLt Richard Koll's PzRgt 11, drove directly towards Cassel. Panzer-Regiment 11 consisted of three tank battalions, each with an authorised strength of 15 PzKpfw IIs, 17 PzKpfw IVs and 34 Skoda PzKpfw 35(t)s. In March 1935, the Wehrmacht confiscated 219 of the 10.5-ton Czech tanks, delivering 130 to PzRgt 11. Only one ton heavier than the PzKpfw II, the 35(t) had a much heavier armament: one 3.7cm cannon and two 7.92mm machine guns. By the time PzRgt 11 approached Cassel it had an estimated 20 PzKpfw IIs, 25 PzKpfw

IVs and 70 PzKpfw 35(t)s operational. Koll began his assault at 1000hrs. While battalions on both flanks were held up by outposts, some two dozen tanks advanced from the south. The battle soon became a contest between British anti-tank guns and the tanks' main gun and machine guns. British 25mm and 2-pdr anti-tank rounds ricocheted off the PzKpfw 35(t)s' 25mm front armour until the gunners switched their aim to the tank tracks, or waited until the tanks passed and hit the 16mm side/15mm rear armour. Bdr Harry Munn described the battle: 'We fired, they moved, halted and fired. After some 15 shells had been fired, [the gun loader asked] "When are you going to hit the bloody thing?" . . . so I shouted to [the gun layer] "Hit [it] in the tracks, Frank!" Just as the tank moved we fired, hitting the track propulsion wheels . . . The tank halted abruptly, swinging to one side. Our next shell must have disabled the turret, as they opened the escape hatch and ran for their lives towards their lines . . .' By the end of the day the 209th Battery had claimed 40 tanks destroyed. Finally, at midnight Koll abandoned the fruitless assault and the surviving Panzers were withdrawn. Depicted here are the crew of disabled PzKpfw 35(t) 713 (1) captured by a squad of 2nd Glosters (2), while an abandoned RHA 18-pdr field gun (3) still points through a loophole made in the city wall. (Artwork by Howard Gerrard, © Osprey Publishing)

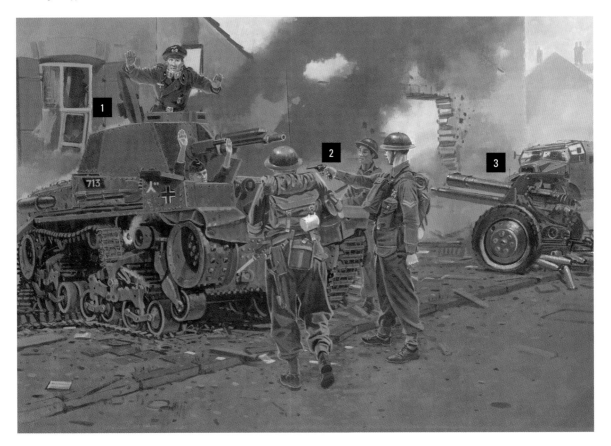

At dawn on 28 May Reinhardt's XLI Corps advanced to Hazebrouck and Cassel to cut off the French retreat. The Panzers swiftly penetrated the British 44th Division's defences. However, the division's remnants made a determined last stand on high ground at Mont des Cats during the 29th, which allowed the 2,500-man remnants of 5th Brigade to straggle northwards behind them, through Watou. Meanwhile, the 6th Panzer Division and the Leibstandarte-SS Adolf Hitler overwhelmed the British 144th Brigade's defence of Wormhoudt and surrounded the 145th Brigade in Cassel. After mounting a ferocious defence of the town of Cassel, the British survivors tried to break out during the night of 30/31 May, but most were captured in the attempt.

Along the coast, Kirchner's 1st Panzer Division besieged Gravelines and the adjacent Fort Philippe. Guderian, however, anticipating the 340km (211 mile) movement south-east to join List's Twelfth Army for the forthcoming *Fall Rot* operation, withdrew the 1st Panzer Division's tanks to the town of Boulogne for replenishment. At this point the Panzers deployed between the River Yser and the coast were also replaced by Gen d.Inf von Wietersheim's recently-reinforced XIV Corps (Motorised). This powerful corps formation now controlled Hubicki's 9th Panzer Division, Wiktorin's 20th Motorised Infantry Division, the independent Motor-Rifle Brigade 11, the elite Infantry Regiment 'Großdeutschland' and the infamous Leibstandarte-SS Adolf Hitler.

The Allied North in Retreat and the Belgian Collapse (21–28 May)

Meanwhile, the German operations against the northern Allied front continued to unfold even as the Panzers surged westwards towards the Channel coast. Earlier, on 19 May, the new French Chief of the General Staff (and Supreme Allied Commander) Général d'Armée Weygand had flown back from the French colony of Syria. He was utterly shocked to discover how bad the strategic situation had already become. On the 20th he flew to Calais and at Ypres met the senior commanders of the three British, French and Belgian armies now trapped in south-western Belgium and northern France by the Panzer advance further south. Here Weygand outlined his plan to cut off Army Group A's thrust to the coast. He noted that the enemy's 'Panzer corridor' was only 40km (25 miles) wide between the town of Arras and the River Somme.

Therefore, Weygand argued, this narrow German-held corridor was vulnerable; it could be severed if powerful simultaneous Allied counter-attacks were launched from north and south on the 22nd, before the lagging German infantry divisions had closed up and secured the corridor's flanks. These attacks were to be conducted from the north by the BEF's three divisions and the four formations of the French 1ère Armée, and from the south by the reconstituted French 7e Armée. To enable the BEF to participate, the Belgians would withdraw to the River Lys and extend their current front to the west. Billotte, however, remained sceptical about

Born in January 1890, GenLt Joachim von Kortzfleisch commanded the XI Corps in GenObst von Reichenau's Sixth Army. In this photo taken during 1944 he can be seen wearing the coveted Knight's Cross. (Photo by Heinrich Hoffmann/ullstein bild via Getty Images)

Exhausted Belgian gunners sleep atop their guns as their horse-drawn artillery unit retreats westward. In the face of vicious assaults by the German Eighteenth Army's infantry divisions, the defending Belgian units resisted stubbornly. The retreats they undertook were not caused by their own failures but by the enemy outflanking them to the south due to the French collapse. (Photo by Keystone-France/ Gamma-Keystone via Getty Images)

whether his battered forces could mount the proposed southward riposte, and so eventually the counter-attack at Arras became largely a British-only affair. Sadly, Billotte was fatally injured in an automobile accident returning from these meetings, and this unfortunate event created a temporary vacuum in command at a critical moment in time.

During the 20th the BEF encountered the first serious German assaults against its units defending along the River Escaut; simultaneously, General Gort began planning for a possible retreat back to Dunkirk. By this time the British generals increasingly mistrusted the Belgians, being convinced that they might capitulate at any time, and had lost any confidence in the French leaders' military abilities. With seven divisions holding 50km (31 miles) of the Escaut Line, and with the British 5th and 50th divisions dispatched for the spoiling attack at Arras, General Gort had all his formations committed to battle. Lacking an Allied leader (Billotte's successor was not appointed until 25 May), the British and Belgian forces withdrew from the Escaut on the evening of 22/23 May. Four British divisions retreated to the French frontier, between Maulde and Halluin, where the new Belgian line – manned by 13 exhausted divisions – turned sharp right to follow the River Lys from near Halluin to Ghent.

With both wings retiring, gaps appeared between the two forces and the Germans quickly mounted attacks against this vulnerable seam. The Eighteenth

Army assaulted the Belgian left on the Terneuzen Canal, forcing Lieutenant-Général de Neve de Roden's Belgian Corps de Cavalerie and the Ve Corps back from Ghent. Meanwhile both Kortzfleisch's German XI Corps and Wäger's XXVII Corps pressured the bulk of the Belgian and British armies. Between these groupings the German IV Corps forced its way across the River Lys astride Courtrai, driving the Belgian 1st and 3rd Divisions back toward Roulers, thus severing the ground link with the BEF.

Meanwhile, on 23 May – as already related – Guderian's XIX Corps (Motorised) invested the towns of Boulogne and Calais, Reinhardt's XLI Corps rolled up to the canals stretching from Saint-Omer to Béthune, and Hoth's XV Corps (Motorised) forced Lord Gort to abandon the town of Arras. With seven Panzer divisions in his rear areas, Gort hastily deployed the three divisions freed by the most recent withdrawal, parcelling out their various brigades to man the Canal Line between La Bassée and Wormhoudt. Thus, Gort could only employ Frankforce's two divisions to counter-attack at Arras. Meanwhile, the southern arm of Weygand's plan never managed to cross the Somme.

Since it was not included in Hitler's *Haltbefehl*, Bock's Army Group B continued its westward advance during the 25th. That day, Kortzfleisch's German XI Corps forced Lieutenant-Général Deffontaine's Belgian VIIe Corps back to Roulers and Thielt, while the German IV Corps drove back the Belgian right wing (Lieutenant-Général Bogaerts' IV Corps). Opening a breach, three German divisions advanced towards the towns of Ypres and Dunkirk. After hearing that

ABOVE Maj Gen Harold E. Franklyn commanded the British 5th Division in France, and later led the temporarily created Frankforce for the Cambrai riposte. He is seen here outside his divisional headquarters at Wambrechies on 22 January 1940. (© IWM, O 1188)

LEFT The scene as seen by an infantry section of the British 7th Guards Brigade near the t'Coolenhof farm. Just out of view to the bottom left of this photo, several infanteers hunker down in their trench. Their .303-cal. Small Magazine Lee Enfield (SMLE) rifles are at the ready, lying on the forward shoulder of the trench. The soldiers can see, in the background, the village of Furnes, parts of which are on fire after artillery bombardments. (© IWM, HU 1134)

RIGHT In the wake of Belgium's capitulation, long columns of captured Belgian soldiers marched dejectedly to the rear while German horse-drawn artillery passes them heading for Nieuport. Although the fighting in this area had ended, the roads were clogged with surrendered troops and civilian refugees and this slowed the German approach to Dunkirk. (© IWM, HU 75891)

BELOW After the eventual Belgian capitulation on 28 May 1940, a pair of triumphant German soldiers raise a Nazi swastika flag above the Royal Palace of Laeken, in Brussels, the home of Léopold III, King of the Belgians. (Photo by ullstein bild/ullstein bild via Getty Images)

the southern branch of Weygand's plan was cancelled, Gort abandoned his planned ripostes, dispatched Frankforce to fill the Lys-Ypres gap, and planned to withdraw the rest of the BEF behind it. Général d'Armée Blanchard meanwhile dispatched the 2e DLM to extend the Allied line north of Ypres. Next, at 1230hrs on 26 May 1940, Weygand ordered the French 1ère Armée, the BEF and the Belgian Army to regroup behind the line of the Aa Canal, the Lys and the Canal de Dérivation, to form a bridgehead covering Dunkirk. Amidst now-pervasive inter-Allied mistrust, the BEF began planning its withdrawal from Dunkirk but without informing either of its two allies. At noon on 26 May, the British government ordered Gort's forces to fight their way back to the west and then use all the beaches and ports to evacuate them to England: the next day Gort's sole mission became to evacuate to England the maximum number of British forces.

If things had become desperate for the BEF, they were *in extremis* for the Belgians. Léopold's army was being bent into a separate pocket. Pushed back from the Lys, in the centre Lieutenant-Général Michem's battered IIe Corps, Vaerstraete's VIe Corps and Deffontaine's VIIe Corps held the defensive line that ran from Roulers through Thielt on to Nevele. The six marching infantry divisions of Geyer's German IX Corps and Kortzfleisch's XI Corps immediately began to assaulting this new defensive position. Meanwhile, both de Neve de Rode's Corps de Cavalerie and Vandenbergen's Belgian Ve Corps attempted to defend the line of the Lys Canal against the attacks launched by Wobig's

XXVI Corps. Finally, to help shore up their collapsing defensive last stands, the Belgians also had to commit their sole remaining reserve – the two infantry divisions of Lieutenant-Général Vanderveken's Ier Corps. These two formations rushed to the collapsing Belgian right flank and desperately attempted to hold along the railway line from Ypres to Roulers.

The Belgian Army was now physically separated from the BEF, was completely exhausted and no longer had any further reserves. In addition, the Belgian forces had no means of following the Allies to the town of Dunkirk. By late on 25 May King Léopold had reluctantly to accept that his army's situation was now utterly hopeless. The next morning Wobig's German XXVI Corps successfully assaulted across the Canal de Dérivation close to the villages of Ronsele and Balgerhoeck. At the same time the infantry formations of Geyer's IX Corps attacked the forces defending Nevele. In the centre, XI Corps' assaults successfully opened a gap between Thielt and Izegem. This tactical triumph rendered open the route to the towns of Bruges and Ostend.

During the 27th, King Léopold informed the Allied commanders that his forces had reached the limits of their endurance and could no longer continue the fight. With their backs to the sea, their ammunition exhausted, and the hospitals overflowing, the Belgians had done all they could. At 1800hrs King Léopold opened negotiations for the surrender of his army and his nation. Shortly before midnight King Léopold reluctantly accepted Hitler's demand for unconditional capitulation. The ensuing ceasefire commenced at 0500hrs the next morning. The bitter battle for Belgium was now over. But the battle for the beleaguered Dunkirk pocket was just about to begin.

The Battle for the Dunkirk Cauldron (29 May–4 June)

During 26 May the first Royal Navy vessels arrived at Dunkirk's shattered docks to undertake Operation *Dynamo* – the evacuation of the BEF from the port. This day Lord Gort was ordered to withdraw towards the coast and begin the evacuation. During the 27th, however, only 7,669 British troops were successfully evacuated from the beaches, although the next day this rose to 17,804 personnel. Meanwhile, the heroic last stand of the 1ère Armée around the town of Lille bought precious time for the other French forces to fall back into the Dunkirk perimeter. Back on the 25th, moreover, British III Corps commander Lt Gen Ronald Adam moved his HQ to Dunkirk to coordinate the actions of the 250,000 British troops caught in the pocket with that of the French. Upon his arrival, Adam found that Général de Corps Fagalde had already established a strong defence in depth around the city using French troops.

What remained of the French 21e Division Infanterie had already deployed behind the line that ran from Gravelines through Watten to the town of Cassel. Meanwhile, the remnants of the French 68e Division Infanterie had entrenched

As the Royal Navy's rescue ships reached Dunkirk harbour, this is the scene that greeted them. The Saint- Pol oil refinery burns fiercely in the background. Meanwhile, a paddle-wheel minesweeper steams into the harbour while in the foreground HMS *Vanquisher* readies herself to follow. The end of the eastern mole is visible to the left, while the end of the western mole, with its distinctive lighthouse, is to the right. (© IWM, C 1720)

along the canal line that ran from Mardyck through Spycker to the village of Bergues. Adam now placed his British 144th Brigade on the left flank of the secondary line at Wormhoudt. The Allies quickly mapped out a defensible 48km (30 mile) perimeter using as many contiguous water barriers as possible. With Fagalde's forces already holding the perimeter's western side, newly-arriving French troops would be placed west of the canal that ran from Dunkirk through to Bergues. In the British portion of the defensive perimeter Adam placed Lt Gen Alan Brooke's II Corps furthest east, covering the two canals forming the corner at Nieuport and extending to Furnes. Meanwhile, Lt Gen Michael Barker's I Corps would defend the centre sector that ran through Furnes. Finally, Adam's own III Corps would fill in the sector that ran between there and the village of Bergues.

Subsequently, the British forces soon established embarkation assembly areas at three beaches. Malo-les-Bains, an eastern suburb of Dunkirk, became the evacuation beach for Adam's III Corps. Further to the east Bray-Dunes Plage became the rescue site for Barker's I Corps. Finally, and furthest to the east the beach of La Panne Bains was the designated evacuation location of Alan Brooke's II Corps. Subsequently, between 26 and 28 May, as described above, the Allied forces gradually fell back on to the perimeter around Dunkirk in the face of continuing bitter German assaults.

During 29 May 1940 the Allies' 48km (30 mile) long defensive perimeter around the town of Dunkirk began to take a more solid shape. This was despite two complications. Firstly, the Belgian Army's capitulation had created a vacuum on the eastern side of the Dunkirk–Lille Pocket. Even worse, it was only on the previous morning that Blanchard was appalled to discover that the BEF was already evacuating its forces from Dunkirk; the British had not informed him of their imminent departure. This unilateral action was very likely to compromise the entire continuing defence of the city.

Throughout 29 May – and despite sustained German Air Force attacks on the beaches – Allied shipping managed to evacuate 47,310 men from the Dunkirk pocket. The German ground assaults conducted that day were hampered by the mass redeployment of their ground formations and Luftwaffe squadrons southward to the Somme river in preparation for the launching of *Fall Rot*. These orders removed Guderian's and Reinhardt's Panzer corps from the siege of Dunkirk. This redeployment of the Panzers was tactically sensible, as tanks were

of little use against the Allied defences established along marshy water barriers or the region's urban centres. The Eighteenth Army, moreover, was approaching from the east, and its infantry forces were more suitable for the tactical tasks associated with liquidating the Dunkirk pocket.

That said, during 29 May GenLt Kauffmann's 256th Infantry Division did mount an assault on Nieuport, but this proved unsuccessful in the face of tenacious Allied resistance. Meanwhile, the withdrawing British forces also managed to repel the German assaults on the village of Furnes. Simultaneously, Maj Gen Henry Curtis's British 46th (North Midland and West Riding) Division withdrew to new positions along the sector of the Basse Colme Canal that ran from the village of Bergues through to Hoymille.

Meanwhile, between them Maj Gen Montgomery's British 3rd Division and Martel's 50th Division held the line from Noordschote to Poperinghe. As this defence unfolded, Franklyn's British 5th Division and Maj Gen Holmes' 42nd (East Lancashire) Division both fell back into the main defence line across the sector that ran from Linde through to Bambecque on the River Yser. Through these lines filed the retreating units of Maj Gen Alexander's 1st Division and Maj Gen Loyd's 2nd British Division as they moved westward to be evacuated. Meanwhile, to the south of the BEF's rearguard, Maj Gen Osborne's badly mauled British 44th (Home Counties) Division withdrew from the high ground of the Mont des Cats and reached the evacuation beaches the next day. Finally, surrounded at Cassel, the 145th Brigade continued to hold the hilltop town in readiness for a breakout attempt the following night.

Meanwhile, further south, Hoth's XV Corps closed the trap on the six battered divisions of Prioux's 1ère Armée, which now defended the area around Lille. In capturing the villages of Lorgies, Furnes, and Lomme, Walsporn's 5th Panzer Division and Rommel's 7th Panzer Divisions between them all but encircled

ABOVE LEFT Lt Gen Sir Alan Brooke, the BEF's II Corps Commander, came away from the battle of Dunkirk with his reputation as an effective leader unbesmirched. He subsequently rose to become Chief of the Imperial General Staff. He is seen here in 1943, just to the left of the Union ensign on the staff car, while visiting senior British and Canadian commanders. (Photo courtesy of Libraries and Archives Canada, PA-034134)

ABOVE RIGHT One of the five British Fleet Air Arm 825 Squadron Fairey Swordfish Mk I aircraft lost on the 29 May raid on Bollezeele in support of the Dunkirk garrison; it is seen crash-landed in a field south of Bergues. The RAF lacked dedicated ground-attack aircraft for close air support of the troops defending the Aa Canal, and so the FAA attempted to fill this gap with its anachronistic Swordfish biplanes. (© IWM, HU 58737)

Hell From Above, 29 May 1940

As the third wave of dive-bombers approached Dunkirk harbour, they were immediately attracted to the ten vessels clustered at the end of the eastern jetty. Berthed on the harbour side of the mole were (from the end, landward) the destroyer *Grenade* (Cdr Richard Boyle), six armed trawlers of Minesweeping Groups 51 and 61 (Sub Lt Robin Bill, aboard *Fyldea*) moored in two rows of three and the destroyer *Verity* (Cdr Robert H. Mills). Along the sea side of the jetty were the large Isle of Man packet RMS *Fenella* (Capt W. Cubbon) and paddle-wheel Thames excursion steamer *Crested Eagle* (Lt Cdr Bernard Booth, RNR). Beginning their attacks at 1750hrs, *Grenade* **(1)** was soon hit twice, one bomb exploding in a forward fuel tank and starting raging internal fires. Fourteen ratings were killed and another four mortally wounded. Recognizing the ship was doomed, Cdr. 'Jack' Clouston's Royal Naval pier party slipped the ship's lines so that it would not sink at its berth but the tide swung it around until it drifted stern-first into the harbour channel. Meanwhile *Fenella* **(2)**, having embarked 650 troops, had a bomb plunge through her promenade deck, killing 15. Two other bombs hit the mole alongside, exploding among the jetty's boulders, wrecking the engine room and perforating her hull below the waterline. The ship began to settle and list and those on board evacuated forward on to the *Crested Eagle*. *Fenella* slowly sank at her berth. Another salvo of bombs rained down upon the trawlers. The *Polly Johnson* (Lt F. Padley, RNR; outboard in the first row) was heavily damaged by two near misses that wiped out the 3in. gun crew and she soon departed in company with

Arley (Skipper A. Duffield, RNR), but had to be abandoned and scuttled en route. The *Brock* (Skipper A. U. Setterfield, RNR) also got under way, leaving *Fyldea* **(3)** (Skipper G. Whammond, RNR) moored to the mole. The *Calvi* **(4)** (Skipper Bertram Spindler, RNR; outboard in the second row) had a bomb go down a ventilator shaft and through its bottom and sank upright. Further down the jetty, *Verity* had been straddled by bombs for about 35 minutes when Cdr Mills, seeing that the air attacks had driven the troops from the mole, got under way empty, skirting the burning *Grenade* and the *Calvi's* wreckage as she left the harbour. Loaded with 600 shell-shocked troops, *Crested Eagle* **(5)** got under way at approximately 18.30hrs, pulling away from the mole in a wide turn to port and was pounced upon by the last of the Stukas. Four bombs rained upon it, setting the aft end of the ancient wooden ship fiercely ablaze. Lt Cdr Booth quickly realised his ship was doomed and ran the burning wreck aground near Zuydcoote Sanitorium where the 200 surviving troops and crew – many of them severely burned – were rescued by three minesweepers and the destroyer *Sabre*. Meanwhile, fearing that the sinking, blazing *Grenade* would block the harbour channel, Cdr Clouston ordered the trawler *John Cattling* **(6)** (Skipper G. W. Aldan, DSC, RNR) to tow *Grenade* out of the channel. Burning fiercely from stem to stern, *Grenade* was pulled to the west side of the outer harbour where, at approximately 2000hrs, her magazines exploded. (Artwork by Howard Gerrard, © Osprey Publishing)

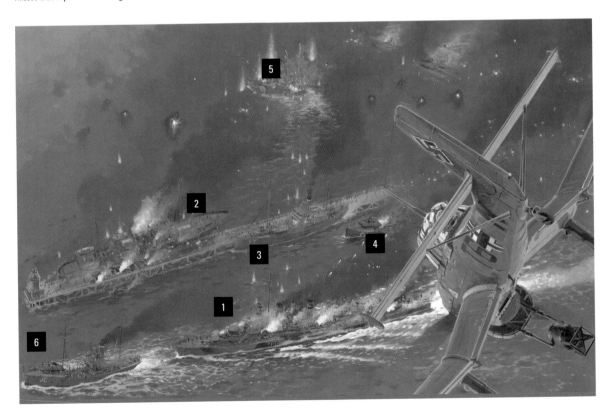

Prioux's beleaguered remnants. Subsequently closing in from the east, the spearheads of Wäger's German XXVII Corps even captured Prioux himself. When subsequently Wäger's vanguard pushed westward to close on Armentières, they successfully linked up with elements of the 7th Panzer Division. This meeting completed the encirclement of the six depleted and demoralised divisions of what remained of the once mighty French 1ère Armée. After two more days of hard fighting, some 35,000 exhausted French troops finally surrendered.

Luckily for the Allies, during 30 May the principal German focus remained the redeployment of significant forces to their designated assembly areas in readiness for the launching of *Fall Rot*, rather than on the crushing of the Dunkirk pocket. Three infantry divisions from GenObst von Reichenau's Sixth Army did, however, launch limited assaults across the Basse Colme Canal that afternoon. These attacks were either repulsed, or merely made slow progress in the face of determined Allied resistance. Overall, the day proved that the Germans' disjointed command arrangements were unsatisfactory, and a complete restructuring of the forces arrayed against the town of Dunkirk occurred over the next 36 hours.

With four infantry corps now under command, Küchler's Eighteenth Army assumed responsibility for all operations against the Dunkirk perimeter, as well as the mopping up of the last scattered French remnants in the now overwhelmed former pocket around Lille. Küchler's command now deployed seven infantry divisions, an independent motorised rifle brigade, and as its spearhead force, GenLt Ritter von Hubicki's 9th Panzer Division. Subsequently, during the following night the British 145th Brigade, surrounded at Cassel, tried to exfiltrate out toward the beaches. However, fierce German ripostes overwhelmed the small detachments attempting to escape, and these were eventually forced to surrender near Watou. In total that day some 53,823 Allied troops (including 8,616 French personnel) were rescued; Adams' British III Corps HQ staff were also evacuated that day.

ABOVE LEFT During January 1940 senior Canadian officers (the four to the left) visited the BEF in France. On the extreme right is Maj Gen Harold Alexander, who ably commanded the 1st British Division in the 1940 campaign. Next to him is Maj Gen Paget, who – as related in Chapter Two – later commanded Sickelforce during the Anglo-French intervention in Norway. (Photo courtesy of Libraries and Archives Canada, PA-034177)

ABOVE RIGHT Maj Gen Bernard Montgomery effectively led the 3rd British Division in the 1940 campaign and was evacuated to the UK with his reputation intact. Later, as a full general and then a field marshal, he commanded the Allied troops that mounted the June 1944 D-Day landings and subsequently liberated most of northern France. Here he is seen on 13 September 1943 awarding a Canadian Corporal the Military Medal at Catanzaro in Italy. (Photo courtesy of Libraries and Archives Canada, PA-130065)

RIGHT To disrupt the Allied naval evacuation from Dunkirk the Germans concentrated their heavy 17cm and 21cm artillery pieces in the area between Nieuport, Gravelines and Mardyke. Here a 21cm (8.3in) Mörser 18 L/30 heavy howitzer is seen in action; it had an impressive maximum range of 16,720m (18,290 yards). (© IWM, MH 9200)

BELOW By 30 May 1940 the Germans had decided to place all the elements from the four separate corps that were engaging the Dunkirk perimeter under the command of Gen d.Art Georg von Küchler's German Eighteenth Army. During the 1939 Polish campaign Küchler had commanded the eight divisions controlled by the Third Army. (Photo by ullstein bild/ullstein bild via Getty Images)

By the morning of 31 May, some 92,000 British and 156,000 French troops had been cornered in the ever-shrinking Dunkirk perimeter, which they were defending with desperate determination. That day the Allies faced a coordinated series of German assaults to break into the perimeter. By then the German Eighteenth Army deployed 120,000 troops against them. This might seem to suggest that the Allies enjoyed numerical superiority; but of course, tens of thousands of these Allied troops were not defending the Dunkirk perimeter but instead waiting on the beaches for embarkation back to England. Across the eastern flank, meanwhile, three German divisions attacked the British line in the sector that ran from Bulscamp through Furnes and on to Nieuport. Simultaneously, during the day some 53,230 British troops – mainly from the II Corps' 3rd, 4th and 5th Infantry Divisions – were evacuated from the pocket.

The next day, with the Luftwaffe fully alert that the Allied ground forces were escaping en masse by sea, their squadrons mounted 485 sorties against the evacuation beaches. Meanwhile, Küchler's forces staged further coordinated assaults designed to crack open the perimeter. On the eastern front GenLt Wobig's XXVI Corps pushed through in the sector around Nieuport while Geyer's IX Corps spent the day advancing to the Franco-Belgian frontier. Meanwhile, the assaults mounted by units of Ulex's X Corps split the perimeter at the seam between the French and British forces. In exploiting this success, the German advance forced back each side of the rupture, widening the breach; this enabled Ulex's reinforcing units to pass through and advance from Bergues into the fringes of Dunkirk itself. To the east of Bergues, meanwhile, German attacks also forced the British 126th Brigade back to the Canal des Chats. Again, despite these setbacks, the day's dogged Allied defensive stand allowed a further 64,429 Allied troops to be evacuated by sea back to the United Kingdom.

With the BEF almost entirely evacuated by the early hours of 2 June 1940, the remaining French forces continued fervently to defend the perimeter. That morning,

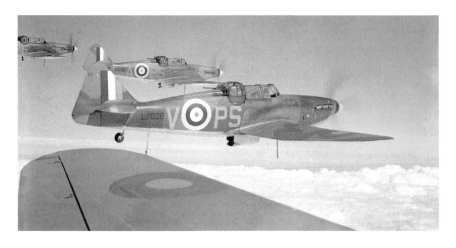

LEFT During the battle for Dunkirk, the RAF strove to disrupt the Luftwaffe's strikes on the embarking troops and those personnel manning the defensive perimeter. The inexperienced crews of No 264 Sqn's Defiant fighters reported grossly exaggerated numbers of kills. On 29 May they claimed 37 enemy aircraft kills, whereas the real figure was just two. (© IWM, CH 884)

a local French counter-attack near Hoymille even delayed the German resumption of attacks. Finally, that afternoon the main German assaults resumed. These were spearheaded by the 61st Infantry Division, recently committed from the army reserve, and by Hubicki's 9th Panzer Division. The latter advanced along the main road to the village of Spycker, which its late evening assaults secured by 2300hrs.

Küchler's main effort, however, remained in the central sector. Here, GenMaj Cranz's German 18th Infantry Division resumed its attacks around the village of Bergues at 1500hrs. The leading German units advanced, but slowly in the face of determined Allied resistance until a desperate counter-attack halted them short of the Canal des Moëres. That evening 54 British and 43 French evacuation vessels arrived and in the early hours evacuated the remaining 7,208 British troops still waiting to be rescued. Operation *Dynamo* was by then complete.

The evacuation of the last British troops from Dunkirk by the early hours of 3 June left Général de Corps Fagalde with some 25,000 French troops manning the shrunken perimeter and another 22,000 waiting ready for embarkation. It was also estimated that another 25,000 rear-area troops remained unaccounted for, bunched in thousands of tiny undisciplined groups cloistered in cellars or cowering amid the dunes. On the morning of the 3rd, Fagalde again tried to upset the Germans' planned assaults with a pre-emptive spoiling attack near Galghouck. Unperturbed by this, however, Cranz's German 18th Infantry Division soon repulsed the riposte and

LEFT Images like this have become iconic representations of the Dunkirk evacuation. Because Luftwaffe attacks had made much of the harbour unusable, thousands of soldiers were evacuated directly from the beaches. As the larger ships with deeper draughts could not come in close to the shore, the troops had to wade out deep into the water and wait patiently in long lines for a ship to take them home; amazingly, good discipline endured in these most arduous circumstances. (Photo by Time Life Pictures/Pictures Inc./The LIFE Picture Collection via Getty Images)

THE DUNKIRK PERIMETER IS CLOSED, 30 MAY 1940

The Dunkirk defensive perimeter as it was established on 30 May 1940, the Allied forces within it, harbour embarkation facilities, the three beach evacuation points and the German units facing and attacking the perimeter.

GERMAN FORCES

A 9th Panzer-Division's Aufkärungs-Abteilung 9
B 9th Panzer-Division's Schützen-Regiment 10
C 9th Panzer-Division's Schützen-Regiment 11
D 9th Panzer-Division's Panzer-Regiment 33
E 9th Panzer-Division's Artillerie-Regiment 102
F SS-Regiment 'Leibstandarte Adolf Hitler'
G 20th. Infanterie-Division (mot.)
H 18th Infanterie-Division
I 254th Infanterie-Division
J 14th Infanterie-Division
K 216th Infanterie-Division
L 56th Infanterie-Division
M 208th Infanterie-Division
N 256th Infanterie-Division

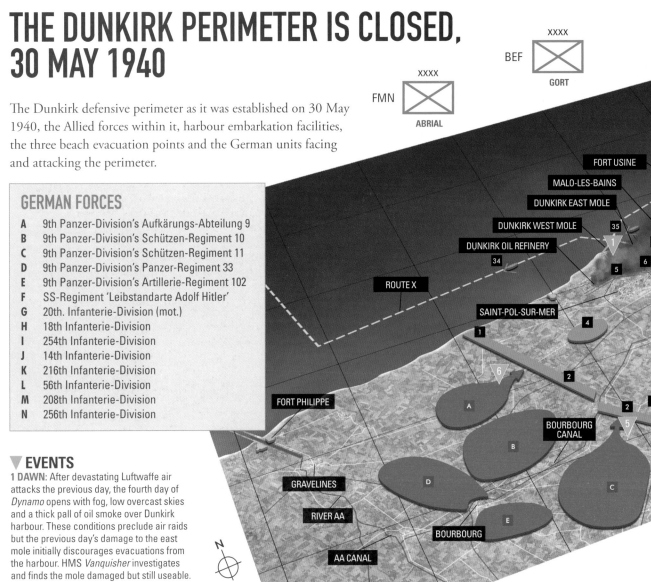

▼ EVENTS

1 DAWN: After devastating Luftwaffe air attacks the previous day, the fourth day of *Dynamo* opens with fog, low overcast skies and a thick pall of oil smoke over Dunkirk harbour. These conditions preclude air raids but the previous day's damage to the east mole initially discourages evacuations from the harbour. HMS *Vanquisher* investigates and finds the mole damaged but still useable. Despite the late start, 24,311 troops are evacuated from the harbour during the day.
2 MIDDAY: Gunboat HMS *Locust* begins to tow the severely damaged escort sloop HMS *Bideford* back to England. They arrive 36 hours later.
3 1415HRS: Steaming via Route Y four French torpedo boats evacuate troops from Quai Félix Faure. At 1645hrs the *Bourrasque*, while dodging German artillery fire off Nieuport, leaves the swept channel, hits a mine and sinks with the loss of 150 men.
4 MID-AFTERNOON: Loading from the surf on to the small boats becomes increasingly chaotic, resulting in swamped and capsized boats and drowned troops. Seeing the need for a pier of some sort, near La Panne Lt Harold Dibbens leads the 102nd Provost Company and Royal Engineers' 250th Field Company in pushing a line of lorries and other abandoned vehicles into the surf,

shooting the tires to prevent them from becoming buoyant and lashing planking across their tops to form the first 'provost jetty', jutting some 150m (492ft) into the surf. So successful is this effort that on the evening of 30-31 May, another nine 'provost jetties' are constructed between Malo-les-Bains and La Panne.
5 1400–2000HRS: Ordered to drive back the French 225e RI in order to bring their 10.5cm artillery into range of Dunkirk Harbour, light tanks from the 9. Panzer-Division's PR 33 assist

their SR 11 in attacking towards Spycker. Artillery bombardment begins at noon, followed by assaults two hours later. However, determined French defence, utilizing its well-emplaced artillery and anti-tank batteries, holds its ground. A follow-up attack at 2000hrs, attempting to use nightfall to their advantage, is similarly repulsed.
6 LATER IN THE EVENING: To draw off French forces defending against SR 11's attacks, 9. Panzer-Division's Aüfkl-Abt. 9 attacks across the disused Mardyck Canal. Again the French troops, heavily supported by artillery and anti-tank guns, repulse the assault.

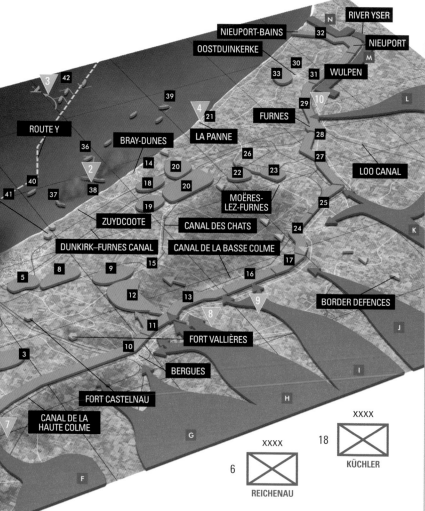

RIVER YSER

NIEUPORT-BAINS

OOSTDUINKERKE

NIEUPORT

N

32

M

30

33

31

WULPEN

29

L

ROUTE Y

39

FURNES

28

3

42

LA PANNE

21

4

27

BRAY-DUNES

26

23

LOO CANAL

36

14

20

22

2

18

20

25

MOËRES-
LEZ-FURNES

24

38

40

19

41

37

ZUYDCOOTE

CANAL DES CHATS

17

DUNKIRK–FURNES CANAL

CANAL DE LA BASSE COLME

15

K

5

8

9

16

12

13

9

BORDER DEFENCES

11

8

J

FORT VALLIÈRES

10

BERGUES

I

3

H

FORT CASTELNAU

CANAL DE LA
HAUTE COLME

7

G

F

```
        xxxx
                            xxxx
         6                18
                            KÜCHLER
      REICHENAU
```

7 APPROXIMATELY 2000HRS: In an attempt to cross the Canal de la Haute Colme and split the seam of the French defences between the 225e and 341e RI, the SS-Regiment 'Leibstandarte Adolf Hitler' attacks from the south. Although timed to take advantage of SR 11's evening attack towards Spycker, the inundation south of the canal, the water obstacle of the canal itself and spirited French defence by the 3e Coy of the 225e RI neutralise the assault.

8 1500 AND 2000HRS: The 18. Infanterie-Division moves up to Bergues and the Canal de la Basse Colme and launches its first attack from Warhem, which is repulsed by the 5th Bn The Border Regiment (from 42nd Division's 126th Brigade). At dusk the 139th Brigade begins to pull out of the line to move to Malo-les-Bains for evacuation, their place being taken by the French 137e RI. A renewed attack at 2000hrs, in coordination with the attacks by units on the western side of the perimeter, successfully establishes a bridgehead but fierce French counter-attacks drive the Germans back across the canal.

9 1600HRS: Arriving at the Canal de la Basse Colme, the 254. Infanterie-Division hastily goes into the assault, attempting to cross the canal at two places and relieve pressure on the 18. Infanterie-Division to the west. However, the British defence is stout and the 2nd Coldstream Guards beat back the western attack while the 1st Duke of Wellington's defeat the one launched from Hondschoote.

10 2200HRS: After an initial repulse late in the day and under a strong artillery bombardment, in the early darkness elements of the 56. Infanterie-Division wade across the canal and infiltrate British defences north of Furnes, establishing a bridgehead. Once discovered, a determined counter-attack by the 1st Coldstream Guards drives the Germans back across the canal and restores the defensive line.

Day of the Defiants, 31 May 1940

Conceived in 1935 as the replacement for the Hawker Demon, the Boulton Paul Defiant was not intended to be a 'fighter'. Instead it was designed as a 'bomber destroyer' – intended to engage only enemy bombers while its contemporary, the Hawker Hurricane, fended off escorting fighters. The aircraft mounted a Boulton Paul-built version of the French de Boysson four-gun turret and had no fixed forward-firing armament, so Defiant pilots were trained to close with enemy bomber formations from the flank, or by flying across their noses slightly below the bomber's level, in what was known as a 'crossover' attack. In this way the turret gunner would turn to fire 'broadside' against the enemy. The initial attack was to be concentrated on the lead bomber, thereby disrupting the defensive cohesion of the enemy formation. At 1840hrs Sqn Ldr Philip Hunter led a dozen Defiants to Dunkirk having coordinated with Hurricanes of No. 111 Sqn to have them in close cover/line astern with Spitfires from No. 609 Sqn shadowing to one side and above. Soon three of the faster Spitfires dived on a large formation of Heinkel bombers, claiming one shot down, while Hunter climbed his formation to engage and the Hurricanes turned to occupy nearby Bf 109Es. True to doctrine, Hunter and three others closed from below on the flanks of a bomber in the leading group and 16 Browning .303in. machine guns chattered away, riddling its belly. This aircraft (from Stab/KG 27) was last seen

circling down towards the sea with one engine on fire and apparently crashed offshore, it and its crew being listed as missing in action. Hunter then moved his Defiant (1) to the leader of another group of bombers, the aircraft (1G+AN) (2) of Oblt Kalischewski, leading the 5. Staffel formation. His gunner, Leading Aircraftman F. H. King, damaged it while other Defiants engaged the remaining Heinkels as they scattered. Plt Off G. Hackwood and Leading Aircraftman Lillie found themselves beneath another and Lillie opened fire at 50m (164ft), exploding the left engine. This bomber is believed to be the machine that crashed near Saint-Folquin (between Dunkirk and Calais), killing all aboard. Plt Offs Barwell and Williams (3) engaged another 5. Staffel machine (1G+IN) (4), riddling the underside of the pilot's cabin, and reportedly it 'nosed forward and dived slowly towards the sea'. It returned to base damaged with the pilot mortally wounded. Return fire from the belly gunner damaged Barwell's aircraft, forcing him to ditch on the way home. Return fire also damaged another Defiant, the wounded gunner baling out and the pilot returning to crash-land at Manston. Failing to return were Flt Lt Nicholas Cooke and his gunner Cpl Albert Lippert (5). This engagement proved what Defiants could do if permitted to use their practised tactics, but at a high cost. (Artwork by Howard Gerrard, © Osprey Publishing)

then launched its own attacks in the centre. These assaults gradually drove the defending French troops back to the western bank of the Canal des Moëres.

During the day of 3 June, and the ensuing night, an assorted fleet of 64 British and 63 French craft evacuated a further 46,792 French troops (and six British stragglers) back to England from Dunkirk's beaches. Indeed, at the sites of embarkation, an undisciplined mob of 10,000 fear-stricken French rear-area stragglers poured on to the dunes trying to reach the safety of one of the naval craft. When the final rescue vessels departed during the early hours of 4 June, some 40,000 French troops were left stranded in a small enclave that now merely extended around the town of Dunkirk itself.

The German ground assaults on the reduced French defensive perimeter resumed at dawn on the 4th. But by this point most of the remaining defenders realised that continued resistance was futile, and that there was no prospect of

ABOVE LEFT Although Operation *Dynamo* extracted enough troops to form sufficient divisions to defend the UK, these formations lacked most of their heavy equipment, which had been lost in France. Here near Bray-Dunes a Vickers Mk VI tankette and a Bedford OX 30-cwt lorry have been abandoned and disabled by being driven into a canal. (© IWM, HU 58729)

ABOVE RIGHT A snapshot of the human drama of war. A group of British infanteers sit in their foxholes in the dunes of the beaches at Dunkirk. Pain and suffering is etched on their faces, as they watch in anguish and exhaustion as the Allied rescue fleet is sunk or blown out of the water before their unbelieving eyes.

being evacuated by sea. Consequently, soon white flags of surrender began appearing everywhere across the town. The German 18th Infantry Division quickly crossed the Canal des Moëres and advanced into the devastated city right up to the harbour's Eastern Mole. At 1000hrs the remaining battered and demoralised French remnants – some 38,000 troops – officially surrendered to the Germans. In total, Operation *Dynamo* and the evacuations preceding it successfully brought home 221,504 British and 170,475 French troops, albeit largely without any heavy equipment. Indeed, in early June 1940 there were only 54 anti-tank guns, 420 field guns and 163 heavy guns available in the whole of the United Kingdom, insufficient to repel a German invasion.

The German Preparations for *Fall Rot* (29 May–8 June)

In the wake of the stunning strategic success achieved in just 10 days by *Fall Gelb*, the German forces in the West frantically reorganised in preparation for the start of *Fall Rot*, the subsidiary campaign designed to conquer the rest of France. Both sides' efforts now became focused on the new front that separated the Wehrmacht's formations from those of the French along the Somme, Oise and Aisne rivers, as well as along the Maginot Line fortifications to the south-east.

Although the Germans lacked the three-to-one numerical superiority to which the attacker should typically aspire, they now enjoyed a clear advantage in both tactical acumen and command and control. In addition, the German forces had already achieved a stunning strategic triumph over the Allies and this significantly bolstered their fighting spirit, just as the morale of the French defenders continued to plummet. Many on the Allied side simply could not believe the scale of the military calamity that had already befallen them. In these circumstances, successfully halting the renewed German ground onslaught would be an immensely challenging task for the beleaguered French forces. But the only viable prospect the French held of saving France from German subjugation was somehow to hold the imminent onslaught along the flimsy defences of the Weygand Line.

On 4 June 1940 the Allied front line ran from the Channel coast in the west, eastwards to the defences of the Maginot Line fortifications and then southwards down to the Swiss border. Across this frontage the three German army groups deployed between them a total of 116 divisions. Within this total were included 10 Panzer and eight motorised divisions that deployed a total of 2,100 combat-fit tanks. In the previous week, the German Army had devoted extensive efforts to reconstitute, reorganise and refresh its hard-fighting armoured formations after the attrition and exhaustion inflicted upon them during *Fall Gelb*.

Facing them were a total of 92 French divisions with 1,200 tanks. These forces were controlled by two separate higher commands. Général d'Armée Prételat's Groupe d'Armées 2 controlled the 330km (205 mile) western sector of the front that ran from the Channel coast through to the western end of the Maginot Line fortifications near the town of Longuyon. Meanwhile, the recently-constituted French Groupe d'Armées 3, now commanded by Général d'Armée Besson, held the rest of the front along the Maginot Line from Longuyon through to the Swiss border.

On paper Prételat's command fielded some 43 divisions, but many of these were significantly depleted by the bitter battles of the previous few weeks, while troop morale also remained fragile. The French held behind the front line in this sector three armoured divisions and three light cavalry divisions as a mobile

BELOW LEFT During 4 June, after all of the naval evacuation vessels had departed, the remaining French troops left stranded in the Dunkirk perimeter surrendered. Here a section of German infanteers is moving along the beach, while out to sea the wreck of an Allied warship, sunk either by Luftwaffe attacks or by German heavy artillery fire, can be seen. (Photo by SeM/ Universal Images Group via Getty Images)

BELOW RIGHT The Allies mounted frantic repair efforts to reopen Dunkirk's docks, which had been pulverised by enemy aerial attack. With the eastern mole finally reopened for embarkations, HMS *Vivacious* came alongside the battered structure, squeezing in between the jetty and the wreck of the minesweeping trawler *Calvi*.

THE EVE OF THE RENEWED GERMAN ONSLAUGHT, *FALL ROT*

Even while the Eighteenth Army obliterated the Dunkirk enclave, many dozens of German formations from Army Groups A and B were redeploying south and south-east in preparation for the start of the *Fall Rot* offensive. On 4 June 1940 the German front line ran from the Somme estuary westward along the River Somme through Péronne, along the valley of the Oise to the Aisne south-east of Sedan. The 79 divisions deployed by Army Group B in the west and Army Group A in the east had been assembled along this 275km (170 mile) frontage. Facing them were the 50 divisions of (from west to east) the French 10e, 7e, 6e and 2e Armées. French forces, demoralised by the military debacle that had already befallen them, now faced the huge challenge of somehow stemming the impending renewed Blitzkrieg onslaught.

reserve force, designed to plug any significant German penetrations of the main line of resistance. However, all six of these formations had been badly battered by the previous actions, and were well understrength in personnel and equipment. In most of these six formations, for example, the remaining operational tanks were just 25 per cent of the authorised strengths; this gave the French a paltry total combat-fit fleet of around just 400 tanks. Another 500 French tanks were parcelled out in squadron-sized packets to reinforce the defensive power of the French infantry divisions. In the skies above France, moreover, the Luftwaffe enjoyed overwhelming numerical superiority against the battered remnants of the Armee de l'Air. Things did not augur well for Prételat's Groupe d'Armées 2.

The French High Command correctly anticipated that the western sector of the front line – which ran along the Somme, Oise and Aisne rivers – was going to be the focus of German offensive *Schwerpunkt*. The German operational logic was to advance along the direct route toward the French capital, Paris, as well as to the key ports located on the north-western and western French coasts. To resist this impending onslaught, Weygand tried to beef up the defensive combat power of the forces of Prételat's French Groupe d'Armées 2.

Weygand ordered Prételat's troops to rapidly construct defensive field fortifications along the southern banks of the Somme, Oise and Aisne rivers to create what became known as the Weygand Line. The French also swiftly withdrew several divisions from the Maginot Line defences opposite the River Rhine, as well as from the Alpine front facing Italy; these forces rushed westward to reinforce the Groupe d'Armées 2 front. Moreover, the divisions of Besson's French Groupe d'Armées 3 that remained manning the Maginot Line also detached numerous small columns of replacements that were sent west to help the formations defending the Somme, Oise and Aisne rivers to make good the losses incurred during *Fall Gelb*. The French defences were also reinforced along the extreme left flank by the Channel coast by the remaining remnant of the British Expeditionary Force. This force centred around the British 1st Armoured Division. As a reserve position, the French also began constructing defences along the Seine and Marne rivers.

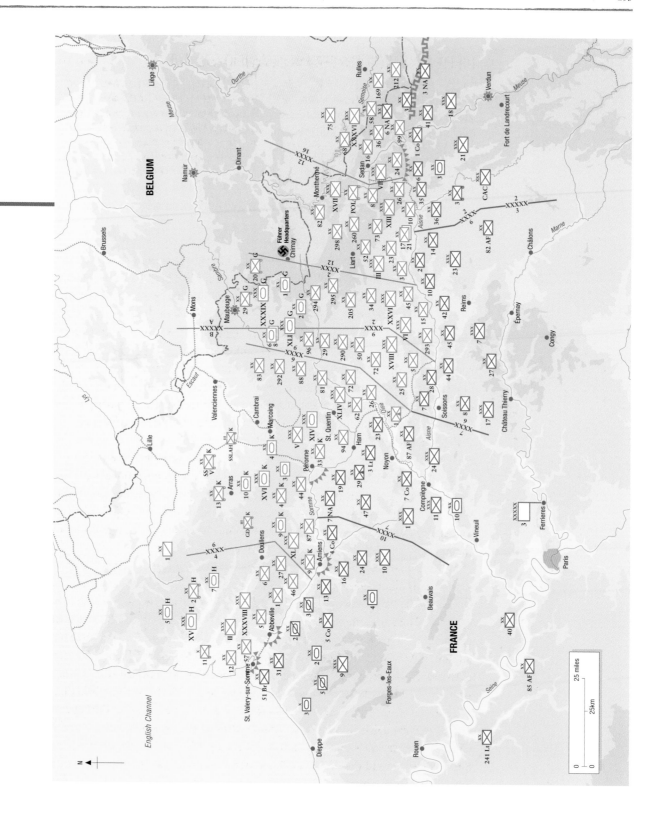

Along the eastern sector that ran from the town of Longuyon down to the Swiss border, the Groupe d'Armées 3 manned the powerful Maginot Line defences. Besson commanded this higher formation, which on paper controlled some 39 divisions. About half of these manned the Maginot Line itself while the remaining formations acted as a local mobile reserve behind the line. Seven were fortress infantry and six were colonial divisions; all were understrength to an extent after sending detachments to reinforce Prételat's Groupe d'Armées 2 in the west. Unfortunately, Besson's entire command did not field a single armoured or mechanised formation; indeed, the 300 tanks it did control were parcelled out in squadron-strengths to support its infantry formations.

Further south still, three divisional-sized second-rate infantry formations and five fortified sector commands of Général d'Armée Olry's *Armée des Alpes* (Army of the Alps) completed the French order of battle. This higher command held the front-line positions that faced the mountainous border with north-western Italy. Finally, a further six low-grade infantry divisions manned the central interior regions of France. Would this order of battle prove sufficient to halt the impending German onslaught?

From 29 May to 4 June, as the bitter battle for Dunkirk raged, the German Army Groups B and A reoriented their forces; meanwhile GenObst Ritter von Leeb's Army Group C's 25 divisions continued to threaten the French Maginot Line fortifications. Along the western sector on 4 June 1940, Army Group's A and B between them fielded 91 divisions, including ten Panzer and eight motorised divisions. Each command now sported its own army-equivalent Panzer group. After meteoric promotion to army-level status Guderian now controlled three mobile corps – the XIX, XXXIX and XLI Corps, while Panzer Group Kleist controlled a further two mobile corps.

The final German *Fall Rot* strategic plan envisaged that Army Groups B and A, each spearheaded by their respective Panzer groups, would attack south on either side of Paris. Kleist's Panzers were to charge south-west toward the Atlantic coast. In the meantime, Guderian's Panzers were to advance south towards the city of Reims, and then bear left to threaten the rear of the French forces still fixed in dogged defence of the Maginot Line fortifications. Leeb's Army Group C would ensure that these forces remined fixed in and around the Maginot Line by mounting its own offensive actions, code-named Operations *Bear* and *Tiger*.

The planned daring high-tempo armoured thrusts mounted by Army Groups A and B would thus split up the defending French forces into three isolated parts. Once the French forces had been dismembered in this fashion, subsequent German operations would ensure that each isolated French contingent could be comprehensively defeated in detail. In particular, the German advance would surround the Groupe d'Armées 3 as it still manned the Maginot Line. This fortification system was not a continuous fortified front, but rather a mish-mash

During 6–9 June, in the early stages of *Fall Rot,* the German offensive reached and passed the town of Soissons. Here German soldiers pose for a photograph beside the National Highway 2 to Paris, in the area between Soissons and Villers-Cotterets in the Aisne valley, France, on 9 June 1940. (Photo by adoc-photos/Getty Images)

of different elements. It consisted of the primary Fortified Regions (like Metz), the second-cycle lateral extension to these Regions, and then the weaker casemate lines of the Rhine defences and those in the Sarre Gap. While it varied geographically in its defensive power, taken as a whole the Maginot Line was the most extensive and powerful fortification then in existence.

Army Group B Overwhelms the Weygand Line (5–7 June)

The new German *Fall Rot* offensive against the French defences then hastily being thrown together along the line of the Somme, Oise and Aisne rivers – the Weygand Line – commenced in a staggered fashion. The start date for each of Bock's four armies depended on how quickly their respective forces could redeploy and ready themselves for the forthcoming southward assault, after the heavy fighting during *Fall Gelb*. Indeed, while the first attacks by elements of Bock's Army Group B, deployed to the west, occurred on 5 June, it was not until the 9th that the first forces of Rundstedt's Army Group A, positioned further to the east, commenced their own respective parts of the general offensive. Indeed, the process of hastily redeploying and reconstituting for *Fall Rot*, on the immediate back of waging *Fall Gelb*, was an enormous organisational challenge. The German forces surmounted these obstacles with awe-inspiring military efficiency.

On 5 June 1940, after fierce Luftwaffe aerial attacks, the nine divisions of Bock's subordinate Fourth Army first attacked the so-called Weygand Line, along the westernmost sector that ran for 63km (39 miles) between the English Channel and Amiens. Facing this attack was the French 10e Armée. Given the German numerical and tactical superiority, as well as their buoyant fighting spirit, the fierce French resistance encountered that day achieved the significant success of limiting German gains. Indeed, the attacking German infantry divisions only managed to secure an 8km (five mile) advance south from the bridgeheads already established across the River Somme at St Valery and Abbeville.

Meanwhile, Hoth's XV Corps (Motorised) – which still controlled Walsporn's 5th and Rommel's 7th Panzer Divisions – mounted its own assault on crossings of the Somme at locations equidistant from these existing bridgeheads. In the face of fierce resistance, the Panzers established two small bridgeheads that day. Meanwhile, to the east, the German Sixth and Ninth Armies – which were still not ready for a general offensive south – mounted some limited attacks to gain better jumping-off points for their forthcoming offensives. First, XIV Corps (Motorised) assaulted across the River Somme at Amiens and secured a bridgehead south of the river. These attacks were spearheaded by Hubicki's 9th Panzer Division and by Schaal's 10th Panzer Division. Secondly, and in the face of staunch defensive actions by the French 7e Armée, the 3rd and 4th Panzer Divisions of Hoepner's XVI Corps (Motorised) gained additional ground for manoeuvre within the bridgehead over the River Somme that had already been established to the west and south of the town of Péronne.

During the second day of *Fall Rot*, 6 June 1940, the Allied defensive positions began to crumble in the face of the immense combat power the assaulting German forces were generating against them. Along the far western sector, the British 51st Highland Division was forced by German pressure to retreat back to the line of the River Bresle, which exposed the left flank of the neighbouring French forces. Meanwhile, Hoth's 5th and 7th Panzer Divisions continued their attacks south until their two respective bridgeheads had been joined together.

Subsequently, driving south against the weak seam that existed between the French 9e and 10e Corps, the Panzers made good progress in the face of dislocated resistance. To protect Hoth's left (eastern) flank, GenLt von Manstein's XXXVIII Corps now joined the German drive south across Fourth Army's extreme eastern flank, astride the town of Picquigny. Further east still, the 3rd and 4th Panzer Divisions from Hoepner's German XVI Corps (Motorised) successfully broke through the French defences and swiftly advanced south-south-west toward Roye.

With the western section of the Weygand line penetrated in numerous places, on the evening of 6 June, Général d'Armée Weygand bowed to the inevitable and reluctantly accepted that this defensive position could no

GenLt Ferdinand Schaal daringly commanded the 10th Panzer Division in both the Polish and Western campaigns. He is seen here (in the centre) on 11 August 1939 with (left) SS-Gruppenführer Karl Hermann Frank, the Secretary of State for the Reich protectorate of Bohemia-Moravia, and (right) Gen Erich Friderici, the commander in that protectorate. (Photo by ullstein bild/ ullstein bild via Getty Images)

longer be held without triggering a large-scale French collapse. Consequently, he ordered Prételat's Groupe d'Armées 2 to give up the River Somme position and withdraw a further 26km (16 miles) to the south. That night the battered forces of the 10e and 7e Armées were to disengage and move south. They were to attempt to establish a new line anchored on the River Bresle in the west; this planned new line of resistance would then run south-east down to the town of Aumale. The line was then supposed to run east-south-east beyond Oresmaux until it reached the city of Noyon.

Consequently, during the morning of 7 June the four Panzer divisions subordinated to Hoth's and Hoepner's corps commands had surged rapidly south through open terrain, largely unopposed by the French, who had redeployed further south. Indeed, by the end of the day the three infantry divisions of Gen d.Art Haase's German III Corps had advanced to, and already attacked, the new British position established on the River Bresle. Indeed, Hasse's vanguard forces had quickly established two threatening bridgeheads to the south of the river. Just to the immediate east, beyond the town of Aumale, Hoth's 5th and 7th Panzer Divisions – in the face of negligible French resistance – had charged a further 16km (ten miles) south-south-west to threaten Forges-les-Jeux. In a vain attempt to halt this threatening Panzer breakthrough the French 10e Armée had committed its only mobile reserve. This was the newly-arriving British 1st Armoured Division, which was then moving north towards the town of Forges-les-Jeux. Simultaneously, Hubicki's 9th Panzer Division and Schaal's 10th Panzer Division surged south-west to reach a point 16km (ten miles) beyond Oresmaux. Finally, in the extreme east, Hoepner's two Panzer divisions raced south-west to expel the French 47e Division from the town of Roye. By the evening of the 7th, therefore, along this 64km (40 mile) western stretch of the Weygand Line, France's last hope of stymieing the seemingly unstoppable Panzer onslaught had already failed. A decisive German breakout to the south seemed almost inevitable.

Further to the east, along the left flank of the sector held by Reichenau's German Sixth Army, two of its divisions initiated their own southward assaults on the French line. To the immediate east, moreover, the five marching infantry divisions of the German Ninth Army mounted their own respective offensive from the German positions previously established along the Oise-Aisne Canal. Facing the latter's assaults were the colonial and fortress regiments controlled by the 6e Armée and by the extreme eastern wing of the 7e Armée.

Despite some French defensive successes on both flanks during 6 June, in the centre the two infantry divisions from Gen d.Inf Beyer's XVIII Corps made good progress to the west of Pinon. These formations surged south toward the River Aisne either side of the city of Soissons. This threatening penetration forced the 6e and 7e Armées to fall back to the River Aisne to maintain some sort of defensive cohesion. During 7 June, even before many of the French forces in this section

Gen d.Inf Ernst Busch's Sixteenth Army formed part of Army Group A's invasion of southern Belgium and northern France. After falling into disfavour with Hitler in 1944, Busch was put on the reserve list. But he was recalled in the war's final days to lead Supreme Command North-west, deployed across the Emsland and Schleswig-Holstein. (Photo by ullstein bild/ullstein bild via Getty Images)

had managed to withdraw behind the Aisne, the rapid German exploitation to the south had already successfully established two dangerous bridgeheads across the River Aisne.

Army Group A Commences its Offensive (9–15 June)

After days of frantically intense preparation, on 9 June Rundstedt's Army Group A, located to the east of Bock's Army Group B, also joined the unfolding *Fall Rot* offensive. Across its western sector, Army Group A assaulted the positions established along the River Aisne by the 6e Armée (deployed on the extreme eastern flank of the sector of Prételat's Groupe d'Armées 2). Further east, Rundstedt's army group attacked the positions manned by the westernmost flank formations subordinated to Besson's Groupe d'Armées 3. The Army Group A sector commenced in the west at the juncture of the Oise-Aisne Canal with the River Aisne, north-east of Soissons. Rundstedt's front then ran eastward along the River Aisne before continuing across the bridgehead over the River Meuse to the south of the town of Sedan. Army Group A's sector of responsibility ended just past the western end of the Maginot Line near the town of Longuyon.

Meanwhile, across its western flank – along the Aisne north of the city of Reims – the German Army Group A deployed the Second Army's eight divisions together with the upgraded Panzer Group Guderian. The latter now fielded three corps (motorised) that between them deployed four Panzer and two motorised infantry divisions. Across his central sector, along the River Aisne and the Aisne-Meuse Canal, Rundstedt deployed 16 infantry divisions from the Twelfth Army. Finally, across the eastern sector, which ran across the southern face of the Sedan bridgehead and along the Maginot Line's western extremities, the German Sixteenth Army's 11 divisions were deployed.

The objective of the German Army Group A was to burst out south into the open country beyond the River Marne, giving its forces the tactical opportunity to wheel left (eastwards) behind the western sector of the Maginot Line fortifications. Such a breakout also provided German Army Group A's armoured formations with the opportunity both to wheel right (south-westward) to outflank Paris, and to head south into France's central-southern heartlands.

After heavy initial artillery and air strikes, at 0630hrs on 9 June Rundstedt's western and central sectors commenced their respective offensives. In the east, Gen d.Inf Busch's Sixteenth Army merely remained poised, ready to assault the western fringes of the Maginot Line fortifications. The recently constituted Panzer Group Guderian spearheaded the offensive by attacking the French defences along the River Aisne west of the town of Rethel. To the west and east, meanwhile, German infantry divisions also assaulted this river line. By evening, in the face of fierce French resistance, Guderian's Panzer divisions had secured two small bridgeheads over the river. During 7 June the Germans successfully exploited south from these bridgeheads in the face of slackening French resistance. Finally, that evening the French were compelled to begin withdrawing south towards the River Marne, a redeployment that was to be completed under the shrouding cover of darkness.

This successful swift German break-in operation thus provided Group Guderian's armour with the possibility of charging south-eastward to outflank the Maginot Line defences. In addition, the French withdrawal from the River Aisne to the River Marne inadvertently exposed the western extremity of the Maginot Line to attack from the rear. Therefore, on 11 June the infantry divisions of Busch's Sixteenth Army assaulted through the gaps emerging in the fortress line between the subdued Fort La Ferté and the town of Longuyon. On the 12th, Weygand reluctantly decided to accept reality and withdraw the bulk of his forces further south, effectively leaving the Maginot Line's western sector to its own fate – German encirclement. Into this operational void poured Guderian's four Panzer divisions, aiming to boldly and quickly exploit this significant and rare operational-level opportunity.

The Fall of the French Capital, Paris (10–14 June)

Between 8 and 10 June 1940 the formations controlled by Panzer Group Kleist, as well as the German Fourth and Sixth Armies (all from Bock's Army Group B), continued to surge south-west toward the lower Seine to the west of Paris, in the face of desultory French resistance. The wider German plan was that these forces would continue to advance south past the capital city, thus outflanking it from the west. At the same time, the advance of the German Ninth Army – from the western flank of Rundstedt's Army Group A – up to and beyond the River Marne would outflank the French capital from the east. This double envelopment would have the effect of separating Paris from the mass of the forces controlled by the French Groupes d'Armées 2 and 3. Cut off from any prospect of relief, the Germans hoped that the French capital would quickly capitulate, sparing them from the need to carry on protracted and costly urban fighting in its labyrinth of streets and alleyways; they had learned a painful lesson from the Polish defence of Warsaw in autumn 1939.

On 10 June, meanwhile, Weygand had created the Army of Paris, seemingly as a force that would tenaciously defend the capital against enemy attempts to seize it. However, during that fateful day the strategic situation for France deteriorated significantly. First, Italy declared war on France, forcing her beleaguered forces to defend yet another front. Second, the rapidly advancing German spearheads had secured dangerous bridgeheads across the lower Seine in two places. These forces were thus now threatening the capital. Later that day the French government hurriedly packed up and relocated south to the city of Tours. Early the next day, however, Weygand decided that he would soon declare Paris

ARMY GROUP B'S PANZER CHARGE THROUGH NORMANDY AND BRITTANY, 15–21 JUNE

During 5–9 June 1940. the right wing of GenObst Fedor von Bock's German Army Group B initiated *Fall Rot* and successfully overwhelmed the initially-determined Allied defence of the River Somme. Subsequently, the 14 divisions deployed by Panzer Group Kleist, as well as those deployed by the German Fourth and Sixth Armies, successfully forced crossings of the lower River Seine to the west of Paris. Subsequently, during 14–20 June Hermann Hoth's 5th and 7th Panzer Divisions audaciously charged south-west through Normandy and Brittany in the face of dissolving French resistance. Indeed, by the 21st the German mobile formations had captured all the key cities in this part of France: Cherbourg, Brest, St. Malo, Rennes and Lorient.

an 'open city' that would not be defended, thus sparing its civilian population from the horrors of a protracted siege; this intent was not immediately publicised to the population, however, to prevent mass panic from erupting.

By 13 June 1940 the advancing German forces had reached various points located many miles beyond Paris to the south-west and south-east; in the meantime, other German marching-infantry formations had closed on the city from the north. On that very same day, the French government informed Parisians that the city was not to be defended. The steady stream of panicked French refugees hell-bent on fleeing the city soon turned into a vast flood of terrified humanity that choked every single road to the south of the city, making French tactical manoeuvre all but impossible. That evening, moreover, the first forward detachments from the German 9th Infantry Division reached the city's suburbs. Subsequently, during the early hours of 14 June, German and French representatives discussed the arrangements regarding the city's immediate capitulation. At 0600hrs both parties signed the pertinent surrender documents. That morning German marching-infantry columns filled the entire city and soon Nazi Swastika flags flew from all of the city's key buildings. Paris had fallen to the Wehrmacht with barely a shot being fired.

Army Group B Conquers North-Western France (15–21 June)

From 10 to 14 June significant elements of GenObst von Bock's Army Group B had crossed the lower Seine west of Paris and continued to advance rapidly south-west through Normandy in the face of collapsing French resistance. By then Paris had already fallen. Prime Minister Paul Reynaud had been facing intense internal political pressure to negotiate a ceasefire with the Germans, something he refused to countenance. As a result, he was finally forced out of power on the 16th. A new, anti-war, party led by the new Prime Minister Marshal Henri Philippe Pétain – the World War I hero who had been recalled from his ambassadorial duties in Spain – took the helm in the midst of France's darkest crisis. The French

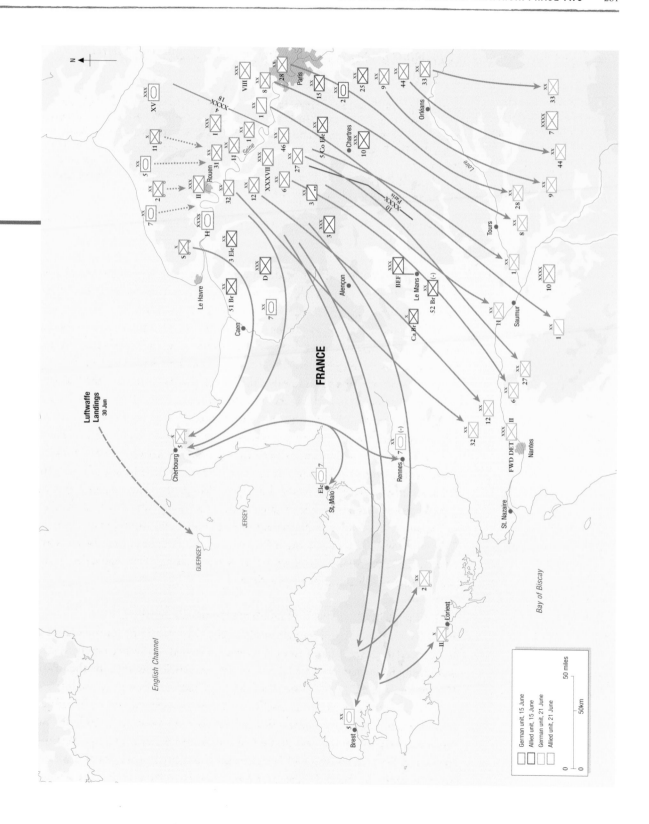

The Fight for Casemate Oberroedern-Nord, 20 June 1940

The German assault on Casemate Oberroedern-Nord was a desperate fight. During the preparatory bombardment a Stuka bomb hit the casemate's protective ditch. The explosion breached the casemate's exterior wall, breaking up several interior walls in the bottom level. Smoke and dust blew through the casemate and the crew panicked. Meanwhile, fire from 88mm anti-tank guns disabled two of the casemate's armoured cupolas, hitting each more than a dozen times **(1)**. The loss of these cupolas left the forward side of the casemate blind and defenceless. A third cupola, recessed in the casemate's roof, was not visible to the crews of the 88s and therefore was not engaged **(2)**. Once the 88mm guns stopped firing, German infantry and combat engineers emerged from a nearby ravine, crossed the anti-tank **(3)** and barbed-wire **(4)** obstacle belts, and infiltrated around the side and rear of the casemate. As the Germans closed in for the final assault, Oberroedern-Nord's commander, Lt Vialle, rallied his soldiers who then fired every available weapon at the attackers, including a 47mm anti-tank gun, 7.5mm machine guns,

handheld 50mm mortars and even the commander's revolver. When German troops moved in to breach the casemate's armoured door and disable the weapon embrasures **(5)**, the casemate crew used special grenade launchers (called *goulottes*) mounted in the walls of the casemate to drop hand grenades into the protective ditch and keep the German soldiers away. Realizing the danger of the situation, Lt Vialle signalled the neighbouring Casemate Aschbach-Est to lob 50mm mortar rounds on Casemate Oberroedern-Nord **(6)**. Despite the intense French defensive fire, the German soldiers made several attempts to take the casemate; but each was repulsed and the attack stalled. Meanwhile, deadly accurate fire from the twin 7.5mm machine guns of Oberroedern-Nord's undamaged cupola blocked the arrival of German reinforcements and the route of withdrawal. Trapped, the German soldiers hunkered down in bomb craters until dive-bomber attacks against Casemate Aschbach-Est and other nearby fortified works provided cover for a hasty withdrawal. (Artwork by John White, © Osprey Publishing)

government by then had relocated to the port-city of Bordeaux in south-western France, far away from the rampaging Panzer advance. Committed to salvaging something from the military disaster through negotiation, on 17 June Marshal Pétain's government opened the first tentative ceasefire feelers with Nazi Germany.

GenObst Erwin von Witzleben (left) commanded the German First Army, part of Leeb's Army Group C. During 14 June Witzleben's forces initiated the Operation *Tiger* offensive against the French Maginot Line defences located between Faulquemont and Saarguemines. Here Witzleben is speaking with GenObst Curt Haase in France during spring 1941. (Photo by ullstein bild/ullstein bild via Getty Images)

During 15–21 June, meanwhile, Army Group B's forces – spearheaded by Hoth's 5th and 7th Panzer Divisions – rapidly surged southward, overrunning the entirety of Normandy and Brittany. With no thought about the risk of exposed flanks, Rommel's 7th Panzer Division raced through Normandy and the Cotentin Peninsula to capture the port-town of Cherbourg, as well as St Malo, by the 19th. His armoured division then turned south to reach, and capture, the town of Rennes by the 20th. Meanwhile, Walsporn's 5th Panzer Division had stormed westward through the Brittany peninsula to capture the key port-city of Brest. Finally, Hoth's remaining subordinate formation, GenLt Bader's German 2nd Motorised Infantry Division, had secured the key French Atlantic Coast naval base at Lorient.

Further to the east, some 12 German infantry divisions from the German Fourth and Eighteenth Armies had meanwhile advanced south as fast as they could manage in the face of only sporadic determined French resistance. Bypassing the key towns of Alençon, Paris, Le Mans and Chartres, the infanteers marched frantically down to and across the mighty River Loire. Indeed, by 21 June these dozen German marching infantry divisions had crossed the lower Loire on a 330km (205 mile) frontage that ran between the cities of Nantes in the west and Orléans in the east. Apart from a few isolated locations of staunch defensive resolve, the effective resistance the French ground forces could muster was negligible. Even when dogged tactical resistance was initially encountered, the employment of Junkers Ju 87 Stuka close air support and ground flanking assaults typically swiftly overcame these isolated pockets of resistance.

THE DEMISE OF THE MAGINOT LINE, 5–13 JUNE

During 5–13 June, as *Fall Rot* unfolded to the west, Army Group C continued to threaten the as yet unscathed French Maginot Line fortifications. Next, on 14 May – the day that Paris capitulated – the German First Army assaulted the Maginot Line's Faulquemont-Saarguemines sector, while the next day Seventh Army initiated its attack in the area east of Colmar. By 19 June these two German pincers were not far from linking up. To avoid encirclement, the French forces still manning the Line's Bitchte–Hagenau sector abandoned their forts and retreated south-west. As this withdrawal unfolded, however, dozens of French formations found themselves being caught in a much bigger pocket, for by then Guderian's armour had raced south along the Marne valley and closed in from the west to reach the Swiss border and seal the encirclement.

Army Group A Encircles the Groupe d'Armées 3 (12–22 June)

During 12–16 June Panzer Group Guderian, as well as the marching infantry of the German Second and Twelfth Armies, all rapidly surged south-east toward the cities of Verdun, St Mihiel, Chaumont and Langres. In the process these forces threatened the left flank of the substantial forces of the Groupe d'Armées 3 then fixed in defence of the Maginot Line fortifications along the Franco-German border. The pressure on this latter command increased on 14 June, the day Paris capitulated, when the German Army Group C finally moved from mounting feints against the Maginot Line to initiating actual offensive actions. That day, GenObst von Witzleben's German First Army initiated its Operation *Tiger* offensive. Witzleben's forces mounted this assault across the 32km (20 mile) sector of the front that stretched from north of Faulquemont to the town of Saarguemines. In the ensuing 72 hours First Army's forces established a deep and wide penetration of the Maginot Line that included the capture of the key towns of Sarre-Union and Sarrebourg.

The next day, to the south east, the German Seventh Army launched its own attack across the Rhine against the Maginot Line, codenamed Operation *Bear*. Even though the German Seventh Army controlled some of the least combat-ready divisions within the German Army, the defending French forces had already been significantly denuded to reinforce the crisis situation to the north-west. During 15 June five Seventh Army divisions successfully penetrated the Maginot Line to establish a small bridgehead on the western bank of the Rhine. Over the next four days these five divisions pushed westward, capturing the town of Colmar in the process. By the 19th, Seventh Army's spearheads were just 32km (20 miles) away from the advance of First Army's drive south beyond Sarrebourg. To avoid being encircled between these two German advances, the French forces still manning the intact Maginot Line defences between the towns of Bitchte and Hagenau abandoned their forts and retreated south-west. This French redeployment, however, did not prevent the bulk of Besson's Groupe d'Armées 3 from being caught in a pocket, as Guderian's armour had already closed in from the west and south-west to seal the encirclement.

RIGHT The Maginot Line proper
ceased in its western end at Longuyon,
some 45km (28 miles) east-south-east
of Sedan. From near Longuyon,
adjacent to the Franco-Belgian border,
a weaker line of casemates and
bunkers, such as this one, ran
west-north-west until they reached the
River Meuse; the line of bunkers then
ran west-north-west along the Meuse's
southern bank through the town of
Sedan. (Photo by ullstein bild/ullstein
bild via Getty Images)

BELOW Generale Alfredo Guzzoni
commanded the Italian Fourth Army
during the Italian invasion of
south-eastern France. Guzzoni (right) is
seen here on 7 April 1939, during the
Italian occupation of Albania. Italian
Foreign Minister Count Ciano (left) and
Guzzoni together read a telegram from
'Il Duce', Mussolini, congratulating them
on this successful military operation.
(Photo by ullstein bild/ullstein bild via
Getty Images)

Indeed, during 14–16 June 1940 the four Panzer and three motorised infantry divisions of the Panzer Group Guderian had charged south and south-east down the valley of the River Marne to leave the town of Langres and Vitry far behind. In order to maintain offensive momentum and tempo, the Panzers had simply bypassed any localised centres of firm French resistance. However, near the town of Juniville the battered remnants of the 1ère DCr had mounted a surprise counter-attack that temporarily halted the advance of the German 1st Panzer Division. By then Panzer Group Kleist had redeployed to join Army Group A and now charged south into central France across Guderian's exposed western (right) flank.

On 17 June 1940 Guderian's spearheads reached the town of Pontarlier on the Swiss border, thus realising the encirclement of what remained of Besson's Groupe d'Armées 3. The four divisions of XLI Corps (Motorised) sealed the western flank of the pocket, from near the city of Nancy in the north, south-west to beyond the town of Épinal. Meanwhile, the three mobile divisions of the XIX Corps (Motorised) sealed the southern flank of the pocket. Indeed, on the 19 June, XIX Corps (Motorised) from Army Group A linked up with the spearheads of the German Seventh Army (from Army Group C) to the west of Mulhouse.

This German link-up surrounded the remnants of the French 3e, 5e and 8e Armées, plus the Maginot Line's fortress-infantry garrisons: the trapped forces totalled around 400,000 men and 80 tanks. Weygand ordered the encircled formations immediately to mount a breakout attempt toward the west.

However, the morale of the French troops was already very low, and during 20–21 June entire French regiments surrendered en masse to the nearest German formation that they could locate. The war in eastern France was effectively over.

The Final Nail: The Italian Invasion of the Alpine Front (20–22 June)

On 10 June 1940, with France reeling in the face of the German onslaught through the Weygand Line, the country received another deadly blow. For that day Fascist Italy declared war on the Allies, forcing the French to contemplate trying to resist an Italian invasion of south-eastern France. During 11–19 June the Italian Army prepared for offensive warfare against France as the two countries' air forces launched modest raids on one another's bases. Also during this period, of course, France's dire strategic situation continued to exponentially deteriorate as ever greater swathes of territory fell to the rampaging German forces: by 19 June peace feelers had been initiated.

By 20 June, the Italian ground forces were finally ready and consequently their spearheads launched attacks across the mountain passes into French territory. The Italian Army Group West had concentrated 30 Italian divisions with 400,000 troops under the overall command of Crown Prince Umberto of Savoy, Luogotenente Generale del Regno D'Italia. The ultimate objective of the Italian ground offensive was to capture the key Mediterranean port of Marseille.

Facing them were the 200,000 troops of the French Armée des Alpes, which was commanded by Général d'Armée Olry. These forces were organised into three second-rate reserve infantry divisions and several independent fortress commands. Although aided by the difficult mountainous alpine terrain, the defensive power of the Armée des Alpes was severely hampered by the increasing threat to its lines of communication posed by the German armour charging south down the Rhône valley toward its rear areas. Indeed, Lyon had just been declared an open city, which would soon permit the Panzers to use its valuable bridges to cross the mighty River Rhône and directly threaten Olry's rear.

In the final phases of *Fall Rot*, Luftwaffe close air support proved a very useful asset in breaking up the rarely encountered pockets of more determined French resistance. When the advancing Panzer spearheads encountered such staunchly defended islands of firm resistance, Stuka dive-bombers were called in to pound the locations, their dive whistles added an additional psychological effect to their devastating lethal strikes. (© IWM, HU 103326)

The initial Italian attacks in the north were hampered by deep snow and bad weather, and this surprisingly enabled the weak French defending forces to limit the Italian advance to just some small territorial gains. Even on the better ground, amid a kinder climate along the Mediterranean coast, an entire Italian corps only managed to advance 5km (three miles) into the weak French outpost line that screened the town of Menton. In response to these disappointing achievements on 21 June 1940 the Italians requested that the Germans speed up their drive down the Rhône valley to put pressure on the French rear; the request got short shrift from the Wehrmacht. It was only on the offensive's third day, 22 June, that the Italian First Army finally managed to capture Menton.

That evening, however, France signed an armistice with Germany, so the fighting in the Alps gradually died down. Italy and France signed their own armistice on the 24th, which ceded Nice and a slice of the Savoy Alps region to Italian occupation. But the Italian invasion had been an embarrassing disappointment to Germany, and the martial qualities of the Italian Armed Forces seemed to compare very poorly with the astonishing military triumphs that the Wehrmacht had just achieved.

Endgame: The French Capitulation (18–25 June)

By 18 June 1940 a torrent of advancing German forces – spearheaded by the rampaging Panzers – were charging into southern France, with effective French resistance being encountered in only a very few isolated locations. The morale of the vast majority of French troops was extremely low, with the soldiers unable to comprehend the scale of the disaster then engulfing them. Pétain's new French government was similarly demoralised and set their plans on a negotiated settlement that might save part of France from full German occupation.

On 22 June 1940 the French were forced to sign a humiliating surrender agreement at Compiègne, in the same railway carriage where the Germans had capitulated in 1918. Here the German delegation pose for the cameras; we can see (from left) Foreign Minister Joachim von Ribbentrop, Adm Erich Raeder, Wilhelm Brückner, Hitler, GenObst Wilhelm Keitel, Hermann Göring, GenObst Walther von Brauchitsch and Rudolf Hess. (Photo by ullstein bild/ullstein bild via Getty Images)

That same day the French government declared that all communities with populations of over 25,000 citizens were open towns, not to be defended. In the actions that did occur during 18–20 June, the German armoured spearheads found that after a fierce brief initial encounter, the French units they encountered typically soon proved very ready to surrender en masse to them.

On the 19th the new French government initiated peace feelers with the Germans via the Spanish ambassador to France. In the ensuing 48 hours a French delegation, led by Général Huntziger, drove north all day and arrived in Paris. The delegation then drove to the location where Hitler had decided the capitulation would take place. This was a particular train wagon located at Compiègne; it was the very same site where Imperial Germany had been compelled to sign the November 1918 Armistice that ended the Great War. Hitler's choice was an extreme

On 23 June, the day after the French capitulation had been signed at Compiègne, Adolf Hitler posed for this photograph in front of the Eiffel Tower in Paris. This act formed part of his personal tour of celebration to mark the ignominious national humiliation that overwhelming Nazi German military might had inflicted upon the French. (Photo by Heinrich Hoffmann/ Galerie Bilderwelt/ Getty Images)

In celebration of the triumphs achieved, on 19 July 1940 in Berlin Hitler promoted 12 senior commanders from the rank of Generaloberst to Generalfeldmarschall. This included army group commanders Bock, Leeb and Rundstedt, as well as four army commanders (Kluge, List, Reichenau and Witzleben). Hitler also, as this image shows, personally congratulated other senior commanders including (from the right) Hermann Hoth, Heinz Guderian and Ernst Busch. (Photo by ullstein bild/ullstein bild via Getty Images)

gesture of political humiliation and revenge. Within this railway wagon Hitler and his senior Nazi Party leaders and Wehrmacht commanders awaited the French delegation, but then Hitler left as soon as the surrender preamble had been read.

At 18:36 on 22 June 1940 the Armistice between France and Germany was signed. In the terms of the capitulation, Germany occupied the northern two-thirds of France, plus a strip that ran south along the Atlantic coast to the Spanish border. The treaty, however, left unoccupied the poorest southern third of the country, which would be run as an Axis puppet state by the new collaborationist regime. The regime had moved to Vichy in central France, and was subsequently referred to by the city's name. The Vichy regime controlled the existing French Empire and the French Fleet. So as to give time to get the news to disparate French forces, the ceasefire only took effect at 0035hrs on 25 June. In not quite 25 days the Germans had achieved what had eluded them for four years during the Great War: they had conquered central and southern France.

AFTERMATH

In the early hours of 25 June 1940, the guns fell silent across southern France: *Fall Rot* had ended. Between them the Wehrmacht's *Fall Gelb* and *Fall Rot* invasions had conquered all of north-western Europe: the Netherlands, Belgium, Luxembourg, the British Channel Islands, and France; the latter conquest had been modestly assisted by the Italian invasion of south-eastern France on 20 June. These stunning military triumphs brought 57 million Europeans under the horrors of either direct German occupation or Axis-puppet control. Many of them would have to wait between four and five years to be liberated by the Western Allied advance from the June 1944 D-Day landings.

The casualty figures from the 1940 Western campaign go some way to indicating the sheer enormity of German military success. The total German combat casualties – according to Alastair Horne's *To Lose a Battle* – were 156,492 ground personnel. This included some 27,074 troops recorded as killed in action, some 111,034 wounded in action, a further 18,384 missing in action (some of whom undoubtedly had perished), but excluded 6,653 Luftwaffe personnel. If this is incorporated, the total German personnel losses were 163,145. If one adds in the total Italian casualties of 6,055 (which included frostbite 'combat wounds'), this makes an overall Axis casualty figure for the campaign of 169,200.

Given that the peak German strength of personnel committed to the campaign was 3,350,000, the total casualty figure of 163,145 represents a wastage rate of just 4.9 per cent. When the sheer military strength of Germany's

ABOVE Although the 'miracle' evacuation from Dunkirk successfully extracted much of the BEF's manpower back to the UK, most of its heavy weapons and equipment had to be left on the Continent. Here some disabled British Army anti-aircraft guns can be seen abandoned along the promenade at Bray-Dunes. (© IWM, HU 2286)

LEFT The stunning German military triumph in 1940 condemned tens of millions of French civilians to four painful years of brutal German occupation. It was not until the June 1944 Normandy landings that the Western Allies began liberating the French from Nazi tyranny. Here crowds in Paris welcome the arrival of Allied troops in late August 1944. (Photo courtesy of Library and Archives, PA-130252)

The triumphs achieved in 1940 emboldened Hitler to commence preparations for an amphibious assault across the Channel into southern England. But first the Germans had to defeat the Royal Air Force, so that with aerial superiority they could prevent the Royal Navy devastating the naval invasion armada or the thousands of required subsequent naval resupply sorties. Failing to defeat the RAF, the Germans turned to area bombing of UK cities – the Blitz – in a vain attempt to break British morale. Here a Heinkel He 111 bomber is seen over London on 7 September 1940. (Photo courtesy of Library and Archives, PA-037470)

enemies in this campaign is factored in, and the geographical scale of the theatre, the fact that the side on the offensive experienced a loss rate of under five per cent seems to indicate that Hitler's Wehrmacht had, using its Blitzkrieg approaches, achieved a truly stunning and disproportionate military success.

The overall French losses were estimated (and, as he admits, probably under-estimated) by Horne as around 2,190,000 personnel. This total comprised some 90,000 killed in action, 200,000 wounded in action, and around 1,900,000 troops either missing or as prisoners of war). An official French source calculated that there were 85,310 French combat deaths, 120,000 wounded in action, 12,000 missing, and 1,540,000 French prisoners of war. These figures give a total of 1,757,310 casualties, some 98 per cent of the total French strength.

The other Allied powers had smaller absolute casualty figures. The British experienced 66,426 casualties (including 11,014 deaths) and 41,388 soldiers taken prisoner, the Belgians 23,350 casualties plus 200,000 prisoners, the Dutch

9,779 combat losses and 110,000 prisoners, the Polish 5,500 combat deaths and 16,000 prisoners. Often forgotten, the tiny Luxembourg Army suffered seven troops wounded in action during its brief resistance to the German invasion on 10 May. In total, Allied human casualties came to around 2,230,000 personnel. Overall Allied personnel losses were no less than 13 times higher than those of the Axis invaders.

The balance sheet of equipment losses also swung heavily in the favour of the Axis invader. One source estimated that the Germans lost 822 Panzers as complete losses (34 per cent of the total), while the Luftwaffe lost 1428 aircraft (28 per cent of the front-line total). Allied aircraft losses came to 1,274 platforms, while France lost 1,749 tanks, some 43 per cent of its strength; most of the remainder fell intact into German hands.

The Armistice of 25 June 1940 left all of northern and western France under direct German occupation, south-eastern France under Italian occupation, and the rest of southern France under the pro-Axis Vichy puppet state. The subsequent German and Italian occupation of France was brutal and rapacious. Both countries drained the manpower of France for slave labour, and ruthlessly exploited the country's economic capability for the benefit of the occupying nations. Over four years of Axis occupation left over 60,000 resistance fighters dead, a further 30,000 citizens executed for various crimes, as well as 40,000 inhabitants of Alsace, forcibly conscripted into Wehrmacht, as combat deaths. Some 240,000 of the French military held as prisoners of war in Germany died before the war's end in May 1945.

The stunning Axis triumph in the 1940 Western campaign strongly encouraged Hitler to contemplate an invasion of Britain. Though sufficient British personnel had escaped from looming German capture via Operation *Dynamo*, the naval evacuation from Dunkirk, to man the British Army's UK-based formations, these divisions lacked heavy weaponry. In the county of Kent on 12 June 1940 – the most likely German invasion location – the British defending forces lacked a single working anti-tank gun. But to conquer the United Kingdom, the Luftwaffe had to secure air superiority to prevent the mighty Royal Navy destroying the German invasion fleets. However, in the summer of 1940 the RAF fought off the German aerial *Blitz* against Britain. Equally, the German Navy had been badly depleted by the heavy losses suffered in the invasion of Norway.

Consequently, Hitler eventually shelved his fantasises of conquering the United Kingdom. By then, anyway, his strategic planning had returned to the most important struggle within the Nazi *Weltanschauung* (world-view): the titanic existential racial battle of survival of Capitalist Nazism against Communism in Stalin's Soviet Union. In June 1941, the Axis powers launched Operation *Barbarossa*, the invasion of the Soviet Union. The appallingly brutal and massive ideological war of annihilation on the Eastern Front would consume most of Germany's military assets for a further 1,312 days until the war's end in early May 1945.

For both sides North-western Europe became a relative strategic backwater until on 6 June 1944 the Western Allies launched the D-Day invasion of Normandy. In the ensuing 11 months the Western Allies liberated France, Belgium, Luxembourg and the Netherlands. On 8 May 1945 Nazi Germany surrendered unconditionally, and the heinous scourge of Nazism was removed from Europe's battered, war-torn soil.

THE BATTLEFIELD TODAY

In the early 21st century there exists only a very small number of physical, tangible, artefacts and locations across the Netherlands, Belgium and France where an interested individual can get some personal insight into the momentous military events that occurred here during the Western campaign of May–June 1940. With regard to the bitter battle for Belgium, it is perhaps helpful to focus on the actions of the German armoured formation commanders. The main protagonists in the story in Belgium are the corps commander Gen d.Kav Hoepner, and the division commanders GenLt Stever and GenMaj Stumpff.

To fully appreciate the enormity and difficulty of the tactical tasks facing these three Panzer generals, it is best to begin any exploration of the battlefields located around Hannut, Gembloux and Maastricht; the latter is located on the right (eastern) bank of the River Maas. The Wilhelmina Bridge remains much as it was in May 1940, only with the great hinged trapdoor section of the roadway fully in place instead of angling into the water below. Once across the River Maas, the next physical obstacle for an armoured invader is the wide Albert Canal. This water feature is now spanned by a new, very modern bridge at Vroenhoven. As a memorial to the men who lost their lives fighting here, the builders have left the battle-scarred bunker on the bridge's western abutment entirely intact. This preservation effort reflected the recognition that – as the bunker's inscription declares – this very place, located on the Albert Canal, was where World War II started for Belgium on 10 May 1940.

Following the invading Panzers' westward route via the villages of Tongeren and Waremme, it is remarkable what great tank country the plateau between the towns of Hannut and Gembloux really is. This centuries-old military movement corridor comprises gently rolling countryside with flowing undulations, ideal for mechanised manoeuvring. In addition, there are many high points crowned with small woods that make excellent sites for the execution of anti-tank ambushes. The expansive plain is riven with small streams in narrow but deep valleys, invariably forested. Except for the small towns of Hannut, Crehen, and Merdorp along the crest of the broad ridge, most of the villages – and they remain today much as they were in 1940 – are tucked into these ravines, great for concealing French armour until sallying out for a counter-attack, but limiting their fields of fire from defensive positions.

Not to be missed is the *Musée du Corps de Cavalerie Français 1940* (Museum of the French Cavalry Corps 1940), located in Jandrain, the site of an epic French last-ditch defence before Général de Corps Prioux's front line was finally breached. Housed in the former village schoolhouse and meeting hall – Capitaine Laffargue's Command Post during the battle – this small but excellent museum contains a large collection of artefacts and has detailed records of the battle, an invaluable treasure to any military historian researching it. At the time of writing, museum staff member Major Richard de Hennin offers battlefield tours, in English, to those who book ahead of time. This is good because, unlike the battlefields around the village of Stonne, there are no monuments or memorials commemorating what occurred here in 1940.

The only remaining vestige of the battle is the famous water tower located on the high ground between the villages of Jandrain and Jandrenouille – a location that served both as an artillery observation post for the French and a very visible *guidon* (an obvious geographic objective) used by the attacking Panzer units. Plainly evident are the impact marks of 37mm shells and a volley of 20mm cannon fire, as well as numerous small pocks made by the fire of rifles and machine guns. From this dominating position, the entire battlefield of 13 May can be viewed. Noting the sheer closeness of the neighbouring villages makes it easy to visualise how crowded this relatively small – 10km (six mile) square – battlefield was, given that 256 German and 165 French tanks were manoeuvring and fighting upon it.

While in this general area, visiting the *Musée de la Ligne KW* the (Museum of the KW Defence Line) at Chaumont and the *Musée de la 1ère Armée Français* (the Museum of the First French Army) at Cortil-Noirmont is also recommended. In contrast to the rather unspoiled (but unmarked) battlefield around Jandrain, the route of GenLt Ritter von Hubicki's 9th Panzer Division across the River Maas and through Mill to Moerdijk is largely lost in the expansive and unrelenting growth of modern civilisation.

At Moerdijk, on the south side, one battle-scarred *VIS-kazemat* (machine-gun casemate) remains, while on the northern bank a large *B-kazemat* (river casemate housing an anti-tank gun), a *VIS-kazemat*, and several *Pyramide* group bomb shelters can be examined. The original 1936 steel truss highway bridge has been replaced with the A16's dual four-lane concrete spans, the former's long trusses being used to build the A27 motorway across the Bergse Maas, 20km (12 miles) to the east. Off the A16, one can see the bridges at Dordrecht much as they were in May 1940.

Adjacent to the city of Rotterdam, the crucial Waalhaven aerodrome has succumbed to the spread of suburbia. The airfield at Willemsbrug was replaced with a new one in 1981, and the razed inner city has been rebuilt with little likeness to its 1940 state. Most historically important, 10km (six miles) south, at

Near the villages of La Ferté and Villy, close to the Franco-Belgian border, stood the Fort (Petit Ouvrage) La Ferté. This was located in the fortified sector Montmédy, part of the weak westward extension of the Maginot Line proper, which ended further east at Longuyon. It was defended by 103 French fortress infantry troops and gunners. During 14–18 May a bitter fight for the local area and the fort ensued, with the complex eventually falling, but only after raging fires had caused every one of its defenders to perish. (Photo by Pascal STRITT/Gamma-Rapho via Getty Images)

Rijsoord, is the school that in 1940 was briefly GenLt Student's Command Post; it is now the De Poort Institute. In this building hangs a large bronze plaque that commemorates the inglorious day of the Dutch capitulation.

In fact, the only significant site remaining from the Dutch five-day war is the Grebbeberg, which – though heavily wooded now – is preserved so that visitors can see defensive bunkers and reconstructed trenches as they walk up the fairly steep slope from the ancient Hoornwerk bastion to the crest. Atop the hill is the *Militair Ereveld Grebbeberg* (Grebbeberg Military Cemetery) where some 800 Dutch and German soldiers are buried. Although less strategically significant, at the east end of the Afsluitdijk, Fort Kornwerderzand is almost completely preserved and makes an excellent time capsule to take one back to May 1940.

Moving further south, anyone with a deep interest in better understanding the 1940 *Fall Gelb* campaign in the West will want to explore the area around Sedan. After all, the key to explaining the success of the German invasion was undoubtedly the pivotal battle of Sedan, which raged during 13–15 May. Visiting the battlefield today, the military historian and enthusiast will first discover that Napoleon III's decisive defeat in 1870 and the two battles fought there in World War I are well accommodated with monuments, memorials and museums. However, the later defeat that cost the French the 1940 campaign – and four and a half years of freedom – is not nearly so well commemorated.

The most persistent relics of the climactic tactical battle fought at and around Sedan are the many concrete casemates still dotting the countryside, too strong to

The Assault on Fort La Ferté, 18 May 1940

The capture of the French Maginot Line installation Fort La Ferté was a textbook assault on a fortified position. The attack began with a concentrated artillery barrage that blew gaps in the fort's obstacle belts and cratered the ground around the fort **(1)**. Despite its intensity, the barrage did not seriously damage the fort, although its primary weapon – an AM turret – was jammed in a raised firing position, facing to the rear of the fort. As the artillery barrage lifted, a detachment of German combat engineers led by Oblt Alfred Germer carefully approached Block 2 as 88mm flak provided suppressive fire against the fort's armoured cupolas and turret. Using craters for cover, Germer's engineers worked their way to the top of the block and began systematically putting the cupolas out of action with explosive charges. After the first cupola was disabled **(2)**, the engineers detonated 40kg of explosive charges against the side of the turret. Although the explosion was tremendous, it failed to destroy the turret. Next, a 6kg charge was used to blow open one of the turret's weapons embrasures, followed by a 9kg charge shoved through the opening, into the interior of turret. The explosion from that charge, along with secondary detonation of ammunition inside the block, ripped the turret off its base and lifted it into the air **(3)**. The turret then crashed back on its base and landed canted to one side. The engineers then threw several more explosive and smoke charges into the opening at the base of the turret, as well as the block's other armoured cupolas, starting several fires inside the combat block. Smoke from fires caused the French commander, Lt Bourguignon, to order the fort's crew to seek shelter far below ground in the connecting corridor between Blocks 1 and 2. Shortly thereafter, once night fell, Germer's detachment attacked the fort's other combat block in a similar manner, disabling its five armoured cupolas and setting a fire inside Block 1. Refusing to surrender, all 103 members of La Ferté's crew perished, asphyxiated by fumes from the fires raging in the upper stories of the fort's two combat blocks. German casualties were few. Germer was awarded the Knight's Cross for his leadership during the attack. (Artwork by John White, © Osprey Publishing)

demolish except in the most profitable circumstances. For instance, driving west from Sedan towards the village of Donchery along road D724 reveals Blockhouse 46 and Artillery Casemate 47. These two installations were instrumental in the French repulse of the 2nd Panzer Division's initial attempts to force a crossing of the Meuse. Likewise, south-east of Sedan a number of pillboxes, blockhouses and casemates dot route D6E, these having been used by French fortress infantry units in their repulse of the initial assaults made by both of the 10th Panzer Division's rifle regiments. Today, these are but empty tombs dedicated to the men who died inside them trying to defend France from the invader.

Commemorated as such is Maison-Forte (MF10) Saint-Menges – one of eight such installations positioned along the roads from the River Semois into the town of Sedan – which is located along the east edge of the D6, about two miles north of the village of the same name. Additionally, it is also possible to locate the large command bunker of Général Lafontaine and his 55e Division Infanterie staff. This headquarters lies approximately one mile south of Bulson, about 150 yards into the woods just south of Au Jardin de Bulson, on the east side of the D29 road.

For all the completed defensive positions dotting the landscape south of Sedan, when one examines the frontage along the Meuse that was subjected to the 1st Panzer Division's assaults, it is striking that northwards from Casemate 211 – easily viewable just north of the Pont Neuf bridge – there were none for over a mile to the corner of the Iges Canal. While the gunners of Casemate 211 made the crossing of the Infantry Regiment 'Großdeutschland' very costly, the two battalions of Kirchner's Rifle Regiment (Motorised) 1 faced only three rifle squads and a machine-gun team in open positions. The lack of meaningful French resistance allowed the 1st Panzer Division's riflemen and pioneers to pass over – as Guderian described – as though the crossing was being carried out on manoeuvres. Once afoot on the far side the German troops were able to organise quickly a powerful advance through the widely spaced casemates forming the *Ligne Principale de Résistance* (main line of resistance). Upon seeing the battlefield in detail, one appreciates the possibility that, had this section of the River Meuse been fortified with casemates manned with resolute French fortress infantry troops like the rest of the 55e Division's river frontage, the 1st Panzer Division's assaults could have been repulsed just as were both the Panzer divisions on its flanks.

The observant contemporary viewer of this battle-space is also struck by the very restricted French fields of fire – narrow arcs and the limited range of their weapons – provided by gunners ensconced in these widely separated casemates. This makes clear why it was so necessary to position interval troops between the bunkers. These were the troops that panicked and fled. In their absence, it is easy to see how the German riflemen were able to infiltrate between and around the concrete casemates and eliminate one after another by attacking from their blind sides.

While there are few memorials to the actions fought during May 1940 in the vicinity of Sedan, further south, beginning at Stonne, there are numerous memorials and monuments to the stout defence presented by the many component units of Général Brocard's French 3e DCr as well as those of the 3e DIM. This is ironic, as these tactical actions proved irrelevant to the outcome of the *Fall Gelb* campaign. Nevertheless, the displays at the village of Stonne provide the viewer with an up-close look at a well-maintained Char B1 bis tank – its armour marred but unpierced by several noticeable enemy hits – and an APX 47mm SA 37 anti-tank gun. At Sy – the location of the HQ of the artillery regiments of the 3e DIM – can be seen a modernised French Model 1897/1935 75mm field cannon. These and other pertinent sights are well organised along the '*Bataille de Stonne Circuit Historique*' route.

While the museum in the famous *Château Fort de Sedan* contains nothing pertaining to the May 1940 battle, numerous small museums in the Sedan area can be recommended to visitors. These include the *Musée Mai–Juin 1940* (Museum of May–June 1940) in Margut, the *Musée des Spahis* (Spahis Museum) located at La Horgne, the *Musée de la Bataille Mai-Juin 40* (Museum of Battle May–June 1940) at Semuy, and the well-preserved Maginot Line fort at Villy-La-Ferté.

There are relatively few meaningful relics of the events that occurred during *Fall Rot*, the second phase of the German invasion of France. Perhaps the most notable is the railway carriage located at Compiègne. This is a replica of the railway carriage in which the armistices were signed that brought to an end both the Great War and the German invasion of France in 1940. In spring 1945 the Germans destroyed the original carriage, which had been taken to Thuringia in Germany. In 1950 the French positioned a similar wagon in the exact spot where the two armistice agreements were signed. It formed the foundation-point for a museum established at the location. Next to it are a few charred remnants of the actual carriage that had been destroyed in 1945.

CONCLUSION

During the period from September 1939 to June 1940 the world witnessed a fundamental transformation of the balance of power within the continent of Europe. This transformation was achieved entirely by a crushing German force of arms. In just 10 months the Wehrmacht conquered first Poland, then Denmark and Norway, and finally the Netherlands, Belgium, Luxembourg and France. In these 300 days the observing world experienced astonishment at the scale, speed and decisiveness with which the Nazi German military utilised war as an instrument to deliver Hitler's foreign policy, always aggressive rather than defensive.

During September–October 1939 it took the Wehrmacht just 36 days to conquer Poland, albeit with the assistance of a Soviet Red Army invasion of Eastern Poland. In this campaign the German Army developed operations with faster tempo and greater momentum than had been witnessed before. Spearheaded by Panzer and light-mechanised divisions, the German offensive unfolded more quickly than the Poles could react. Supported by effective Luftwaffe air-ground assistance, the German mobile formations out-flanked, enveloped, and encircled numerous Polish forces, leading to a quick and stunning success. The victims of this innovative German operational method retrospectively named it Blitzkrieg.

Just six months later, in early April 1940, the Wehrmacht conquered Germany's small neighbouring country of Denmark and launched expeditionary amphibious assaults on Norway. Given the latter country's difficult mountainous terrain, and Germany's limited maritime transportation capabilities, this campaign was one fought without significant numbers of tanks being involved. Instead, the Germans applied some of the underlying principles of Blitzkrieg during the spring 1940 Norwegian campaign. The most important of these were a high speed (tempo) of ground operations that helped developed momentum, flexibility and agility, aggression, the effective use of air power (mainly for close air support) and the able integration of naval, air and ground forces. It took the Wehrmacht just 61 days of combat during April–June 1940 to conquer Norway and expel the Anglo-French intervention forces they encountered.

If these impressive military successes were not already awesome enough, German martial power reached its apogee during the May–June 1940 Western campaign. Full of confidence, the Wehrmacht undertook an enormous military challenge. Impudently, the German forces simultaneously invaded the Netherlands, Belgium, Luxembourg and France, as well as engaging the British Expeditionary Force in northern France. We should not forget that during the Great War (1914–18) the Kaiser's German Forces, despite four years of combat, did not manage to defeat the Allied defence of Belgian and French soil.

Yet to the astonishment of the watching world, in just ten short days the German *Fall Gelb* invasion (10–20 May) delivered outstanding military triumphs. The Germans conquered all of the Netherlands and most of Belgium, charging an awesomely powerful armoured wedge through the difficult forested terrain of the Ardennes in the Allied centre and through to the Channel coast near Abbeville, trapping the entire Allied northern-located forces. These northern Allied remnants soon capitulated, but many of the encircled forces had managed to escape via the maritime evacuation carried out at Dunkirk (27 May–4 June).

Next, the successful German *Fall Rot* invasion of the rest of France (5–25 June 1940) swiftly brought the country to strategic capitulation. In just 1,120 hours the Wehrmacht had strategically defeated the most potent military power in Europe. In 1940, therefore, the German Armed Forces achieved in just 47 days the climactic military prize that had that eluded them during the four years of combat waged in the Great War. This stunning triumph displayed to the world the awesome combat power of the Germans' operational method. During these ten months of combat the Germans learned and incrementally improved the practise of a style of warfare that retrospectively became known to the Nazis' enemies as Blitzkrieg. Or rather, during this period far-sighted corps and divisional level commanders such as Guderian, Hoth, Reinhardt, Rommel, Veiel and Walsporn proved that their tactical approaches could deliver stunning battlefield success.

This radical new German operational approach envisaged the utilisation en masse of strategically concentrated, rapidly moving, well-balanced, all-arms armoured forces: this was epitomised by the German Panzer division. This operational approach initially envisaged swiftly penetrating the initial enemy defences through exploiting surprise, speed, shock action and aggression, and backed by extensive aerial strikes on both in-contact enemy forces as well as on as-yet-uncommitted reserves. Once the German Panzer divisions had got beyond the enemy's tactical zone of defence, they would conduct audacious,

risk-embracing, rapidly executed, strategic deep penetration operations. These bold armoured advances deep into enemy territory would be carried out with little regard to the risks accruing from their exposed flanks. These high-tempo, high-momentum, armoured thrusts would swiftly overrun rear-area headquarters, depots, transportation nodes, and reserve forces' assembly areas.

The sheer speed and scale of the German advance would cumulatively inflict increasing shock action, dislocation, paralysis and panic on the enemy's forces. The tempo and momentum that the German Panzer formations developed were significantly greater than that developed by the enemies these formations assaulted. The rapid-execution of tactical action enabled Wehrmacht forces to get inside their enemies' decision-making cycles. This helped paralyse their enemies' reactions. By the time an Allied tactical response had emerged, the battlefield situation had so changed that the Allied response was irrelevant. Through these methods, during 1939–40 the German Blitzkrieg swiftly defeated every opponent, however powerful, that the Wehrmacht encountered.

During 1939–40 the German Wehrmacht seemed invincible against any enemy they encountered and this perhaps understandably fostered within the

The German Blitzkrieg approach emerged rapidly in the early 1930s from extremely limited precedents. Indeed, during 1929 the German Army conducted manoeuvres with lorried infantry cooperating with the 'tanks' that the army then possessed. These were – as seen in this image – automobiles around which had been fitted canvas and plywood panels that turned the car into a pretend tank that lacked both a working gun and any genuine armour protection. (Photo by Keystone-France/Gamma-Keystone via Getty Images)

senior German political and military leadership an exaggerated sense of the infallibility of Blitzkrieg. Subsequently, in June 1941 Hitler unleashed his armed forces towards the achievement of his primary, ideologically driven, foreign-policy objective: the annihilation of the Communist Soviet Union and its Slavic populace, which he considered sub-human. In the June 1941 Operation *Barbarossa* offensive, the German forces led a wider Axis alliance in the numerically and geographically largest military campaign the world had ever seen.

In order to achieve strategic victory during the 1940 Western campaign the German Blitzkrieg had only to achieve a single envelopment operation to produce a single *Kesselschlacht* (Cauldron Battle) in the Dunkirk–Lille pocket. In contrast, on the Eastern Front during 1941 both sides waged an ideological war of unprecedented brutality across a geographical vastness some 18 times greater than that of the 1940 Western campaign. Unless the Soviet forces collapsed precipitously under the force of Blitzkrieg, the German Army would have to successfully execute something like ten separate envelopment or double-envelopment operations in order to bring the Soviet forces to strategic defeat.

Despite the Wehrmacht's enormous self-confidence and tactical acumen, in the face of a grimly determined enemy, the scale of the task proved too much for Blitzkrieg to achieve. Despite securing some of the greatest tactical military successes of all time during the 1941 campaign season, the German Blitzkrieg could not quite bring the Soviet colossus to strategic defeat. The terrible consequences of this for Nazi Germany emerged most obviously in late April 1945 when advancing Soviet shock troops placed the Red Banner flag on top of the *Reichstag* (parliament building) in Berlin. During the titanic 1941–45 Eastern Front campaign Blitzkrieg simply proved inadequate in the face of the enormity of the military task being attempted and the sheer Soviet determination to survive at any cost. Therefore, the period between September 1939 and June 1940 undoubtedly represents the high point of the awesome combat power that the German Blitzkrieg could unleash.

GLOSSARY

AASF	British RAF: Advanced Air Striking Force
AdA	French Air Force: *Armée de l'Air,* or 'Army of the Air'
BAR	Polish Army: Browning Automatic Rifle (Polish licensed manufacture of American design
BEF	British Army: British Expeditionary Force
BEF-AC	British Army: British Expeditionary Force (Air Component)
ChA	Belgian Army: *Chasseurs Ardennais,* or 'Ardennes light infantry'
Col	various armies: Colonel
DCr	French Army: *Division Cuirassée* (armoured division)
DIM	French Army: *Division d'Infanterie Motorisée* (motorised infantry division)
DLC	French Army: *Division Légère de Cavalerie* (light cavalry division)
DLM	French Army: *Division Légère Mécanique* (mechanised light division)
Fliegerkorps	German Air Force *Luftwaffe*: Air Corps, comparable to an army corps command
GHQ	British Army: General Headquarters
GQG	French Army: *Grand Quartier Général* (Army General Headquarters)
HMS	British Royal Navy: His Majesty's Ship
JFF	German Air Force (*Luftwaffe*): *Jagdfliegerführer,* 'fighter flying commander'
KG	German Air Force (*Luftwaffe*): *Kampfgeschwader* or 'battle wing,' meaning 'bomber wing'
K-W Line	Belgian Army: The Koningshooikt-Wavre defence line
KOP	Polish Army: *Korpus Ochrony Pogranicza,* Border Defence Corps
le FH	German Army: *leichte Feld Haubitze,* light field howitzer, artillery piece
Luftflotte	German Air Force (*Luftwaffe*): 'Air Fleet,' equivalent of an army group command

MG	German Army: *Maschinengewehr*, machine gun
MP	German Army: *Maschinenpistole*, sub machine gun
OKH	German Army: *Oberkommando des Heeres* (German Army High Command)
OKW	German military: *Oberkommando der Wehrmacht* (German Armed Forces High Command)
OODA	Observe-Orientate-Decide-Act (Loop); the military decision-making cycle
PaK	German Army: *Panzerabwehrkanone*, anti-tank gun
PzKpfw	German Army: *Panzer Kampfwagen* (tank)
RAF	British: Royal Air Force
SF	French Army: fortified sector: *Secteur Fortifié*
SOMUA	French Army tank manufacturer: *Société d'Outillage Mécanique et d'Usinage d'Artillerie*
Spahis	French Army: light horse-mounted cavalry regiments recruited primarily from Algeria and Tunisia
StG	German Air Force (*Luftwaffe*): *Stukageschwader* or 'dive-bomber wing'
Stuka	German Air Force (*Luftwaffe*): *Sturzkampfflugzeug*, Junkers Ju 87 dive-bombing aircraft
TONE	French Army: *Théâtre d'Opérations du Nord-Est* or 'North-East Theatre of Operations HQ', commanded by *Général* Alphonse-Joseph Georges
Veldleger	The Royal Netherlands Army: 'field army'
ZOAN	French Air Force: *Zone d'Operations Aériennes Nord* or 'North Air Operations Zone'

FURTHER READING

PART ONE: THE AUTUMN 1939 POLISH CAMPAIGN

There is considerable literature in the English language on the political and diplomatic events leading up to the outbreak of World War II. Several recent studies by Anita Prazmowska have examined Poland's diplomacy. English language coverage of Polish military operations remains very thin; the best known is Robert Kennedy's *The German Campaign in Poland 1939* (US Army Pamphlet 20-255) 1956. It remains very useful, though it is weak on the Polish side and has several glaring errors.

The Polish side of the campaign is well covered by Polish sources. Several of the late Cold War Soviet-influenced broad surveys are of particularly high quality and offer pungent analysis, but for political reasons are excessively critical of the 1939 Polish leadership. Published by the Warsaw Ministry of Defence publishing house, WMON, examples include the multi-author *Polski czyn zbrojny w II wojnie swiatowej: Wojna obronna Polski 1939*, published in 1979, and Tadeusz Jurga's numerous works on the subject. Other seminal works include E. Kozlowski's *Wojsko Polskie 1936–1939* (1974) on the Polish Army's 1936 modernisation programme, and Marian Zgorniak's *Sytuacja militarna Europy w okresie kryzysu politycznego 1938r* (1979) on the military situation in Europe during the Czech crisis.

All the important studies on the war are far too numerous to mention. Besides books, the Polish military history journal *Wojskowy przeglad historyczne* provides excellent coverage of specialised aspects of the 1939 campaign. Other Polish publications broadly cover a broad range of subjects and include a comprehensive selection of unit and formation histories, histories of the combat arms, studies of the air force and navy, as well as technical histories of the weapons and equipment.

The main historiographical problem with Polish accounts published prior to 1989 is their treatment of the Soviet invasion of 17 September. Fortunately, the problem has disappeared since 1989 and more balanced coverage of the Soviet role, both from Polish and Russian sources, have emerged. Additionally, Polish officers who escaped to Britain in 1940 published some important work: the Sikorski Institute in London has published an essential multi-volume history of the campaign. The émigré literature helps cover research areas off limits domestically under communist rule in Poland, for example, Karol Liszewski's *Wojna polsko–sowiecka 1939* (The Polish–Soviet War of 1939), Polish Cultural Foundation, London (1986).

English-language accounts of Polish operations are much less extensive. There is excellent coverage on popular military enthusiast themes, especially aircraft and the air force. There is also some important scholarly work in diplomatic history, but very little on military policy. On the Polish cavalry in 1939, see Stephen Zaloga's 'Polish Cavalry against the Panzers', *Armour* magazine, January/February 1984. The German secondary literature on the campaign is limited too. One of the better recent accounts is Janusz Piekalkiewicz's *Polen Feldzug: Hitler und Stalin zerschlagen die Polnische Republik*, Lubbe, Bergisch Gladbach (1982). A useful source is the reprinted German general staff daily situation maps for the campaign: Klaus-Jurgen Thies, *Der Zweite Weltkrieg im Kartenbild: Band 1 Der Polenfeldzug*, Biblio Verlag, Osnabruck (1989). Yet, there are few specialised monographs. There is extensive coverage of German aircraft, weapons and uniforms of the 1939 campaign in the enthusiast literature on the war in the English language.

The Soviet invasion of Poland in 1939 was ignored in Soviet Cold War military literature so as not to aggravate already sensitive Polish–Soviet relations. Indeed, the subject remained off limits until 1991, but the literature remains slim due to the near collapse of publishing of serious histories of World War II in contemporary Russia. Polish researchers utilised the short-lived window of opportunity in the Russian archives in the early 1990s to extract many documents, which have been published in a number of collections in Polish books and scholarly journals. One of the few new campaign studies to emerge utilising this archival work was Janusz Magnuski and Maksim Kolomiets' *Czerwony Blitzkrieg* (Red *Blitzkrieg*), Pelta, Warsaw (1994).

Due to the language barriers presented by Polish, German and Russian sources, the additional books listed here are limited exclusively to English accounts:

Bethell, Nicholas, *The War Hitler Won: The Fall of Poland September 1939,* Holt, Rinehart, Winston, London (1972)

Citino, Robert, *The Evolution of Blitzkrieg Tactics: Germany Defends Itself Against Poland 1918–1933,* Greenwood, Westport (1987)

Corum, James, *The Roots of Blitzkrieg: Hans von Seeckt and German Military Reform,* University of Kansas, Lawrence (1992)

Cynk, Jerzy B., *History of the Polish Air Force 1918–1968,* Osprey Publishing, Oxford (1972)

Hooton, E.R., *Phoenix Triumphant: The Rise and Rise of the Luftwaffe,* Arms & Armour Press, London (1994)

Kliment, Charles, and Nakladal, B., *Germany's First Ally: Armed Forces of the Slovak State 1939–45,* Schiffer, Atglen (1997)

Maier, Klaus, et. al., *Germany and the Second World War, Vol. 2: Germany's Initial Conquests in Europe,* Oxford University Press, Oxford (1991)

Norwid-Neugebauer, M., *The Defence of Poland: September 1939,* M. I. Kolin., London (1940)

Sword, Keith (ed.), *The Soviet Takeover of the Polish Eastern Provinces 1939–41,* University of London Press, London (1989)

Peszke, Michael A., *The Polish Navy 1939–1945,* Hippocrene, New York (1999)

Zaloga, Stephen, *The Polish Army 1939–45,* Men-at-Arms 117, Osprey Publishing, Oxford (1982)

Zaloga, Stephen and Victor Madej, *The Polish Campaign 1939,* Hippocrene, New York (1985)

PART TWO: THE SPRING 1940 CAMPAIGNS IN DENMARK AND NORWAY

Because no comprehensive history of the 1940 campaign in Norway and Denmark exists, understanding the many sides of this campaign requires consulting many publications. The best English-language source from the German perspective is Telford Taylor's *March of Conquest: German Victories in Western Europe, 1940,* Simon and Schuster, New York (1958). Taylor relates the German decisions, planning, deployment and operations in detail at the diplomatic, strategic and operational levels. It lacks tactical level analysis, however. The most comprehensive British history of the spring 1940 Norwegian campaign is T. K. Derry's *The Campaign in Norway,* J. R. M. Butler, ed., HMSO, London (1952). This British official history downplays the defensive contributions of the Norwegians, demeans French participation, and overstates Allied damage inflicted on the Germans. The most detailed account of British ground actions is Christopher Buckley's outstanding *Norway,* HMSO, London (1951). From the naval side, Donald Macintyre's *Narvik,* Norton, New York (1960) tells the story principally from the Allied perspective in detail, but suffers from judgemental editorialising.

For an even-handed and detailed account of both naval battles off Narvik, see Peter Dickens, *Narvik: Battles in the Fjords,* Naval Institute Press, Annapolis (1974).

German victory in Norway relied heavily on its near domination of the skies. This story is precisely detailed by Christopher Shores et al, in *Fledgling Eagles,* Grub Street, London (1991), the only detailed account of air actions in the campaign. There are no English-language studies of the Norwegian military defence of its nation. However, two books by Norwegian authors – Johan Waake's *The Narvik Campaign,* George Harrap, London (1964) and Theodor Broch's *The Mountains Can Wait,* Webb Book Publishing, St Paul (1942) – include useful information on Norwegian units at Narvik. For an English-language account of the French participation in Norway, see Captain Pierre Lapie's *With the Foreign Legion at Narvik*, John Murray, London (1941). There are two excellent books on the Polish Brigade: Karol Zbyszewski and Jozef Natanson, *The Fight for Narvik: Impressions of the Polish Campaign in Norway*, Lindsay Drummond, London (1940) and *Polish Troops in Norway: A Photographic Record of the Campaign at Narvik*, M. I. Kolin, London (1943). Together, the above works constitute the core studies of the campaign. For additional works, see:

Ailsby, Christopher, *Hitler's Sky Warriors: German Paratroopers in Action 1939–1945*, Brassey's, Dulles (2000)

'Attack on Vaerlose Airfield', Peter Nellemann (trans), *Small Air Forces Observer*, Vol. 14/2 (54), (April 1990)

Barnett, Correlli, *Engage the Enemy More Closely*, W. W. Norton, New York (1991)

Brayley, Martin, *The British Army 1939–45 (1) North-West Europe*, Men-at-Arms 354, Osprey Publishing, Oxford (2001)

Broch, Theodor, *The Mountains Wait*, Webb Book Publishing, St Paul (1942)

Brown, Eric, 'Blackburn's ill-fated duo: The Skua and Roc', *Air International*, Vol. 13/4, (November 1977)

Chesneau, Roger, *Aircraft Carriers of the World, 1914 to the Present*, Brockhampton Press, London (1998)

Crawford, Alex, *Gloster Gladiator*, Mushroom Models, Redbourne (2002)

Folsom, Russ, 'Panzers in Norway – 1940,' http://hem.fyristorg.com/robertm/norge/Panzer%20Abt.%20z.b.V.40.html

Foss, Christopher (ed.), *Encyclopedia of Tanks and Armored Fighting Vehicles*, Thunder Bay Press, San Diego (2002)

Frischauer, Willi, and Jackson, Robert, *The Altmark Affair*, Macmillan, New York (1955)

Green, William, 'Stopper in the Bottle', *Air International*, Vol 17/4, (October 1979)

Hagen, Kurt Erik, 'Aldi Mer 9. April', *Small Air Forces Observer*, Vol 14/3 (55), (July 1990)

Hogg, Ian, *Fortress: A History of Military Defence*, St Martin's Press, New York: (1977)

Hooten, E. R., *Phoenix Triumphant: The Rise and Rise of the Luftwaffe*, Arms and Armour Press, London (1994)

Kersaudy, Francois, *Norway 1940*, St Martin's Press, New York (1990)

Konstam, Angus, *British Battlecruisers 1939–45*, New Vanguard 88, Osprey Publishing, Oxford (2003)

Lenton, H. T., *German Warships of the Second World War*, Arco Publishing, New York (1976)

Lucas, James, *Alpine Elite: German Mountain Troops of World War II*, Jane's Publishing, London (1980)

Lucas, James, *Storming Eagles: German Airborne Forces in World War Two*, Arms and Armour Press, London (1988)

Mallmann Showell, Jak, *The German Navy in World War Two*, Naval Institute Press, Annapolis (1979)

Mollo, Andrew, *Armed Forces of World War II Uniforms, Insignia and Organization*, Orbis, London (1981)

Morzik, General Fritz, *German Air Force Airlift Operations*, Arno Press, New York (1968)

Pallud, Jean Paul, *After the Battle: The Norwegian Campaign*, After the Battle, London (2004)

Quarrie, Bruce, *German Airborne Divisions: Blitzkrieg 1940–41*, Battle Orders 4, Osprey Publishing, Oxford (2004)

Quarrie, Bruce, *German Airborne Troops 1939–45*, Men-at-Arms 139, Osprey Publishing, Oxford (1983)

Roskill, S. W., *White Ensign: The British Navy at War 1939–1945*, Naval Institute Press, Annapolis (1960)

Shores, Christopher, Foreman, John, et al, *Fledgling Eagles: The Complete Account of Air Operations During the 'Phoney War' and Norwegian Campaign, 1940*, Grub Street, London (1991)

Smith, Peter C., *Into the Assault: Famous Dive Bomber Aces of the Second World War*, John Murray, London (1985)

Sumner, Ian, and Vauvillier, Francois, *The French Army 1939–45 (Vol 1)*, Men-at-Arms 315, Osprey Publishing, Oxford (2000)

Tarnstrom, Ronald, *Germany: The Wehrmacht Strikes: 1940–1942*, Trogen Books, Lindsborg (1989)

Tarnstrom, Ronald, *Sword of Scandinavia*, Trogen Books, Lindsborg (1982)

Thomas, Andrew, *Gloster Gladiator Aces*, Aircraft of the Aces 44, Osprey Publishing, Oxford (2002)

Weal, John, *Messerschmitt Bf 110 Zerstörer Aces of World War 2*, Aircraft of the Aces 25, Osprey Publishing, Oxford (1999)

Whitley, M. J., *Battleships of World War Two*, Arms and Armour Press, London (1998)

Whitley, M. J., *Cruisers of World War Two*, Brockhampton Press, London (1999)

Williamson, Gordon, *German Destroyers 1939–45*, New Vanguard 91, Osprey Publishing, Oxford (2003)

Williamson, Gordon, *German Heavy Cruisers 1939–45*, New Vanguard 81, Osprey Publishing, Oxford (2003)

Williamson, Gordon, *German Light Cruisers 1939–45*, New Vanguard 84, Osprey Publishing, Oxford (2003)

Williamson, Gordon, *German Mountain & Ski Troops 1939–45*, Elite 63, Osprey Publishing, Oxford (1996)

PART THREE: THE SPRING 1940 WESTERN CAMPAIGN

Although there exists a huge literature on the overall 1940 German campaign in the West, surprisingly, very little detailed literature exists in the English language on Army Group B's conquest of Holland and Belgium. While there is ample Dutch coverage of their valiant defence in Dutch, few English sources exist. The best English study is Allert Goossens' 'War Over Holland, May 1940: The Dutch Struggle' (www.waroverholland.nl). Lt. Kol E. H. Brongers' *The Battle for The Hague, 1940*, Uitgeverij Aspekt, Soesterberg (2004) – although more a popular history and limited in its scope – is also well recommended. The epic armoured clash at Hannut is also understudied in the English language. The best account is Jeffrey A. Gunsburg's 'The Battle on the Belgian Plain, 12–14 May 1940: The First Great Tank Battle' in *The Journal of Military History* (April 1992), but it contains inaccuracies.

Even German sources cover the conquest of Belgium and the Netherlands inadequately. Karl-Heinz Frieser's outstanding *The Blitzkrieg Legend: The 1940 Campaign in the West*, Naval Institute Press, Annapolis (2012) relegates the conquest of the Netherlands to a mere 'operational deception maneuver' and only devotes eight unoriginal pages to the tank battle at Hannut.

The German airborne drops and the ensuing battles lack detailed coverage because, though ultimately victorious, they represented disastrous near-defeats. Consequently, they are treated by most authors as a historically insignificant sideshow. Similarly, the significant tank battle at Hannut, because it highlighted the realities and deficiencies of the Panzers has never made flattering German press. Another very good source on the Low Countries' campaign is Douglas Dilday, *Fall Gelb 1940 (2): Airborne Assault*, Campaign 265, Osprey Publishing, Oxford (2015).

In addition, the following secondary sources also provide useful insight on the campaign:

Belgium: The Official Account of What Happened, 1939–1940, Evans Brothers (for the Belgian Ministry of Foreign Affairs), London (1941)

Bond, Brian, *France and Belgium 1939–1940*, Associated University Presses, Cranbury (1979)

Cull, Brian, and Bruce Lander with Heinrich Weiss, *Twelve Days in May*, Grub Street, London (1995)

Decker, Cynrik De, and Jean Louis Roba, *Mei 1940 Boven Belgie* ('May 1940 over Belgium'), Uitgeverie De Krijger, Erembodegem (1993)

Doorman, Lieutenant-Colonel P. L. G., *Military Operations of the Dutch Army, 10th–17th May, 1940*, George Allen & Unwin (for the Ministry of Foreign Affairs), London (1944)

Kruk, Marek, and Radoslaw Szewczyk, *9. Panzer Division, 1940–1943*, Mushroom Model Publications, Petersfield (2011)

Lucas, James, *Storming Eagles: German Airborne Forces in World War Two*, Arms and Armour Press, London (1988)

Mallan, K., *Als de Dag van Gisteren: Rotterdam, 10–14 Mei 1940* ('It Seems like only Yesterday, 10–14 May 1940'), De Gooise Uitgeverij/Unieboek, Weesp (1985)

Molenaar, Colonel F. J., *Luchtverdediging in de Meidagen 1940* ('Air Defence in the May Days, 1940'), Staatsuitgeverij, 's-Gravenhage (1970)

Mrazek, James E., *The Fall of Eben Emael*, Presidio, Novato (1970)

Quarrie, Bruce, *German Airborne Divisions, Blitzkrieg 1940–41*, Battle Orders 4, Osprey Publishing, Oxford (2004)

Schoenmaker, Wim and Thijs Postma, *Mei 1940 – de verdediging van het Nederlandse luchtruim* ('May 1940 – The Defence of the Dutch Airspace'), De Bataafsche Leeu, Amsterdam (1985)

Schuurman, J. H., *Vliegveld Bergen NH 1938–1945*, Uitgeverij De Coogh, Bergen (2001)

Sebag-Montefiore, Hugh, *Dunkirk: Fight to the Last Man*, Harvard University Press, Cambridge, MA (2006)

Speidel, Gen d.Flg Wilhelm, *German Air Force in France and the Low Countries*, USAF Historical Studies No.152 (1958), Air Force Historical Research Center, Maxwell AFB

Steenbeek, Wilhelmina, *Rotterdam: Invasion of Holland*, Ballantine Books, New York (1973)

Thomas, Nigel, *Hitler's Blitzkrieg Enemies 1940: Denmark, Norway, Netherlands & Belgium*, Men-at-Arms 493, Osprey Publishing, Oxford (2014)

Weiss, Dr. Heinrich 'Luftkrieg über Holland 10–15 Mai 1940' ('Air War over Holland, 10–15 May 1940'), unpublished manuscript, n.d.

Undoubtedly, the best German account of their 1940 invasion of France is Karl-Heinz Frieser's *The Blitzkrieg-Legend: The 1940 Campaign in the West,* trans Peter Greenwood, Naval Institute Press, Annapolis (2012). It covers campaign planning, the decisive battle at Sedan, and the resulting Panzer breakthrough to the coast in extraordinary detail, providing for the first time in the English language the German view of many operational issues, from the development of the *Fall Gelb* plan to Hitler's decision to stop the Panzers short of Dunkirk.

However, it omits entirely the airborne invasion of the Netherlands, treats the feint into Belgium as an afterthought, and virtually ignores air power. But for the military enthusiast narrowly focused on Heinz Guderian's ground operations, it is recommended. Unwilling to accept that their previously victorious and much vaunted army could actually be defeated in battle, most French, and many British, histories sustain this premise with aggregate comparisons of tanks, aircraft, and divisions involved, then try to divine some systemic flaw – cultural, social, political, industrial, organisational or psychological – that was responsible for catastrophe. Instead, as Colonel A. Goutard's *The Battle of France, 1940*, trans A. R. P. Burgess, Fitzgibbon, Ives, Washburn, New York (1959) and Jacques Benoist-Méchin's *Sixty Days that Shook the West: The Fall of France, 1940*, trans Peter Wiles, Putnam, New York (1963) correctly describe, there were a host of military failures resulting in manifold, simultaneous defeats on several battlefields.

Also recommended are two excellent 'After the Battle' publications. The first is Jean Paul Pallud's *Blitzkrieg in the West, Then and Now*, Battle of Britain Prints International, London (1991) is exceptionally comprehensive – although the text derives largely from secondary sources – and lavishly illustrated. Equally thorough is Peter D. Cornwell's *The Battle of France, Then and Now*, Battle of Britain Prints International, London (2007), a meticulous aerial combat study. Additional valuable secondary works include:

Alcorn, William, *The Maginot Line 1928–45,* Fortress 10, Osprey Publishing, Oxford (2003)

Barbanson, Erik, with François Vauvillier, *La 1ère DLM au Combat*, Histoire & Collections, Paris (2011)

Battistelli, Pier Paolo, *Panzer Divisions: The Blitzkrieg Years 1939–40*, Battle Orders 32, Osprey Publishing, Oxford (2007)

Bekker, Cajus, *The Luftwaffe War Diaries: The German Air Force in World War II*, Doubleday, New York (1968)

Christienne, Charles, and Pierre Lissarrague, *A History of French Military Aviation*, trans Frances Kianka, Smithsonian Institute Press, Washington, DC (1986)

Deichmann, Paul, General, *Spearhead for Blitzkrieg: Luftwaffe Operations in Support of the Army, 1939–1945*, Ivy Books, New York (1996)

Dilday, Douglas, *Fall Gelb 1940 (1): Panzer Breakthrough in the West*, Campaign 264, Osprey Publishing, Oxford (2014)

Ellis, L. F., *The War in France and Flanders 1939–1940*, HMSO, London (1953)

Gamelin, Général M. *Servir: Les Armies Francaises de 1940,* 3 vols., Plon, Paris (1946)

Guderian, General Heinz, *Panzer Leader*, trans Constantine Fitzgibbon, E. P. Dutton, New York (1952)

Horne, Alistair, *To Lose a Battle: France, 1940*, Little, Brown, Boston (1969)

Jackson, Robert, *Air War over France 1939–40*, Ian Allan, London (1974)

Jacobsen, H. A. *Decisive Battles of World War II: The German View,* Putnam, New York (1965)

Kaufmann, J. E., and Kaufmann, H. W., *Fortress France: The Maginot Line and French Defences in World War II,* Praeger, Westport (2006)

Macksey, Kenneth, *Guderian: Panzer General*, Greenhill Books/ Lionel Leventhal, London:(2003)

Manstein, Field Marshal Erich von, *Lost Victories*, trans Anthony Powell, Henry Regnery, Chicago (1958)

The Rommel Papers, B. H. Liddell Hart, ed., trans Paul Findlay, Harcourt, Brace, New York (1953)

Mary, Jean-Yves, and Hohnadel, Alain, *Hommes et ouvrages de la ligne Maginot,* 13 volumes, Histoire & Collections, Paris (2000–2003)

Taylor, Telford, *March of Conquest: The German Victories in Western Europe, 1940*, Nautical & Aviation Publishing, Baltimore, (1991)

INDEX